Praise For Auto Repair For Dummies

"Ms. Sclar stresses preventive medicine for the automotive patient . . . with a bedside manner that any physician would envy."

> —Reprinted with Permission of *The Dallas Morning News*

"It has dispelled automotive myths and mystique for . . . long-suffering motorists, male and female."

> —Paul Dean, *Los Angeles Times*

"This book may be easily used as a primer for both understanding automotives and performing service and repair on all major car components. If only a few titles are purchased for an automotive collection, this should be one of them."

> —*Library Journal*

"An auto repair manual for people who think they can't do it themselves."

> —*The Times-Picayune,* New Orleans, LA

". . . an idiot-proof guide to painless, money-saving car care."

> —*The Toronto Star*

"An indispensable manual for any do-it-yourselfer."

> —*Auto Advocate*

"If you're tired of macho mechanics who seem to talk to you in a foreign language, who you suspect may be ripping you off . . . and who never seem to completely fix your car, then Deanna Sclar has just what you need."

> —*Fort Worth Star-Telegram*

"Even car owners who consider do-it-yourself car repair with the same trepidation as they would a self-performed tonsillectomy will find valuable material in this volume . . .valuable to anyone who drives."

> —*The News Tribune,* Tacoma, WA

TM

References for the Rest of Us!™

AUTO REPAIR FOR DUMMIES®

by Deanna Sclar

IDG Books Worldwide, Inc.
An International Data Group Company

Foster City, CA ◆ Chicago, IL ◆ Indianapolis, IN ◆ New York, NY

Auto Repair For Dummies®

Published by
IDG Books Worldwide, Inc.
An International Data Group Company
919 E. Hillsdale Blvd.
Suite 400
Foster City, CA 94404
www.idgbooks.com (IDG Books Worldwide Web site)
www.dummies.com (Dummies Press Web site)

Library of Congress Catalog Card No.: 99-88811

ISBN: 0-7645-5089-6

Printed in the United States of America

10 9 8 7 6 5 4 3

1B/TQ/QY/ZZ/IN

Distributed in the United States by IDG Books Worldwide, Inc.

Distributed by CDG Books Canada Inc. for Canada; by Transworld Publishers Limited in the United Kingdom; by IDG Norge Books for Norway; by IDG Sweden Books for Sweden; by IDG Books Australia Publishing Corporation Pty. Ltd. for Australia and New Zealand; by TransQuest Publishers Pte Ltd. for Singapore, Malaysia, Thailand, Indonesia, and Hong Kong; by Gotop Information Inc. for Taiwan; by ICG Muse, Inc. for Japan; by Intersoft for South Africa; by Eyrolles for France; by International Thomson Publishing for Germany, Austria and Switzerland; by Distribuidora Cuspide for Argentina; by LR International for Brazil; by Galileo Libros for Chile; by Ediciones ZETA S.C.R. Ltda. for Peru; by WS Computer Publishing Corporation, Inc., for the Philippines; by Contemporanea de Ediciones for Venezuela; by Express Computer Distributors for the Caribbean and West Indies; by Micronesia Media Distributor, Inc. for Micronesia; by Chips Computadoras S.A. de C.V. for Mexico; by Editorial Norma de Panama S.A. for Panama; by American Bookshops for Finland.

For general information on IDG Books Worldwide's books in the U.S., please call our Consumer Customer Service department at 800-762-2974. For reseller information, including discounts and premium sales, please call our Reseller Customer Service department at 800-434-3422.

For information on where to purchase IDG Books Worldwide's books outside the U.S., please contact our International Sales department at 317-596-5530 or fax 317-596-5692.

For consumer information on foreign language translations, please contact our Customer Service department at 1-800-434-3422, fax 317-596-5692, or e-mail rights@idgbooks.com.

For information on licensing foreign or domestic rights, please phone +1-650-655-3109.

For sales inquiries and special prices for bulk quantities, please contact our Sales department at 650-655-3200 or write to the address above.

For information on using IDG Books Worldwide's books in the classroom or for ordering examination copies, please contact our Educational Sales department at 800-434-2086 or fax 317-596-5499.

For press review copies, author interviews, or other publicity information, please contact our Public Relations department at 650-655-3000 or fax 650-655-3299.

For authorization to photocopy items for corporate, personal, or educational use, please contact Copyright Clearance Center, 222 Rosewood Drive, Danvers, MA 01923, or fax 978-750-4470.

is a registered trademark or trademark under exclusive license
to IDG Books Worldwide, Inc. from International Data Group, Inc.
in the United States and/or other countries.

IDG BOOKS WORLDWIDE

As set forth in a 1979 Settlement Agreement and Release between McGraw-Hill, Inc. and Philip R. Martin, IDG Books Worldwide, Inc. includes the following statement: "Title by permission of Philip R. Martin, author of *Auto Mechanics for the Complete Dummy,* © 1974."

About the Author

Deanna Sclar is the internationally best-selling author of *Buying a Car For Dummies,* a guide to purchasing new and used vehicles, insurance, and more. A former contributing editor to *Family Circle, Boys' Life,* and *Exploring,* she also writes a regular column for the *Los Angeles Times* and has written articles that have appeared in *Redbook, New Woman,* and other national magazines.

As an automotive expert and consumer spokesperson, Deanna has appeared on more than 700 radio and TV shows, including *Good Morning America, NBC Nightly News* with Tom Brokaw, *Today, Sonya Live,* and *The Gayle King Show.* Her *Auto Repair For Dummies* video was a National Home Video Awards finalist. She's co-hosted *Outrageous Women,* a weekly TV talk show, and has produced, written, hosted, and edited several documentaries.

The former "Thumbs Sclar" has restored two classic cars, a truck, and a house. An inveterate gypsy and blue-water sailor, she has crewed her way across the Pacific and Polynesia, sailed and dived the Great Barrier Reef, trekked alone for nine months through southeast Asia and five months through Brazil, and crossed the Atlantic in a small boat with a companion and a cat.

"My goal is to prove that we have control over our lives," she says. "Whether you are working on a car or making a lifelong dream come true, it's a do-it-yourself world. Knowing this has turned my life into a great adventure, and I want to pass the good news on to everybody else!"

ABOUT IDG BOOKS WORLDWIDE

Welcome to the world of IDG Books Worldwide.

IDG Books Worldwide, Inc., is a subsidiary of International Data Group, the world's largest publisher of computer-related information and the leading global provider of information services on information technology. IDG was founded more than 30 years ago by Patrick J. McGovern and now employs more than 9,000 people worldwide. IDG publishes more than 290 computer publications in over 75 countries. More than 90 million people read one or more IDG publications each month.

Launched in 1990, IDG Books Worldwide is today the #1 publisher of best-selling computer books in the United States. We are proud to have received eight awards from the Computer Press Association in recognition of editorial excellence and three from Computer Currents' First Annual Readers' Choice Awards. Our best-selling *...For Dummies*® series has more than 50 million copies in print with translations in 31 languages. IDG Books Worldwide, through a joint venture with IDG's Hi-Tech Beijing, became the first U.S. publisher to publish a computer book in the People's Republic of China. In record time, IDG Books Worldwide has become the first choice for millions of readers around the world who want to learn how to better manage their businesses.

Our mission is simple: Every one of our books is designed to bring extra value and skill-building instructions to the reader. Our books are written by experts who understand and care about our readers. The knowledge base of our editorial staff comes from years of experience in publishing, education, and journalism — experience we use to produce books to carry us into the new millennium. In short, we care about books, so we attract the best people. We devote special attention to details such as audience, interior design, use of icons, and illustrations. And because we use an efficient process of authoring, editing, and desktop publishing our books electronically, we can spend more time ensuring superior content and less time on the technicalities of making books.

You can count on our commitment to deliver high-quality books at competitive prices on topics you want to read about. At IDG Books Worldwide, we continue in the IDG tradition of delivering quality for more than 30 years. You'll find no better book on a subject than one from IDG Books Worldwide.

IDG BOOKS WORLDWIDE

John Kilcullen
Chairman and CEO
IDG Books Worldwide, Inc.

Steven Berkowitz
President and Publisher
IDG Books Worldwide, Inc.

VIII WINNER
Eighth Annual Computer Press Awards ≥1992

IX WINNER
Ninth Annual Computer Press Awards ≥1993

X WINNER
Tenth Annual Computer Press Awards ≥1994

XI WINNER
Eleventh Annual Computer Press Awards ≥1995

Dedication

For my children, Gina and Casey, who are now old enough for cars of their own. May we stay "in tune" forever!

Acknowledgments

Terry Miller of the Auto Parts and Accessories Association (APAA), Tim Sullivan, Rick Johnson, and Jack Trotter — the "godfathers" of the original edition. Your good advice, bright ideas, valuable leads, and unhesitating friendship meant a lot to me. I hope the good Karma flows back your way!

Don Donesley, my first automotive guru, whose classes and advice made this book possible. Thanks for introducing me to three of the finest things in life: cars, beer, and the Mojave Desert!

Tim Tierney and Bob McMinn, of the APAA, who offered valuable suggestions for the revised editions. Thanks for the time and trouble!

Rosemarie Kitchin, Bob Rodriguez, Tom Houston, Anton Veseley, and A. B. Schuman, who provided leads and illustrations for the first revised edition. You are the kind of friendly, helpful people who make working in the automotive field a pleasure indeed!

The old Thursday Evening Auto Class at University High School, a truly communal group who shared ideas, tools, and elbow grease; served as guinea pigs for one another; changed master cylinders by flashlight; and got it all together over beer and pizza afterward. Wherever you all are now, pals, thanks for being your beautiful selves!

John Cutsinger, who provided the kind of backup that every writer needs to free her so she can write. Thanks for the hot meals, the errands run, the unfailing good humor, and the sympathy that only another car-freak can offer.

Paul Dean, John O'Dell, and Ira Siegel, whose technical insights were invaluable in updating this book.

All the wonderful people at IDG Books who held my hand, advised and encouraged me, and worked hard and long on this book, especially Holly McGuire, Acquisitions Editor; Pam Mourouzis, Senior Project Editor; Tracy Barr, "Dummification expert"; Wendy Hatch and Tammy Castleman, Copy

Editors; Heather Prince, Acquisitions Coordinator and Internet wizard; Regina Snyder, Project Coordinator; Brian Drumm, Graphics Technician; Brian Torwelle, Page Layout Technician; Nancy Reinhardt, Proofreader; and Carol Burbo, Indexer. You are absolutely the best editorial team I've ever encountered. May the Fonts be with you!

And, finally, thanks to Tweety Bird, faithful Mustang, who survived all the experiments and mistakes and grew up to be a fine car and a worthy steed, and to Honeybun, my dream car come true.

What's So Special about Auto Repair For Dummies

It Is Not Written for Confirmed "Do-It-Yourselfers." It Is for You If

- You have never held a wrench.
- You are positive that, in your case, manual labor can lead only to disaster.
- You haven't the vaguest idea of how a car works.
- You cannot identify anything you see under the hood of your vehicle.
- You have failed shop or arts and crafts.
- You believe that if you do something wrong, your car can blow up.

To Enjoy This Book, It Would Help If

- You don't believe that working on your car can possibly be fun, but you're willing to give it a try for any reason whatsoever.
- You are sincerely tired of being ripped off because of your own ignorance.

Why Should That Be Enjoyable? Because You Will Be More Delighted Than Anyone Else to Find

- Cars run on principles that are as easy to understand as common sense.
- Most of the devices on your car will not hurt you unless you really go out of your way to hurt yourself.
- Not only can you get a fair deal, but you can save a tremendous amount of money, extend the life of your vehicle, save on fuel, do your bit for the environment, and have a heck of a good time working on your car!
- It's fun because it's so easy and you expected to hate it or be bored or befuddled.

Here's How *Auto Repair For Dummies* Accomplishes These Miracles:

- By starting from scratch (it even shows you what a screwdriver looks like)
- By providing step-by-step illustrated instructions for even the simplest tasks

- By telling you exactly what you need and how to know if you've been given the wrong part
- By covering each system thoroughly in simple terms *before* you get to work on it (it's easier to work on something that you understand)

There Are Fringe Benefits, Too!

- Your vehicle will run better and live longer.
- Automotive technicians will respect you.
- You'll have more money to spend on other things.
- You'll no longer be a dummy.

It Tells You the Truth About

- What makes your vehicle go (and how and why as well)
- The easy work involved in keeping your car well tuned and running right, and how to tell what's wrong if trouble strikes
- A program of "preventive medicine" to avoid trouble, which takes about 15 minutes a month
- Whether you can handle a problem yourself, and how to get it fixed at a fair price if you can't

These Features Will Make Life Even Easier:

- A Practical Glossary of Automotive Terms that are in special type throughout the book so that you can refresh your memory if you've forgotten what something means
- A detailed Index where you can look up a part, a problem, a symptom, or a specific job and find the page you need
- A Maintenance Record so that you can keep track of what you've done and when you did it
- A Specifications Record where you can keep all the information you need to buy the right parts for your vehicle
- A Tool Checklist so that you can tell what you need, what you already have, and what you'd like for your birthday
- Tons of illustrations that show you how things look, where they are, and what to do with them

This Revised Edition Also Tells You

- How to keep your vehicle young and healthy looking, and how to repair the dents, dings, and other hard knocks that life has inflicted on its body

- A whole bunch of stuff about diesel engines, alternatively fueled vehicles, turbocharging, fuel injection, electronic ignitions, anti-lock brake systems, and other innovations that may come into your life, like it or not

- What to do if you meet with The Unexpected

You Have a Few Things to Supply, Too!

- You have to buy the book.

- You have to read it.

- You have to try to do one small, easy job yourself (you can pick the job).

And *That's* What's So Special about This Book!

It is probably the only auto repair manual designed for people who think that they can't do it themselves, feel that they wouldn't like it anyway, but are willing to give it a try. How do I know that it will work for these reluctant readers? Because it is written by a genuine, certified ex-dummy who has found that, despite total ignorance and a complete lack of manual dexterity, working on a car is enjoyable, rewarding, and easy. Believe me: If *I* can do it, so can you!

DEANNA SCLAR

Publisher's Acknowledgments

We're proud of this book; please register your comments through our IDG Books Worldwide Online Registration Form located at http://my2cents.dummies.com.

Some of the people who helped bring this book to market include the following:

Acquisitions, Editorial, and Media Development

Senior Project Editor: Pamela Mourouzis

Acquisitions Editor: Holly McGuire

Copy Editors: Wendy Hatch, Tamara Castleman

Technical Editors: Paul Dean, Ira Siegel

Editorial Coordinator: Maureen F. Kelly

Editorial Manager: Rev Mengle

Production

Project Coordinator: Regina Snyder

Layout and Graphics: Amy M. Adrian, Brian Drumm, Angela F. Hunckler, Kate Jenkins, Brent Savage, Jacque Schneider. Janet Seib, Michael A. Sullivan, Brian Torwelle, Maggie Ubertini, Mary Jo Weis, Dan Whetstine

Special Art: Precision Graphics

Proofreaders: Nancy Price, Nancy L. Reinhardt, Marianne Santy, Rebecca Senninger, Toni Settle

Indexer: Carol Burbo

Special Help
Tracy Barr, Nicole Haims, Jonathan Malysiak

General and Administrative

IDG Books Worldwide, Inc.: John Kilcullen, CEO; Steven Berkowitz, President and Publisher

IDG Books Technology Publishing Group: Richard Swadley, Senior Vice President and Publisher; Walter Bruce III, Vice President and Associate Publisher; Steven Sayre, Associate Publisher; Joseph Wikert, Associate Publisher; Mary Bednarek, Branded Product Development Director; Mary Corder, Editorial Director

IDG Books Consumer Publishing Group: Roland Elgey, Senior Vice President and Publisher; Kathleen A. Welton, Vice President and Publisher; Kevin Thornton, Acquisitions Manager; Kristin A. Cocks, Editorial Director

IDG Books Internet Publishing Group: Brenda McLaughlin, Senior Vice President and Publisher; Diane Graves Steele, Vice President and Associate Publisher; Sofia Marchant, Online Marketing Manager

IDG Books Production for Dummies Press: Michael R. Britton, Vice President of Production; Debbie Stailey, Associate Director of Production; Cindy L. Phipps, Manager of Project Coordination, Production Proofreading, and Indexing; Tony Augsburger, Manager of Prepress, Reprints, and Systems; Laura Carpenter, Production Control Manager; Shelley Lea, Supervisor of Graphics and Design; Debbie J. Gates, Production Systems Specialist; Robert Springer, Supervisor of Proofreading; Kathie Schutte, Production Supervisor

Dummies Packaging and Book Design: Patty Page, Manager, Promotions Marketing

◆

The publisher would like to give special thanks to Patrick J. McGovern, without whom this book would not have been possible.

◆

Contents at a Glance

Cartoons at a Glance

By Rich Tennant

page 201

page 467

page 75

page 503

page 9

page 419

Fax: 978-546-7747 • E-mail: the5wave@tiac.net

Table of Contents

Introduction

● ●

*F*or many people, getting a driver's license is an event that runs second only to getting a diploma or a marriage license. We study, practice, and take the test in a state of high anticipation that's marred only by the fear of failing and being "grounded" forever. Yet most of us succeed in passing and hop happily into our cars, headed for the freedom of the open road. Unfortunately, most of us don't know the first thing about the machines we're licensed to drive — and this can turn a ticket to freedom into a ticket to trouble.

I'm not necessarily talking about physical danger. State motor vehicle bureaus have made fairly sure that, before we can get a driver's license, we know how to drive defensively and can handle a car under poor driving conditions. What I'm referring to is the kind of trouble that comes from depending on other people to care for and repair our vehicles. If you're like most people, you probably tend to drive around until something goes wrong and then incur the expense of replacing worn and burnt-out parts — or the entire engine — when low-cost, regular maintenance could have kept your wheels turning for a long time.

About This Book

Whether you're trying to cut expenses, are tired of being patronized, or have just fallen in love with your first car, this book tells you how your car works, what it needs in the way of tender loving care, and how to keep from getting ripped off if you have to entrust repairs to someone else. By handling the simple maintenance and tune-ups and being able to diagnose trouble and perform the less complex repairs yourself, you'll earn the respect of your family, your mechanic, and your car — and you'll feel pretty good about it!

In this book, I introduce you to the wonders of the internal combustion engine and to the even more wondrous newfangled engines of the future. After you get familiar with the principal parts and systems involved, I gently lead you into basic maintenance and repair tasks that you can do yourself. Don't worry about getting in over your head. If a repair can get you into trouble if you attempt to do it yourself, I tell you how to be sure the work is done properly by a professional at a fair price. I also warn you when you should tackle a job only with an experienced friend or automotive teacher at your elbow. So don't chicken out on me! Start with the easy stuff and then take on the more challenging tasks. You'll love yourself for it, and your vehicle will love you, too. Believe me, I've been there. . . .

How I Became Intimately Involved with My Car (and Why You'll Want to Do It, Too)

Before I moved to California, I was an ordinary urban cliff dweller: I had only a nodding acquaintance with cars. Ours was locked up in a garage, to be summoned forth by my husband for excursions to "the country"; otherwise, I used subways, buses, and taxis. All the maintenance on our car was done by the garage that housed it. My sole contribution to our automotive life was choosing the color whenever we bought a new vehicle, and my main purpose in getting a driver's license was so that I could go to the supermarket during our summers in the country or drive down to the lake for a swim. I rarely, if ever, drove in the city because doing so seemed a cross between foolishness and suicide.

When we moved to California, I must confess that my enthusiasm for a life in the sun was considerably dampened by the knowledge that this would also include a life on the freeway, but then I began to sow my oats. It started with a solo marketing excursion, and then that marvelous feeling of freedom that comes with sliding behind the wheel began to take hold. Before I knew it, I was looking for a car of my own.

Because the family budget had been considerably strained by the move West, the best I could do was a six-year-old Mustang with more than 70,000 miles on it. A friend of mine who had grown up in Los Angeles — and was therefore a qualified automotive expert — checked out the car and pronounced it drivable. He said that it might need "a little work." We took it to a reliable mechanic, who checked it over, tuned it up, and told me that it was "a classic."

Thus reassured, I drove the car to the Department of Motor Vehicles to register it. I parked the car, turned off the ignition, locked it, and found that, sitting there in the middle of the parking lot, the car was singing! A bit puzzled, I rechecked the ignition and the radio, but everything was truly shut off. And still the car sang. By the time I returned, all was quiet. But that night, when I took the family out to dinner, old Tweety Bird began to sing again. Several weeks of filling and refilling the radiator, changing the coolant, putting gunk in the radiator to block any leaks, and so on managed to reduce the singing somewhat. But when I found out, many dollars later, that all she had needed was a new $2 radiator cap, I was made abruptly aware of two things:

- ✔ Tweety was mine, and my responsibility. If she didn't work, I wasn't going to be able to, either.

- ✔ It would be impossible to enter this symbiotic relationship properly if I didn't know anything about her, because the garage bills were going to send both of us down the drain.

So I conned a friend of mine (who happened to have two sets of automotive tools) into taking an auto shop class with me at a local adult education center. I discovered that cars are pretty simple things to deal with. Instead of a bewildering array of weird metal objects and miles of hoses that threatened to blow up if I turned a screw in the wrong direction, I soon found that a car is just a series of simple Rube Goldberg mechanisms linked together (with a computer thrown in now and then that even professional mechanics need specialists to deal with). Most maintenance, tune-ups, and many repairs involve only a few, isolated gadgets, and cars are very good about sending out signals telling you clearly what's wrong — if you know how to hear, see, smell, or feel them.

Before long, it was no longer enough to be able to communicate with a mechanic; I wanted to be the mechanic *myself* whenever possible. I learned that the best way to work on a vehicle is to handle it like a baby — take a firm grip on things and do the job without mincing around. Not only did I save money, but Tweety began running better, and I found that I was having *fun!* To share the good news with everyone else, I sat down and wrote the first edition of this book. I called it *Auto Repair for Dummies* because that's the only title that I would have been willing to take a chance on before I realized how easy this stuff really is.

Doing it yourself can really pay off in terms of dollars and cents. The major difference between doing the work yourself and taking it to a professional is that professional mechanics often try the most potentially lucrative solution first. If that doesn't do it, they try the next thing, and continue to try things until they hit the right one. This method can cost you a bundle.

On the other hand, when *you* do the diagnosing, you can try the cheaper solutions first. For example, if your engine has been overheating constantly, you replace the radiator cap, pressure-test the system, and check the coolant level and the thermostat *before* buying and installing a new water pump. And if it finally comes down to changing the pump, you try to find a rebuilt one and install it yourself (which is usually not difficult). The money you save is well worth the effort.

With this book as your guide to auto repair, you may discover that your car stops being a mystery and begins to be fun to hang around with. You may even, as I did, enter into the closest relationship you'll ever have with an inanimate object. Of course, the term *inanimate* isn't really accurate. When you realize that a car exhibits most of the symptoms of life — it's self-propelled, reacts to outside stimuli, consumes fuel and discharges wastes, and even manages to sing a little tune now and then — it's really hard not to respond to it as though it were another living thing. Of course, how far you go along with this idea is your own business. It's not a prerequisite for getting into auto repair, but it helps.

How I Picture You

In order to make this book as relevant, readable, and enjoyable as possible, I envisioned it as a friendly conversation with the kind of person I felt would want to read it. Here's the mental portrait of my readers that I kept in mind:

- ✔ You're intelligent and may know a great deal about a lot of things (law, business, literature, medicine, and other nonautomotive subjects), but you need some help when it comes to cars.

- ✔ You're tired of living as a "closet dummy" who nods and smiles at the incomprehensible mutterings of your mechanic, only to end up shelling out money for repairs that you neither fully understand nor always need.

- ✔ You've decided that it simply isn't worth the extra money to have other people do things for you that you can do yourself.

- ✔ You're tired of other people assuming (especially if you're a teenager or a woman) that you aren't capable of handling repairs yourself.

- ✔ You're tired of feeling helpless in an emergency and want to be able to troubleshoot and deal with breakdowns and accidents so that you can cope with the unexpected.

- ✔ You want to keep a good vehicle in good condition without paying dearly to have someone else do the maintenance, or you simply want to keep your old heap running just a little longer without spending a lot of money on it.

- ✔ You either want the satisfaction of doing it yourself, or you just want to save a few bucks by not having to rely on the whimsy of fate and the expertise of mechanics for every little hiccup.

- ✔ You want to maintain your vehicle _without_ devoting every weekend, weeknight, and spare lunch hour poring over the intricacies, details, and mysteries of the internal combustion engine.

- ✔ You've realized (I hope!) that a vehicle that runs inefficiently because it's poorly maintained pollutes the environment, and you want to do something to turn that around.

How This Book Is Organized

If you're eager to get started (or at least willing to read on while reserving judgment), then let me tell you a bit about what this book does and doesn't cover. Basically, it covers everything you need to know to care for and maintain your vehicle, from what tools you need (whether you borrow or buy them), to how to perform a tune-up, to how to fix common problems. To help you find information easily, this book is divided into six parts, each containing chapters that deal with a particular topic. The following sections describe the information that you can find in each part.

Part I: Getting Started

If you want the basics, this is the part for you. I cover things that everyone who drives should know, like how decide whether you want to do a job yourself, how to get the hood open, how to use a jack and change a tire, and how to take *anything* apart and put it back together again. A monthly under-the-hood check that can prevent 70 percent of highway breakdowns, and a bunch of easy repair jobs, should transform you from an "I-*can't*-do-it-myselfer" into a hands-on mechanic. I also describe the tools that you'll need at one time or another if you plan to do regular maintenance and simple repairs, and I give you pointers on what you can borrow and what you should buy.

Part II: What Makes It Go?

This part begins with a simple overview of how a standard internal combustion engine works and how various systems work together to get a vehicle started, keep it running, and bring it to a stop. Subsequent chapters provide a closer look at each system — electrical, fuel, cooling, transmission, and so on — on a part-by-part basis. You'll be relieved to know that I explain everything in everyday terms, with no jargon, no unnecessary technical details, and lots of simple illustrations. If alternatively fueled vehicles strike your fancy, you'll find information on how diesel, electric, fuel cell, hybrid, and other innovative engines work, and the advantages and disadvantages of each kind.

Because the key to doing *any* job is to understand what you're working on and how it functions, I strongly recommend that you read the chapter in this part that deals with the system you want to work on *before* you head for the chapter that tells you how to do the specific job.

Part III: Keeping Your Car in Good Condition, System by System

Here, you can find out how to perform regular maintenance on your vehicle: change the oil and coolant, do basic tune-ups, check the tires, maintain the brakes, and more. By following the detailed instructions in this part, you can keep your vehicle running longer and more efficiently and lessen the likelihood of major problems that could send it to "The Great Used-Car Lot in the Sky."

Part IV: Dealing with On-the-Road Emergencies

This part helps you deal with problems that may occur while you're away from home. It shows you how to decipher such symptoms as weird noises, smoke, smells, and leaks to determine what's wrong (we call this *troubleshooting* in Carspeak) and what to do if your car drops dead on the road. If it's safe and fun to do the work yourself, I tell you how to do it. If the job is just too hairy to deal with yourself, I tell what to look for so that, when you do talk to a mechanic, you can describe the problem in the terms the mechanic needs to hear and evaluate whether the service you're getting is good, poor, or even necessary.

This part also tells you how to find a good mechanic, decipher a mechanic's invoice, and get satisfaction on complaints if, despite your best efforts, you run into problems with *anything* you buy.

Part V: Helping Your Vehicle Look Its Best

Because keeping a vehicle clean — inside and out — can extend its life and value, in this part I cover washing, waxing, and removing stains from the body and all the interior surfaces, plus how to repair the small dings, dents, and rust spots that cost big bucks at body shops.

Part VI: The Part of Tens

This part can save you money, time, and sanity. It offers "eco-logical" tips for saving fuel and lists the most important preventive maintenance you can do to keep your vehicle in good condition.

Glossary

If you're unfamiliar with the jargon, automotive terms can sound like pig Latin — familiar but nonsensical. That's why I've provided a practical glossary that tells you what something is and gives you advice about it as well. Throughout the book, glossary terms are set in a special font to remind you to go to the glossary when you see a word that you don't recognize or a term that you don't understand.

Special features

To be sure that you can find whatever you need easily, there's an extra large index, so you can look for a part, system, symptom, or problem when you return to this book for instructions. If you're not sure what to look for, try general terms like "How to" and "Troubleshooting." There's also a Maintenance Record to remind you to get busy if you've let things go too long, and a handy Specifications Record so that you have the numbers of the parts you need when you go to the auto supply store.

Icons Used in This Book

This icon points to suggestions or hints that can make a task easier, save you money, help you avoid hassles, or otherwise make your life easier.

This icon indicates information that you may have encountered elsewhere in the book and need to take into consideration.

This icon appears beside technical information that, although interesting (at least to me), you can skip without risking anything important.

This icon appears beside information that you want to watch out for because it points out events or circumstances that are dangerous or can end up costing you a lot of money.

This icon appears beside rules that you absolutely _must_ follow if you want to achieve success in a particular situation. There aren't many of them, so pay attention when you do come across them!

This icon appears beside real-life stories that provide a relaxing respite from serious subjects and demonstrate what you should — or should not — do to avoid major trouble or to triumph in difficult situations.

Where to Go from Here

You can use this book any way you want to in order to find the information you need. You can read it from cover to cover or jump from section to section as the fancy strikes you. To find a general topic, head to the table of contents. If you're looking for more specific information, go to the index.

No matter how you use the book, I recommend that you tuck it into your trunk compartment or under the front seat to keep it handy when it's time for a tune-up or if you want to make an adjustment or figure out what's gone wrong.

If this book turns you on to auto repair, then by all means extend your knowledge by reading more and more sophisticated literature on your favorite automotive topics. There are excellent books that deal with specific systems, vehicles, and repairs, written for the amateur mechanic. But there's no substitute for hands-on experience. You won't be able to realize any of these goals unless you stop procrastinating and start *working.* If you're feeling timid about actually *touching* your car's inner parts, try doing something simple, like checking the oil dipstick or changing the air filter. Believe me, once the ice is broken, the heady sense of power will carry you through most of the other basic stuff. I hope that you find it as exhilarating as I did, and I know that your car will love you for it.

May you and your car have a long and happy life together!

Part I
Getting Started

The 5th Wave
By Rich Tennant

"It looks to me like your engine is equipped with a 'Clapper' starter motor. Now stand back and let me just try something."

In this part . . .

Ever seen someone try to figure out how to open a can of sardines? They have the key in one hand, the can in the other, and they poke, prod, and pry until they finally decide that saltines alone are fine. If you've ever tried to open the hood of your vehicle or jack it up without the benefit of prior experience (or paying attention when someone else did it), you may feel as confused as they seem. That's why this part covers the things every driver should be able to do, safety tips that everyone who works on cars should know, and the tools you can use to get your vehicle running smoothly again. This part also shows you how to do a monthly under-the-hood check that can reduce the likelihood of major repairs being needed by *70 percent!*

Chapter 1

Things Every Driver Should Know

• •

In This Chapter

▶ Knowing when to do it yourself

▶ Paying attention to safety

▶ Filling 'er up yourself

▶ Getting under the hood

▶ Jacking up the car

▶ Changing a tire

▶ Getting into your car when you lock yourself out

▶ Taking things apart (and putting them back together again)

• •

*1*f you're not particularly mechanically inclined, you may watch those who *are* with admiration and amazement — and exasperation because they have something you don't: an understanding of how things work and how things go together. When they take something apart, they can reassemble it back the way it was. When they say that they want to take a look under the hood, they can actually get the darn thing open. And when they need to change a flat, they don't spend ten minutes trying to figure out which end of the jack is up.

The good news is that you don't have to be born with a wrench in your hand to know how to fix things — even things as seemingly complicated as a car. I know; I've been there. The section in the Introduction called "How I Became Intimately Involved with My Car (and Why You'll Want to Do It, Too)" tells you all about my automotive epiphany.

Of course, the simplest things can sometimes be the biggest hurdles to overcome. After all, if you can't even figure out how to open the hood, how can you check the oil or the coolant level? That's why I begin this book with a chapter on the basics. I explain simple tasks that you use again and again as you work on your vehicle — like how to open the hood, jack up a car, and change a tire. I also include instructions for filling the tank with gas yourself (it's cheaper than full-service), a surefire method for taking *anything* apart and putting it back together again, and safety pointers that *every* mechanic — experienced and beginner — should heed.

You can find a definition in the Practical Glossary of Automotive Terms at the end of the book for any word that's printed in this special type.

Before You Tackle Any Job

It's wonderful to do things yourself. It costs you less, it gives you a sense of power to know that you did it on your own, and you know that the job's been done right. Nevertheless, to avoid getting in over my head, I always ask myself the following questions before undertaking *any* job:

✔ Do I really want to do this? Will it be fun — or horrendous? (I try never to do anything that doesn't *feel* good anymore (unless it's absolutely necessary).

✔ Do I know how to do it? If not, where do I go to learn?

✔ Does it require such expensive tools that it would cost less to have someone do it for me than to buy those tools? Can I borrow the tools I need?

✔ If I goof, can something be seriously damaged? Can I?

✔ How long will it take, and what is my time worth? How much money will I save by doing it myself?

You'll be happy to know that almost every job in this book should pass these tests. If you find one that doesn't, don't hesitate to turn it over to a professional — *after* you read enough to know that the job is definitely necessary, what it entails, whether the work has been done properly, and how to get satisfaction if it isn't. With that in mind, let's get on to the very first thing you need to know in order to work on your vehicle.

Safety Rules

The first time I tuned my car, I was sure that if I made the smallest mistake, the car would explode when I started it. This seems to be a common delusion, but it just isn't so. All you'll get is silence (which can be just as disconcerting, but not lethal after all). This isn't to say that working on cars is free from danger, though. Before you do any work on a vehicle, be sure to observe the following safety rules:

✔ **Don't smoke while you're working on your car — for obvious reasons!**

✔ **Never work on your car unless the parking brake is on, the gearshift is in Park or Neutral, and the engine is shut off.** If you have to run the engine to adjust something, turn it on and off yourself to avoid the risk that a friendly helper may misunderstand and turn the engine on while your hands are in the way.

✔ **Be sure that the parts of the engine you're working on are nice and cool so that you don't get burned.** If you're doing a job that calls for a warm engine, be very careful.

✔ **Never jack a car up unless the wheels are properly blocked.** I go into more detail about this later in this chapter in the "The Safe Way to Use a Jack" and "How to Change a Tire" sections.

✔ **Use insulated tools for electrical work.**

✔ **Before using a wrench or ratchet on a part that's "stuck," make sure that, if it suddenly comes loose, your hand won't hit anything.** To avoid the possibility of being injured because your hand slams into something, *pull* on wrenches whenever possible rather than *pushing* on them.

✔ **Take off your rings, long necklaces, or other jewelry.** If they get caught on parts, they — and you — can be damaged.

✔ **Tie back long hair.** If your hair accidentally gets into a moving fan or belt, you can literally be scalped.

✔ **If you're working with toxic chemicals, such as antifreeze, cleaners, and the like, keep them away from your mouth and eyes, wash your hands thoroughly after using them, and either store them safely away from pets and children or dispose of them in a way that's good for the environment.** (For examples, see the next paragraph and the sidebar "How to dispose of empty gasoline cans safely," later in this chapter.)

✔ **Know that gasoline is extremely dangerous to have around.** Not only is it toxic and flammable, but the vapor in an *empty* can is explosive enough to take out a city block. If you must keep a small amount of gasoline on hand for a lawn mower or chain saw, always store it in a ventilated gasoline can designed specifically for that purpose. Unless you're going far into the wilds, *never* carry a can of gasoline in or on your vehicle.

✔ **Work in a well-ventilated area to avoid breathing in carbon monoxide if you have to run the engine, or breathing in toxic fumes from chemicals and gasoline.** If possible, work outdoors in your driveway, your backyard, or a parking lot. If you must work in your garage, be sure to keep the garage door open and move the vehicle as close to the door as possible.

✔ **Keep a fire extinguisher handy.** You can find reasons for this that may surprise you in Chapter 2.

So much for the scary stuff. It's all a matter of common sense, really. And remember: Making a car blow up is almost impossible unless you drop a match into the fuel tank. If you do something incorrectly, the worst thing that will probably happen is that the car won't start until you get it right.

How to dispose of empty gasoline cans safely

Although gasoline simply burns, gasoline plus air forms an explosive vapor that can literally take out your entire neighborhood. For this reason, it's wise not to store or carry gasoline unless you're heading far away from any source of fuel (and use only a specialized, vented gas can in that unlikely event). If you have an old gasoline can around, get rid of it! Immediately add water until it's full and, as soon as you can, take it to a recycling center that handles toxic waste. If there's no center nearby, ask your local service station if they'll dispose of it for you.

Some people keep gasoline around to clean parts with. This is extremely dangerous. Mechanic's solvent, available at gas stations and auto supply stores, works better and has been treated with a flame retardant to keep it from burning too freely.

How to Fill 'Er Up Yourself

More and more gas stations are shifting toward self-service. If you've been reluctant to abandon the luxury of the full-service lane, chances are that it's going to get more and more difficult to find one. Knowing how to fill 'er up yourself not only prevents you from being stranded with an empty tank when there's no one available to fill it for you, but it also saves you money on every gallon, every time.

Always extinguish your cigarette before you start to pump gasoline. If the flame comes in contact with gasoline fumes, it can cause an explosion.

Here's how to pump your own gas:

1. **Look at the price window on the pump.**

   If a price is registered there, have the attendant clear the machine so that the price window reads "$0.00."

2. **Move the lever on the pump to ON.**

3. **Unscrew the cap from your fuel tank.**

4. **Unhook the pump nozzle and hose from the pump and place the nozzle into the fuel tank opening.**

5. **Squeeze the trigger on the pump nozzle to allow gasoline to flow out of the hose and into your fuel tank.**

   There's usually a little latch near the trigger that keeps the trigger open so that you don't have to stand there holding onto it. Don't worry about overflows; gas pumps shut off automatically when your tank is almost full.

Engaging the trigger latch gives you time to take advantage of the other free services at the gas station. You can wash your car's windows or check the air pressure in your tires and add air if they need it. (There are instructions for doing so in Chapter 19.)

When the gasoline stops flowing, the trigger clicks closed and the numbers in the pump window stop moving. Remove the nozzle from the fuel tank and hang it back on the pump.

Never "top off" a tank by adding fuel after the pump has shut off automatically. If you overfill your tank, the fuel may overflow the fill hole or leak out onto the road through an overflow outlet. This is not just a waste of your money; spilled gasoline ruins asphalt, pollutes the air, and is a fire hazard. This kind of leakage is especially prone to happen if it's a hot day and the gasoline in your tank expands.

6. **Replace the cap on your fuel tank.**

How to Open the Hood

How can you do even simple "under-the-hood" jobs — such as checking the oil, antifreeze, and transmission fluid; refilling windshield wiper fluid; and checking accessory belts — if you don't know how to get the hood open?

The good news is that opening the hood of a car is easy and uncomplicated — if you know how to do it. Although the location of the hood release may differ from one vehicle to the next, all releases work in pretty much the same way:

- ✔ In newer models, the hood release is often inside the vehicle, somewhere near the steering column or on the floor next to the driver's seat. (It generally displays the word *Hood* or a picture of a car with its hood up.) In older models, the hood release is behind the grill or behind the bumper.

- ✔ All vehicles have a safety catch that stops the released hood from popping all the way open. The purpose of the safety catch is to prevent the hood from accidentally coming open and obscuring your vision while you're driving.

- ✔ Once the hood is up, it usually stays up on its own, unless you need to prop it up with a safety rod.

If you haven't the faintest idea of how to get your hood open, head for the full-service bay the next time you go in for gas and ask the attendant to show you how to open the hood. You may pay a little more for fuel, but the lesson will be worth it, and you can get your windows washed and your tire pressure checked for nothing! (If you're really short of cash, just ask for $5 worth of gasoline; the difference in cost will be negligible.)

Here's how to open the hood of your car yourself:

1. **Find your hood release and pop open the hood.**

   Either consult your owner's manual, or try to remember the last time a service station attendant opened the hood of your car. Did he or she ask you to pull a lever inside the vehicle? Or did he or she go directly to the front grill?

   If the hood release is at the front of the car, look around and through the grill and feel under the grill and behind the bumper to find a handle, lever, arm, or button. Then pull, press, or push front to back and side to side on the thing you find until it releases the hood. If the hood release is inside the car, press, push, or pull it until you hear the hood pop open.

   The hood will open a little, but it will probably be stopped by the safety catch: a metal lever that, when pressed one way or the other, releases the hood so that it can open all the way.

2. **With one hand, raise the hood as far as it will go. With the other hand, feel along the area between the hood and the grill for the safety catch. Release it and then raise the hood the rest of the way.**

3. **Secure the hood if necessary.**

   If the hood stays up all by itself, fine. If it doesn't, look for a safety rod that's attached either to the underside of the hood or to the bottom edge of the hood opening. Either lift or lower the rod (depending on where it's located) and fit the end of it into the slot that's provided to hold it in place.

   On some vehicles, the hood is held up by two gas-pressurized cylinders known as *hood shocks*. If the gas has leaked out of these units, be careful because the hood could come down at any moment. If that's the case, replace these units or secure the hood with a broom handle or similar object.

The Safe Way to Use a Jack

The most obvious reason to jack up a car is to change a tire, but other jobs, such as inspecting brakes, may also require you to get under the vehicle. (Even if you're reed-thin enough to squeeze yourself between the pavement and the underside of your car, you still need room to move around and manipulate tools.) Chapter 2 has detailed information about the different types of jacks, as well as items such as jack stands (essential) and creepers (nonessential, but nice). This section explains how to use a jack safely and efficiently. The next section shows you how to change a tire after the vehicle is in the air.

Jacks are used only to get a vehicle off the ground. They should _never_ be used to hold a vehicle in place. Even if you're simply changing a tire, you need to make sure that you've blocked the other wheels so that the car doesn't roll off the jack. _You must use jack stands when you work underneath your car;_ if you don't, you run the risk of serious injury or even death. People have been crushed to death when vehicles that were improperly secured fell on them.

Before you attempt to jack up your vehicle, observe the following safety precautions:

✔ **Never change a tire on a freeway or highway.** Not only can you be seriously injured, but you can also fall prey to carjackers. Don't exit the car on the side nearest traffic; use a cellular phone to call road service or the AAA. If you have no cellular phone and a public phone isn't near enough to make a call and get right back into your car, hang a white rag or a white piece of paper out of the driver's side window and wait for the highway patrol to rescue you.

✔ **Always park a vehicle on level ground before you jack it up.** If you get a flat tire on a hill and can't coast to the bottom without killing the tire completely, then park close to the curb, turn the wheels toward the curb, and block the downside wheels securely to prevent the car from rolling. Even after taking these precautions, however, I'd be nervous.

✔ **Never jack up a vehicle without blocking the wheels.** Even if the car is on level ground, use bricks, wooden wedges, or metal wheel chocks to block the wheels at the opposite end of the car from the end that is to be raised. Doing so keeps the vehicle from rolling after it has been jacked up.

Keep the blocks in the trunk of your car so that you won't have to go hunting around if you have to change a tire when you're away from home.

If you find yourself faced with the job of changing a tire and you have nothing with which to block the wheels, park near the curb with the wheels turned in. This may not keep you from getting hurt if the car rolls off the jack, but at least innocent motorists and pedestrians won't have to deal with a runaway driverless car!

✔ **Be sure that your gearshift is in Park (or in First if you have a manual transmission) and that the emergency brake is on _before_ you jack it up.** The only time you don't want the emergency brake on is when you have to be able to rotate a _rear_ wheel or remove rear brake drums to inspect the brakes. In such a case, make sure that the front wheels are blocked _securely,_ preferably with chocks designed for the purpose. (Chocks are available at a low cost at auto supply stores, and they stow neatly in the trunk.)

Once you've observed the safety precautions just listed, follow these steps:

1. **If you're going to remove a wheel to change a tire or check your brakes, remove the hubcap (if there is one) and loosen the lug nuts *before* you jack up the car.**

   Once the car is jacked up, the wheel will turn freely, which makes getting a hubcap off harder and makes starting the nuts almost impossible. Instructions for removing a hubcap and loosening lug nuts are in the next section, "How to Change a Tire."

2. **Place the jack under the part of the vehicle that it should contact when raised. If you are using jack stands, place them near the jack.**

   Where you place your jack depends on whether you're planning to do a one-wheel job, such as tire changing or brake checking, or a two-wheel, whole-end repair job. To find out the proper place to position the jack for your particular vehicle, check your owner's manual. If you have no manual, ask the service department at your dealership to show you the proper place, or follow these rules:

   Never place the jack so that the weight of the vehicle rests on something that can bend, break, or give. If your manual is incomprehensible or lacks this kind of information, try to place the jack so that it touches either the car frame or the big bar that supports the front wheel suspension. You can also place jacks near the rear-wheel axle. Until you become more proficient at this, I'd stick to jacking up one wheel at a time. It may mean more work, but the practice is good for you.

3. **Lift the vehicle by using the jack. How you accomplish this depends on the type of jack you're using (see Figure 1-1):**

   • If you have a *hydraulic* jack, place the handle into the appropriate location and pump up and down. Use nice, even strokes, taking the jack handle from its lowest to its highest point on each stroke to cut down on the labor involved.

   • If you have a *tripod* jack, turn the crank.

   • If you have a *scissor* jack, insert the rod or wrench over the knob and then crank.

Figure 1-1:
The type of jack you have determines whether you crank, turn, or pump.

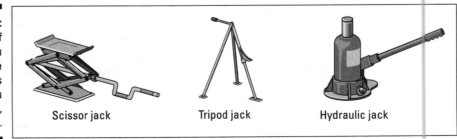

Scissor jack   Tripod jack   Hydraulic jack

4. **If you have jack stands, place them under the car, near the place where the jack is touching the vehicle (see Figure 1-2). Raise the stands until they are high enough to just fit under, and lock them in place. Lower the jack until the car is resting on the jack stands. Then remove the jack.**

Substituting boxes, stones, or bricks for jack stands is very dangerous. They can slip out or break while you're under the car. A jack can do the same thing, so if you're going to work under your car (and you will if you plan to change your own oil and do your own lube jobs), be sure to buy a pair of jack stands. The money you save by getting under there yourself will pay for the stands in no time. You can find information about buying jack stands in Chapter 2.

Figure 1-2:
Jack stands hold your vehicle up safely.

5. **Before you begin to work, wiggle the car a little to make sure that it's resting securely on the jack or the jack stands.**

Doing so also tells you whether you have the wheels blocked properly. It's better if the vehicle falls while all four wheels are in place. (It will bounce just a little.)

If you remove a wheel and begin to work without making sure that you jacked up the car and blocked it securely, it can do a lot of damage to itself — and to you — if it falls. (This is not meant to frighten you away from jacking up your car and working on or under it. It's just to emphasize the fact that a few simple precautions will remove any danger.)

6. **When you're finished working, lower the vehicle to the ground.**

If you're using a tripod or scissor jack, simply turn the crank in the opposite direction. If you're using a hydraulic jack, use the rod to turn the pressure release valve. The jack will do the rest of the work for you.

How to Change a Tire

Even if you're a member of the AAA or CAA, there's always a chance that you'll find yourself stuck with a flat tire on a remote road with no telephone in sight. On these occasions, all traffic generally vanishes, leaving you helpless unless you know how to change a tire yourself. Everyone should have a general idea of what's involved:

1. **Secure the vehicle so that it won't roll.**

2. **Jack up the vehicle, following the instructions in the preceding section, "The Safe Way to Use a Jack."**

3. **Remove the old tire.**

4. **Put on the new tire.**

5. **Put away the jacking stuff and the old tire.**

6. **Drive happily into the sunset.**

But the job gets sticky in a couple of places. Unless you're properly equipped, you can find yourself out of luck and in for a long wait for help to come along. The following sections explain in detail, and in order, how to change a tire. To make sure that you have the tools you need, read the section called "More Things to Carry in Your Car" in Chapter 2, and then stock up.

If you own a luxury car with an air suspension, you need to turn the system off before jacking up your car. Vehicles with air suspensions have an on/off switch located in the trunk area.

Removing a hubcap

If you have an older car that still has hubcaps (instead of the wheel covers on more recent models), the first task in changing a tire — after you pull to the side of the road and finish banging the heel of your hand against the steering wheel in frustration — is to remove the hubcap of the injured tire. The following steps tell you how:

1. **Use a screwdriver or the flat end of a lug wrench (see Figure 2-20 in Chapter 2) to pry off the hubcap.**

   Just insert the point of the tool where the edge of the cap meets the wheel, and apply a little leverage (see Figure 1-3). The cap should pop off. You may have to do this in a couple of places; it's like prying the lid off a can of paint.

Figure 1-3:
You can use
a screw-
driver to pry
a hubcap
loose.

2. **Lay the cap on its back so that you can put the lug nuts into it to keep them from rolling away and heading for the nearest sewer.**

After you remove the hubcap, the next task is to loosen the lug nuts.

Loosening the lug nuts

Lug nuts are those big nuts that hold the wheel in place. Most garages retighten them with a power tool, and unless you've done the job yourself by hand, they're going to be pretty hard to loosen. (Take my advice in Chapter 2 and buy a *cross-shaft* lug wrench. Figure 2-20 shows what one looks like.)

Before you begin, you have to ascertain whether the lug nuts on the wheel you're working on are right-hand threaded or left-hand threaded. This isn't a "left-handed hammer" joke; the threads determine which way you turn the wrench. The lug nuts on the right side of a vehicle are always right-hand threaded, but the nuts on the left side *may* be left-hand threaded. Look at the lug nuts on your car; in the center of the lugs you should see an R, an L, or no letter at all:

✔ A lug with an R or with no letter is right-threaded. Turn it *counterclockwise* to loosen it.

✔ A lugs with an L is left-threaded. Turn it *clockwise* to loosen it.

For the purposes of sanity, I'll assume that your car has right-threaded nuts. If you have a couple of lefties, just turn the wrench in the opposite direction as you follow these steps to loosen the lug nuts:

1. **Find the end of the wrench that fits the lug nuts on your car, and fit it onto the first nut.**

Always work on lug nuts in rotation. That way, you won't forget to tighten any later.

2. Apply all your weight to the bar on the *left*.

This starts turning the nut *counterclockwise*, which loosens it.

If the nut has been put on with a power tool and you can't get it started, a piece of hollow pipe, fitted over that left-hand arm of the cross-shaft wrench, magically adds enough leverage to start the nut easily (see Figure 1-4). After you replace the nut yourself, this aid is no longer necessary. But remember, the longer the arms on your lug wrench, the more leverage you have.

Figure 1-4: A hollow pipe and a cross-shaft wrench can loosen the tightest lug nuts.

Don't remove the lug nuts completely; just get them loose enough so that you can remove them by hand *after* raising the car (a feat explained in an earlier section of this chapter, "The Safe Way to Use a Jack").

Changing the tire

Once the vehicle is safely jacked up and the lug nuts are off, follow these instructions to change the tire:

1. Remove the spare from the trunk if you haven't already done so.

Actually, it's easier to do this before jacking up the car. If you haven't checked your spare recently, keep your fingers crossed that it has enough air in it! Roll the spare to the scene of the action.

2. Grasp the flat tire with both hands and pull it toward you.

The flat tire sits on the exposed bolts that the lug nuts screwed onto. As you pull the flat off, it should slide along the bolts until, suddenly, it clears the end of the bolts and you find yourself supporting its full weight. Tires are heavy, and you'll be quite happy to lower it to the ground (if you haven't already dropped it).

3. **Roll the flat along the ground to the trunk to get it out of the way.**

4. **Lift the spare onto the lug bolts.**

   Because tires are heavy, you may have a little trouble lifting the spare into place — especially if you're not accustomed to lifting heavy things. If this is the case, a bit of ingenuity may help; see the sidebar "A little ingenuity goes a long way" for details.

5. **After you have the spare tire in place, replace the lug nuts and tighten them by hand.**

   Give each lug nut a jolt with the wrench to get it firmly into place, but wait until the car is on the ground before you really try to tighten the lug nuts.

   Remember, right-hand threaded nuts tighten in a clockwise direction; lefties go the other way.

6. **Replace the jack, lift the car off the jack stands (if you used them), and lower the car to the ground.**

7. **Once the car is resting on the ground, use the lug wrench to tighten the lugs as much as you can.**

   You don't want to twist them off the bolts or ruin the threads, but you don't want the wheel to fall off, either. Use your hollow pipe if you're worried about tightening them sufficiently, or step on the right-hand arm of the lug wrench after the nut is tight.

8. **If your car has hubcaps, place the hubcap against the wheel and whack it into place with the heel of your hand.**

   Cushion your hand with a soft rag first so that you won't hurt it. And don't hit the hubcap with a wrench or hammer — you'll dent it. Whack it a couple of times, in a couple of places, to be sure that it's on evenly and securely. (Even secondhand hubcaps can cost from $20 to more than $100 apiece to replace.) If it's too much of a hassle, or if you don't have the time to replace the hubcap, you can take it home and install it later; it's mostly ornamental, and you can drive for a while without it. But *do* replace it soon because it helps keep dust and dirt out of your brakes and bearings.

9. **Put the flat in the trunk where the spare was located, and put your tools away.**

   Don't forget to remove the wheel blocks, and *don't forget to have that flat fixed!*

A little ingenuity goes a long way

I have a friend who is a female of small stature. When her first flat occurred while she was on the road, she found herself in the infuriating position of being unable to lift the heavy spare onto the lug bolts — while a macho truck driver, whose offers of help she had spurned, enjoyed the scene. (He'd decided to hang around and watch the "little lady" change her tire.) After hearing her sad tale, I suggested that she cut an old wooden crate into a ramp that could get the tire high enough to fit onto the lug bolts and that she keep the ramp in the trunk of her car for future tire changes. She did it and is now gloriously independent once more. Here's how to make a ramp like hers:

1. **Measure the distance from the ground (A) to the bottom of the tire (B) while the car is jacked up.**

2. **Nail some boards together to form a ramp of the same height as AB in Step 1.**

3. **Now you can roll your wheel up the ramp and just push it into place without having to lift it yourself!**

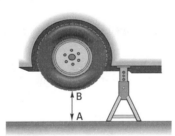

1. Measure the distance from the ground (A) to the bottom of the tire (B) while the car is jacked up.

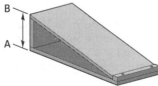

2. Nail some boards together to form a ramp of the same height as AB in Step 1.

3. Now you can roll your wheel up the ramp and just push it into place without having to lift it yourself!

Make sure that your flat tire is repaired properly. Instead of dismounting the tire from the wheel rim, inspecting it, fixing it, and remounting it, some service stations simply plug the flat from the outside. Several states now outlaw this procedure, known as "outside-in" repair. To avoid this, tell the service facility that you *don't* want the tire plugged from the outside; you want the flat corrected the proper way.

 If you get caught in the middle of nowhere with a flat tire and are unable to change it yourself, you can get rolling again without riding on the flat. If you carry an aerosol can of nonflammable inflator/sealant, simply screw the nozzle of the can onto the valve stem of the flat tire, and it fills the tire with air and some sort of goo that temporarily seals the puncture. Because there's still some question about how permanent this fix is and its ultimate effects on your tire, use inflator/sealant *only* in emergencies, get to a service station as soon as possible, and ask the attendant to try to remove the stuff before fixing the tire.

You may not find the prospect of changing your own flat tires especially alluring. But isn't it nice to know that if a crisis does occur and you're not near a phone or don't have the time to wait for the auto club, you can get yourself rolling again in less than 15 minutes?

 If reading these instructions makes you think that you'd rather languish by the side of the road for hours than undertake changing a tire yourself, you might consider outfitting your vehicle with *run-flat* tires. Although these tires will set you back a couple of hundred bucks, you'll be able to drive with a flat to the nearest service station without ruining the tire.

To make the job easier should an emergency arise, you may want to go out and check the lug nuts on your car now. If they're on hideously tight, loosen them with a lug wrench and a pipe and retighten them to a reasonable tension so that you won't have to struggle at the side of the road.

Getting Back into a Car When You've Locked Yourself Out

Here's an "emergency" that may not be dangerous, but certainly can be exasperating!

 If you tend to be feather-headed and leave the keys in your car fairly often, you may be tempted to hide an extra key somewhere on the vehicle. However, I must warn you that unless you're very clever about where you hide it, you may be inviting someone to steal your car or its contents. Those little magnetic boxes that stick to the metal surface of the body or frame are the best bets here, but *be sure to place your box in an obscure and hard-to-reach area where it can't jiggle loose and fall out.* I leave the choice of area up to you — if I publish a list of suggestions, the Car Thieves of America will nominate me for their annual Helpful Dummy Award! Be imaginative. Struggling a little to reach that extra key is better than giving the car away easily. And *don't* hide your house key with it. You don't want to give *everything* away, do you?

Assuming that you've decided not to risk hiding that extra set on your car, here's how to get in without a key:

- ✔ **If you have the old-style door locks with little buttons that go up and down,** obtain a wire coat hanger, straighten it out, and bend the end of it into a little hook. Insert it between the rubber molding and the side window or vent window and then, carefully, with the dexterity of a jewel thief, hook it around the door button and pull it up.

- ✔ **If you or your auto manufacturer has had the foresight to replace these buttons with the new, smooth kind,** your vehicle has less of a chance of being stolen, but you will have a harder job getting into it without a key. You may be able to use the hanger to hook one or to push the gizmo near the door handle, but most of them will straighten out your hanger before they condescend to budge. Sorry!

- ✔ **If you're in a parking facility or near a service station,** the attendants often have a gadget called a "jimmy" that can be slid between the window and the door and used to operate the locking mechanism. It certainly doesn't hurt to ask. If they have one, ask them to do the job for you and be generous with your thanks. They've just saved you a lot of time and money.

- ✔ **If you call a locksmith,** you'll have to prove that you own the vehicle before any work can be done, and you'll probably also have to pay immediately. (Let's hope that you didn't lock your wallet in there along with your keys.) If your key is lost outside your car and your steering wheel locks, the locksmith may have to dismount the steering wheel and remove the lock — this can cost you lots of money, plus time and aggravation, before you can drive off again.

There's good news, however. Each car key is coded by the auto manufacturer, and if you have the key code number, a locksmith can make you a new key as long as you have identification and can describe the vehicle in terms of its vital statistics. General Motors car keys have little coded tags that you knock out of the key and keep; other U.S. cars come with little metal tags with the number on them; and most foreign carmakers engrave the number right on the keys.

As a valuable favor to yourself, write down the code number where someone at home can read it to you in an emergency. Also record it — without identifying what it is — in your pocket address book or in your wallet *before you lose your keys.* If you don't know the code number for your keys and you bought the car, new or used, from a dealer, the dealer may still have the number on file. Failing that, a good locksmith may be able to analyze a key in fairly new condition and come up with the proper code for it.

✔ **If you happen to lock yourself out of the car while you have the trunk open,** you may be able to move the rear seat out of the way and gain access to the rear of the car (or you can hide an extra ignition key in the trunk).

✔ **If you get totally freaked out and decide to break a window,** break the little vent window, if you have one. It's cheaper to replace, and sometimes the latch breaks before the glass does.

If you have to break the glass, wrap something around your hand and use a stone or other heavy object. Keep your head away from flying glass, although most auto glass should be shatterproof. And *don't* break a window that will interfere with visibility while you're driving home to face the jeers of your family and friends.

How to Take Anything Apart — and Get It Back Together Again

I've never been able to follow the instructions to put my kids' toys together, but I can take a wheel assembly apart and get it back together again, slowly but accurately, by using the following procedure. The bonus is that this procedure works for *anything* that you need to take apart and put back together again — brakes, toasters, bicycles, and so on.

1. **Get a *clean,* lint-free rag and lay it down on a flat surface, near enough to reach without having to get up or walk to it.**

   As you remove each part, you're going to lay it on this rag. Consequently, the rag shouldn't be in an area where oil or dust or anything else can fall on it and foul the parts. If you're going to use something that blasts air for cleaning purposes, leave enough of the rag uncluttered to lap it over the parts resting on it.

2. **Before you remove each part, stop and ask yourself the following questions, and if you're worried about forgetting, make notes:**

   • What is this thing?

   • What does it do?

   • How does it do it?

   • Why is it made the way it is?

   • How tightly is it screwed on (or fastened down)?

Most amateurs tend to put things back very tightly, in hopes that the part won't fly off. But some things, like bolts that hold gaskets in place, shouldn't be tightened too securely, because the gasket would be squeezed out of shape and whatever it's holding in would get out, or the bolt threads could be stripped. So try to remember (or make notes about) how hard each thing was to remove. The note needn't be long — just something like "Part #6: Hook at end of arm on left hooks on to knob to right of Part #7." Add a picture if it helps.

3. **As you remove each part, lay it down on the rag** *in clockwise order, with each part pointing in the direction it lay when it was in place.*

   This is the key to the whole system. When you're ready to reassemble things, the placement and direction of each part tells you when to put it back and how it went.

4. **If you're making notes, assign each part a number indicating the order in which you removed it — Part #1, Part #2, and so on.**

   If you work systematically and understand the function of each part, you won't be left with those "extra" nuts and bolts at the end of the job. You can even put numbers on the parts with masking tape if you're afraid that the rag may be moved accidentally.

5. **When you're ready to reassemble everything, begin with the last part you removed, and then go counterclockwise through the parts.**

> **Never, never do a job in a hurry.**

Allow yourself plenty of time. If things get rough, have a soft drink or a cup of coffee. You may get a whole new perspective when you go back to work. Turn on your answering machine or take the phone off the hook, keep the kids and the dog away, and relax. If you hit a snag, sit quietly and think about it — don't panic. If the parts fit together before, they'll fit together again.

Chapter 2

The Way to Your Car's Heart Is through Your Toolbox

. . . .

In This Chapter

▶ Getting the best tools for your money

▶ Determining which tools you need to buy (and which ones you can just borrow)

▶ Stocking a trunk compartment toolbox

▶ Making your list and checking it twice: A tool checklist to take with you to the auto parts store

. . . .

Whether you're trying to cook up a decent meal, paint a picture, run an office, or work on your car, you're only as good as your tools. Just as you can't slice tomatoes super-thin with a bent, rusty, dull knife, and you can't type a professional-looking letter on a broken-down typewriter, you can't do any kind of job on your engine if you lack the means to loosen or remove parts, clean or **gap** them, reinstall them, adjust them, and test the results.

Before you run off to return this book because you aren't prepared to spend a lot of money on tools that you'll probably never use again after you ruin your engine or cut off your thumb, let me tell you that all you really need are a few basic implements, and they're not very expensive. (I'll deal with the engine and your thumb later.) In this chapter, I list and describe the tools you need for working on your vehicle. You may be surprised at how many of them you already own, and in the event that you do need to buy a few, I give you pointers on getting value for your money.

Shopping for Tools

Tool prices vary widely, but if you keep your eyes open and know where to go, whom to talk to, and what to look for, you can get a good value at a fair price.

- ✔ Shop for tools in a major auto parts chain store, and stick to well-known brands.

- ✔ Watch the newspaper for sales; most chains have them regularly, and you can save a lot of money.

- ✔ Buy each kind of tool in sets of different sizes rather than buying at random. You can save money this way.

- ✔ Look for high-grade steel with no rough edges.

- ✔ Pick out friendly-looking salespeople and ask them what kinds of tools they buy. Most of them are auto enthusiasts who will be delighted that you're planning to do your own work (and be a future customer), and they'll be happy to point out the best buys.

Buying everything at once isn't necessary to get started on your car; use the beg, borrow, and steal-from-the-family-toolbox methods if you must. The important thing is to get to work!

Screwdrivers

There are two basic types of screwdrivers: *standard,* or *slot, screwdrivers* (the most common type) and *Phillips screwdrivers.* The difference between a standard screwdriver and a Phillips screwdriver is the shape of the head, as shown in Figures 2-1 and 2-2. You use Phillips screwdrivers with Phillips screws, and standard screwdrivers with — you guessed it — standard screws.

Using a screwdriver of the wrong type or size can damage the screw, the screwdriver, and even *you* if your hand slips while you're struggling to use the tool. Always use a screwdriver with a tip that's the same width and type as the head of the screw you're working on.

Because you usually can't use a standard screwdriver on a Phillips screw or vice versa (except for some Phillips/slot head screws that can be tightened or loosened by a standard blade type or Phillips head screwdriver), and because your car is fitted with both types of screws in a variety of sizes, you need several of each type (not just for your vehicle, but for almost anything around the house).

Shafts vary in length too, which is useful because a longer shaft provides greater access to "buried" screws, while a shorter shaft gets into tight places more easily. Handles also vary. It's important to have large, easy-to-grip handles to help you loosen tight screws.

You can get all the screwdrivers you need for relatively little money. Look for sales on plastic- or rubber-handled screwdrivers in sets of varying sizes.

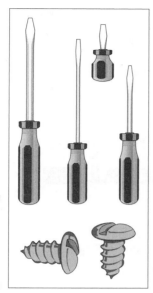

Figure 2-1:
Standard
screws and
screw-
drivers.

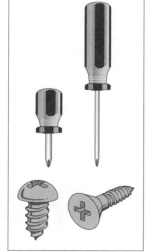

Figure 2-2:
Phillips
screws and
screw-
drivers.

Screwholders

Screwholders are perfectly marvelous for hanging onto screws that have to
fit into tiny places. Instead of hanging onto a screw with the fingers of one
hand while wielding the screwdriver with your other hand, you simply fit the

screw into the screwholder and use the screwholder instead of a screwdriver to tighten the screw. One type of screwholder has a magnet to hold the screw; another (see Figure 2-3) has a little gizmo that grabs the screw when you twist the screwholder. Both are lovely.

Figure 2-3:
A screwholder can help you get screws into hard-to-reach places.

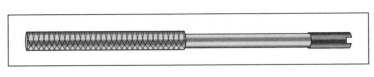

Wrenches

Wrenches are probably the most basic tools for auto repair. You need a couple of different kinds in different sizes. There are several basic types of wrenches, some for very specialized purposes, but the following sections cover the kinds you need for most jobs. Look for sets made by well-known toolmakers, and try to buy them on sale. (For more pointers on buying tools, see the beginning of this chapter.)

The turning of the screw

If you find yourself confronted with a screw that's difficult to start unscrewing, try giving the screw a slight twist in the *opposite* direction (clockwise), as though you were trying to tighten it. Then loosen it (counterclockwise). If this trick doesn't work, tap the screwdriver on the head with a hammer, which may loosen the screw a bit. If strong-arm tactics aren't getting you anywhere, you can try squirting the troublemaker with penetrating oil. (Don't use penetrating oil on a running engine or on any really hot areas, because it could ignite.) Remember to keep your temper with difficult screws; otherwise, you risk stripping the threads and turning a fairly simple job of replacing what you've loosened into a hair-puller.

Most wrenches are available in both standard — also known as SAE (Society of Automotive Engineers) — and metric measurements. You must know which system of measurement your engine is based on. Originally, most foreign vehicles (except British ones, which had their own thread standard) were based on the metric system, while domestic engines used SAE standards based on fractions of an inch. Today, most American vehicles have a mix of SAE and metric nuts and bolts. Foreign cars or foreign components used on American cars (a practice that's becoming quite common) use metric nuts and bolts — even the inch-based British. Check your owner's manual or ask your dealer to see whether your vehicle requires metric or standard SAE tools before you buy anything.

Combination wrenches

When shopping for wrenches, you'll come across *open-end wrenches* and *box-end wrenches,* but the very best kind to get are *combination wrenches,* which have an open end and a closed end on each wrench (see Figure 2-4). These wrenches come in sets of several sizes, and each wrench is made to fit a nut of a specific size, whichever end you use. See the sidebar "How to use a combination wrench."

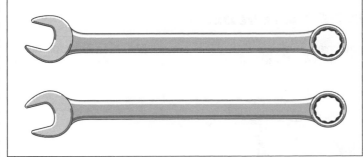

Figure 2-4: Combination wrenches, with one open end and one boxed end, are your best bet.

Offset wrenches

Some combination wrenches are sort of S-shaped. Called *offset wrenches,* these are good for working in hard-to-reach spots. You may want to add a couple to your tool kit.

The most useful offset wrench is the *distributor wrench,* shown in Figure 2-5, which you use to adjust your car's timing. (You need this tool only if your car has a *non-electronic* ignition system.) Be sure to get one to fit the distributor hold-down clamp on your vehicle.

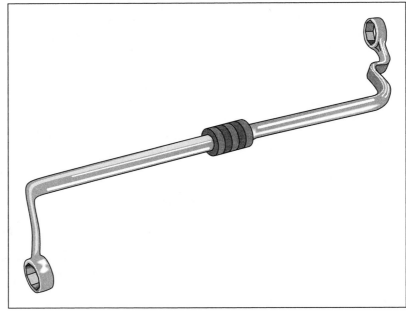

Figure 2-5:
An offset
distributor
wrench is
probably the
most useful
offset
wrench.

Ignition wrenches

Ignition wrenches (see Figure 2-6) are simply sets of combination wrenches in very small sizes for ignition work. You can get a set for a couple of dollars.

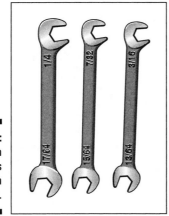

Figure 2-6:
Use ignition
wrenches
for ignition
work.

How to use a combination wrench

Here are a few tips for using a combination wrench:

✔ To use the open end of a wrench most effectively, place it around the nut you want to remove and then move the wrench to the right so that the nut moves in a counterclockwise direction. If the nut sticks, give it a squirt of penetrating oil or a tap on the head with a hammer.

✔ You can use your free hand to keep the wrench down over the nut. This gives you some control and prevents the wrench from flying off the nut.

✔ When you move the wrench as far as it can go, you loosen the nut 15 degrees. (That's why the slot is at an angle.) By simply turning the wrench over so that the other surface of the same end is around the nut, you can move the nut another 15 degrees without having to place the wrench at a different angle.

✔ Always use the proper size wrench. If the wrench that you use is too big, it can slip and round off the edges of the nut, which makes the nut harder to tighten later on. It can also round off the inside edges of the wrench, with the same results. (Of course, a wrench that is too small won't fit over the nut.)

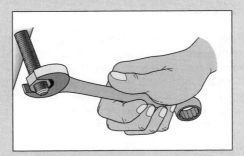

Allen (or hex) wrenches

Some of the screws or fastenings on your vehicle may have odd-shaped holes in the centers of their heads that require special *Allen wrenches* — L-shaped rods that fit into the holes (see Figure 2-7). If the center hole is hexagonal, the wrench you need is sometimes called a *hex wrench*. You can buy a set of assorted-sized Allen wrenches for under $15.

Figure 2-7:
Allen
wrenches.

Socket wrenches

A good set of socket wrenches, shown in Figure 2-8, can really make the difference between enjoying your work and killing yourself over it. Socket wrenches come in sets for a wide variety of prices, depending on quality and how many there are in the set. Sets can include either a mix of SAE and metric sockets, all SAE, or all metric pieces. Unless you've decided to become a mechanic, you can buy an inexpensive set of basic socket wrenches suitable for your vehicle for less than $25.

Figure 2-8:
A socket
wrench set.

Your set of socket wrenches should contain the following basic items:

- ✔ **A variety of ¼-inch or ⅜-inch drive heads or sockets:** The ½-inch, ⁹⁄₁₆-inch, and ¾-inch sockets are the ones you'll use the most, unless you need a metric set. The metric sizes most often used are 10, 11, 12, 13, and 14 mm.

  The word *drive* refers to the size of the square hole in each socket where it attaches to the ratchet handle. It's easy to remember that the smaller the drive, the smaller the job you use it for. A ¼-inch drive is for tiny areas; ⅜-inch drive is for the next range of sizes, typically up to SAE ¾ or 18 mm metric; ½-inch drive is for up to SAE 1⅛, or up to 25 mm; and other drives up to 2 inches are for really big jobs (you won't need one of these monsters). You can use adapters to convert sockets of one drive to fit handles of another drive.

- ✔ **A spark plug socket:** This is the large socket with a soft lining to hold the spark plug securely without damaging its soft jacket when you remove and insert it, or when you drop it on the floor by mistake. Spark plugs come in two sizes, so make sure to get the size that fits the spark plugs in your car. Your owner's manual may note the spark plug size.

- ✔ **At least one ratchet handle, to which you can fit any of the sockets:** Most sets have two or three handles with at least one adapter. You may want to add additional adapters to extend the handle to different sizes and adapt it to different drives. Figure 2-9 shows the wide variety of sockets, handles, and adapters available.

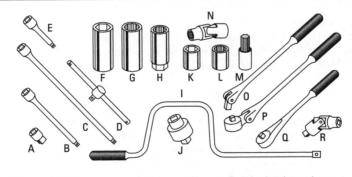

Figure 2-9:
The parts of a socket wrench: adapters, ratchet handles, and extenders.

A	-Adapter	K	-Regular 6-point socket
B, C, E	-Extension bars	L	-Regular 12-point socket
D	-Sliding T handle	M	-Hollow screw socket bit
F	-Deep 6-point socket	N	-Universal 12-point socket
G	-Deep 12-point socket	O	-Flex handle
H	-Spark plug socket	P	-Flex head rachet
I	-Speeder handle	Q	-Reversible rachet
J	-Rachet adapter	R	-Universal joint

> ✔ **A flex-head handle:** Although not strictly necessary, a flex-head handle is very useful. It enables you to hold the ratchet handle at any angle when working in tight places — and engines are full of tight places!
>
> ✔ **Socket extenders:** These indispensable items help you get your socket head way down into the bowels of your engine compartment to reach those almost-unreachable nuts and bolts.

The way to tell a good socket wrench set is to look at the number of teeth in the ratchet handle. Most have 20 to 30 teeth. The really good ones have up to 60 teeth. The more teeth the handle has, the better it can fit into tight places. This is because you have to move the handle only a few degrees to turn the nut as much as a cheaper handle would in many degrees. In other words, a ratchet handle with 24 teeth must be moved 15 degrees to reach its limit. A handle with 60 teeth has to be moved only 6 degrees to turn a nut as far. You can find instructions for using a socket wrench in the section called "Removing spark plugs" in Chapter 12.

Torque wrenches

A torque wrench, shown in Figure 2-10, is designed to tighten a nut, bolt, or screw to an exact degree. A torque wrench is extremely handy because, until you become familiar with a job, you always run the risk of undertightening or overtightening things.

If you're replacing a spark plug and you don't tighten it enough, it will work itself loose and fail to deliver a spark. If you overtighten a spark plug, you can strip the threads or crack the plug. Similarly, parts that have gaskets can leak if the bolts that hold them aren't tightened enough. But if you overtighten the same bolts, the gaskets will be crushed, causing the fluid to leak anyway.

Most really good torque wrenches are expensive, but a cheaper one is good enough to serve your purposes. If you'd rather not spend the money until you're sure that you're really going to like working on your car, borrow a torque wrench just to get the feel of how tight a nut, bolt, or other part should be. Or you can just forget the whole thing. I've never used a torque wrench; my set of socket wrenches accomplished everything quite well for the work in this book. If you *are* planning to buy a torque wrench, get one with a slim profile, because torque wrenches are bulky anyway and often don't fit into tight places.

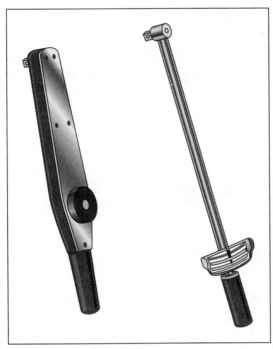

Figure 2-10:
Dial torque
wrench
(left) and
deflecting
beam torque
wrench.

If you use a torque wrench, keep the following in mind:

✔ Grip a torque wrench well down the shaft (not up close to the dial) and operate it smoothly.

✔ Tighten a series of nuts or bolts in a sequence that distributes the pressure evenly, instead of in strict clockwise or counterclockwise order.

✔ When tightening a series of bolts, tighten them all just until they're snug. Then go back and tighten them all a bit more. Then go back and tighten them all the way to the torque specifications. Doing so ensures that the entire part you're tightening is under even pressure, prevents leaky gaskets, and increases the life of the bolt and the part. This and the preceding tips are good to follow when you're using any kind of wrench to tighten anything.

✔ Before using a torque wrench, make sure that the nut or bolt turns freely so that the torque wrench gets a true reading of the proper nut tightness. You can use a lubricant such as WD-40 on the threads and run the nut up and down a few times to free it before using the torque wrench on it.

Adjustable wrenches

An adjustable wrench, sometimes called a *monkey wrench,* is a useful addition to your toolbox. (See Figure 2-11.) You probably already have one in the house. You can adjust the jaws to fit a variety of nuts and bolts simply by turning the wheel. I like the very small and medium sizes because they fit into tight spaces easily.

Figure 2-11:
An adjustable wrench has many uses.

Hammers

You may associate hammers solely with carpentry, but they're useful in automotive work as well. In auto repair, you use a hammer to "sweet talk" something loose (like a nut or bolt that's on too tight). You *don't* use a hammer to whack the tar out of your engine.

Make sure that you use the right kind of hammer. You should have a *ball-peen* hammer (see Figure 2-12). A *carpenter's hammer* (or *claw hammer*) isn't really designed for auto repair.

Figure 2-12:
Use a ball-peen hammer, rather than a claw hammer, for car repair.

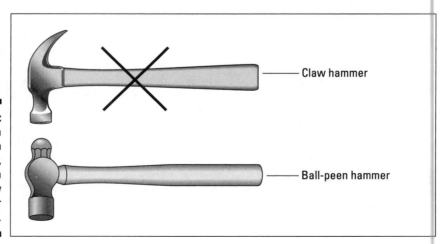

Claw hammer

Ball-peen hammer

If all you have is a carpenter's hammer and you don't want to buy another one, you can probably make do with it. Just be sure that the hammer you use doesn't have a loose head. If the shaft isn't securely sunk into the head, the head can fly off and damage your car, you, or an innocent bystander. Claw hammers can also be dangerous because a hard, solid impact can cause the claws to break off, with dismal results.

Pliers

Almost everyone has *needle-nosed* and *slip-joint* pliers (see Figure 2-13); if you rummage through the family toolbox, you'll probably discover that you have them, too. Both types of pliers are useful for auto repair.

If you have to buy pliers, the very best kind to get are *combination slip-joint pliers.* You can adjust these general-purpose tools to several widths with a sliding pin. They usually have a wire-cutting slot built into them as well. If you're the only person on your block who doesn't possess these, by all means rush out and buy them before dark. Again, they needn't be expensive. Just make sure that they work easily, are made of forged hardened steel, and seem to be well finished.

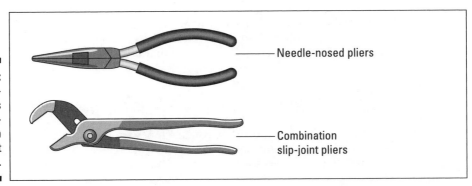

Figure 2-13:
Needle-
nosed pliers
and combi-
nation
slip-joint
pliers.

Needle-nosed pliers

Combination
slip-joint pliers

If you're *really* into tools, you may also want to buy the following pliers, but you can easily get along without them:

✔ **Robogrip pliers** are a useful variation of slip-joint pliers that automatically lock in position when you have a grip on the part that you want to manipulate.

✔ **Adjustable vice-grip pliers** are useful for persuading recalcitrant stuff to loosen or twist — if, for example, you round off the edges of a nut so that normal tools won't loosen it. When set properly, the jaws lock onto a metal part very tightly, and you can pull, push, or twist almost anything with them.

How to use pliers

A couple of notes on the use of pliers:

✔ If you're working on electrical wiring and don't want to get shocked, make sure that the handles of your pliers are covered with rubber to insulate them. If the handles are naked metal, slip a length of rubber hose over each handle, leaving the hose in one piece. Doing so not only insulates the pliers,

but the rubber also straightens out when you release the pliers, causing them to spring open quickly.

✔ Never use combination slip-joint pliers on nuts and bolts — they round off the corners, making them harder to replace. Besides, nuts and bolts are what you have all your lovely wrenches for.

Gauges and Meters

Despite the simple principles behind how an engine works (if you want the lowdown, head to Chapter 3), many auto repair tasks require fairly precise adjustments: You put only so much oil into the engine. You add only so much air to tires. You tighten some nuts and bolts only so tight. You leave a gap of a precise size between spark plug electrodes. Several tools are available to help you determine when enough oil, fluid, air, pressure, or whatever is enough. This section highlights those that are most useful.

Wire, taper, and flat feeler gauges

This section covers tools that you use for "gapping" spark plugs, points (on cars with *non-electronic* ignition systems), and valves. These tools are very inexpensive — some stores even give them away as premiums. Although I usually discuss specialized tools in the chapters that call for them, I want to mention these now so that you can pick them up while you're at an auto supply store buying other stuff:

✔ **Wire and taper feeler gauges:** You use these gauges for gapping spark plugs (see Figures 2-14 and 2-15). *Gapping* simply means sliding the proper-sized wire or taper gauge between the spark plug electrodes to make sure that the surfaces are the proper distance apart. Doing so ensures that the spark can jump across the gap with the proper intensity.

✔ **Flat feeler gauges:** You use these gauges to adjust valves and ignition contact points, relatively simple jobs that are impossible to do properly without a feeler gauge (see Figure 2-16). Look for these gauges as part of a set of tools — or as freebies in auto parts stores — before you buy them separately.

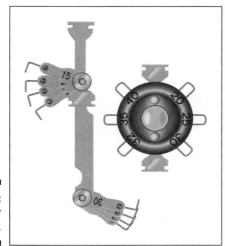

Figure 2-14:
Wire feeler
gauges.

Figure 2-15:
A taper
feeler
gauge.

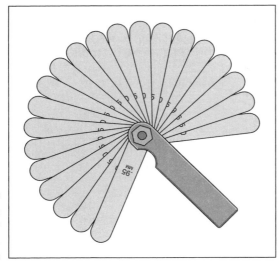

Figure 2-16:
A flat feeler
gauge.

Cars with electronic ignitions don't need tune-ups, and they require special expensive tools for adjustments. If your car has an electronic ignition, forget about buying a feeler gauge for gapping points. You can consult your owner's manual to see whether your car's ignition is simple enough to adjust yourself and what tools you'd need, but chances are that you'll be happy to have a professional maintain the system for you. The good news is that electronic ignitions usually don't require adjusting if they're set correctly in the first place.

Compression gauges

You use compression gauges, shown in Figure 2-17, to check the pressure that builds up in each cylinder as your engine runs. These gauges also reveal worn or damaged piston rings and valves. If your vehicle is new, you probably won't have this problem for some time, but if you have an older or secondhand vehicle, this easy-to-use gauge is a good investment. It can help you spot trouble and save money. The screw-in kind is easiest to use but usually costs a bit more.

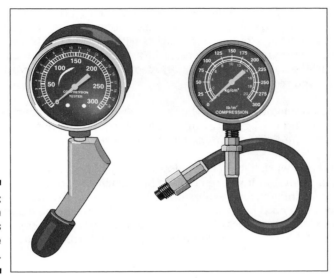

Figure 2-17:
Compression
gauges
measure
pressure.

Work Lights

Whether you plan to work on your car in your home garage, in your driveway, at the curb near your house, or in the auto shop at a local school, you'll find that the lighting will be inadequate once you get under the hood — or under the car, if you're that adventurous. A work light can provide all the illumination you need and enable you to shine the maximum amount of light right on the work area and not in your eyes (see Figure 2-18).

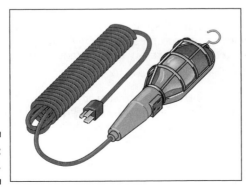

Figure 2-18:
A work light.

When you shop for a work light, be sure to get one that has a protective cage around at least half the bulb and a cord that's long enough and properly insulated. (Go for at least a 25-foot cord. Lights with shorter cords are cheaper, but if you need to buy an extension cord to get the light to your car, you may end up spending more in the long run.) Also look for the Underwriter's tag to be sure that you're getting quality.

The typical work light cage has a hook at the top so that you can hang the light inside the hood of your car or on a nearby part. The hook is very handy, but *don't hook the light to anything that carries electricity!*.

You'll find that a work light is useful for a variety of home repairs and for outside work at night, but if you're going to be working far from an electrical outlet, you may need a long extension cord in addition to a work light. Luckily, neither a cord nor a work light is an expensive item. You may also want to consider a work light that gets its power from your car's battery. I've also seen portable battery-powered fluorescent lanterns that are useful for night work and for camping.

Jacks

Most new cars come with a jack to be used when changing tires. If you have a secondhand car, or if your jack has been lying around neglected, you may need to buy one. If you think that you need a new jack, you can buy the scissor type, but I suggest that you invest in a 1.5-ton hydraulic jack, which is faster and safer and not terribly expensive (refer to Figure 1-1 in Chapter 1).

Whatever type you buy, make sure that the jack is suited to your car's body design. To determine the type of jack you need and to find out how to use the jack that came with the vehicle, check your owner's manual or ask someone at an auto parts store.

Check your jack periodically and lubricate it. Never use a jack without the base plate, and never jack up your car unless the wheels are properly blocked. You can find instructions and safety tips for using a jack and changing a tire in Chapter 1.

Make sure that your jack is in the trunk of your car at all times. It's very depressing to know how to change a flat, only to find when a flat occurs that your jack is in your garage and your car is on the road.

Tool kits

If, as you read this chapter, you're made painfully aware that you're going to have to go out and buy practically everything, you may want to look into prepackaged tool kits. Nearly every major supplier carries an inexpensive basic automotive tool kit with everything you need for maintenance and minor repairs already in it. If you're totally tool-poor, one of these may prove to be the best buy. Make sure that you're getting good quality, however. It's better to have a couple of tools that work well than to have a large assortment of junk.

While I'm on the subject, empty toolboxes are inexpensive and worth buying. They keep tools clean and in good shape, and, most important, all in one place. Look for a lightweight, plastic toolbox that fits easily into the trunk of your car. Although your tools are useful around the house, it's nice to have them handy if you get stuck away from home.

Jack Stands

If you plan to work under your vehicle, you also need a pair of jack stands (refer to Figure 1-2 in Chapter 1). With these, you jack up the car, place the jack stands under the car close to where the jack is, and then remove the jack so that the weight of the vehicle rests on the jack stands, and not on the jack, which can collapse or roll over. The stands keep the car off the ground with less danger of slipping and enable you to jack up more than one side of the vehicle at a time. Get two jack stands and read the instructions in Chapter 1 before you use them.

Substituting boxes, stones, or bricks for jack stands is very dangerous. They can slip out or break while you're under the car. A jack can do the same thing, so if you're going to work under your vehicle (and you will if you plan to do your own lube jobs), be sure to buy a pair of jack stands. The money you save by getting under there yourself will easily pay for the stands in no time.

Creepers

If you're going to spend a lot of time under your vehicle, you may want a creeper, which is basically just a board with casters under it. (See Figure 2-19.) You lie on it and move around easily.

Figure 2-19:
A creeper
makes
working
under your
car more
comfortable.

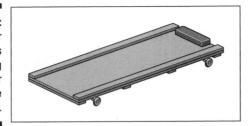

If you're good at carpentry, you can make a creeper yourself from some ply-wood and a couple of old roller-skate wheels. If you're fed up with buying things, try lying on an old bedboard or a ratty old blanket instead.

If you're not yet game for a lot of under-the-car work and you just want to change your tires, change your oil, and be done with it, forget about the creeper and just be sure that you have a jack and jack stands that work properly, and that you know how to use them safely (see Chapter 1). Your owner's manual can tell you how to operate the jack that came with your vehicle, or you can take the jack to an auto supply store and ask someone there to show you how it works.

Fire Extinguishers

A fire extinguisher isn't really a tool, but it's a *must* for your vehicle. Get the 2¾-pound dry chemical type.

An engine fire won't necessarily ruin your car — if you can extinguish it quickly. A gasoline leak can be ignited by a stray spark from your spark plug wires. The resulting fire looks awful, but it's really burning on the *outside* of your engine. If you put it out quickly, your vehicle may suffer little or no damage.

Cigarette butts can also land on your backseat, causing a fire, and fires can be caused by ruptured fuel lines, flooded carburetors, and faulty wiring as well, so an inexpensive fire extinguisher may not only save you money; it may also save your life. If the flames are anywhere near the fuel tank, forget the hero-ics; just run for it and throw yourself to the ground if you think that the tank may explode.

Because your fuel tank is located right under your trunk compartment, keep your extinguisher under the *front* seat of your car, in a suitable bracket that will prevent it from rolling under the pedals when you stop the car.

Funnels

You use funnels to fill your radiator, add oil, and add transmission fluid to your car. Steal a large one from the kitchen, or buy one at an auto supply or hardware store. Either metal or plastic is fine. Just be sure to clean it thoroughly after each use.

Some automotive funnels come with a short hose attached so that you can insert the hose directly into a narrow opening in a space that's too small for the funnel to fit into.

More Things to Carry in Your Car

You can pack your toolbox with the best tools that money can buy, but all those fancy gadgets and gizmos won't do you any good if they're in your garage at home when your car breaks down 30 miles from civilization. Don't tempt fate: Keep these tools and materials onboard at all times (you probably have most of this stuff already, so there's no excuse for being unprepared):

- ✔ **Rags:** Rags should be clean and lint-free.

  Get rid of gasoline-soaked rags — they're highly combustible. Never keep them in closed places. Don't use an oily rag on anything that isn't oily already. Because your car contains a variety of substances that must be kept away from other substances, throw out or wash dirty rags, and use a clean one each time you start a job. Keep a clean, lint-free rag in your glove compartment; you'll need it to wipe your oil or transmission dipstick.

- ✔ **Spare parts:** If you replace your spark plugs and your points, save the old ones if they're not too worn. Carry them in your trunk compartment toolbox for quick replacements if something goes wrong with those in your engine. Just be sure to replace these substitutes with new ones immediately, because they won't hold up well. The same goes for old, not-too-cruddy air filters, rotors, and other minor gizmos. A couple of extra nuts, bolts, and screws also help, in case you lose the ones you have or strip them accidentally.

- ✔ **Emergency parts:** Buy extra accessory belts, extra coolant hoses, an extra thermostat, an extra radiator cap, and extra fuses — they're inexpensive and could get you out of a lot of trouble on a long trip.

- ✔ **Spare tire:** Check your spare tire often. It's humiliating to go through the work of changing a tire only to find that your spare is flat, too. If your spare is worn beyond belief, most garages will sell you a not-too-hideous secondhand tire at a low price. Make sure that it's the right size.

✔ **Lug wrench:** A lug wrench is sometimes provided, along with a jack, on new cars (see Figure 2-20). You use it to remove the wheel or lug nuts when you change your tires. If you buy a lug wrench, get the *cross-shaft* kind, which gives you more leverage.

✔ **Jumper cables:** One of the most common automotive malfunctions is the loss of power to start it, either from an old or faulty battery or from leaving the headlights on by mistake. If you're in this situation, you can either wait for the AAA or a nearby garage to come and bail you out, or, if you're in a safe, well-populated area, you can stop a passing car, whip out your jumper cables (shown in Figure 2-21), attach them in seconds, and "jump a start" from the Good Samaritan's car to your own. Most people are willing to lend their cars to this sort of operation because they lose nothing but a few minutes of their time, but it's up to you to decide whether you want to risk getting car-jacked if the Good Samaritan turns out to be a devil in disguise. Chapter 21 has instructions for the proper way to jump a start.

You can buy a set of jumper cables for much less than you'd have to pay a garage to send someone to start your car. Good cables cost more because they have more strands of better-conducting wire, which let more "juice" flow between the vehicles with less loss of voltage.

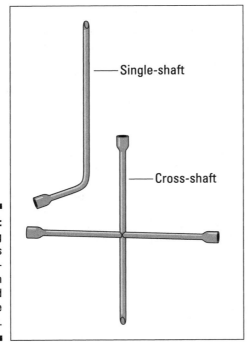

———Single-shaft

———Cross-shaft

Figure 2-20:
Lug wrenches are essential when you need to change a tire.

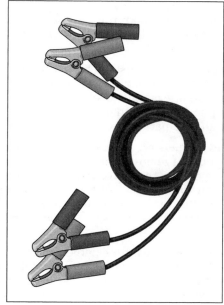

Figure 2-21:
You use
jumper
cables to
jump-start
a car.

Sometimes the success or failure of an attempt to jump a start depends on the quality of the jumper cables and their grips. If you get a cheap set, here's an easy way to make them work better: Go under the plastic sheath that covers the place where the cables meet the grips and squeeze the connection tight with a pair of pliers. Doing so improves the connection, and sometimes the cheap set of cables works beautifully — at least for the first few times. The best way to stay out of trouble is to pay a little extra for a quality set of cables.

✔ **Snow and ice equipment:** If you live in an area that's cold in winter, try to carry tire chains or a bag of sand in case you find yourself dealing with icy conditions. (Rock salt is no longer used for this purpose because it corrodes metal and is considered an environmental hazard.) A small shovel may prove useful for digging your tires out, and a scraper can clear your windshield if you've been parked in the snow and it's iced over. A can of de-icing fluid is useful in icy weather.

✔ **Flashlights and reflectors:** A flashlight is always a good addition to your glove compartment. It can help your kids locate dropped toys on the floor of the car, enable you to see under the hood if your car breaks down, and serve as an emergency light for oncoming traffic if you have to stop on the road for repairs. A flashlight with a red blinker is safest for this purpose. Of course, you have to be sure to put in fresh batteries now and then or to carry a couple of extras.

An inexpensive set of reflector triangles can save your life by making your stopped vehicle visible on the road. You can use flares, but they can be dangerous, and many states have rules regarding their use on highways.

✔ **First-aid kit:** It's a good idea to keep a first-aid kit in your workshop and in your vehicle. Choose one that's equipped with a variety of bandages, tweezers, surgical tape, antibiotic ointment, something soothing for burns, and a good antiseptic. You can find one of these kits for very little money at a drugstore or an auto parts store.

✔ **Hand cleaner:** Most hand cleaners are basically grease solvents. They range from heavy-duty stuff that removes the skin along with the grease, to soothing, good-smelling creams that leave your skin feeling reborn, to precleaners that you put on your hands *before* you start working so that the grease slides off easily afterward. Some of these cleaners can also be rubbed into work clothes to remove grease and oil stains before you launder them.

✔ **Gloves:** Keep a pair of gloves in the car for emergencies. Thin, tough, and comfortable dishwashing gloves are available at any discount store or supermarket. They cost little and keep the grease from under your fingernails. One problem, however, is that gasoline or solvent may melt them. If you prefer, industrial rubber gloves, available at swimming pool supply stores, aren't affected by gasoline, solvent, or battery acid.

✔ **Spare tools:** If you can't carry your toolbox in your car all the time, try to leave a couple of screwdrivers, some standard-size combination wrenches, an adjustable wrench, and a can of penetrating oil in your trunk compartment. Some very handy gizmos that combine a variety of basic tools into one all-purpose, weird-looking instrument are also available.

✔ **Hat:** To keep the dust and grease out of your hair, and to prevent long hair from being caught in moving parts, wear a hat that you can afford to get dirty. A wooly watch cap or a baseball hat worn backwards works just fine.

✔ **Cellular phone:** This device is useful when you're stuck on a road somewhere with a dead car or when you have an accident. You can call your loved ones or friends for help or call the auto club (some cell phones have an AAA or 911 call button) or the police.

✔ **Miscellaneous stuff:** A roll of duct tape, a roll of electrician's tape, a sharp knife, and scissors also come in handy.

Tool Checklist

Table 2-1 (on the following page) is a handy checklist to help you keep track of what you have, what you need, and what you think you can do without. Photocopy the page and take it to the store. (Asterisked tools are optional, but definitely worth buying. Tools with two asterisks are only for vehicles with non-electronic ignitions.)

Table 2-1	Tool Checklist		
Tool	*Have*	*Don't Have*	*Need Sizes*
Standard screwdrivers			
Phillips screwdrivers			
Screwholder*			
Combination wrenches			
Offset distributor wrench**			
Ignition wrenches**			
Allen wrenches			
Socket wrench set			
Flex-head extension*			
Extra handles and adapters*			
Torque wrench*			
Adjustable wrench			
Ball-peen hammer			
Combination slip-joint pliers			
Wire and taper feeler gauges			
Flat feeler gauge			
Compression gauge*			
Work light*			
Jack and jack stands			
Creeper*			
Fire extinguisher			
Funnel			
Spare tire			
Cross-shaft lug wrench			
Jumper cables*			
Flashlight			
First-aid kit			

Chapter 3

Preventive Maintenance: A Monthly Under-the-Hood Check

• •

In This Chapter

▶ Preventing 70 percent of the causes of highway breakdowns

▶ Checking the air filter

▶ Checking accessory belts

▶ Checking the battery

▶ Checking the radiator

▶ Checking hoses

▶ Checking the fluid levels

▶ Checking the wiring

▶ Checking the windshield wipers and tires

• •

*W*e all know people who are chronic tire kickers. These people habitually walk around their cars, kicking the tires to make sure that they aren't flat, before they get in and drive off. These same people habitually open and close all the cabinet doors in the kitchen and check the gas jets to make sure that they're completely off every time they go past the stove. We tend to laugh at them, yet they're probably rarely caught with flat tires, open cabinets, or leaking gas. You can learn from these people and make a habit of checking the little things under the hood of your car — maybe not *every* time you go somewhere, but definitely once a month and before starting out on long trips.

If the idea of committing yourself to a regular under-the-hood checkup seems less than alluring, look at it this way: *Spending 15 minutes a month on this under-the-hood check can prevent 70 percent of the problems that lead to highway breakdowns!* If you need more motivation, check out the sidebar "The benefits of a well-maintained car."

The benefits of a well-maintained car

For tangible evidence of how taking care of your car can benefit you, I offer this: Years ago, when I was married, I showed my husband (who used to run at the sight of anything mechanical) how to do everything in this chapter and perform a tune-up (the topic of Chapter 12). After he changed his spark plugs and serviced his distributor, his mileage increased from 10 miles per gallon to 17.5 miles per gallon. He was so impressed that, the next weekend, he changed his radiator hoses, fixed a windshield-washer pump that had gotten stuck, and became a con-firmed do-it-yourselfer. This was a relief to me, because I had visions of taking care of *two* cars, and that's *one* car too many for a working girl — unless she's a garage mechanic!

Convinced? Then what you need to check regularly is anything that can run out of fluid, lose air, jiggle loose, or fray after use — in other words, things like **accessory belts**, tire pressure, and **coolant** level. This chapter explains what to look for, how to look for it, and what to do if you discover that some-thing needs to be replaced or refilled.

I've provided a Maintenance Record sheet at the back of this book. Make a copy for each of your vehicles to keep track of what you check and what you replace. You'll find a Specifications Record at the back of the book as well. To avoid having to return parts that don't fit your vehicle, just make a copy of this "spec sheet" for each of your vehicles, fill in the appropriate part num-bers, and take it with you to the auto supply store.

Once a month, in the morning, before you've driven your car, arm yourself with a clean, lint-free rag and the tools mentioned in this chapter and open the hood of your vehicle. (If you've never done that, see "How to Open the Hood" in Chapter 1.) Then check the items in the sections that follow. It may take longer the first time you do it, but after that you should be able to whip through this check in about 15 minutes.

If the coolant, oil, transmission, brake, or power-steering fluid level is very low, fill it to the proper level and check it again in a couple of days. If it's low again, ask a mechanic to find out why you're losing fluid and correct the problem.

Check the Air Filter

Look for the **air cleaner** (see Figure 3-1). In carbureted engines, the air cleaner is usually large and round with a snorkel sticking out of the side to facilitate the intake of fresh air. Some fuel-injected engines also have a round air cleaner; others use a rectangular one.

If you unscrew the wing nut on the lid of your air cleaner and undo any other devices that hold it down, you'll find the **air filter** inside. To see whether your air filter needs to be replaced, just lift it out (it isn't fastened down) and hold it up to the sun or to a strong light. Can you see the light streaming through it? If not, try dropping it *lightly,* bottom side down, on a hard surface. Doing so should jar some dirt loose. (Don't blow through the filter — you can foul it up that way.) If the filter is still too dirty to see through after you've dropped it a few times, you need a new one. Chapter 13 has instructions for buying and replacing air filters.

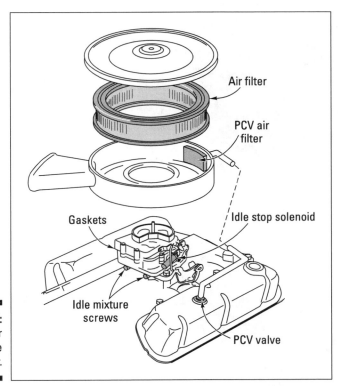

Air filter

PCV air filter

Gaskets

Idle stop solenoid

Idle mixture screws

PCV valve

Figure 3-1: The air filter is inside the air cleaner.

Because the air filter extracts dirt and dust particles from the air, you should change it at least once a year or every 20,000 miles, whichever comes first — unless yours gets very dirty before then. If you do most of your driving in a dusty or sandy area, you may need to replace your air filter more often.

Check the Accessory Belts

Take a look at all the belts (see Figures 3-2 and 3-3) that drive the fan, the alternator, and other parts of your car. If any of the belts "gives" more than half an inch when you press on it, you may be able to adjust it *if* it is otherwise in good condition. If a belt is cracked or frayed inside or outside, or if the inside surface is glazed and shiny, you should replace it. Chapter 14 has instructions for adjusting and replacing accessory belts.

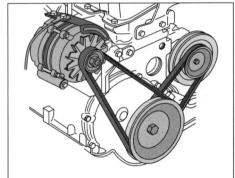

Figure 3-2:
Accessory
belts.

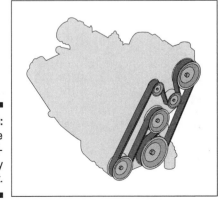

Figure 3-3:
Serpentine
multi-
accessory
drive belt.

If only one belt appears to be driving all the accessories in your car, see the section called "Check the Serpentine Multi-Accessory Drive Belt," which follows this one.

Check the Serpentine Multi-Accessory Drive Belt

In most modern vehicles, a single, long, flat drive belt (shown in Figure 3-3) drives all the engine accessories. This belt winds its way around every accessory pulley, and on the way winds tightly around a "tensioner" pulley that keeps the belt to the correct tension. In cases where it is possible to adjust the tensioner, you usually find something that indicates the correct belt tension.

It isn't easy to figure out whether a belt is at the right tension just by looking at it, but if the belt is loose, you will hear squeaky noises when you accelerate sharply. (With the hood up and the emergency brake on, have a friend accelerate the engine while you listen. Be sure to keep your hair and clothing away from the belt.) If the belt squeaks, have a professional replace both the belt and the tensioner because, in many cases, radiators and air conditioning condensers may have to be removed to allow access to the belt.

Check the Battery

The battery is part of the ignition system and stores electrical current that your car uses to start. The battery also passes electricity along to the parts of your vehicle that need electricity to function. (For more information about the ignition system in general and the battery in particular, see Chapters 5 and 12.)

A battery, like other parts of your car, is subject to wear and tear and should be checked regularly. In particular, you want to pay attention to the battery's trouble spots, shown in Figure 3-4. A battery that's kept clean and filled with water should last a long time.

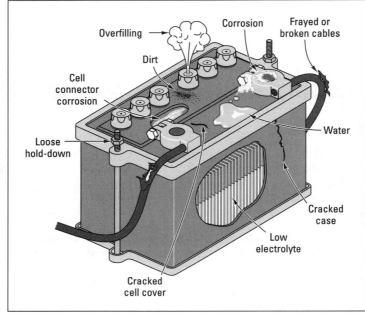

Overfilling

Corrosion

Frayed or
broken cables

Dirt

Cell
connector
corrosion

Loose
hold-down

Water

Cracked
case

Low
electrolyte

Cracked
cell cover

Figure 3-4:
The parts of
the battery
that you
want to pay
attention to
during a
regular
check.

To check your battery, follow these steps:

1. **If you have a battery with removable caps or bars on top, remove them. (See Figure 3-5.)**

   These days, most batteries are sealed.

   Never open a battery with a lit cigarette in your mouth. (For that matter, never smoke while working around your car!) Batteries are filled with an acid that generates hydrogen gas, so you want to be careful when working around them. If you get the liquid on your skin or clothes, wash it off with water immediately.

2. **If your battery is not sealed, look inside the battery.**

   If you have a sealed battery, you won't be able to do this, so disregard Step 3 and move on to Step 4.

3. **If the liquid inside the battery doesn't reach the tops of the plates, add distilled water or water with a low mineral content until it covers them.**

   Be very careful not to add liquid past the top of the fins inside the battery.

4. **If you see powdery deposits on the terminals, clean them off.**

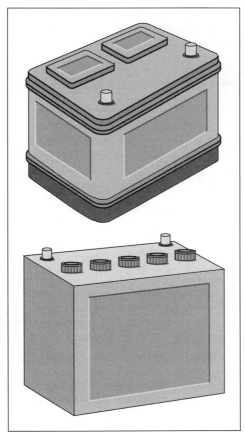

Figure 3-5:
Battery
covers with
removable
caps or
bars.

The cruddy deposits that form in lovely colors on the top of your terminals are made by battery acid. Before you clean this stuff off, remove the
cables from the positive terminal and negative terminal by undoing the
nut on each cable clamp and wiggling the cable until the clamp comes
off the terminal post.

Always remove the cable clamp from the negative terminal first. (It's the
one that's marked with a – sign.) *Replace the positive cable first and the
negative cable last.* If you attempt to remove the positive clamp first and
your wrench slips and touches something metal, your wrench can fuse
to the part like an arc welder.

Brush the deposits off the terminal posts and cable clamps with an old
toothbrush or disposable nonmetallic brush and a mixture of baking
soda and water. Sprinkle the baking soda straight from the little yellow
box that keeps your refrigerator smelling nice, dip the brush in water,
and scrub the deposits away.

If your cables and clamps won't clean up completely with baking soda and water, rotate a round battery terminal cleaner brush (see Figure 3-6) on each terminal to shine it up and ensure a good, solid electrical connection. You can also shine up the insides of the cable clamps by using the clamp cleaner that is usually sold as one unit with the terminal brush. If you can't find these brushes, use a *soapless* steel wool pad.

Figure 3-6:
A battery
terminal
brush and
clamp
cleaner.

5. **Dry everything off with a clean, disposable, lint-free rag.**

   Try to avoid getting the powdery stuff on your hands or clothes, but if you do, just wash it off with water *right away,* and neither you nor your clothes will be damaged.

6. **To prevent these corrosive deposits from forming again, coat the terminals with grease or petroleum jelly.**

7. **Examine the battery cables and clamps to see whether they are badly frayed or corroded.**

   If the damage looks extensive, the cables and clamps should probably be replaced; otherwise, the battery may short-circuit and could damage onboard computers.

   In most modern cars, computers control the engine fuel and ignition systems and automatic transmission functions. When messing about with batteries and their cables, be extremely careful not to make a mistake and inadvertently send a shot of unwanted voltage into one of the computers and destroy it. They're not cheap to replace! Carefully remove and replace battery cables, always removing the *negative* cable first and replacing it last.

If you don't want to lose all those precious radio presets when you disconnect the battery, you can make a cheap tool with a cigarette lighter socket and a 9-volt battery. (Most electronics stores can set this up for you.) Plug the 9-volt battery into your cigarette lighter socket before disconnecting the battery, and when you're done, you'll still have all those radio presets. That process also helps maintain memory for your onboard computers for your engine and transmission.

Take these precautions: Tie the cables back while you're working on the battery so that they don't flop back over onto the terminals. Always remove the negative cable if you plan to work on wiring under the hood. Do not allow anything made of metal to connect the terminal posts; this can damage the battery. And if the cables are connected to the posts at the time, you can destroy the onboard computers.

8. **If you've been having trouble starting your car, if your headlights seem dim, or if the battery is old and has bars or caps that you can remove and look inside, buy a battery tester (see Figure 3-7) and use it to check whether the battery acid concentration is high enough.**

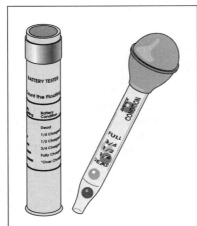

Figure 3-7:
Battery
tester.

These testers cost only a few dollars. You simply draw some of the battery fluid (electrolyte) into the tester and look at the floating balls inside it. A scale on the tester tells you the condition of the battery fluid. If you get a very low reading, you can try having the battery refilled and recharged at a service station. If they tell you that your battery should be replaced, replace it. It's no fun to get caught with a dead battery, because you can't drive to the store to get a new one!

If you have a *sealed* battery and you own or can borrow a voltmeter, attach it across the battery terminals (red to positive and black to negative). With all accessories off and the battery at 70 degrees Fahrenheit, the voltage reading should be 12.6 volts or slightly lower at lower temperatures. Or just stop off at your local service station and have them test the battery.

9. **Check the battery case and the terminals.**

   If you see major cracks in the battery case or obvious terminal damage, the battery should be replaced regardless of its electrical performance.

When replacing the battery, buy a new one with a reputable brand name at an auto parts store, battery service, or department store; don't risk getting stranded by a cheap battery that malfunctions. But don't overbuy, either; it's foolish to put an expensive battery with a five-year guarantee in a vehicle that you intend to get rid of in a year or two.

Don't just dump your old battery into the trash, where it's a hazard to the environment. Because batteries are recyclable, you can trade in your old battery for a discount on the price of a new one and walk away content knowing that the old one will be back in service before long.

Check the Radiator

The radiator cools your engine and needs water and coolant (sometimes called *antifreeze*) to function. (Chapter 8 familiarizes you with the parts of the cooling system and how they work; Chapter 14 tells you how to flush your cooling system and do minor repairs on it; and Chapter 21 tells you what to do if your car overheats on the road.)

Always use a 50/50 mixture of coolant and water to fill or top off the cooling system. Use plain water only in an emergency. Most modern engines have aluminum cylinder heads, which require the protective anticorrosive properties of antifreeze to prevent corrosion. For the purposes of brevity, I'll refer to that 50/50 mix simply as "liquid" or "coolant" from now on.

Never add coolant to a *hot* engine! If you need to add more liquid, wait until the engine has cooled down to avoid the possibility of being burned or cracking your engine block. To check the level of the liquid in your cooling system and add more, if necessary, do the following:

✔ **If your car has a coolant recovery system (a plastic bottle connected to the radiator that holds an extra supply of liquid, shown in Figure 8-2 in Chapter 8):** There's no need to open the radiator cap. Just check to see whether the liquid reaches the "Full" line on the side of the bottle. If it doesn't, add a 50/50 mix of water and coolant to the bottle until it reaches the "Full" line.

Some coolant reservoirs are pressurized and have a radiator cap instead of a normal cap. Do not open these when the engine is hot, or hot coolant may be ejected.

✔ **If your car has no coolant reservoir:** You need to open the cap on your radiator, peek down the hole and, if necessary, add liquid. The next two sections show how to do so.

Opening a radiator cap safely

Never try to remove a radiator cap from a hot engine; the escaping steam can burn you. Wait for the engine to cool down. Test for a cool engine by grasping the large upper radiator hose. If the hose is hot to the touch and/or feels like it has a lot of pressure inside it, continue to wait until it's cool enough for you to open the cap safely.

To open the cap (as shown in Figure 3-8), place a cloth over the cap and turn it counterclockwise to its first stop. This allows the pressure to escape. If you see liquid or a great deal of steam escaping, retighten the cap and wait for things to cool down. If not, continue to turn the cap counterclockwise to remove it. Tilt the cap away from you as you remove it so that whatever steam remains lands on the engine or under the hood, and not on you.

Figure 3-8:
Removing a radiator cap safely.

Checking and adding coolant to a radiator

If you have no reservoir, here's how to check the coolant level (after you get the radiator cap off) and add liquid, if necessary:

1. **Look down the hole in the top of the radiator; you should be able to see the liquid an inch or so below the place where the cap screwed on.**

If the liquid is below the fins in the radiator, or you can't see it at all, the level is too low.

2. **If the level is too low, pour a 50/50 mixture of water and coolant down the radiator hole until it covers the fins or reaches an inch or so below the cap.**

Keep the following points in mind as you check the coolant in your radiator or coolant reservoir:

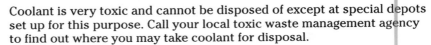

- ✔ **Coolant is usually red, green, blue, or yellow. If it looks colorless, looks rusty, or has things floating around in it, flush your cooling system and add new coolant.** Instructions for when and how to do so are in Chapter 14.

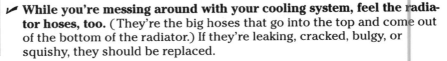

- ✔ **If the coolant has a sludgy, oily surface, immediately take the car to your mechanic to check for internal head gasket leakage.** The service facility will have special equipment for performing this check.

  Coolant is very toxic and cannot be disposed of except at special depots set up for this purpose. Call your local toxic waste management agency to find out where you may take coolant for disposal.

- ✔ **While you're messing around with your cooling system, feel the radiator hoses, too.** (They're the big hoses that go into the top and come out of the bottom of the radiator.) If they're leaking, cracked, bulgy, or squishy, they should be replaced.

For more information about replacing hoses and adding water or coolant to the radiator, see Chapter 14; to find out what to do if your car overheats anyway, head to Chapter 21.

Check the Hoses

To check your car's hoses, walk around the hood area and squeeze every hose you encounter. If you find any that are leaking, bulgy, soft and squishy, or hard and brittle, replace them. Replacing a hose is easy and inexpensive. You'll find instructions for how to do so in Chapter 14.

It pays to replace hoses *before* they break; any savings in time or effort aren't worth the aggravation of having your trip come to an abrupt halt on the freeway because of a broken hose. Most tow trucks don't carry spare hoses (they'd have to carry too many different kinds, and they don't have the time to change hoses on the road), and you may end up paying an expensive tow charge for a couple of dollars' worth of hose that you could have replaced ahead of time in about ten minutes.

Check the Oil Dipstick

Oil reduces the friction in your engine and keeps it running smoothly. You should check your oil at least once a month to make sure that there's enough oil and that it isn't contaminated.

To find out whether your car needs oil, do the following:

1. **When the engine is cold (or has been off for at least ten minutes), pull out the dipstick (the one with a ring on the end of it that sticks out the side of the engine, as shown in Figure 3-9) and wipe it off on a clean, lint-free rag.**

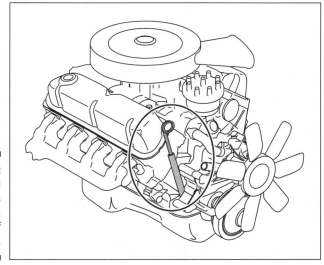

Figure 3-9: The oil dipstick is located on the side of the engine.

Why you should check the oil yourself

The problem with driving into a gas station and allowing the attendant to check your oil is that the dipstick will always read a little low because so much of the oil is still inside the hot engine rather than in the oil pan. By adding more oil until it reaches the "Full" level on the stick, the attendant may overfill the engine and damage it. For this reason, always wait at least ten minutes after you shut off the engine before allowing anyone to check the dipstick. If you don't feel like sitting around at a gas station, the best time to check your oil is first thing in the morning, when the car has been sitting all night and the engine is cold.

2. **Shove the stick back in again.**

   If the dipstick gets stuck on the way in, turn it around. The pipe it fits into is curved, and the metal stick bends naturally in the direction of the curve if you put it back in the way it came out.

3. **Pull the dipstick out again and look at the film of oil on the end of the stick (see Figure 3-10).**

Figure 3-10:
This is one time when you want to follow directions from a dipstick.

4. **Notice how high the oil film reaches on the dipstick and the condition of the oil.**

   If your oil looks clean enough but only reaches the "Add" level on the dipstick, you need to add oil. You can get some oil the next time you fill up at the gas station, or you can buy a bottle at an auto supply store and add it yourself. Chapter 15 can help you to determine the proper weight oil for your vehicle; it also provides instructions for locating the place to pour in the oil.

   If your oil looks clean enough but only reaches the "Add" level on the dipstick, you need to add oil. You can get some oil the next time you fill up at the gas station, or you can buy a bottle at an auto supply store and add it yourself. Chapter 15 can help you to determine the proper weight oil for your vehicle; it also provides instructions for locating the place to pour in the oil.

   If the oil is dirty and grimy or smells of gasoline, it probably needs to be changed. You can pay a mechanic or an oil-change place to change it for you, but why not head to Chapter 15 to find out how to change the oil yourself? The task is easy and can save you a lot of money. I know that it's easy because, during one of my appearances on his show, Regis Philbin changed the oil in a car in five minutes without getting a spot on his Italian silk suit!

5. **Put the dipstick back in.**

Check the Automatic Transmission Fluid

To check your automatic transmission fluid, look for a dipstick handle toward the rear of the engine, sticking out of your transmission (see Figure 3-11) or transaxle (if your vehicle has front-wheel drive).

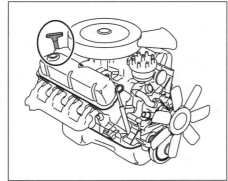

Figure 3-11:
Where to find the dipstick for an automatic transmission.

If you have a car with a manual transmission, disregard this step. The fluid level in a manual transmission must be checked with the vehicle on a hoist to enable the technician to reach a plug in the bottom of the transmission. It's best not to monkey around with this yourself. The next time your car is in for repairs or lubrication, have the mechanic check the transmission fluid level for you as well. However, it's a good idea to know what type and viscosity of fluid goes into your transmission and to make sure that's what the technician plans to use. Some newer manual transmissions use automatic transmission fluid; others use engine oil.

To check your automatic transmission fluid, do the following:

1. **With the gearshift in Neutral or Park and the emergency brake on, let your engine run. When the engine is warm, pull out the dipstick. (Don't turn off the engine.)**

2. **Wipe the dipstick with a clean, lint-free rag; then reinsert it and pull it out again.**

3. **If the transmission fluid doesn't reach the "Full" line on the dipstick, use a funnel to pour just enough transmission fluid down the dipstick tube to reach the line. Don't overfill!**

There are several types of transmission fluid. Each is made for a specific type of automatic transmission. Newer transmissions from the major auto-makers require different fluid than vehicles as little as two years old. Because so many different kinds of transmissions are around these days, check your owner's manual or dealership to find out which type of fluid your car requires, and enter that type on your Specifications Record.

4. **Dip the tip of your index finger into the fluid on the dipstick and rub the fluid between your finger and the tip of your thumb.**

The transmission fluid on the dipstick should be pinkish and almost clear. If it looks or smells burnt or has particles in it, have a mechanic drain and change the fluid.

If your car hesitates when your automatic transmission shifts gears, the first thing to check is the transmission fluid level — *before* you let any mechanic start talking about servicing or adjusting your transmission or selling you a new one. Many symptoms of a faulty transmission are the same as those for being low on transmission fluid. Obviously, adding transmission fluid is a lot cheaper than replacing the whole transmission system! See Chapter 17 for advice.

Check the Brake Fluid

On the driver's side of your vehicle, usually up near the firewall, is a big, round thing called the vacuum brake booster. Just in front of that, sitting on and connected to the brake master cylinder, is the brake fluid reservoir, a plastic canister that contains (you guessed it) brake fluid. (Older vehicles don't have a plastic reservoir; instead, the master cylinder is a little metal box with a lid that you must remove to check the fluid level.)

When you put your foot on the brake pedal, the fluid in the master cylinder (see Figure 3-12) moves down the brake lines to the front and rear brakes. If there's insufficient brake fluid, air is introduced into the brake lines and your car won't stop properly. Therefore, it's important to keep enough brake fluid in your brake fluid reservoir. (This situation is not as scary as it sounds; most master cylinders have two chambers as a safety feature. This way, if one well of brake fluid suddenly goes dry because of a leak in the brake lines or something like that, the other chamber still has enough fluid in it to stop the car.)

If your vehicle has anti-lock brakes (ABS), consult your owner's manual before checking your brake fluid. Some require you to pump the brake pedal approximately 25 to 30 times before opening and inspecting the fluid reservoir.

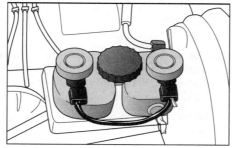

Figure 3-12:
The master cylinder on many popular cars.

To check your brake fluid, do the following:

1. **Open the top of your brake fluid reservoir.**

   If you have the kind with a little plastic reservoir on top, just unscrew the cap of the reservoir. If you have a metal master cylinder that contains the reservoir, use a screwdriver to pry the retaining clamp off the top (see Figure 3-13).

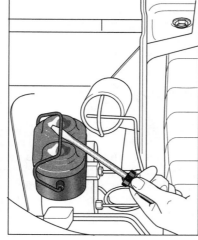

Figure 3-13:
Releasing the lid of a metal master cylinder with a screwdriver.

Always clean the top of the cylinder or reservoir carefully before opening it. A small amount of dirt falling into the fluid can cause the internal seals of the master cylinder to fail. Your brakes will begin to lose effectiveness and ultimately fail completely.

2. **Look to see where the fluid level lies between the low- and high-level indicating marks on the plastic reservoir, or inside the master cylinder, to make sure that the brake fluid level is within half an inch or so of the cap.**

If the level isn't high enough, add the proper brake fluid for your vehicle. (You can find instructions for buying the proper brake fluid in Chapter 18.) Also keep the following points in mind:

- **Don't get brake fluid on anything that's painted — brake fluid eats paint.** If you spill any, wipe it up immediately and get rid of the rag. Because brake fluid is toxic, take anything with more than just a couple of small spots of fluid on it to a toxic waste center.

- **Don't get grease or oil in your brake fluid — either one may ruin your hydraulic brake system.**

- **Don't leave a can of brake fluid standing around open.** Brake fluid soaks up moisture to keep it from settling in the hydraulic components and corroding them. If moist air gets to brake fluid for as little as 15 minutes, the fluid is ruined. So keep the can tightly closed until you're ready to use it, and if you have some fluid left over, take the can to a toxic waste center for disposal.

If your car has a manual transmission and the brake fluid reservoir is empty when you check it, you may have to "bleed" the brake system. See Chapter 18 for step-by-step instructions.

Because brake fluid deteriorates with use, it should be replaced by a mechanic if it looks dark in color. In any case, have the fluid changed every two years. Doing so protects the hydraulic components from internal corrosion and premature brake failure.

Check the Power-Steering Fluid

To check the power-steering fluid, locate the power-steering pump in your car (see Figure 3-14). If you can't find it, your owner's manual should tell you where it is. Unscrew the cap and see whether the fluid reaches the fill mark on the dipstick (or whether it's near the top of the bottle). If the level is low, check your owner's manual or dealership to see what kind of fluid your power steering pump requires. Mark this type on your Specifications Record for future reference.

Check the Wiring

Feel the wires that you encounter under the hood. If they feel hard and inflexible, if bright metal wires show through the insulation, or if the wires look corroded or very messy where they attach to various devices, they may need to be changed before they short out. Until you really get to be an expert, have a professional do the rewiring for you.

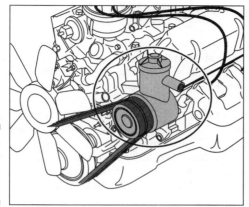

Figure 3-14:
The power-
steering
pump.

To figure out whether your ignition wires are electrically sound and not leak-ing to surrounding engine parts, put the car in Neutral or Park and put the emergency brake on. Start your engine, and lift the hood at night in a place where no light shines on your car. Look down at the engine until your eyes are accustomed to the dark. If your ignition wires are leaking, you'll see flash-ing lights — almost like a small fireworks display within your engine compartment. Have the ignition wires replaced if you see this.

Check the Windshield-Washer Fluid

Under your hood is a plastic bottle or bag that connects to the washers on your windshield wipers. Is it full of liquid? If not, you can fill it with any one of a variety of windshield-washer solutions — you can even use a home window cleaner. *Don't use detergent.* It can leave a residue that can plug up your lines, and it isn't easy to drive with suds all over your windshield!

Pay attention to the kind of washer fluid you get. Some kinds are concen-trated, which means that you need to mix them with water before you add them. If you live in an area that gets cold in the winter, you can buy a pre-mixed washer solution that contains **antifreeze**. This solution comes in quart and gallon sizes and keeps your windshield clean while preventing the liquid from freezing up in cold weather.

Other Important Checks

Although they're not found under the hood, you should check the following two areas as part of your monthly routine.

Check and replace windshield wipers

If your wipers have been making a mess of your windshield, buy new blades or new inserts for them. The rubber wiper inserts are inexpensive and usually just slide into place. The metal blades into which the inserts fit are a little more expensive, but if your old ones look corroded or generally aren't in good shape, you should replace them as well. The metal blades frequently come in packages with conversion parts for different cars. Consult your auto parts store for the type and size of blades you need and for instructions on inserting the blades if you can't figure out how to do so just by looking at them. Be aware that some vehicles have different-sized wipers for the driver and passenger sides, and that other vehicles have only one wiper. If your vehicle has a rear window wiper, don't forget to check that, too.

Check the tires

Tires that are low on air pressure wear down faster and make your car harder to steer. Tires that have too much pressure may blow out or steer erratically. Try to keep your tires inflated to within the manufacturer's specified range. To do so, buy an accurate tire gauge (they aren't expensive) and check the pressure in each tire. Chapter 19 has instructions for performing this easy task and checking your tires for signs of a variety of problems.

If you've done this monthly under-the-hood check, congratulations! You now know that your vehicle has what it needs in terms of fuel, oil, water, and other exotic beverages. You can be reasonably sure that it won't leave you stranded on the highway because of a faulty hose, wire, or belt, and you did it all yourself! Doesn't it feel good? There's nothing like working on your own car for instant rewards. Get in and drive it around. It feels smoother, right? The pickup is better. The car is happier, and you can hear the engine purring. Your vehicle knows that you care about it, and your efforts have drawn the two of you closer to one another. Silly romanticizing? Well, I have either an extremely affectionate car or a wild imagination.

Part II
What Makes It Go?

The 5th Wave   By Rich Tennant

"Sure I work on diesels. Bring her around and we'll put her on the lift."

In this part . . .

You can't repair anything on a vehicle until you know how it works. In this part, I explain what makes a vehicle run, walking you through system by system. Despite the fact that the only interaction your vehicle usually seems to demand from you is a key in the ignition and a foot on the gas pedal, you may be surprised to find that cars really aren't magic. Also included in this part is a chapter on special vehicles and how they work: diesels and alternatively powered vehicles.

Chapter 4

The Inner Secrets of Your Car Revealed

*O*ne of the major events that marked the transition of early man from "wise monkey" to a more civilized critter was the ability to get something else to do his work for him. Along with such major technological breakthroughs as the club and spear, the control of fire, and the invention of the loincloth was the eventual use of round logs (later called "wheels") to move things and people. Wheeled carts of various types were pushed or pulled by humans and animals for centuries until some early science-fiction freak decided to invent a machine that could move itself, and the first engine appeared.

Today, most people possess vehicles that can move themselves. True, you have to tell your car when to go and when to stop, and you have to steer it in the proper direction and keep it in good running order, but any vehicle is basically a set of wheels with an engine to turn them.

The **internal combustion engine**, which still forms the "heart" of most vehicles, is a lightweight, fairly efficient, and relatively uncomplicated piece of machinery. It works on a mixture of gasoline and air to produce enough power to turn a shaft that turns the wheels. The basic gizmos on your car are simply the things that bring the fuel and air together in the proper quantities, ignite them, and channel the resulting power to the wheels. All the rest of the stuff is there to make this happen with ease and efficiency, to provide you with some control over what's going on, and to give you a place to sit and to stow your groceries.

For a look at the future, check out the **alternatively fueled vehicles** described in Chapter 7.

In this chapter, I give you a brief overview of how each of the basic systems in a vehicle with a standard internal combustion engine functions and how these systems work together to make the vehicle run. Don't worry about what model you own; every vehicle with an internal combustion engine works on the same principles. By viewing your vehicle as a series of simple systems, each with a specific job to do, you can stop seeing it as a dismaying collection of wires, hoses, and gizmos and be able to deal with it easily and confidently. Once you've gotten a general idea of how things work, the rest of the chapters in Part II explore each system in detail. When you've become familiar with how a system functions, you're ready to tackle the chapter in Part III that shows you how to work on that system.

Every car manufacturer makes sure to do something a little bit differently than the competition does so that it can get patents and say that its vehicles are the best. Also, the location and looks of the engine and transmission in rear-engine cars and front-wheel drive vehicles are different from those with traditional front engines and rear-wheel drive. Therefore, if any part of your vehicle is not exactly where it is in the pictures in this chapter, don't panic. Believe me, the part is in there someplace, or your car wouldn't go. If you have trouble finding something, your owner's manual should have a diagram (which was probably gibberish to you until you bought this book) showing the location of each principal part. You can also ask a friend who has a similar vehicle, or your friendly automotive technician, to point out these "missing" parts. I'm willing to bet, however, that if you read this chapter carefully with an eye on your own vehicle, you can locate almost all the parts yourself.

Although you certainly don't need them to get through this book, it's good to have both an owner's manual and a service manual for every vehicle you own. If you don't have an owner's manual, ask your car dealer to get one for you or to tell you where you can get one. Service manuals are also available for every vehicle, and I strongly suggest that you get one of these as well. Every auto repair facility cannot stock a service manual for each year, make, and model of every vehicle, and if you lend your service manual to an independent service facility that is working on your car, you can save money by reducing the time it would take them to figure out the proper way to repair it. Also, if you get to the point where you want to do more than basic repairs, one of these manuals will be indispensable. The drawings in service manuals show you where every little screw and washer fits so that you won't end up with a couple of "extra" parts at the end of the job, and they show you how to do each job in the most efficient manner.

You can obtain a service manual at the parts department of your local dealership, or write to the company that made your vehicle and print "Service Manuals" on the envelope. The car manufacturer will be very happy to sell you one. If you have an older vehicle, you can find new or used service manuals or instruction books for it in bookstores. Public libraries often have surprisingly large collections of service manuals, too.

Whenever you encounter an unfamiliar term set in this font, you'll find it in the glossary at the end of the book. This glossary not only defines the word but usually provides practical information about it as well.

What Makes It Start?

Although people tend to think that most vehicles are totally powered by gasoline, many parts — the radio, headlights, clock, and so on — actually function on electricity. Of course, you could get along without these devices if you had to, but did you know that it also takes electricity to get your car to *start?* An ignition system works in conjunction with your car's electrical system to provide the power that allows your starter to make your engine turn over. Once your engine turns over, it can begin to run on gasoline, just as you expected it to.

The following is a blow-by-blow explanation of what happens when you start a car. Most vehicles still have traditional gasoline-powered engines; if yours doesn't, you can find information about alternatively powered vehicles in Chapter 7.

To get the most from this chapter, take the book out to your vehicle and try to find as many of the parts as possible as you read along. (If you don't know how to get the hood open, you can find instructions in Chapter 1.) Just *touching* the weird-looking gizmos under the hood helps you get past any doubts and fears you may have about getting more intimately involved with your vehicle. But then, isn't it always that way?

1. When you turn the key in your car's ignition switch to Start, you close a circuit that allows the current to pass from your battery to your starter via the starter solenoid switch. (See Figure 4-1.)

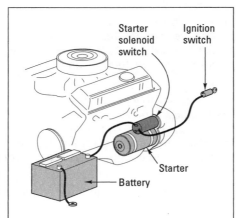

Starter
solenoid
switch

Ignition
switch

Starter

Battery

Figure 4-1:
The starting
system.

2. The starter makes the engine turn over (that's the growling sound you hear before the engine starts running smoothly). Chapter 5 tells you exactly how it does this.

3. Once the engine is running, fuel (gasoline) flows from the fuel tank at the rear of the car, through the fuel lines, to the fuel pump under the hood. (See Figure 4-2.) Chapter 6 explores the fuel system in detail, and Chapter 13 shows you how to keep it in tune.

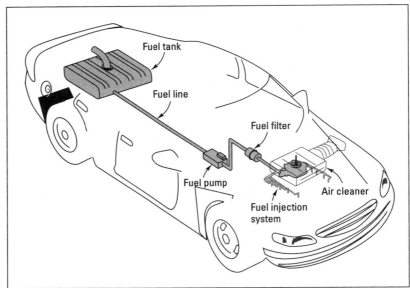

Figure 4-2:
The fuel
system .

4. The fuel pump pumps the gasoline through a fuel filter into the intake manifold. (In carbureted cars, the gasoline is pumped into the carburetor, but nearly everything else is similar in cars with fuel injection.)

5. Each pound of fuel is mixed with 15 pounds of air to form a vaporized mixture, like a mist. Because fuel is much heavier than air, this mixture works out to something like 1 part of fuel to 9,000 parts of air, by volume. In other words, your engine really runs on air, with a little fuel to help it!

6. This fuel/air mixture passes into the cylinders in your engine. A cylinder, as shown in Figure 4-3, is a hollow pipe with one open end and one closed end. Inside each cylinder is a piston, which fits very snugly and moves up and down. The piston moves *up,* trapping the fuel/air mixture in the upper part of the cylinder and compressing it into a very small space.

7. A spark from a spark plug *ignites* the fuel/air mixture, causing an explosion.

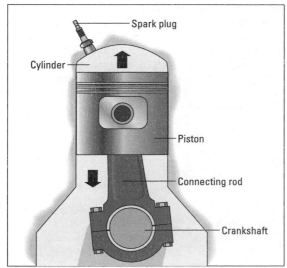

Figure 4-3:
A cylinder
and piston.

8. The explosion forces the piston back *down* again, with more power than it went up with.

9. Attached to the bottom of the piston is a connecting rod, which is attached to a crankshaft, which leads, eventually, to the drive wheels of your car. As the piston and the connecting rod go up and down, they cause the crankshaft to turn. As shown in Figure 4-4, this is pretty much the same motion you use to pedal a bike: Your knee goes up and down while your foot pedals 'round and 'round.

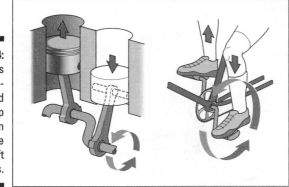

Figure 4-4:
The pistons
and con-
necting rod
move up
and down
to turn the
crankshaft
in circles.

10. At the other end of the crankshaft is a box of gears called the transmission. If your car has a conventional engine with rear-wheel drive (see Figure 4-5), the transmission is under the front seat. If it has a transverse engine and front-wheel drive (see Figure 4-6), the transmission is under the hood of the car. On rear-engine cars, both the engine and the transmission are under the rear deck lid, where the trunk would ordinarily be found.

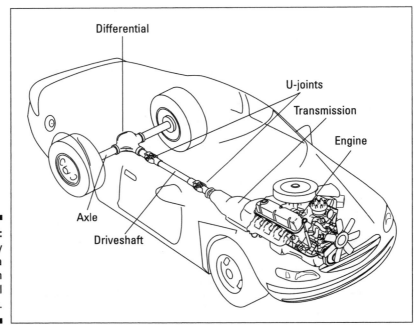

Differential

U-joints

Transmission

Engine

Axle

Driveshaft

Figure 4-5:
Cutaway view of a car with rear-wheel drive.

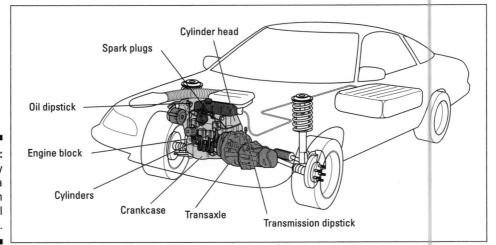

Cylinder head

Spark plugs

Oil dipstick

Engine block

Cylinders

Crankcase

Transaxle

Transmission dipstick

Figure 4-6:
Cutaway view of a car with front-wheel drive.

11. If your car has a manual transmission, you'll also find the clutch located between the crankshaft and the transmission. The clutch tells the transmission when to connect or disconnect the engine from the rest of the drive train. In a car with an automatic transmission, this is done automatically.

12. When you shift into Drive (or First, if you have a manual transmission), a set of gears causes the rest of the crankshaft (which is called the driveshaft after it leaves the transmission) to turn at a particular speed. See Figure 4-7.

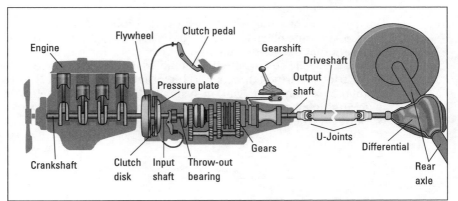

Figure 4-7:
The
drive train.

13. The driveshaft runs to the rear wheels of conventional rear-wheel-driven vehicles and ends in another set of gears called the differential. The differential turns the power of the engine and the transmission 90 degrees into the axles that connect the drive wheels of the car. Because on most vehicles, the axle is set at right angles to the driveshaft, you can see that the differential is really changing the direction of the power so that the drive wheels can turn. Chapter 9 looks at drive trains and transmissions in detail, and Chapter 17 helps you deal with them.

Cars with front-wheel drive or with rear engines do not require driveshafts because the power source is located right between the wheels that are going to drive the car. On these vehicles, the transmission and the differential are combined into a single unit called the transaxle, which connects directly to provide power to the drive wheels.

14. The drive wheels turn and push the vehicle forward (or backward), and off you go.

And you thought you just had to turn on the ignition and step on the gas!

What Makes It Run?

Now let's take a look at what some other systems do to keep the car moving happily down the road. Because these systems work simultaneously and just keep on doing the same thing over and over, there's no need to take them step-by-step.

The ignition system

Once your car has started running, the ignition system (see Figure 4-8) continues to provide electric current to the spark plugs so that they can provide the spark that causes the fuel to burn. To do so, the current passes from the alternator to the coil, where it is amplified. From the coil, the current goes to the distributor, which directs it to the proper spark plug at the proper time. Chapter 5 examines the ignition system and the rest of the electrical system in greater detail, and Chapter 12 shows you how to keep its various parts working together in harmony.

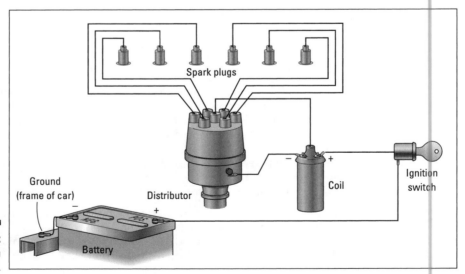

Figure 4-8:
The ignition
system.

The cooling system

Because the temperature at which the combustion of fuel and air takes place is around 4,500 degrees Fahrenheit, the temperature must be quickly lowered below the boiling point, or your engine would break down rapidly. To keep your engine cool, water and coolant circulate from your radiator through pipes in your engine called water jackets. A water pump keeps the water circulating, and a fan helps keep the engine cool when you're stopped at a light and there's no air rushing through the fins in the radiator. (See Figure 4-9.)

Chapter 8 explores this system in greater detail, and Chapter 14 shows you how to do simple jobs like flushing the system and replacing the coolant. It also shows you what to do if your car overheats.

The lubrication system

Oil constantly circulates through your engine to keep its moving parts (pistons, connecting rods, crankshaft, and the like) lubricated to move freely and to reduce the friction that causes your engine to heat up. An oil pump keeps the oil circulating, and an oil filter keeps it clean. The rest of the lubrication system (see Figure 4-10) is devoted to keeping the moving parts outside the engine from rubbing against one another and wearing each other away. To find out more about this system and how to change your oil and oil filter, see Chapter 15. Chapter 16 tells you how to lubricate other parts of your car.

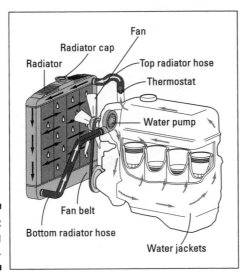

Figure 4-9:
The cooling
system.

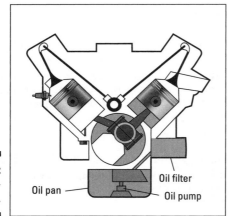

Figure 4-10:
The lubrica-
tion system.

The exhaust system

The exhaust system, shown in Figure 4-11, is the waste disposal system of
your car. Exhaust gases from the burnt fuel/air mixture that was ignited in
the cylinders pass through exhaust pipes to the tailpipe at the rear of the
vehicle (these gases contain carbon monoxide, which is poisonous). On the
way, antismog pollution-control devices remove some of the harmful substances. A muffler controls the noise of the escaping gases; if it fails, you can
get a ticket, probably for disturbing the peace! There is little you can do to
maintain or repair this system except to have the tailpipe or muffler replaced
if it breaks or wears out. You'll hear about its parts again as you wend your
way through the book.

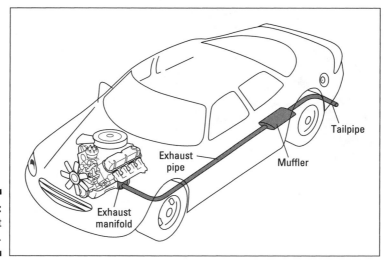

Figure 4-11:
The exhaust
system.

What Makes It Stop?

Still with me? Good! Now all you need to know is what goes on when it's time for the car to stop. (See Figure 4-12.)

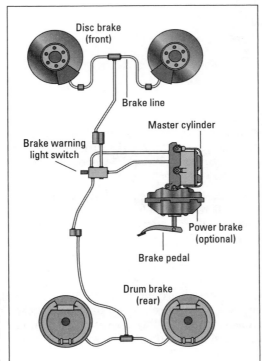

1. To stop your car, you step on the brake pedal.

2. The brake pedal pushes against another piston in a cylinder located under the hood of your car. This is called the master cylinder, and it is filled with a liquid called brake fluid.

3. When the piston in the master cylinder is pushed by your brake pedal, it forces the brake fluid out of the master cylinder into tubes called brake lines, which run to each wheel of your car.

4. The wheel has either a disc brake or a drum brake. To keep it simple, I'll just look at disc brakes here. (Drum brakes work on the same general principles; see Chapter 10.) A disc brake is composed of a flat steel disc (surprise!) sandwiched between a pair of calipers, as shown in Figure 4-13. These calipers contain one or more little pistons that are forced into the disc by the brake fluid.

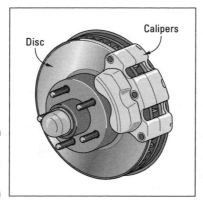

Figure 4-13:
A typical
disc brake.

5. **Brake pads** located between the disc and the pistons grab the disc with their rough asbestos surfaces and force the disc to stop turning. This forces the wheel to stop turning. When the wheels stop turning, the car comes to a stop.

6. When you take your foot off the brake pedal, the whole process is reversed: The brake pads release their hold on the disc, the fluid moves back up the brake lines to the master cylinder, and the wheels can turn freely again.

Four-wheel disc brakes are standard on most new vehicles. Other vehicles have disc brakes on the front wheels and drum brakes on the rear wheels. A few older cars have drum brakes all around. Chapter 10 tells you all about both kinds of brakes and how **power brakes** and **parking brakes** work, and Chapter 18 shows you how to check the brake system on your car to see whether it's in good shape and how to do simple brake work.

Now that you've got the general picture of how the various systems in your car work together, the rest of this part goes into detail about each system. Then Part III shows you how to keep each automotive system functioning smoothly with simple maintenance and easy repairs. If your car is behaving erratically, check out Chapter 20 for a guide to various symptoms and what they mean. If you encounter something that you can't handle, Chapter 22 tells you how to find a good service facility and become its favorite customer.

Chapter 5

The Electrical System: Your Car's Spark of Life

In This Chapter

▶ How the starting system works

▶ How the charging system keeps things going

▶ How the ignition system fires things up

*T*he electrical system provides your vehicle with that vital spark that makes it start and keeps it running. Here are some of the services that the electrical system performs:

- ✔ It provides the initial power to get your engine started, through the **starting system**.

- ✔ It fires the spark plugs so that they can cause the fuel and air to "combust" and drive your engine, through the **ignition system**.

- ✔ It fires the fuel injectors on fuel-injected engines through a computerized engine-control system.

- ✔ It generates electrical power for the various systems in your vehicle that depend on electric current, through the **charging system**.

- ✔ It stores excess current for future needs, in the **battery**.

- ✔ It runs a mixed bag of electrical gadgets, like your car's horn, headlights, and so on, through various **circuits**.

The following sections break down the electrical system into its basic functional subsystems.

The Starting System

The starting system, shown in Figure 5-1, is the portion of the electrical system that gets your car started. When you turn your key in the ignition switch to "Start," the action closes a circuit that lets electrical current flow from your car's battery to its starter. On the way, the current passes through a little device called the **starter solenoid**, which becomes important only if it malfunctions. Basically, all the solenoid does is pass the current along; you don't adjust or replace it unless it breaks down.

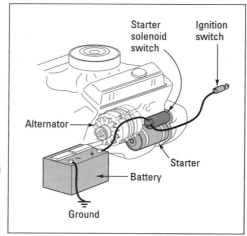

Figure 5-1:
The starting
system.

The following sections describe each part of the starting system.

Because actually seeing and touching something is worth a thousand words, it's a good idea to take this book out to your vehicle and trace the path of the electric current to each part in the system. Don't be shy now! (If you need them, you can find instructions for opening the hood in Chapter 1.) If, as you try to trace the wiring through the starting system, you find a couple of parts that I haven't mentioned yet (like a little square box called a **voltage regulator**), just hang in there. Like the solenoid, you don't have to fuss with these parts unless they fail, and if they fail, they have to be replaced by a professional.

The battery

The battery is the big box that sits under the hood. (See Figure 5-2.) It's filled with acid and distilled water and has a set of plates inside it. The battery stores electric current for starting the car, turning on the lights, and powering the ignition system. It also stabilizes the voltage in the electrical system and provides current whenever the electrical demands exceed the output of the charging system. Quite a helpful little gadget!

On the battery, attached to either the top or the sides of the box, are two large metal terminals. One is a positive terminal; the other is a negative terminal. You can tell which is which because the positive terminal is usually larger and may have a "+" or the word "Positive" on or near it.

On many vehicles, there's a red cap on the positive terminal, and the battery cable leading to it may be red as well. The cable to the negative terminal is usually black. The clamps on the cables that you use to jump-start a dead battery are usually colored red and black so that you can tell which one goes where. You can find instructions for jump-starting a dead battery in Chapter 21.

As you can see in Figure 5-1, most cars are *negative ground,* which means that the wire from the negative terminal is attached to the frame of the vehicle to ground it, and the wire from positive terminal leads to the starter, ignition, and so on. (Some foreign cars are *positive ground* — or positive *earth,* as they call it in England — and this simply means that the wire from the positive terminal is attached to the frame of the car to ground it.)

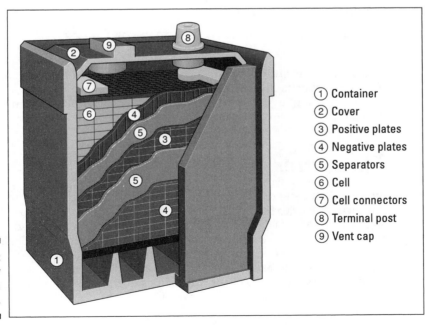

① Container
② Cover
③ Positive plates
④ Negative plates
⑤ Separators
⑥ Cell
⑦ Cell connectors
⑧ Terminal post
⑨ Vent cap

Figure 5-2:
Cutaway
view of a
battery.

I know *what* the problem is; I just don't know *where* it is . . .

After I took my first class on the electrical system, I went out one morning and found that my car wouldn't start. I remembered my instructor saying that if you hear a clicking noise (that's your solenoid) but your engine won't start running, you probably have a loose wire somewhere between the ignition switch and the starter. So I opened the hood (it was only the second time I'd gotten that far) and peeked in. Sure enough, I saw a cluster of wires on the firewall in front of my steering wheel. (The firewall is the divider between the interior of your car and the under-the-hood area. It runs from the windshield down.) I could see where the wires ran to the battery, along the frame of the car, but after that I got lost. I ended up calling the AAA.

When the AAA truck arrived, I proudly informed the technician that I knew what was wrong. "It's just a loose wire between my battery and my starter," I announced. "Then why didn't you fix it yourself?" he asked. "Because I don't know which gadget is the starter!" He was nice enough to keep from laughing, and I felt better when the problem *did* turn out to be a loose wire on the starter. He also pointed out the starter and showed me where the wires ran that connected to it.

Today, most batteries are sealed and don't require much maintenance. However, deposits do form on the terminals, and they can impede the flow of current. Chapter 3 tells you how to check your battery and remove these deposits.

The starter

After the battery sends the current to the starter solenoid (refer to Figure 5-1), the current goes to the starter. The starter is the device that makes your engine turn over. (Figure 5-3 shows what a starter looks like, and Figure 5-4 shows how a starter works.) It's an electrical motor with a gear called a *starter drive* at one end. The starter drive engages a *ring gear* on a flywheel that's bolted to the back of the engine crankshaft. When you turn your key in the ignition switch, the starter drive slides down the shaft and engages the ring gear. This spins the flywheel, which starts the crankshaft turning so that the pistons can go up and down, the spark plugs can fire, and the engine can start running. As soon as the engine is started, the starter has done its job, and you should let go of the key. As your key returns to the "On" (or "Run") position, where it stays until you shut off the engine, the starter drive disengages from the flywheel, and your engine continues running on the fuel and air that are being pumped into its cylinders.

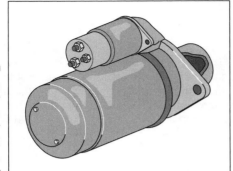

Figure 5-3:
A starter
with a
starter
solenoid
attached.

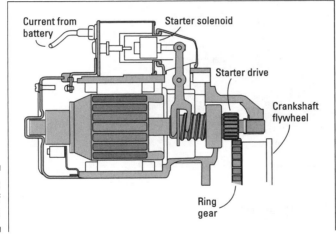

Current from
battery

Starter solenoid

Starter drive

Crankshaft
flywheel

Ring
gear

Figure 5-4:
Anatomy of
a starter.

If you keep the key in the "Start" position after the engine starts running, you'll hear a strange noise. That noise is the clutch in the starter drive that allows the engine to spin faster than the starter. Even though this one-way clutch prevents starter damage once the engine starts, it's not a good idea to hold the key in the "Start" position once the engine is under its own power. Try not to keep the starter engaged this way for longer than ten seconds at a time. If the vehicle doesn't start, allow the starter to cool down for one to two minutes before attempting to start it again. Failure to do so can overheat the starter and damage it. And *don't turn the key to the "Start" position when the engine is running*. If you do, you can damage the gear on the starter and the ring gear on the flywheel.

The Charging System

After you start your engine, it (usually) runs at a nice steady rumble. This is possible because as soon as the pistons in the cylinders start to go up and down, your car begins to run on its usual diet of fuel and air (read all about it in Chapter 6). When you let go of the key and your ignition switch moves from "Start" to "On," the electric current stops flowing to the starter but continues to flow through the charging system and the rest of the electrical system. (See Figure 5-5.)

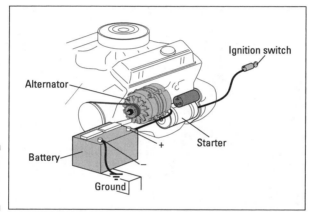

Figure 5-5:
The charging system.

The alternator

The running engine drives a belt that enables your alternator (or *generator*) to produce electric current for the rest of the trip. Here's how it does this:

Your alternator (see Figures 5-5 and 5-6) replaces the electricity that was taken from the battery when you started the car. Then, every time your battery sends out some of its "juice," the alternator replaces it.

The basic difference between an alternator and a generator is that alternators appear on newer cars and produce *alternating* current (AC), which is internally converted to the direct current needed to drive various gadgets. Generators are usually found on cars built before 1964. They simply generate direct current (DC) and pass it on. But to keep things simple, I'm just going to call the gadget an alternator, because no matter which you have on your vehicle, it does the same thing in the long run.

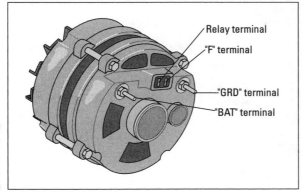

Relay terminal

"F" terminal

"GRD" terminal

"BAT" terminal

Figure 5-6:
The
alternator.

When the alternator is generating electric current, it is said to be *charging*. Although most cars just have dashboard "idiot lights" that go on if the alternator isn't charging, some older cars have gauges with a "D" at one end and a "C" at the other that show whether the system is charging or discharging.

Many newer cars have a *voltmeter,* which indicates system voltage. With the engine running and all accessories off, the system voltage should be 13.5 to 14.5 volts. If not, something may be wrong with the charging system.

The alternator also supplies your electrical system with current to run the car radio, headlights, and so on. I get to those at the end of this chapter.

The voltage regulator

The voltage regulator (see Figure 5-7) is a device that controls the *alternator.* On older cars, it's mounted somewhere under the hood. On newer cars, it may be mounted inside the alternator or inside the **PCM** (Powertrain Control Module). The PCM is a computer that controls the operation of the fuel, ignition, and emission-control systems on newer cars. If the voltage regulator fails, the alternator is powerless.

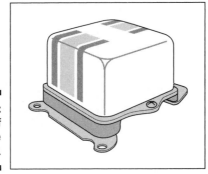

Figure 5-7:
One type of
voltage
regulator.

The Ignition System

The purpose of the ignition system is to *ignite*, or fire, the spark plugs in order to generate power to run the engine. To do so, the battery sends current to the ignition coil. Then that high voltage goes on to the spark plugs — either through a distributor, if you have an older vehicle, or directly to the spark plugs, if you have a newer one.

Most vehicles built prior to 1974 use a non-electronic distributor ignition system, as shown in Figure 5-8. Most vehicles built from the mid-1970s to late 1980s use an electronic distributor ignition system like the one in Figure 5-9. Today, most vehicles use a *distributorless* electronic ignition system such as that shown in Figure 5-10. To make it easier for you to identify the sections in this chapter that deal with the type of system on your vehicle, I've placed the following symbols next to them:

- ✔ ⓨ = old-style, non-electronic ignition system
- ✔ ⓕ = electronic ignition system
- ✔ ⓖ = distributorless ignition system

If you haven't already done so, consult your owner's manual, a service manual, or your dealership to find out which type of system your vehicle has.

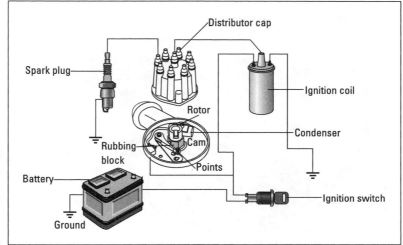

Figure 5-8:
A non-electronic ignition system.

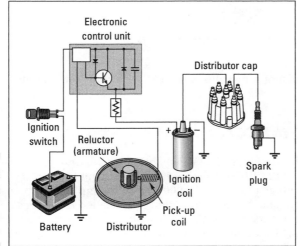

Figure 5-9:
An electronic ignition system.

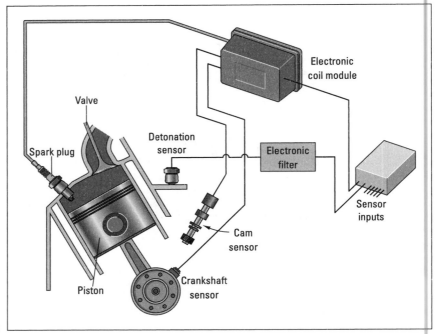

Figure 5-10:
A distributorless electronic ignition system.

All three types of ignition systems use the following components.

The ignition coil

The ignition coil (see Figure 5-11) transforms the relatively small amount of electrical *voltage* (12 to 14 volts) that it receives from the battery into a big enough jolt of voltage (15,000 to 60,000 volts) to jump the spark plug gap. On most cars, a set of *spark plug wires* (sometimes called *ignition cables*) carries the high voltage to each spark plug. A distributorless system has an electronic coil module that does the same thing (refer to Figure 5-10).

The spark plugs

The spark plugs (see Figure 5-12) deliver the spark of voltage to the combustion chamber just when the fuel/air mixture is at the point of greatest compression. The resulting explosion provides the power to propel your vehicle. Chapter 12 tells you how to "read" your spark plugs for clues as to how your car is running and provides instructions for removing, gapping, and replacing spark plugs.

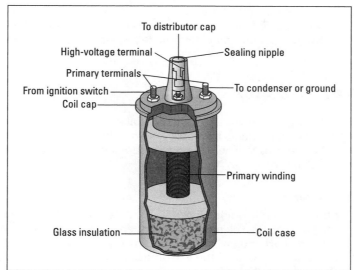

Figure 5-11:
The
anatomy
of a coil.

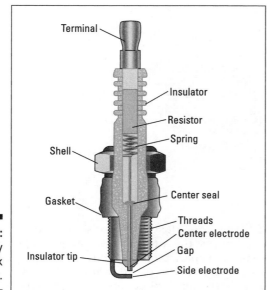

Figure 5-12:
Anatomy
of a spark
plug.

Here's where I get into the characteristics of the different types of ignition systems to be found on various vehicles. You can read about all of them or go directly to the parts found on your vehicle's system and skip the others.

The distributor

The distributor gets the voltage from the coil and distributes it to each spark plug in turn. It also contains the rotor and, on older cars, a set of breaker points, and a condenser. The following sections give you a closer look at the parts of a distributor.

The distributor cap

The distributor cap (shown in Figure 5-13) sits atop the distributor to protect the parts inside from the elements. Current enters and leaves the distributor via the coil and spark plug wires that run through holes in the cap. Chapter 12 shows you how to remove the distributor cap so that you can get a closer look at what's inside. It also tells you which types of distributors should *not* be tampered with.

Figure 5-13:
Distributor caps for non-electronic and electronic distributors.

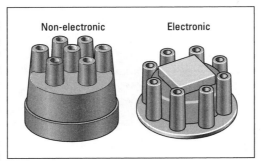

Non-electronic   Electronic

The rotor

The rotor (see Figure 5-14) sits atop the distributor shaft inside the distributor. As the distributor shaft turns, the rotor rotates with it and points toward the terminal at the base of each spark plug wire so that each plug can fire in the correct order. For example, when it's pointing at the terminal of the wire leading to your Number 1 spark plug, it directs the current to that spark plug at precisely the time when the fuel/air mixture in the Number 1 cylinder is waiting to be exploded.

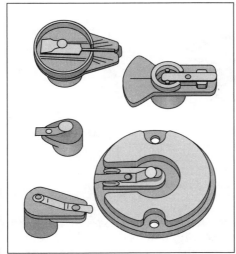

Figure 5-14:
Types of
rotors.

The following parts are attached to a **breaker plate** on the floor of a _non-electronic distributor,_ as shown in Figure 5-15.

Points

On these distributors, the points (short for "breaker points") trigger the flow of electricity so that it arrives at the spark plugs at just the right _point_ in time and at the right intensity. As you can see in Figure 5-16, the points are two pieces of metal, one stationary and one moveable, that are joined at one end so that they can touch and then draw apart.

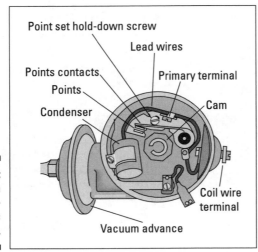

Point set hold-down screw

Lead wires

Points contacts

Primary terminal

Points

Condenser

Cam

Figure 5-15:
Inside a
non-
electronic
distributor.

Coil wire
terminal

Vacuum advance

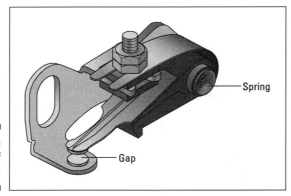

Figure 5-16:
A set of
points.

The way they do this is simple: Attached to the base of the shaft that the rotor sits on is a roundish wheel with bumps on it called a cam wheel. The bumps are called cam lobes, and there is one for each spark plug. As the cam wheel turns on the shaft, each cam lobe contacts the moveable point and pushes the points *open*.

The tiny space created between the open points is called a **gap**. Each time the points open, electric current passes to the rotor, which directs the current to a particular spark plug wire. This causes that spark plug to "fire," producing a spark that ignites the fuel/air mixture in its cylinder. The points are then brought back to the *closed* position by a spring.

Problems with points

The gap between the points must be set at a precise width to ensure that each spark plug fires at just the right time and intensity. If the gap is too wide, the spark plugs fire before the piston has reached the top of its path. This can cause *pre-ignition,* which causes knocking and engine damage. If the gap is too narrow, the spark plug fires after the piston has compressed the fuel/air mixture and has started back down. The loss of compression results in poor combustion, loss of power, greater fuel consumption, and more pollution. If the points can't close enough to allow the current to pass properly, your car stops completely. If they can't get far enough apart to break the circuit, the current arcs across continuously and the points burn out quickly.

This whole problem is referred to as *having your points out of adjustment,* which leads to poor ignition and faulty timing. That's why, when you tune up your car, one of the first things you do is check with a feeler gauge to see whether your points are correctly "gapped." Of course, if your points are badly worn or corroded, you replace them and carefully gap the new points. For information about tuning up your car and gapping the points, see Chapter 12.

The condenser

The condenser (shown in Figure 5-17) is an electrical "sponge" that keeps the points from burning up. This small metal cylinder prevents the electricity from arcing across the gap when the points are open, which would cause the points to burn. Condensers should be replaced periodically, along with the points and rotor. Chapter 12 shows you how to do so.

Figure 5-17:
A
condenser.

Other parts found only on electronic distributors

Electronic distributors employ electronic parts. The good news is that they tend to be relatively trouble-free. The bad news is that if they break down, you have to pay a professional to replace them. They include the following parts:

- An **ignition module** is a transistorized component that triggers the ignition coil to fire high voltage. The module is a "non-wear" component that replaced the old-style "breaker" points in the early to mid-1970s. It is usually found in or around the distributor.

- A **triggering mechanism** inside the distributor — or on the crankshaft — controls the timing of the ignition module. On some vehicles, this is a magnetic pulse generator called a *pick-up coil*. Other vehicles use a *Hall-Effect switch* or a photoelectric sensor inside the distributor to trigger the module. It probably doesn't make much difference which type your vehicle has, because there's no need for you to develop a personal relationship with it.

Other parts found only on distributorless ignition systems

 Distributorless ignition systems also use a solid-state ignition module, along with the following additional electronic parts (refer to Figure 5-10):

- ✔ A **crankshaft sensor** is a trigger device that tells the ignition module when to fire the spark plugs.

- ✔ A **camshaft sensor**, found on *some* distributorless ignition systems, is a trigger device that synchronizes when the proper ignition coil should be fired.

Other Electrical Gadgets

The alternator also supplies the electrical current for the sound system, headlights, taillights, directional signals, defroster, heater, air conditioner, and other electrical gadgets via electrical wiring under the dashboard. Although most of these components require professional repair, the following parts are pretty easy to deal with yourself:

- ✔ **Fuses** control the flow of current to electrical components the same way they do in the home. They are located in a fuse box that is usually found under or near the dashboard. Your owner's manual should show you where the fuse box on your vehicle is, or you can crawl under the dashboard and trace the wires from your sound system until you reach the fuse box. See Chapter 12 for instructions on checking fuses and replacing a burnt-out fuse.

- ✔ **Windshield wipers** need to be checked and replaced periodically. Chapter 3 provides tips on checking and replacing your windshield wipers and windshield washer fluid.

- ✔ **Directional signal flashers** on your dashboard do more than tell you whether the directional signals are flashing. They also are designed to provide clues to malfunctions elsewhere on your car! Chapter 20 tells you how to decipher these clues and rectify the problems that they indicate.

- ✔ **Headlights** are not too difficult to adjust and replace on most vehicles. Chapter 12 provides instructions for doing both jobs.

Chapter 6

The Fuel System: The Heart and Lungs of Your Car

*T*he fuel system, shown in Figure 6-1, stores and delivers fuel to the combustion chambers of the engine so that it can be burned efficiently. Although most fuel systems have some basic components in common, fuel systems do vary: Some employ **fuel injectors** to get the fuel to the engine, and others rely on **carburetors**. (If your vehicle has a **diesel engine**, be sure to read Chapter 7 as well.)

In this chapter, I introduce you to both carbureted and fuel-injected systems as I trace the flow of fuel from the **fuel tank** to the **engine block**. When you know what each part does and where to find it, it's easy to see how all the parts work together to provide your vehicle with "GO power."

If a picture is worth a thousand words, actually looking at and maybe even touching something is worth a thousand pictures. If possible, take this book out to your car, open the hood, and visit with the parts of the fuel system as you read about them.

When you encounter terms in **special type** that are unfamiliar to you, you can find out all about them in the glossary at the end of this book.

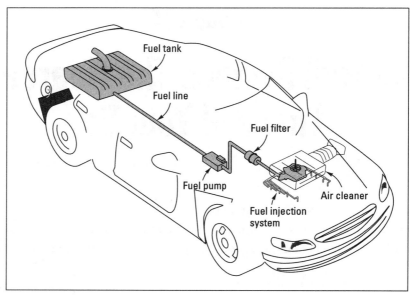

Figure 6-1:
A fuel
system.

Basic Fuel System Components

Whether your vehicle is 20 years old or 20 days old, it probably has the following basic parts in its fuel system. (For additional parts found in carbureted vehicles, see the section called "Following the Fuel through Carbureted Engines." To find out about additional fuel system features in fuel-injected vehicles, see the section called "Following the Fuel through Fuel-Injected Systems," later in this chapter.)

Fuel tank

The fuel tank is a metal or plastic composite container, usually located under the trunk compartment, although some vehicles have some fairly interesting alternative locations for it. If you're not sure where your fuel tank is and you can't find it just by looking, your owner's manual or mechanic can show you where yours is located.

Inside the fuel tank is a little float that bobs up and down on the surface of the fuel, sending messages to the fuel gauge on your dashboard so that you can tell when you have to buy more gasoline. (Chapter 13 tells you why you should always try to keep your fuel tank full.) Although some vehicles run on diesel oil or other alternative fuels, presently most are gasoline-powered, so I usually refer to fuel as gasoline.

Fuel lines and fuel pump

The fuel pump (see Figure 6-2) pumps the gasoline through the fuel lines, which run under your car from the fuel tank to the carburetor or fuel injectors. Older cars with carburetors use a mechanical fuel pump that's driven by the engine. Engines with fuel injection use an electric fuel pump that may be located in or near the fuel tank.

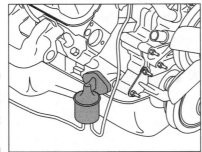

Figure 6-2:
The fuel
pump at
home.

A number of things can cause fuel system problems. Before you let anyone talk you into replacing your fuel pump, make sure that it really is the culprit by following the instructions in the "Testing Your Fuel Pump" section in Chapter 13.

Fuel filter

The fuel filter does exactly what its name implies — it filters the fuel. As the fuel passes along the fuel line on its way to the fuel injectors or carburetor, it passes through the fuel filter. A small screen inside the fuel filter traps the dirt and rust that would otherwise enter your fuel (especially if you ride around most of the time with a near-empty tank). Some vehicles have additional fuel filters between the fuel tank and the fuel pump. It's important to change your fuel filter(s) according to the manufacturer's maintenance schedule. Chapter 13 can help you locate and replace the fuel filter(s) on your vehicle.

Air cleaner and air filter

The air cleaner cleans the air before it's mixed with fuel. In carbureted engines, the air cleaner is usually large and round with a snorkel sticking out of the side to facilitate the intake of fresh air. Some fuel-injected engines also have a round air cleaner; others use a rectangular one.

To find a rectangular air cleaner, follow the large air inlet hose away from your engine. If you'd like to remove the air cleaner to take a look at the air filter inside it or the parts underneath it, follow the simple instructions in Chapter 13.

Inside the air cleaner is an air filter that removes dirt and dust particles before they can get into the fuel injectors or carburetor. To keep your car functioning efficiently, be sure to change the air filter at least once a year or every 20,000 miles, whichever comes first — more often if you've been driving in a dusty or sandy area. Chapter 13 can help you judge whether an air filter needs to be changed and shows you how to do this surprisingly easy job.

Following the Fuel through Carbureted Vehicles

Most vehicles employ one of two popular — but very different — types of fuel systems: Many older cars have carburetors, while most newer vehicles have fuel injectors. Some cars — especially foreign cars and sports cars — have more than one carburetor. Vehicles with fuel injection or diesel engines have none, but they do have air cleaners. Figure 6-1 shows both a carbureted and a fuel-injected system.

With both systems, the fuel may start out in the same place (the fuel tank) and end up in the same place (the engine), but the path it takes varies quite a bit depending on whether your vehicle has a carburetor or fuel injectors. In this section, I explain what happens to the fuel once it passes through the basic elements of the fuel system (discussed in the preceding section, "Basic Fuel System Components") in a carbureted vehicle. If your vehicle has fuel injectors instead of a carburetor, read "Following the Fuel through Fuel-Injected Vehicles," later in this chapter.

The main job of the carburetor, shown in Figure 6-3, is to mix the proper proportions of air and fuel together and pass them along in the proper quantity to the engine. In the following sections, I explain how the various components of the carburetor work together to accomplish this feat.

The float bowl

Air travels down the carburetor barrel, and on its way, it passes a small pipe that leads to a fuel reservoir called a float bowl. The float bowl is a small chamber located in the carburetor (see Figure 6-4). It contains a small amount of raw fuel to ensure a readily available fuel supply when you start or accelerate the car, which is more efficient than having to pump each new portion of gasoline all the way from the fuel tank at the rear of the vehicle.

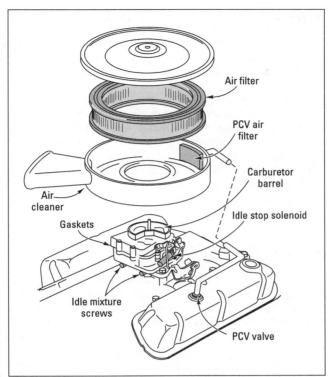

Figure 6-3:
The carburetor.

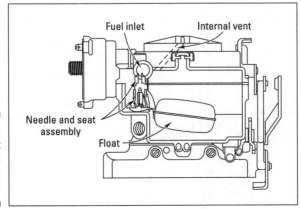

Figure 6-4:
The float bowl is inside the carburetor.

The amount of fuel that stays in the float bowl is controlled by a little float (surprise!) that bobs up and down on the surface of the fuel in the chamber. A hose from the fuel pump keeps the float bowl filled. If your car has too little fuel in its float bowl, it will hesitate or stall when you want that extra surge of power or when you try to start it in the morning.

The float in the float bowl is adjustable, but adjusting it involves taking apart at least a portion of the carburetor. Taking it apart isn't too hard, but putting the thing back together again can get hairy, so if you think that your carburetor needs overhauling, let a professional do the job. Of course, overhaul kits with instructions are available. If you're determined to do the job yourself, look for a good auto repair course and do it under an instructor's supervision. (See the section "Float Level Adjustments" in Chapter 13 for more information about adjusting the float.)

The venturi

Because the faster the air moves, the more liquid it can pick up, the carburetor was very cleverly designed so that air picks up speed as it passes through the carburetor barrel. Here's what happens: Inside the barrel is a chamber called a venturi (see Figure 6-5), which gets narrower as it nears the opening that leads to the float bowl. When the air gets to this narrow part of the venturi, it picks up speed, creating a vacuum just at the point where the opening occurs. This vacuum draws the fuel out of the float bowl and mixes it with the air, creating what's called the fuel/air mixture. The air and the fuel travel in this form to the cylinders, where combustion occurs.

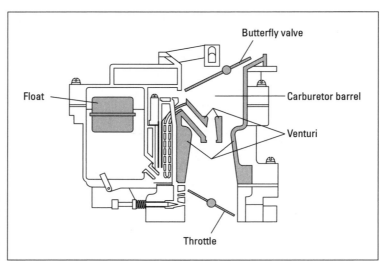

Figure 6-5:
The
carburetor.

An explosive idea

In case you're wondering why air is such an important part of the fuel system, remember that liquid gasoline will not explode — oh, it'll burn all right if you drop a match into it, but it won't explode. And it's the pressure caused by the rapid expansion of exploding gases that drives the engine. The only way to get gasoline to explode is to mix it with air — hence the necessity of the fuel/air mixture.

This, incidentally, is why so many accidents occur with near-empty gasoline cans. People tend to think that an almost-empty can of gasoline is harmless, but this is when it's at its most dangerous! The "empty" can still contains a tiny bit of gasoline, and you need only one part of gasoline to 9,000 parts of air to get a combustible mixture! If a lot of gasoline is sloshing around in the can, there may be *too much* gasoline to explode. But if there's just a bit of gasoline vapor, or fumes, it can mix with the air in the "empty" can, and any kind of spark can set off a really big explosion. A gasoline/air vapor combination is more explosive than TNT! For this reason, *never carry gasoline in anything but a specialized vented gas can, and keep that can filled up.* What's more, unless you're going far from any source of fuel, don't carry (or store) gasoline at all, and get rid of any old cans you have around. (See the sidebar called "How to dispose of empty gasoline cans safely" in Chapter 1).

The choke

At the top of the carburetor barrel, looking up at you after you remove the air cleaner, is the choke (see the sidebar "Automatic chokes"). The choke limits the supply of air entering the venturi in order to enrich the fuel/air mixture. The choke consists of a little adjustable butterfly valve that can open and close. When you go out to start your car in the morning, the choke helps you start and warm up the engine faster. Here's how: When your car is cold, as much as one-third of the gasoline can condense on the cold metal parts of the carburetor, leaving only two-thirds of the fuel/air mixture on its way to the engine. This amount is not enough for proper combustion, so your car won't start properly. To enrich the mixture, the butterfly valve on the choke stays closed, inhibiting the supply of air.

The choke only *limits* the air supply; it doesn't prevent all the air from coming in. The resulting fuel/air mixture is richer than the stuff you usually drive on, but the choke returns to normal after the car warms up.

Automatic chokes

Cars used to have manual chokes, which you controlled by a knob on the dashboard. Today, most cars have **automatic chokes** that work by means of a spring that coils and uncoils in response to the amount of heat present. This spring eventually causes the butterfly valve to open and close.

If you have an automatic choke, chances are that it's controlled by a thermostat located on the outside of the carburetor, either at the top of the barrel near the butterfly valve, or near the carburetor at the end of a long rod. The first type looks like a little round cap with little arrows on it that say "Lean" and "Rich." By turning this knob, you can adjust the proportion of air that's allowed into the carburetor barrel past the butterfly. The second type (see the figure below) uses a rod attached to the thermostat to make the butterfly open and close. For tips on checking and adjusting the choke, see Chapter 13.

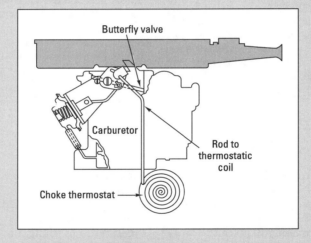

Butterfly valve

Carburetor

Rod to thermostatic coil

Choke thermostat

The accelerator pump

Have you ever wondered what makes your car speed up when you step on the gas pedal? It's a very simple device called an **accelerator pump** — so unsophisticated that you'd think the inventor would have been embarrassed to suggest such a gadget. When you step on the gas pedal to accelerate, a rod connecting the pedal to a little lever on the outside of the carburetor pushes on a little piston inside the carburetor, which squirts a little extra fuel into the venturi. That extra fuel creates a richer fuel/air mixture, which explodes with a bigger bang in your cylinders, giving your car that extra push called acceleration. If your car hesitates when you step on the gas, your accelerator pump may not be working properly. Chapter 13 has instructions for checking and adjusting your accelerator pump.

The throttle

The throttle controls the amounts of fuel and air that come into the carburetor (refer to Figure 6-5). The more air, the higher the vacuum in the venturi. The greater the vacuum in the venturi, the more fuel is drawn out of the float bowl and mixed with the air. The richer the fuel/air mixture, the faster the car goes At high speeds, the throttle is wide open to allow a lot of air to come into the carburetor. At low speeds, the throttle closes so that less air can get in.

The big lever on the outside of the carburetor (see Figure 6-6) is the *throttle arm*. It's attached to the gas pedal and controls the throttle, which is a butterfly device (very much like the butterfly valve) located at the bottom of the carburetor, where it joins the intake manifold.

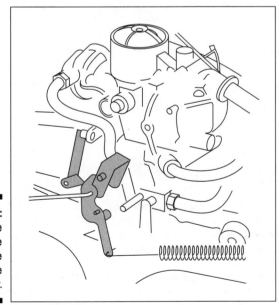

Figure 6-6:
The throttle arm on the outside of the carburetor.

The idle speed screw

The idle speed screw is a little screw located at the bottom of your carburetor, on the outside, right near the throttle. It keeps the throttle from closing completely when your foot is off the gas pedal and the car is idling. (*Idling* is what the car does when it just sits there humming to itself without moving. Cars idle while they wait for stoplights to turn green.)

The idle speed screw is easy to adjust and can do wonders for your engine performance and fuel consumption if it's set properly after you tune your ignition system. If you turn it clockwise with a screwdriver, your car idles faster; turn it counterclockwise, and your car idles more slowly. Chapter 13 has more detailed instructions. (Don't get the idle speed screw confused with the idle mixture screw, however. Figure 6-7 shows you what each of them looks like.)

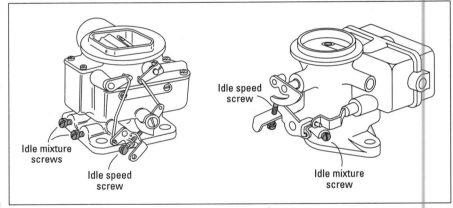

Figure 6-7:
The idle speed and idle mixture screws on a popular carburetor.

The idle mixture screw

The idle mixture screw looks like the idle speed screw, but it controls the proportion of air and fuel that get to your engine while your car is idling. By turning this screw, you can determine how rich the fuel/air mixture is. If you adjust it properly, you can get maximum engine performance and still save fuel.

A carburetor with more than one barrel can have more than one idle mixture screw. The screw (or screws) may reside in a variety of places, depending on your vehicle. Figures 6-3 and 6-7 show a couple of possible locations. You can identify an idle mixture screw by the fact that, if you turn it counterclockwise, the end of the screw comes out of the carburetor. However, because of state and federal smog standards, most car manufacturers place *limiter caps* on the idle mixture screws or hide them behind metal plugs to prevent owners from adjusting them. If the idle mixture screw(s) on your vehicle are adjustable, you can find instructions for adjusting them in Chapter 13.

The idle air bleed screw

Some cars *don't* have an idle speed screw. Instead, they have an idle air bleed screw (or *idle air adjusting screw,* as it is sometimes called) that determines how much extra air is allowed to come in when the throttle is closed. When the throttle is closed during idling, some air should still come through to prevent the formation of carbon and gum deposits that tend to collect around the throttle area.

By turning this screw clockwise, you can decrease the amount of air that gets in and slow down your idle. By turning it counterclockwise, you get more air and more idle speed. Air bleed screws are usually found on Lincolns, Cadillacs, and other big cars. Chapter 13 tells you how to adjust the idle air bleed screw.

The idle stop solenoid

Some newer vehicles not only have an idle speed screw and an idle mixture screw but have an idle stop solenoid as well. Cars with engines with controlled exhaust emissions tend to idle at faster speeds. Often, if such an engine is shut off abruptly, the engine simply can't stop fast enough and keeps going, or dieseling. The idle stop solenoid prevents the car from continuing to idle after you shut it off.

More bang for your buck

To increase the amount of fuel/air mixture that's passed along to the engine, auto manufacturers have developed carburetors with more than one carburetor barrel. A double-barrel carburetor has two venturis, and a four-barrel carburetor has four. You generally find these on large engines, like V-8s, where more fuel and air are needed fast to supply all those cylinders with stuff to feed on. In a four-barrel carburetor, two of the four barrels are reserved for extra power at high speeds or stress. You can see why V-8 engines consume more fuel than most four- or six-cylinder engines do. Of course, they put out more power, too. And if you like to drive a big, impressive vehicle around — or if you want to drive up hills at high speeds — that's the kind of engine you need. Just don't confuse *power* with *efficiency.* A smaller engine will do just as good a job if it's not hauling a lot of extra junk around.

To see whether your vehicle has an idle stop solenoid, look for a little can-shaped device attached to the carburetor near the throttle. When it's time to tune your carburetor, read the instructions for adjusting the idle stop solenoid in Chapter 13.

The intake and exhaust manifolds

The fuel/air mixture travels past the throttle at the bottom of the carburetor to the intake manifold, a cluster of iron pipes usually found near the top of the engine, between the carburetor and the engine block. Another set of manifold pipes, called the exhaust manifold, carries carbon monoxide and other vapor wastes away from the engine for disposal. You usually find the exhaust manifold either lower down on the same side of the engine as the intake manifold or on the other side of the cylinder head.

Figure 6-8 traces the fuel/air mixture's progress from the carburetor to the engine block. To pick up the trail from there, see "The Engine Block: Where the Fuel System and the Ignition System Meet" at the end of this chapter.

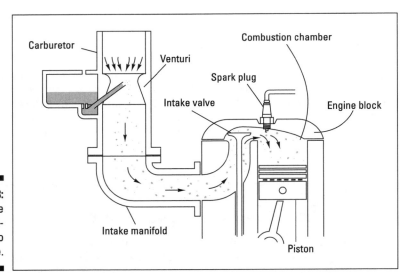

Figure 6-8:
The path the fuel/air mixture takes to the engine.

Following Fuel through Fuel-Injected Vehicles

If your vehicle is less than 20 years old, it probably doesn't have a carburetor. Unless it's run by electricity or another alternative fuel, it probably has a gasoline or diesel engine with a fuel injection system. (For information about diesel, electric, and other alternatively fueled engines, see Chapter 7.)

Today, just about every new vehicle is fuel-injected. Although they're more expensive to service than carburetors, in recent years fuel injection systems with computerized electronic sensing devices have shown sufficient sensitivity, accuracy, and dependability to repay their cost with better performance, greater fuel economy, cleaner exhaust emissions, and more controllable power. Some of the newest models are reported to be 95 to 100 percent clean-burning! Innovations in design are constantly producing cheaper and more durable systems.

At present, most fuel injection systems are too difficult to adjust or repair yourself, but if you know a bit about how they work, you can communicate with your technician more knowledgeably, saving yourself time and money.

Fuel injection systems aren't as new as you might think. The 1957 Chevrolet Corvette featured an optional fuel injection system. Those first fuel-injected engines used *mechanical* injectors (also called *nozzles*) that were nothing more than spring-loaded *poppet valves*. In such an engine, when fuel in a mechanical injector reaches a predetermined level, the injector opens and allows the fuel to mix with air as it travels to the combustion chamber.

Today's engines use *electronic* fuel injectors that are controlled by a computer. A transistor in the computer (often called the *injector driver*) turns the injector on by completing a circuit to allow electric current to flow through a solenoid in the injector. A spring-loaded valve opens, and fuel is injected into the engine. The amount of time that the computer keeps the current applied to the injector is known as the *injector pulse width*. The computer controls the fuel/air mixture by controlling that pulse width. The computer changes the pulse width to make the mixture richer or leaner based on information it gets from various sensors, including the temperature of the engine coolant and air, the speed and load on the engine, the throttle position, and the oxygen level in the exhaust gases.

Fuel injectors are located either in a throttle housing (called *throttle body fuel injection*) or in the intake port (called *multi-port fuel injection*) just ahead of the intake valve. The following sections explore each of these in detail.

Throttle body fuel injection

Throttle body fuel injection is a carburetorless system that mixes the fuel and air together right in the throttle of the car instead of using individual fuel injectors to pump the fuel into each cylinder. (See Figure 6-9.) These systems are less complicated than individual fuel injection systems and are generally cheaper. Some of these systems use solenoids to spray the fuel into the airstream in the throttle through a fuel injector nozzle. Here's how a throttle-body fuel injection system works:

1. An electrical fuel pump pumps fuel to the throttle body assembly. The throttle body assembly looks similar to a carburetor and houses the fuel injector(s) and a fuel pressure regulator.

2. The fuel pressure regulator maintains proper fuel pressure and meters unused fuel back to the fuel tank.

3. A computer controls one or two fuel injectors mounted in the throttle body assembly. The computer applies electrical current to the injector solenoid for the proper duration *(pulse-width)*, and fuel under pressure is then injected and mixed with air as it passes through the throttle on its way to the engine.

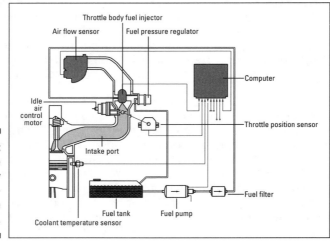

Figure 6-9:
How the throttle body fuel injection system works.

Multi-port fuel injection

Multi-port fuel injection is another type of carburetorless system. It mixes fuel and air together right in the intake port just ahead of the intake valve. (See Figure 6-10.) Vehicles with multi-port fuel injection have a separate fuel injector for each cylinder. Here's how these systems work:

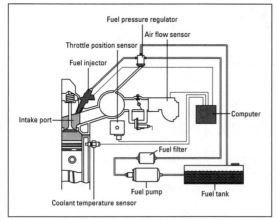

Figure 6-10:
How multi-port fuel injection works.

1. An electrical fuel pump pumps fuel to the fuel rail assembly, to which the fuel injectors are mounted. The fuel rail assembly may also contain the fuel pressure regulator, which maintains proper fuel pressure and meters unused fuel back to the fuel tank. Fuel injectors, one for each cylinder, are attached at one end to the fuel rail and at the other to the intake port in the engine.

2. The computer applies electrical current to the injector solenoid for the proper pulse-width, and fuel under pressure is then injected into the intake port just ahead of the intake valve.

Some multi-port fuel-injected engines feature fuel injectors that fire in *sequence,* which means that each injector opens individually just before its intake valve opens. This type of system is more efficient than a system whose injectors fire simultaneously. (For example, if you have a six-cylinder multi-port fuel-injected engine that's simultaneously fired, three of the six injectors are pulsed together, and then the other three injectors are pulsed.) In addition, emission levels are lower in a sequentially-fired system, but such a system requires a separate electrical circuit for each injector.

The Engine Block: Where the Fuel System and Ignition System Meet

Whether accomplished through a carburetor or a fuel injection system, after the air and fuel unite in the form of a vapor, and the spark plugs are ready to provide that all-important spark of ignition, all that's needed is a spot for that passionate meeting to take place. The rendezvous occurs in your engine's cylinders, and it's truly a triumph of timing (as all successful rendezvous must be!).

In this section, I describe the major parts of the engine and explain how they create the power that drives the car.

Major engine components

Inside the engine are several fascinating parts (see Figure 6-11).

At the top are the cylinder heads. These contain the mechanisms that allow the valves to open and close, letting the fuel/air mixture into the cylinders and allowing the burnt exhaust gases to leave. Below the cylinder heads is the engine block itself. This piece contains the cylinders, which in turn contain the pistons.

Improvements to fuel injection systems

One exciting way that fuel injection systems are being perfected is the tendency to replace moving parts with stationary ones, and "solid" parts with intangible substances. By reducing the number of mechanical parts, car manufacturers hope to reduce production costs and create devices that are less susceptible to breakdown due to physical stress.

Years ago, the Robert Bosch Company developed an air-flow-controlled (AFC) fuel injection system called L-Jetronics. At first, this system used an air flap that responded to the air moving through the throttle by wiping a contact across a resistor. This action sent signals to a computer. By monitoring the volume of air, the computer could then regulate the amount of fuel to be injected into the cylinders. Then someone thought, "Why bother with an air flap that takes two- or three-tenths of a second to respond to a change in air flow?" Systems using platinum wires and sonic waves swiftly followed, and then completely computerized systems were introduced.

Now, I'm all in favor of simplification — ever since my mother taught me to always buy the washing machine with the fewest gadgets on the principle that the fewer parts involved, the fewer things there are that can break down — but I keep having this fantasy that if they continue to replace mechanical car parts with miniaturized and computerized equipment, eventually we may lift the hood of the car and find nothing but a little black box! At that point, when things go wrong, we'll probably have to seek the services of a wizard rather than a mechanic! The upside is that using less metal, plastic, and rubber places less strain on our dwindling supply of raw materials. It also reduces the amount of energy consumed by production (as well as driving) and the number of disposal facilities required to process all the worn and broken stuff we throw away. Let's hope that the trend continues, wizards and all.

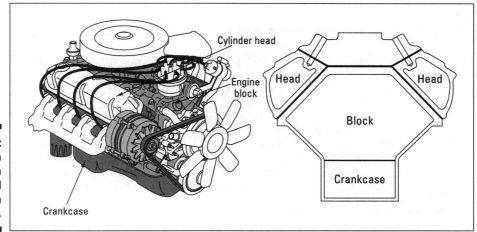

Figure 6-11:
The main
parts of an
internal
combustion
engine.

So what's a cylinder? A cylinder is a hollow iron pipe (see Figure 6-12) capped at one end with a spark plug inserted into and through that cap so that the plug's electrodes are available for action.

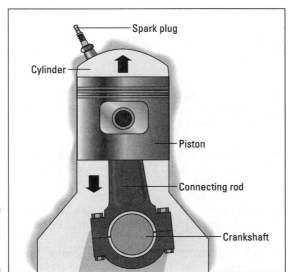

Figure 6-12:
Anatomy of
a cylinder.

Poor maintenance results in poor performance

Poor maintenance can cause the rings and cylinder walls to become thinner with wear, creating a gap between them that allows gases to bypass the rings. This reduces compression in the cylinders and, as you see in the following section on the four-stroke power cycle, you don't get as big a bang for your buck, and your car loses power. Piston rings can be replaced, but it's an expensive job. Before you allow anyone to undertake a "ring job," check the compression to see whether your car really needs it (instructions appear in Chapter 13) and be sure that the car's blue-book value warrants such a costly investment. You may save money in the long run by trading in the old "fuel hog" for a more efficient vehicle.

The cylinders on vehicles with rear-wheel drive run from the front of the engine back toward the firewall at the rear of the engine compartment. On vehicles with front-wheel drive, the engine is usually combined with the transmission into a single unit called a transaxle. These engines are called transverse engines because they're set sideways between the wheels of the car and their cylinders run from side to side (see Figure 6-13).

"Straight" (or "in-line") engines have a single row of cylinders, V-type engines have two parallel rows of cylinders. On rotary engines (found on some Mazdas) the cylinders radiate outward from the center like spokes on a wheel.

Each cylinder has a number, determined by the particular engine's cylinder sequence. You can find descriptions and illustrations of the cylinder sequence for a variety of engines in Chapter 13.

Inside each cylinder is a metal piston, which fits snugly against the walls of the cylinder so that nothing can get past it. On the outside of the piston are piston rings that ensure a snug fit.

The cylinder also has other openings besides the ones for the spark plug and the piston. These are for the intake valves and the exhaust valves.

At the bottom of the engine is the crankcase, which houses the crankshaft and the oil pan. Water circulates throughout the engine to keep it cool, and oil circulates to keep the parts moving freely.

Now that you've met the "players," you're ready to get on to the main event they're designed to participate in: the fiery meeting of air, fuel, and fire known as the *four-stroke power cycle*.

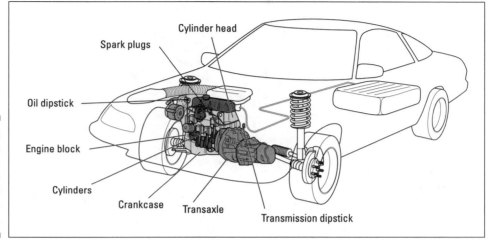

Figure 6-13:
The main parts of a transverse internal combustion engine.

The four-stroke power cycle

The piston rides up and down inside the cylinder on a connecting rod that attaches to the crankshaft, causing the crankshaft to turn. Each movement of the piston is called a *stroke.* Four strokes — down, up, down, up — complete the cycle that creates the power to drive the engine. This process is aptly called the four-stroke power cycle. The four-stroke power cycle varies slightly, depending on whether your vehicle's engine is a conventional internal combustion engine, a stratified charge engine, or a diesel engine. I cover the first two here and the diesel power cycle in Chapter 7.

In a conventional internal combustion engine

Here's what happens on each stroke of the piston in a conventional internal combustion engine:

1. **Intake stroke:** (See Figure 6-14.) When the piston moves *down,* it creates a vacuum in the top portion of the cylinder (where the piston was at the end of its last upstroke). Air can't get in from the bottom of the cylinder because the rings on the piston seal it off. Then the intake valves, conveniently located at the entrance of the intake manifold to the cylinder, open up and let the fuel/air mixture into the cylinder. This mixture rushes in to fill the vacuum left by the piston.

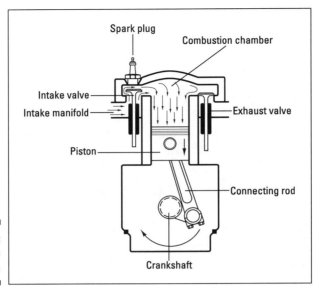

Figure 6-14:
The intake
stroke.

2. **Compression stroke:** (See Figure 6-15.) The piston moves back *up,* compressing the fuel/air mixture into a tiny space between the top of the piston and the top of the cylinder. This space is called the combustion chamber and also happens to be where the electrode end of the spark plug enters the cylinder. The difference between the total space inside the cylinder and the space inside the combustion chamber is called the compression ratio. It indicates that the pressure has been raised from normal air pressure of 15 psi (pounds per square inch) to hundreds of psi, which makes the resulting explosion much more intense.

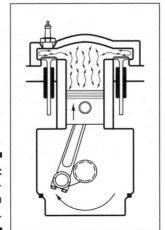

Figure 6-15:
The com-
pression
stroke.

At this point, the intake valves have closed, so the compressed mixture can't get out. (The intake and exhaust valves create airtight seals to ensure that nothing can get past them when they are closed.)

3. **Power stroke:** (See Figure 6-16.) The spark plug produces a spark across the gap between its electrodes. This spark ignites the compressed fuel/air mixture. Then the burning fuel/air mixture explodes, creating intense pressure that forces the piston *down* again. The power that pushed the piston down is transmitted, via the connecting rod, to the crankshaft. It then travels, via the drive train, through the clutch, the transmission, the driveshaft, the differential, and so on, to the wheels. (A quick overview of this process appears in Chapter 4.)

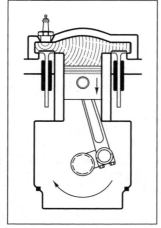

Figure 6-16:
The power
stroke.

4. **Exhaust stroke:** (See Figure 6-17.) The piston moves *up* again, pushing the burned gases up with it. Then the exhaust valve opens and lets the burned gases out into the exhaust manifold. From there, the burned gasses travel through the exhaust system (which, on newer cars, includes anti-pollution devices), through the muffler, and out the tailpipe into the environment.

The cylinders don't fire all at once. To keep the engine properly balanced with all that action going on, they fire in a particular order called the firing order. So while one cylinder is going through Stroke One, another will be at Stroke Two, and so on. The firing order varies from one engine to another and Chapter 12 has descriptions and illustrations of the firing orders for a variety of engine types.

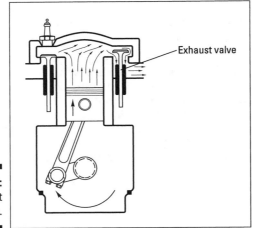

Figure 6-17:
The exhaust
stroke.

Now you can see why an ignition tune-up is so important. If done properly, a tune-up ensures that a full measure of electricity is transferred from the battery, amplified by the coil, and directed by the distributor to the proper spark plug at the proper time. If the spark is insufficient, or if it arrives before or after the fuel/air mixture is at full compression by the piston, the result is less power and poorly burned fuel. Increased air pollution and fuel consumption is a high price to pay for stretching the intervals between tune-ups! Chapters 12 and 13 show you how to keep your electrical system and fuel system in tune.

In a stratified charge engine

In their efforts to design and build cars with a greater degree of fuel efficiency, automakers have had to deal with a frustrating paradox. It takes a *lean* fuel/air mixture (one that has relatively little fuel in proportion to air) to provide maximum fuel economy and cut down on the hydrocarbons and carbon monoxide that pollute the air, but it takes a *rich* mixture to attain greater power and cut down on nitrogen oxides, which also pollute the air. How could a vehicle enjoy the benefits of both mixtures while avoiding the pitfalls? One answer came in the form of the stratified charge engine:

Stratified charge engines are basically the same as conventional internal combustion engines, with one major difference: Stratified charge engines provide both a lean mixture *and* a rich mixture of fuel and air to the cylinders, and they keep the two mixtures separated until the vital moment when combustion takes place. Then the spark plug fires the rich mixture, which in turn ignites the leaner mixture. Because the fuel/air ratio for a conventional engine is around 15:1, and a stratified charge engine can use a mixture as lean as 30:1 (some have even worked successfully with mixtures of 200:1!), you can see why these new engines have stacked up such sensational ratings for fuel efficiency and clean emissions.

The basic design of a stratified charge engine varies with the manufacturer. One of the most outstanding was pioneered by Honda in its CVCC. It used a pre-chamber (short for precombustion chamber) to keep the rich mixture from mixing with the lean one. The following steps explain how the four-stroke power cycle works in a stratified charge engine:

1. **Intake stroke:** The cylinder head has a little chamber, called a *pre-chamber,* which has its own little intake valve. The spark plug is also located in this chamber. On the intake stroke, the little auxiliary intake valve opens and allows a very rich mixture of fuel and air to enter the pre-chamber. On the same stroke, the main intake valve opens up and brings a very lean mixture of fuel and air into the cylinder itself. Figure 6-18 shows a cylinder in a stratified charge engine during the intake stroke. Compare it to the conventional cylinder in Figure 6-14.

2. **Compression stroke:** The lean mixture is compressed at the top of the cylinder in the combustion chamber, and the two mixtures are brought into contact with one another.

3. **Ignition stroke:** The spark plug fires the rich mixture in the pre-chamber, where it burns fiercely and ignites the leaner mixture in the combustion chamber. This action forces the piston down and provides the power that moves the car. Because the lean mixture burns more slowly, the fuel is burned more thoroughly, which is why stratified charge engines get better mileage and put out cleaner exhaust fumes.

4. **Exhaust stroke:** The exhaust valve opens and sends the burned gases out of the car, via the exhaust system.

Other stratified engines use a depression in the piston's surface to provide space for the rich mixture to be ignited, instead of a pre-chamber. This *open chamber* design has performed efficiently in a variety of vehicles.

Turbocharging

Turbocharging means to use a blower or a turbine to force greater amounts of air into an engine's cylinders. This process produces more power in both diesel and conventional vehicles because cars run on air more than they run on fuel. The more air the engine can take in, the bigger the bang is during the power stroke. At first, cars were turbocharged to perform better on race-tracks, but when car manufacturers began to use smaller engines on larger cars to lighten their weight and conserve fuel, turbocharging provided a way to increase the engine's power so that these big cars wouldn't be sluggish on the road.

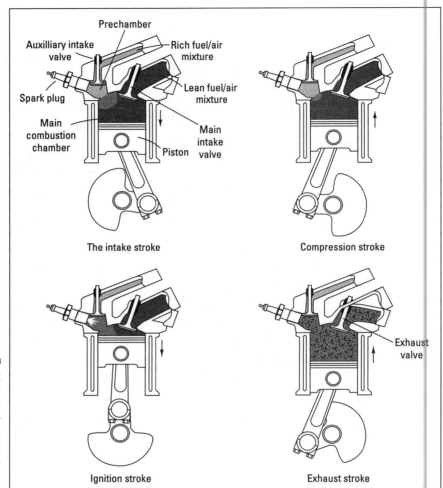

Figure 6-18:
The four-stroke power cycle in a stratified charge engine.

When it came to designing diesel cars, the problem was even more pressing: how to change a car with a reputation of being noisy, underpowered, and smoky into a faster, quieter, more efficient vehicle that could meet the EPA requirements. The results have been heartening indeed. A turbocharger can increase the power on a diesel car by 50 percent while lowering its fuel consumption by 20 to 25 percent! And, what's more, because the turbine itself is powered by the hot gases that normally would go out of the exhaust pipe, you don't need to provide anything extra to drive it. What a wonderful example of recycling!

The nitty-gritty on turbocharging

If you just can't get enough of this turbocharging stuff, the following gets a bit more specific about how turbocharging works:

1. The hot exhaust gases leave the exhaust manifold in much the same manner as they usually do. But instead of going directly through the exhaust system and out of the car via the tailpipe, they first pass through a turbine, which is nothing but a fan that's set in motion by the velocity of the passing gases.

2. A shaft connects the fan to a compressor, which blows fresh, filtered air into the cylinders. (On a gasoline-powered car, it takes the fuel/air mixture supplied by the carburetor and blows it into the cylinders.)

3. The excess and used exhaust fumes pass from the turbine to the exhaust system and continue on their way to the tailpipe and out into the air in their usual manner.

4. The more load on the engine, the hotter and faster are the exhaust fumes that turn the turbine. The faster they turn it, the more air the compressor sends to the engine and the faster the engine can go. This unique way of converting exhaust gas energy into mechanical power has a nice merry-go-round effect.

Sounds simple, doesn't it? Well, usually the first thing an engineer learns is "The simpler, the better," or, as the Zen monks put it, "Less is more." (Ecology, engineering, and philosophy all in a couple of paragraphs! Maybe I ought to change the name of this book to *Zen and the Art of Auto Maintenance.*)

Don't confuse turbocharging with supercharging. A supercharger is a pump that compresses the fuel/air mixture and forces it into the cylinders of a gasoline-powered car. Because superchargers are usually belt-driven by the engine instead of by exhaust gases, they use engine power to increase engine power. Because they're not fuel efficient, they generally are used only to increase the speed of "high-performance," low-efficiency vehicles.

Turbocharging kits are available that you can install on conventional vehicles to increase their power and performance. However, because turbocharging places considerable stress on engines that weren't designed with turbocharging in mind, you run the risk of damaging your engine and voiding all existing warranties if you decide to boost Old Faithful with a turbo kit. So investigate the situation carefully before you go this route. Some owners have had marvelous success, and their engines have lived to tell the tale; others haven't been as lucky. Generally speaking, I would never attempt to turbocharge the original engine of an older car, nor would I tinker with anything but a ruggedly built engine in top condition. If Old Faithful is beginning to show the strain of passing years, it would be wiser to recycle the old workhorse and buy yourself a turbo-powered filly!

Chapter 7

From Horses to Hybrids: The Dope on Diesels and Alternatively Powered Vehicles

* *

In This Chapter

▶ Weighing the advantages and disadvantages of diesel-powered vehicles

▶ Understanding, troubleshooting, and maintaining diesel engines

▶ Starting a diesel on frosty mornings

▶ Finding a good diesel mechanic

▶ Exploring alternative fuels with advantages over gasoline

▶ Identifying popular candidates to replace the internal combustion engine

* *

*E*ver since mechanically propelled vehicles replaced horses as the primary mode of transportation, people have been trying to invent engines that enable vehicles to go faster, cost less, and use fuel more efficiently. After relatively brief romances with steam and electricity, the internal combustion engine became the primary source of automotive power. In the United States and many other parts of the world, gasoline is the preferred fuel for passenger vehicles, while diesel fuel often powers trucks and agricultural and construction equipment. In many parts of the world where gasoline is in short supply, most of the passenger vehicles have diesel engines, too.

In recent years, environmental concerns about the impact of automotive exhaust on air quality — plus the fact that the world's supply of petroleum is rapidly diminishing — have created an intense effort to develop vehicles that run on alternative fuels. Vehicles that run on liquid gases of various kinds, electric vehicles (EV), and vehicles driven by exotic hybrid engines and fuel cells are being touted as prime candidates for "Car of the Future."

The first section of this chapter tells you everything you need to know about vehicles with diesel engines. The rest of the chapter brings you up-to-date on the alternatives that are currently considered to have the most potential for supplanting the internal combustion engine in years to come.

Diesels For Dummies

This section is structured as a mini-version of *Auto Repair For Dummies* devoted entirely to diesel-powered vehicles. It spells out both the advantages and disadvantages of owning a diesel-powered vehicle and explains how a diesel engine works. It also provides instructions for maintaining and troubleshooting diesels and for finding a good diesel mechanic when your best efforts just aren't enough.

Although diesel-powered vehicles are almost universal in a large part of the world where gasoline is almost unavailable, diesel engines are used mainly for heavy equipment in the United States and Canada. Diesel-powered cars exist, but — except for a short period in the 1980s, when fuel shortages made them popular because they got 25 percent more miles per gallon than gasoline engines — they have acquired a reputation for being noisy, underpowered, smelly, and cantankerous. This is not always the case, however. Mercedes-Benz, who pioneered the diesel car as a luxury vehicle decades ago, still makes diesel-powered vehicles that many consider unsurpassed for beauty, performance, high resale value, and high price tags. Volkswagen, whose VW Rabbit was the first peppy, moderately priced diesel car, still offers diesel-powered vehicles, and other manufacturers also offer diesel cars and trucks. If you're considering buying a diesel-powered vehicle, take a good look at the next section before you decide.

The good and bad about diesels

To accurately compare diesel vehicles with traditional gasoline-powered vehicles, you need to consider a number of pros and cons.

PRO: Diesels get great mileage.

CON: So do vehicles with fuel-efficient gasoline-powered engines, which often cost a couple of thousand dollars less than diesels. You can buy a lot of gas for a couple of thousand dollars!

Diesel fuel is not available at many service stations, and although it used to be cheaper than gasoline, it now often costs as much — or more — than gasoline, and it may become even more expensive, depending on availability and demand.

PRO: Diesel fuel contains more usable energy than gasoline.

CON: Although diesel fuel is considered more efficient because it converts heat into energy rather than sending the heat out the tailpipe as gas-powered vehicles do, it doesn't result in flashy "high performance." A gasoline-powered vehicle is like a racehorse — high-strung, fiery, and fast — whereas a diesel vehicle is more like a workhorse — slow, strong, and (hopefully) enduring.

PRO: Diesels have no spark plugs or distributors. Therefore, they never need a tune-up.

CON: Diesels still need regular maintenance to keep them running. You have to change the oil and the air, oil, and fuel filters, and you may need to bleed excess water out of the system. This chapter shows you how to do these things yourself, but if you neglect the maintenance, and the fuel injection system breaks down, you'll probably have to pay a diesel mechanic big bucks to get things unsnaggled.

PRO: Diesels are built more ruggedly to withstand the rigors of higher compression. Consequently, they usually go much longer before they require major repairs than conventional vehicles do. (Mercedes-Benz holds the longevity record with several vehicles clocking more than 900,000 miles on their original engines!)

CON: Do you really want to hang on to the same vehicle for 900,000 miles? Also, there have been cases where automakers have simply plunked diesel engines into vehicles that were originally designed to be gasoline-powered. Because these vehicles weren't constructed to stand up to the stresses imposed by the high compression that diesel engines require, they suffered failures that contributed to their swift decline in popularity.

PRO: Turbocharged diesels have better fuel efficiency and are much more powerful and responsive than traditional diesel vehicles.

CON: Turbocharging will probably get cheaper and even more efficient as time goes on, but you can buy a turbocharged, gasoline-powered vehicle and have the advantages of both.

PRO: Diesels have become easier to start in cold weather.

CON: Although they're better than they used to be, diesel engines are still more difficult to start on cold days than gasoline engines are.

PRO: Diesels put out much less carbon monoxide than ordinary vehicles do, which means less air pollution.

CON: This is a major misconception. Diesels put out 30 to 90 percent more nitrogen oxides and carbon particles (soot), and recent studies show that diesel emissions can cause cancer. As a result, recent legislation is aimed at getting diesel-powered vehicles off the road completely unless they can find a way to meet increasingly stringent EPA standards.

By the time you read this book, the diesel pros and cons may have changed. Government pressure to produce low-emission diesel engines for trucks, buses, and farm and construction equipment by the early 2000s has resulted in increased efforts to develop low-sulfur diesel fuels, specialized catalytic converters, and advanced filters and other devices to cut down or destroy toxic emissions, as well as dual-fuel engines that run on natural gas but can switch to diesel if the gas supply runs out.

Ultimately, you're going to have to check out what's available and make up your own mind. However, based on the current situation, unless you do a lot of driving in parts of the world where gasoline is scarce and diesel fuel is plentiful, I'd stick to gasoline or consider one of the alternatively powered vehicles described later in this chapter.

If you do decide to buy a diesel vehicle, be sure to choose one that allows you to do most of the maintenance yourself, without requiring a great deal of time, money, or skill. Check the owner's manual and talk to diesel mechanics to be sure that the oil is easy to change, because you're going to have to change it quite often. Also make sure that the oil, air, and fuel filters are easy to reach and change, and that you can bleed and prime the fuel system easily. Before you buy the vehicle, make the dealer show you where all these items are located and what you must do to maintain them.

What makes it go?

The basic difference between a diesel engine and a gasoline engine is that in a diesel engine, the fuel is not ignited by an outside power source like a spark plug, nor is it mixed with air in a carburetor. Instead, the fuel is sprayed into the combustion chamber through a fuel injector nozzle, just when the air in the chamber has been placed under such great pressure that it's hot enough to ignite the fuel spontaneously. (You can find more information about diesel fuel later in this chapter.)

Most conventional engines have compression ratios of around 8:1, which means that the volume of each cylinder is eight times larger with the piston at the bottom of the cylinder than with the piston at the top of the cylinder. Diesel engines may employ compression ratios of above 20:1. Because of this fact, and the fact that the compressed air can reach very high temperatures, diesel engines must be built for greater strength and endurance. (See Figure 7-1.)

Because diesel fuel is less volatile than gasoline and is easier to start if the combustion chamber is preheated, manufacturers have installed little glow plugs, which work off the battery, to prewarm the air in the cylinders when you first start the car. They have also designed a variety of heaters to help get things going in extremely cold weather. (See "Getting started on a frosty morning" later in this chapter.)

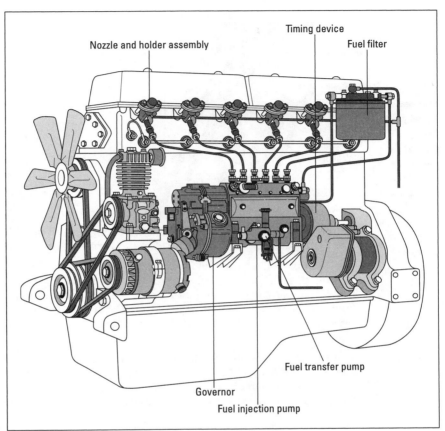

Nozzle and holder assembly

Timing device

Fuel filter

Fuel transfer pump

Governor

Fuel injection pump

Figure 7-1:
A diesel
engine.

Here's a step-by-step view of what happens when you start up a diesel-powered vehicle. The details may vary from one car to another, but the action remains pretty much the same. (It might be fun to compare this description with the short overview of how conventional engines work in Chapter 4.)

1. When you first turn the key in the ignition, you're asked to wait until the engine builds up enough heat in the cylinders for satisfactory starting. (Most vehicles have a little light that says, "Wait," but a sultry computer voice may do the same job on some vehicles.) When you turn the key, the glow plugs kick in and begin to warm up the air in the cylinders. (See Figure 7-2.) Usually, you don't have to wait long — probably no more than half a minute in moderate weather. Developments in glow plugs have dramatically reduced starting time.

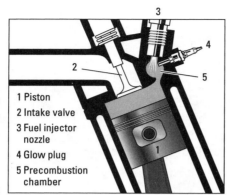

Figure 7-2:
Glow plugs
warm up the
air in the
cylinders.

1 Piston
2 Intake valve
3 Fuel injector
   nozzle
4 Glow plug
5 Precombustion
   chamber

2. When everything is warm enough, a "Start" light goes on. When you see this light, you step on the **accelerator** and turn the ignition key to "Start."

3. **Fuel pumps** deliver the fuel from the **fuel tank** to the engine. On its way, the fuel passes through a couple of **fuel filters** (see Figure 7-3) that clean it before it can get to — and clog up — the **fuel injector** nozzles (see Figure 7-4). Proper maintenance of these filters is especially important in diesels, because fuel contamination can clog up the tiny holes in the injector nozzles.

4. The **fuel injection pump** is truly the heart of the diesel engine. (See Figure 7-5.) It sends fuel to a series of mini-pumps called **fuel transfer pumps**, each of which is responsible for delivering fuel at a pressure of over 1,000 psi (pounds per square inch) to one of the fuel injector nozzles. (See Figure 7-6.)

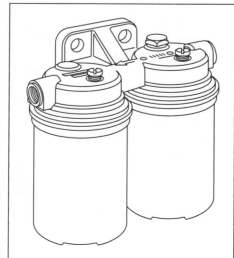

Figure 7-3:
A diesel
fuel filter.

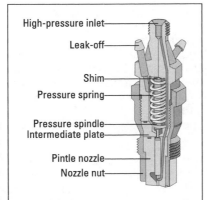

Figure 7-4:
Anatomy
of a fuel
injector.

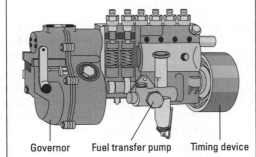

Figure 7-5:
Fuel
injection
pump.

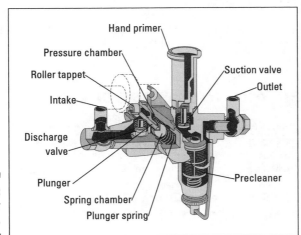

Figure 7-6:
Fuel transfer
pump.

The fuel injection pump's brain is the *governor* (refer to Figure 7-5), which has a very important job: It controls the exact amount of fuel that's sent from each mini-pump to the nozzles and makes sure that the engine doesn't go so fast that it damages itself with excessive heat and pressure. Some governors are built right into the injection pump; others work off the crankshaft or the pump's timing gear; still others measure the speed of the air coming into the engine. All governors are affected by the pressure of your foot on the accelerator, the temperature in the cylinders, the altitude, the speed of the vehicle, and the load that the vehicle is carrying.

At this point, the action moves to the cylinders, where the fuel, air, and "fire" meet. While the preceding steps have been taking place to get the fuel where it needs to go, another process has been running simultaneously to get the air where it needs to be for the final, fiery "power play."

5. On conventional diesels, the air comes in through an air cleaner that's quite similar to those in ordinary vehicles. However, turbochargers have been developed that ram greater volumes of air into the cylinders and may provide greater power and fuel economy under optimum conditions. A turbocharger can increase the power on a diesel vehicle by 50 percent while lowering its fuel consumption by 20 to 25 percent! (See "Turbocharging" in Chapter 6 for details.)

6. As you've read, turning the key started the glow plugs warming up the air in the cylinders. On many engines, the glow plugs are located right in the combustion chambers of the cylinders. On others, they have been placed in little precombustion chambers (refer to Figure 7-2), which the glow plugs can heat more quickly and easily.

7. From here, combustion spreads from the smaller amount of fuel that's placed under pressure in the precombustion chamber to the fuel and air in the combustion chamber itself.

Now take a closer look at each step of the power cycle that converts all this into power to drive the vehicle.

The diesel four-stroke power cycle

Although some diesel engines operate with two-stroke power cycles, chances are that the vehicles you'll encounter use a four-stroke power cycle, which is comparable to the power cycle of a gasoline engine (see Chapter 6). The following explains how the diesel's four-stroke power cycle works:

✓ **Stroke 1 — Intake stroke (see Figure 7-7):** The piston descends, the intake valve opens, and air is drawn into the cylinder.

Figure 7-7:
Intake
stroke.

✔ **Stroke 2 — Compression stroke (see Figure 7-8):** The intake and exhaust valves are closed as the piston moves upward and places the air under extreme pressure. As the pressure increases, the air heats up to the *flash point* (the point at which it causes the fuel to undergo spontaneous combustion). Just before that point is reached, fuel injectors spray fuel into the combustion chambers at the precise instant when ignition is to take place.

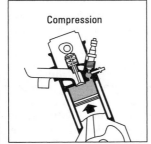

Figure 7-8:
Compression
stroke.

✔ **Stroke 3 — Power stroke (see Figure 7-9):** With intake and exhaust valves closed, the fuel ignites, and combustion forces the piston down. This driving power is transmitted through the transmission and the rest of the drive train to the wheels, which causes the vehicle to move.

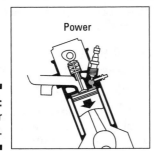

Figure 7-9:
Power
stroke.

> ✔ **Stroke 4 — Exhaust stroke (see Figure 7-10):** The exhaust valve opens as the piston rises and pushes the burned gases out of the cylinder.

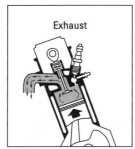

Figure 7-10:
Exhaust
stroke.

Diesel fuel

Diesel engines run on diesel fuel, which is more efficient than gasoline because it contains 10 percent more energy per gallon than gasoline does. It is also safer than gasoline because its vapors don't explode or ignite as easily as gasoline does.

Diesel fuel (sometimes called diesel oil) comes in two grades: Diesel #1 and Diesel #2 (or 1-D and 2-D). Just as gasoline is rated by its octane, diesel fuel is rated by its cetane, which indicates how easy it is to ignite and how fast it will burn. (The higher the cetane number, the more volatile the fuel.) Most diesel vehicles use fuel with a rating of 40 to 55. Most diesel automakers specify Diesel #2 for normal driving conditions. Truckers use Diesel #2 to carry heavy loads for long distances at sustained speeds because it's less volatile than #1 and provides greater fuel economy.

Diesel fuel is also measured by its viscosity, which has to do with its thickness and ability to flow. Like any oil, diesel fuel gets thicker and cloudier at lower temperatures. Under extreme conditions, this fuel can become a gel and refuse to flow at all. Diesel #1 flows more easily than Diesel #2, so it's more efficient at lower temperatures. The two types of oil can be blended, and most service stations offer diesel fuel blended for local weather conditions.

If you plan to drive in very cold weather, choose diesel fuel rated at least 10 degrees lower than the coldest temperatures you expect to encounter. Consult your owner's manual for specifics.

Diesel fuel emissions have been found to be extremely toxic to humans and other living things. Until safer forms of this fuel are developed, be careful not to inhale the fumes while you're pumping it into your fuel tank.

The good news is that safer diesel fuels *are* being developed. The top contender, Fischer-Tropsch, is a liquefied natural gas that contains no sulfur and can be used in conventional diesel engines. With the proper converter, it has the potential to be as clean as natural gas. This fuel would be very expensive to create and market, so if you really love diesel engines, it would be wise to lobby for government subsidies and incentives to make this fuel (or comparable diesel fuels) affordable. For more about this topic, see "Designer diesel," later in this chapter.

The diesel fuel sold at truck stops is often cheaper than at service stations, and the fuel is fresher, too. Freshness is important because diesel fuel can easily become contaminated by the water vapor that condenses in fuel tanks, and by fungus and other microbes that can clog filters and fuel injectors.

If you find yourself at a station that arouses your suspicions, look for slimy stuff on the nozzle of the fuel pump. If, despite these precautions, the fuel in your tank becomes contaminated, see "Curing a sick diesel" later in this chapter.

Try to fill up at a truck stop on a Saturday morning, when commercial trucking action is light. Weekday evenings are the worst times to buy. Muscling a small vehicle into a crowd of big rigs isn't easy!

The electrical system

Diesels require more stored energy for starting than conventional vehicles do, especially on cold days. Instead of just using the battery to enable the starter to crank the engine, as gasoline-powered engines do, a diesel must have sufficient power to enable the glow plugs to warm the combustion chambers and then must build up enough heat and compression in the cylinders to ignite the fuel. For this reason, diesels must possess considerably more battery capacity than conventional vehicles. Some diesels come equipped with two batteries, while others feature a single oversized battery, which may be more than 50 percent bigger than one found on a conventional car.

It's useless to try to jump-start a diesel from a conventional gasoline-powered engine with a battery of lower capacity.

Aside from this, electrical systems on diesels are pretty much the same as those on conventional vehicles, with alternators, solenoids, and starters performing their usual functions. For information about these components, see Chapter 5.

Emergency substitutes

Theoretically, diesel engines should be able to run on kerosene, certain airplane fuels, and home heating oil, but *do not use these in your vehicle under any circumstances.* Standards of refining, filtering, and blending these oils differ widely, and they can ruin your engine, void your warranties, and create a whole lot of trouble for you.

If you find yourself getting low on fuel in a remote area, look for diesel fuel at trucking companies, food processing plants, electric plants, hospitals, and farms. These places usually have diesel engines on the premises, and some Good Samaritan may take pity on you and let you have some.

If you absolutely cannot find a source of diesel fuel, *as a last resort* borrow some home heating oil or buy some Jet-A fuel at a local airport. Diesel mechanics consider this stuff to be like rotgut whiskey — it will get you there, but it's not the best stuff for your system! So run on these fuels only long enough to get to the nearest source of proper fuel.

Caring for your diesel

Regular maintenance is absolutely imperative if you want a diesel engine to last, and every diesel owner will probably need to handle certain pitfalls and problems. To help you deal with maintenance and repair issues — even if you're not the one doing the work — this section covers the regular maintenance that a diesel engine needs, how to get your engine started when the weather turns cold, and what you can do to heal a sick diesel.

Although diesel engines require no ignition tune-ups and tend to last longer without major repairs than gasoline engines, they do require regular low-cost maintenance, mostly in the form of frequent oil and filter changes.

If you own a conventional vehicle and you get sloppy about maintenance and don't change the oil often enough, you'll probably end up with an engine that's aged prematurely. If you own a diesel and do the same thing, you may end up with an engine that's prematurely dead. The same goes for changing filters: A dirty fuel filter can impair a conventional vehicle's performance, but dirty fuel can clog a diesel's fuel injection system, and you may need expensive professional help to get back on the road again.

As a rule, you won't be able to clean or adjust a diesel's fuel injectors yourself, but they can last 100,000 miles or more if you take proper care of the vehicle. If you maintain your vehicle according to the directions in the owner's manual, you should have few problems. After all, truckers have always preferred diesels because they find them to be tough, reliable, and cheap to run and maintain.

Most diesels are designed so that the owner can perform regular maintenance chores without an undue investment in time and money. The following
sections cover these tasks in general terms; your owner's manual should contain the rest of the information you need.

If it doesn't, or you have no manual, amble on over to your dealership's parts
department and ask to see a copy of the service manual. A quick look at the
proper sections in the manual should tell you whether you can do the job
yourself. If you're not sure, ask someone in the service area to show you
where the oil, air, and fuel filters are located and what's involved in changing
or servicing them. Most mechanics are pretty nice about that kind of thing.
If the job really is easy, they won't make enough on it to make lying to you
worthwhile; if the job isn't so easy, you'll be happy to have them do it for you.

Changing the lubricating oil

Because diesel fuel is sometimes called diesel oil, be aware that the oil you
have to change is not the fuel oil, but the oil that *lubricates* the engine. This
job requires lubricating oil that's specially designed for diesel engines, rather
than the lubricating oil designed for gasoline-powered vehicles. After you
understand that distinction, the actual work involved is the same as it is for
conventional vehicles — except that you have to do the task more often. Be
sure to check your oil dipstick *at least once a week* (following the instructions
in Chapter 3) and change the oil filter every time you change the oil (see
Chapter 15 for additional instructions).

Don't be surprised if you change the lubricating oil in your diesel, run the
engine for two minutes, and check the dipstick only to find that the new oil
has turned pitch black; this is normal.

Your owner's manual tells you what kind of oil to use and the maximum intervals you can wait between changes, but I believe that the more often you
change the oil on *any* vehicle, the longer the vehicle will live and the healthier it will be. That goes double for diesels because extreme heat and pressure
help to contaminate the lubricating oil more quickly.

Because the procedure is the same, all the instructions for changing oil and
oil filters in Chapter 15 are relevant, *except for the oil classification codes.*
(The classification codes for automotive oils tell you which oil to use under a
specific set of conditions.) These are the codes for diesel lubrication oils:

- ✔ **CA:** For use with low-sulfur, high-quality fuels only

- ✔ **CB:** For use with high-sulfur, low-quality fuels on vehicles subjected to
  low to medium stress

- ✔ **CC:** Protects against rust, corrosion, and high temperatures under
  medium to severe conditions

- ✔ **CD:** For use under severe conditions

CC is the lubricating oil currently designated for most popular diesels, but check your owner's manual to be sure. The manual also specifies a viscosity grade in the form of a number preceded by the initials SAE. This grade refers to the "weight" of the oil and the temperature conditions under which it will flow. Diesel lubricating oil comes in the same range of weights as oil for conventional vehicles, and you can find all the necessary information in the section "Knowing Which Kind of Oil to Buy" in Chapter 15.

Changing the air filter

The air filter setup on most diesels is the same as it is for gasoline-powered vehicles, with the filter located inside the air cleaner under the hood of the car. You can find directions for reaching the air filter in the "Changing your air filter" section in Chapter 13.

You have to take one big precaution when you change the air filter on a diesel: Always shut off the engine of a diesel before you try to change the air filter. Diesel engines produce exceedingly powerful suction, and the air intake goes directly to the engine. Because almost anything can fly or drop into it — from nuts and bolts to your favorite hairpiece — you risk serious damage to the engine if you open the air cleaner with the engine running.

Changing the fuel filters

Most diesels have two fuel filters — a "primary" filter located between the fuel tank and the engine — which cleans the fuel before it gets to the fuel transfer pump — and a "secondary" filter up near the engine — which gives the fuel a final cleaning before it gets to the fuel injectors. Both are usually easy to change, and your owner's manual should show you how to do this job. On some diesels, the job is much like changing the oil filter on a conventional vehicle: You unscrew the old one, moisten the gasket of the new one with fuel, and screw it into place. Others have filters with replaceable cartridges; you just remove the old one and pop in the new one.

There's one catch to changing the fuel filter, however. The next section has the details.

Bleeding and priming the fuel system

Whenever you change the fuel filter or run out of fuel in a diesel, you must bleed the air bubbles out of the fuel system and then prime it to get a new supply of fuel circulating. Because cranking the engine does the job but also wears down the battery, most diesels include a manual *primer pump* and an *air-bleed screw* for this purpose. On many vehicles, you simply pump the primer's handle to get the fuel moving and then turn the air-bleed screw until a hissing noise tells you that the air is escaping. Just keep pumping until all the air leaves and the noise ceases; then tighten the air-bleed screw and replace the pump handle.

Because bleeding and priming the fuel system is something that may occur fairly often, I suggest that you check the equipment and procedure for any model you're interested in purchasing to be sure that you can do this job quickly and easily.

Water separators

Because diesel fuel can easily become contaminated by water, many diesel cars feature a gadget called a **water separator**, which is usually located on or near the primary **fuel filter**. If your vehicle doesn't have one, I strongly suggest that you have one installed. This part shouldn't be terribly expensive, and it can save you a bunch of money on repairs.

You can usually drain both integral and optional water separators by turning a little drain valve called a *petcock* and emptying the water from the collection chamber of the separator.

It's a good idea to check the water separator weekly at first to see how fast it fills up under normal conditions when you're driving on fuel from your usual source. If the fuel contains a lot of water, you may want to consider buying it elsewhere.

Getting started on a frosty morning

Metal cylinder walls become very cold whenever the temperature drops, so most cars are harder to start in cold weather. Because diesel engines require much higher temperatures to fire the fuel, they have always been harder to start in cold weather than gasoline-powered vehicles are. To warm things up before the engine can run, a variety of heaters have been developed that keep various parts of the vehicle warm and snuggly even when it isn't being driven. Some of these gadgets may be on the vehicle when you buy it; others you can buy and install later on if the need for them arises.

If you're planning to buy a diesel, be sure to ask which heating devices are included in the purchase price. If you live in a cold climate or do much traveling, it may be a good idea to have several devices available for extreme weather conditions. The next sections describe some of your options.

Block heaters

Many diesels come equipped with electrically powered **block heaters** that are built right into them to keep the **engine block** warm overnight. You simply park the vehicle and plug the heater cord into a heavy-duty three-pronged extension cord; then plug the extension cord into a 110-volt electrical socket that can handle a three-pronged plug. Don't skimp on the length of the extension cord — it can be 50 feet to a socket from a motel parking lot! I've been told that in Alaska, where a heater is vital, electrical outlets have been built right into some parking meters. I doubt that anyone tries to beat those meters, especially at −40 degrees.

If your vehicle doesn't have a block heater, you can buy one and have it installed. Various types are available, but *immersion*-type heaters are the most popular.

When buying a heater, consult the charts at the dealer to match the wattage of the heater to the size of your engine and the range of weather you expect to encounter. A high-wattage heater will run up your electric bills unnecessarily if you have a small engine or don't expect the temperature to go below zero very often.

Battery warmers

If your diesel won't start in cold weather and you remembered to plug in the block heater, your battery may be the culprit. Batteries can lose 35 percent of their power at 32 degrees Fahrenheit and as much as 60 percent at 0 degrees. Because the battery has to supply the glow plugs with sufficient juice to get things warmed up, a frostbitten battery isn't of much use on an icy morning.

This problem has two remedies: You can buy a battery with greater capacity (providing that there's room for one under the hood), or you can buy a battery warmer. The two most popular models are the "hot plate" warmer, which simply slides under the battery like a cookie sheet and warms its little toesies, and the "electric blanket," which wraps around the battery and uses more current to deal with really frigid situations. Both simply plug into a nearby 110-volt socket.

Oil warmers and other gadgets

You can buy a heated dipstick to heat the oil in the engine crankcase (just trade it for your normal dipstick and plug it into an electrical outlet) and a host of other gadgets to warm the coolant in the engine and the fuel in the fuel lines. (Most people don't need all this stuff, but for my readers in Alaska, Canada, and other cold climates, I thought I'd cover the subject thoroughly. . . .)

I recently came across a handy hint that may work in a pinch: On a day when your block heater isn't able to combat the cold effectively, try turning on your electric hair-dryer and putting the nozzle into the car's air intake. The warm air should help your engine warm up faster.

What not to do on a frosty morning

Never use engine-starting fluids to start your engine — no matter how eager you are to get underway. The ether in these fluids can ignite at such low temperatures that you risk a fire or an explosion — either of which can mean severe damage to both yourself and your precious diesel. Although the containers do give instructions, measuring the "safe" proportions required is just too hard. If you feel that you must use this stuff, you can find starting-fluid injection kits that are safe and effective; you may want to have one of these installed. Just stay away from those "convenient" spray cans!

Curing a sick diesel

As I mentioned earlier, diesel vehicles can become contaminated by a fungus. Yep, that's right, a *fungus!* It usually happens when you buy diesel fuel that's already "infected" or when the diesel fuel in your tank has been exposed to moisture.

If you suspect that your vehicle has caught a dose of fungus, check its filler pipe and cap for yucky-looking matter, or dip a clean stick into the fuel tank and inspect that. An advanced case of fungus smells like rotten eggs. To cure it, use a biocide designed to kill fuel fungus. Your dealer probably can suggest the proper product and the right amount to use. Or you can ask someone at an auto parts store, a marine chandler, or a home heating or chemical company for advice.

Add biocide only when you're filling the tank with fuel — never to an empty or almost empty tank. If your tank's really been fouled up, your best bet probably is to drain it and have it steam-cleaned, or clean it yourself with a commercial cleaner designed for fuel tanks, and then refill the tank and add the biocide.

If you're planning to store your vehicle for a while, fill the fuel tank completely so that no space is left for water vapor to condense out of the air. Then dose the tank with biocide to prevent fungus from forming.

Here's something that I learned while cruising the South Pacific, where diesel fuel is often contaminated and there's usually only one place to fuel up: If sailors suspect that the diesel fuel they're buying may be dirty, they place a nylon stocking over the end of the nozzle of the fuel hose to strain out contaminants. If the stocking gets fouled up, they dose the tank with biocide immediately.

Finding a reliable diesel mechanic

If you need professional help, either with maintenance or for repairs, and your vehicle is out of warranty, you may want to check around for a good independent diesel mechanic, if only to compare prices or get a second opinion on major surgery. One way to find a good independent diesel mechanic is to look in your local Yellow Pages under "Automobiles, Repair" (or something similar) for a shop whose ad carries the logo of the Association of Diesel Specialists. The ADS authorization goes to repair facilities that send their mechanics to factory schools for instruction, maintain standards of cleanliness, and meet requirements for stocking the tools and parts to deal properly with a variety of diesel systems. (Chapter 22 is devoted to finding and maintaining a good relationship with a mechanic and shows you how to get satisfaction in a dispute over labor or services.)

Cars of the Future: Alternatively Powered Vehicles

The future is fast approaching! As I mentioned at the beginning of this chapter, the intense pressure to clean up and preserve the environment is beginning to pay off. Nuclear-powered cars are still pretty far in the future, but federal and state clean-air laws, along with growing public and auto-industry awareness of the need to cut down on pollutants, are bringing about change. And that change is coming pretty rapidly.

The next edition of *Auto Repair For Dummies* will probably include chapters that deal in depth with vehicles that supercede gasoline and diesel engines. There are many contenders in the field. In this section, I give you a look at the technology awaiting you just down the road.

ICE isn't melting away

Carmakers spent the past 70 years perfecting the internal combustion engine — or *ICE,* as today's automotive engineers and product planners call it. Now companies are spending billions of dollars researching better ways to use alternate fuels, such as compressed natural gas. They're also working to improve electric vehicles (EV) — eerily quiet vehicles that whoosh along the road with plenty of power and no tailpipe emissions — and to come up with radically new alternative fuels and alternative power plants.

The gasoline engine isn't going to disappear, at least not any time soon. Improvements to the internal combustion engine have made it far cleaner and more efficient than ever before, and there's no indication that the industry is going to abandon it. In fact, Honda recently unveiled a gasoline engine that is so clean that it almost meets California's tough zero-emissions standard.

Because such engines are so much less polluting, and because the costs to business and society of eliminating gasoline-powered engines are so staggering (where will all those gas station owners, oil refinery workers, and engine mechanics go?), weaning the world away from the internal combustion power plant will take generations.

But the bywords these days are *ecology* and *economy.* Waiting in the wings, like the freshly diapered New Year's baby waiting to usher out the wrinkled Old Year, are a number of alternative fuels and alternative means of getting power to the wheels. Cars may very well end up being called something like *personal transportation modules* in New Millennium-speak!

Alternative fuels

At present, the leading contenders include methanol, propane, designer diesel fuel bred in the laboratory, and, finally, electric power from hydrogen — a gas that can be distilled from something as simple as water. (That's what the H in H_2O stands for, after all.)

These fuels sound like science fiction, but they're really not exotic. Vehicles that consume such fuels will still get their power from a mechanical or electro-mechanical engine. A gear-driven driveshaft will still turn the wheels. But instead of a powerful V-8 engine with dual exhausts and a four-speed automatic transmission, the next generation's hot car might just have a whining electric motor with a direct transmission that has a single forward position: Drive.

Californians are already getting a taste of the future because of a rule that 4 percent of the new cars sold in the state by 2003 must be emission-free and 6 percent must meet super-ultra-low-emission standards. That's more than 100,000 zero- and near-zero-emission cars that must be ready for the road in just a few years! (New York and several other states have adopted similar rules.)

None of the major auto companies want to invoke the wrath of California. It is, after all, the most populous state, and its residents buy about 10 percent of all the vehicles sold each year. To be kicked out of California, which is the penalty carmakers face if they don't comply with the state's stringent clean-air rules, would have a disastrous impact on the old bottom line.

So the auto industry has launched a major effort to develop so-called *ZEVs*, or *zero-emission vehicles*. Automakers have also developed a number of low- and ultra-low-emission cars and trucks by replacing gasoline with cleaner-burning fuels such as propane and natural gas.

Although most alternative fuels require different kinds of fuel tanks and fuel pumps and modified carburetors and fuel injection systems, everything else in the engine works pretty much like a standard car. The fuels, no matter how exotic, still power internal combustion engines. The most common alternatives to gasoline and diesel are compressed natural gas (CNG), propane, and alcohol fuels such as methanol and ethanol. All are cleaner than gasoline, and each comes with advantages and disadvantages. One common problem is availability. Whereas government and private fleet vehicle operators have refilling stations in their garages for the kinds of alternative fuels they use, relatively few public filling stations pump compressed natural gas or ethanol.

 Adventurous private owners who want to take long trips in their alternatively-fueled cars have to locate publicly available filling stations along their routes and call ahead to make sure that they can stop in for a tankful. The best place to do the checking is on the Internet. The federal government maintains a helpful site called the Alternate Fuel Data Center at www.afdc.doe.gov.

Compressed natural gas (CNG)

Compressed natural gas is already in use in more than 75,000 vehicles in the United States and more than 1 million worldwide, according to the Virginia-based Natural Gas Vehicle Coalition. CNG is a common fuel for forklifts, airport shuttles, and transit buses and for pool cars for government and private fleet operations that are trying to meet state and federal clean-air requirements.

The biggest difference between conventional and CNG vehicles is in the fuel tank (see Figure 7-11). Because CNG is compressed, it's stored under pressure at either 3,000 or 3,600 pounds per square inch, which requires special tanks that can withstand that pressure. The tanks are usually cylindrical because the laws of physics dictate that curving surfaces can hold up under pressure better than flat ones can. The fuel is measured in units called *gasoline-gallon equivalents,* or *g.g.e.*

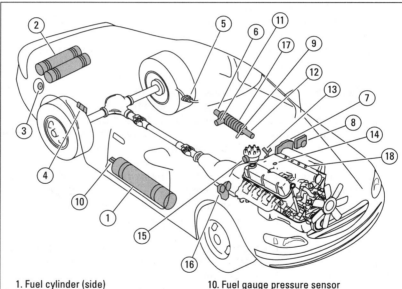

1. Fuel cylinder (side)
2. Fuel cylinders (rear)
3. Fuel fill receptacle
4. Check valve
5. Manual shut-off valve
6. Fuel pressure regulator
7. Powertrain control module
8. Fuel injector driver module
9. Pressure relief discharge tube
10. Fuel gauge pressure sensor
11. High-pressure fuel shut-off solenoid
12. Engine coolant hoses (2)
13. Fuel temperature sensor
14. Fuel pressure sensor
15. Low-pressure fuel shut-off solenoid
16. Fuel shut-off solenoid relay
17. Pressure relief device
18. Fuel injectors (8)

Figure 7-11:
A CNG
(compressed
natural gas)
vehicle.

Natural gas delivers about six times less energy than the same volume of gasoline, so the tanks typically have been larger than a standard gas tank to give the vehicles the same range as their gasoline-powered cousins. One drawback is that the size and number of CNG tanks that most cars and light trucks need uses up valuable cargo or passenger space.

Fuel lines also have to be high-pressure lines, and the fuel delivery system, usually fuel injection, has to be specially made for CNG. But after the gas is mixed with air and injected into the engine's combustion chamber, it works the same as gasoline.

A significant difference occurs at the tailpipe, however. CNG produces far fewer pollutants than either gasoline or diesel, which means that most CNG vehicles qualify for low- to ultra-low-emission standards. DaimlerChrysler even makes a full-size van in California, powered by a CNG-fueled V-8 engine, that is classified as super-ultra-low emission vehicle.

Propane

Propane works much the same as CNG except that it typically is added as a liquid under far less pressure than natural gas. It also is closer to gasoline in terms of the energy derived from each gallon. Propane-powered vehicles need special fuel tanks, but they're not as expensive as the $15,000-plus high-pressure tanks used on most CNG cars and trucks.

Propane is used primarily for fleet vehicles that make day trips. It also is used in farm equipment. Its principal drawback is that it's not as clean-burning as natural gas. Propane is a more complex hydrocarbon, and when it burns, it emits more pollutants.

Alcohol fuels

Alcohol fuels have been around for years, typically mixed with gasoline at a ratio of 15 percent gas, 85 percent methanol or ethanol. The gasoline is added to help with ignition in cold weather, and so that if the fuel catches fire, it will burn with a colored flame. In their pure states, methanol and ethanol burn with a clear flame, which can create a dangerous situation in the event of a fuel fire.

Ethanol is distilled from corn and wheat and is often used in farm vehicles. In addition, it can be used in flexible-fuel and dual-fuel vehicles, although it usually isn't because ethanol filling stations are hard to find — only about 540 of them exist in the entire United States. Methanol, which is distilled from hydrocarbons like coal and natural gas, isn't much used because it isn't as clean as ethanol. As with CNG, use of these fuels requires modification to the fuel storage and delivery systems on cars and trucks.

Designer diesel

One perhaps surprising entry into the clean-fuel arena is *designer diesel.* It is called that because, unlike traditional diesel fuel that is refined from sulfur-laden crude oil, these new diesel fuels have been scientifically designed in the laboratory to be free of sulfur and many of the other impurities that have given diesel a reputation as a dirty fuel. One test refinery in Oklahoma is even producing diesel from natural gas.

Designer diesels are important because the auto industry is looking to a new generation of environmentally friendly, efficient, small diesel engines — usually turbocharged — to augment gasoline and electric power in cars and trucks of the future. One reason is that diesel is more efficient than gasoline. A diesel engine in good tune usually uses about 24 percent of the energy in the fuel for propulsion power. Gasoline engines most often run at around 20 percent when in good shape.

So diesel, if it's cleaned up, has many good points. In fact, the Partnership for a New Generation of Vehicles (PNGV), a nationwide effort by the major domestic carmakers and the federal government to produce the New Millennium's optimum vehicle, has fixed on these small diesel engines coupled with electric motors as the best hope for achieving its goal of producing a hybrid five-passenger car that can get 70 to 80 miles per gallon with extremely low emissions.

Alternative power plants

Alternative fuels lead to a whole new arena of alternative power plants: the innovations that will likely reduce the dependence on the standard internal combustion engine (ICE).

Hybrids

Actually, the first kind of alternative power system uses a small ICE as a critical component. The system is called a hybrid power plant because it's a mix — neither fish nor fowl. It combines small internal combustion engines and electric motors to get maximum power with minimum emissions and maximum fuel economy.

There are two kinds of hybrids (see Figure 7-12 for an illustration):

✔ **A series hybrid** uses a gasoline or diesel engine, coupled with an alternator, to generate the electricity that the electric motor needs to do its work. The electric motor, though, is what actually propels the vehicle, using its power to rotate a driveshaft or a set of drive axles that turn the wheels.

✔ **A parallel hybrid** uses both motors for propulsion. They can run in tandem, or one can be used as the primary power source with the other kicking in to assist when extra power is needed for starting off, climbing hills, and accelerating to pass other vehicles.

The ICE in a parallel hybrid also generates enough electricity to charge a small set of storage batteries mounted in the vehicle's engine compartment or somewhere on the frame. The batteries then provide power for the electric motor when it's called on to do its job.

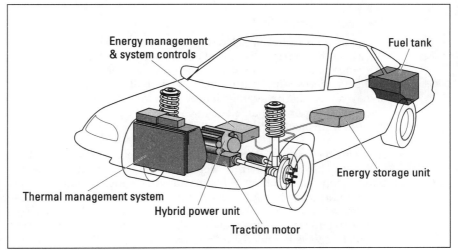

Energy management & system controls

Fuel tank

Energy storage unit

Figure 7-12: A hybrid engine.

Thermal management system

Hybrid power unit

Traction motor

An electronic motor controller sends out the marching orders to the two motors, basing its judgment calls on information received from sensors that tell it things like how hard the driver is pressing on the accelerator or how much strain the internal combustion engine is under.

Having the ICE generator on-board eliminates the need for the costly recharging systems in use on the current crop of battery-driven electric vehicles. If equipped with the same-size gas tanks as conventional ICE-powered vehicles, hybrids have much greater range because of their significantly improved gas mileage.

Honda and Toyota have developed the first commercial hybrid cars. Both are scheduled to go on sale in the United States as year 2000 models. Honda's hybrid — code named the VV — uses a 3-cylinder, 1-liter gasoline engine and an electric motor whose size hadn't been disclosed at press time. The gas engine provides the main power, with the electric kicking in as a sort of *supercharger* when more power is needed.

Toyota's car, the Prius, features a 1.5-liter gas engine and an electric motor rated at 40 horsepower. It works like the Honda, with the electric motor providing extra power when needed. Toyota claims that this car will go 800 miles on a 13.2-gallon tank of gas. The Prius went on sale in Japan in 1998 as the world's first commercially available gas-electric hybrid. Both cars have ultra-clean emissions. And, best of all, both will be priced at under $20,000!

The Toyota and Honda cars are parallel gas-electric hybrids, while Ford, General Motors, and DaimlerChrysler are concentrating on parallel diesel-electrics as part of their work with PNGV.

Electric vehicles (EV)

The same companies are also in the forefront of work on development of a truly usable electric vehicle that accelerates well, has a decent top speed and the range of a conventional gasoline-powered vehicle, seats at least five, and refills its energy supply as quickly as we refill gasoline tanks today. It should also fit as well in the average family's budget as it does in the garage. The section called "Operating an electric vehicle" at the end of this chapter tells you what driving an electric vehicle is like.

Actually, the battery electrics now on the road have several of those characteristics. They do accelerate well, although the extremely heavy battery packs keep them from qualifying as anyone's idea of a hot rod. (However, a private carmaker in southern California does build a two-seat electric sports car that goes from 0 to 60 mph in just 4.2 seconds, which is up there in Chevy Corvette and Dodge Viper territory.) And most of today's electrics will cruise on the freeways at speeds of 75 to 85 mph, depending on how heavy and aerodynamic the vehicle is and how the factory has regulated, or governed, the motor to limit top speed. Nissan's Altra EV, for example, has its top speed limited at 75 mph.

Electric cars and trucks also can haul big loads and climb steep hills with relative ease. That's because, unlike an internal combustion engine that needs to build up revolutions before the maximum pulling power, or **torque**, kicks in, an electric motor provides almost all of its torque from the start. Unfortunately, fast acceleration, hill climbing, and cruising at speeds above 50 miles per hour all consume extra electricity, which cuts down on an electric vehicles' already limited range.

You don't see many electrics in use right now. Although retail sales and leasing started in late 1997, by the middle of 1999 fewer than 2,500 electric vehicles had been sold or leased throughout the United States, mainly in California, where state mandates required them. In comparison, during the same period, about 24 million conventional cars and light trucks were sold or leased.

EVs have been slow to catch on, largely because the industry still considers them experimental and isn't mass-producing them. In fact, some automakers that had begun active sales of EVs have recently stopped making them. That's because the idea that electrics can use storage batteries as their power source, the same way a flashlight draws its power from a battery, hasn't paid off.

Storage-battery technology hasn't achieved the breakthrough needed to let auto-makers store enough energy to give electric cars anywhere near the range they need to compete with vehicles powered by conventional engines. As a result, the average electric car in use in 1999 was getting about 70 miles on a full charge in real-world use, and it took between 4 and 6 hours to recharge those batteries. That means that a 200-mile family trip from New York to Boston, a 4-hour excursion in the average gasoline-powered car, became a 10- to 12-hour journey in an electric. And because storage batteries don't hold much of a charge in extreme cold, the range of a battery-electric vehicle drops way down as the thermometer edges near zero.

So why are some people still excited about EVs? Because tremendous work is being done on alternatives to the storage battery — alternatives that could make emission-free private transportation a reality instead of a mere promise.

Fuel cells

The best answer may well be the fuel cell, a relative old technology that's being adapted and improved in the search for a way to make electric cars more user-friendly. You can see an example of a fuel cell in Figure 7-13.

The fuel cell was invented in the mid-1800s and was put into everyday use by the military and the aerospace industry more than 40 years ago. Nowadays, many hospitals and fast-food restaurants have fuel cells that provide them with electricity so that they are not dependent on a public electrical grid that can black out with no warning.

Essentially, a fuel cell is a processing plant that creates electrical current from hydrogen and oxygen, which is passed over a catalyst, usually a micro-scopically thin sheet of platinum. The electrical current is then fed directly to the vehicle's electric motor for propulsion. Cells are linked together into "stacks" to increase the electrical output. A test car just unveiled by Mercedes-Benz, the Necar 4 (which stands for New Electric Car 4), uses two stacks, each with 160 cells.

The beauty of a fuel cell is that it takes the place of a storage battery and produces electricity directly from a plentiful element: hydrogen. Once perfected, fuel cell-electric cars will have the range and "refill-ability" of gasoline-powered cars. Of course, the method of getting hydrogen to the car in the first place is still up in the air.

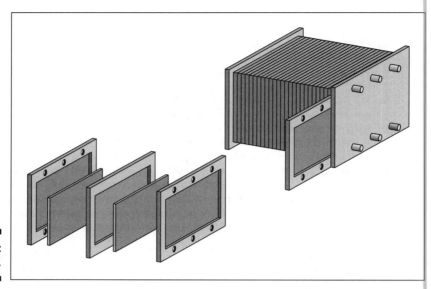

One method would require construction of thousands of hydrogen filling stations where motorists would pull in to fill their cars' tanks with either liquid or gaseous hydrogen. Still to be resolved, of course, is how to finance construction of such a delivery system or infrastructure.

The industry also has not yet settled on what form of hydrogen to use. Gaseous hydrogen, like CNG, would have to be stored in tanks that could withstand thousands of pounds of pressure. But liquid hydrogen has to be stored at unbelievably cold temperatures — 423 degrees below 0 — and then must be warmed up to function properly in a fuel cell.

A fuel-cell electric car that ran directly on hydrogen would produce virtually no emissions — the only thing dribbling out of the tailpipe would be a trickle of distilled water formed in the interaction of the hydrogen and oxygen inside the cell!

But because of the problems inherent in getting hydrogen to cars, some in the industry are considering another type of system. It appears that the hydrogen needed for a fuel cell to operate can be produced on-board a car or truck, distilled, if you will, from a hydrocarbon fuel such as gasoline, methanol, or ethanol. The process requires the fuel to be turned into a vapor under high heat. That process produces carbon monoxide and a few other pollutants, so it isn't as clean as a system that uses hydrogen directly, but it's still far cleaner than an internal combustion engine.

Those problems aside, the cells that industry uses are far too large for automobiles, and a good deal of work has gone into figuring out how to shrink them. Automakers have developed fuel cells that are small enough to put into test vehicles, although they are still 30 to 50 percent too heavy for commercial use. They still are about 10 times too costly to be considered for commercial use. But their time is coming. DaimlerChrysler has said that it will have fuel cell cars in the retail market by 2004. And the other major automakers won't be far behind.

Operating an electric vehicle

After automakers conquer the problems of how best to produce the electricity that an electric car needs, the rest is pretty easy. The electrics on the market today handle remarkably well and can hold their own on busy freeways. They're not the cars to take on a long trip, but for commuting and most daily use, they're no different from their gasoline-powered cousins once you get past the fact that there's no engine under the hood and that you don't have to pull into a gas station unless you have to use the restroom or you get a nail in one of the special, low-rolling resistance tires.

What *is* under the hood is a powerful electric motor — all the necessary wires and plumbing, plus all the equipment for conventional heating and air conditioning, **power brakes**, and **power steering**. You even find a conventional 12-volt battery to provide start-up power and keep the clock, power locks, and other electrically controlled devices in operation when the power plant is shut down.

Inside, an electric car looks much the same as any other. (All but the EV-1 started life as conventional ICE vehicles and were modified to become electrics.) The biggest difference is on the instrument panel. Instead of a fuel gauge that shows how full the tank is, electric vehicles have digital readouts that show how much charge is left in the battery and how economically — or not — you are driving. And those with *regenerative* braking systems have a gauge or readout that shows when power is being generated and stored. (Regenerative braking uses the energy of the braking action to generate electricity to replace a very small part of what is consumed when accelerating.) Several electric cars also have a readout that estimates the number of miles remaining before they run out of juice.

Some, like Nissan's Altra EV, also have a digital **tachometer** that tells you how fast the electric motor is revolving. And it's much faster than the **crankshaft** in a gasoline-fueled car! Driving down the freeway at 74 mph and glancing down at the tach to see that you're cruising at 16,000 rpm is unsettling!

The other oddity — and it's fun to watch the guys at the car wash try to figure this out — is that an electric vehicle doesn't do much of anything when the key is turned on. Sometimes a small cooling fan kicks in, and the "On" or "Ready" indicator light on the dashboard lights up. But that's it. No roar, no sputter. Pump the accelerator all you want; you get no action. An electric motor doesn't rev up until you engage the transmission.

When you engage the transmission, you send a signal to the motor controller, which boosts the voltage to the motor in response to the pressure you place on the accelerator (which looks and feels just like a gas pedal). As the voltage increases, the motor spins faster. The power is transmitted to the drive axle through a series of gears, just as the power from a conventional vehicle's revolving crankshaft is transmitted. (If you've forgotten how it does that, review Chapter 4.) The difference is that, because an electric vehicle delivers full torque at all times, the transmission has only a single speed. There's no need to shift into higher or lower gears to increase the motor's efficiency.

So it's a simple matter of getting in, turning the key, shifting into Forward or Reverse, and driving away. You may see a cloud of dust — it depends on where you parked — but you won't see a cloud of fumes or hear a rumble of exhaust. Just the whine of an electric motor ramping up.

Many problems must be overcome before the gasoline-driven internal combustion engine is relegated to museums and classic car collections. But the industry and various governments are spending billions of dollars to develop functional electric and hybrid vehicles for personal use. The Car of the Future is a matter of when, not whether. It may already be on the road by the time you read this book!

Chapter 8

The Cooling System Up Close

• •

• •

*W*ith all that "air, fuel, and fire" stuff going on in its engine, your vehicle needs something to help it keep a cool (cylinder) head! Because water is usually cheap, plentiful, and readily available, auto manufacturers have found it to be the simplest answer to the problem. (Except for a few who found that air is even cheaper and more abundant. They designed the air-cooled engine. If you have a pre-1975 Volkswagen, you won't find a drop of water in it.)

Of course, nothing is as simple as it seems. Automakers add a couple of gimmicks to keep the water from boiling too easily. These include a water pump to keep it moving; a fan and a radiator to cool it off; a pressure cap to retard boiling; a thermostat to help the engine quickly reach and maintain the proper temperature; and antifreeze/coolant to raise the boiling point and keep the water from rusting the engine and freezing in winter. Put them all together, and you have your vehicle's cooling system (see Figure 8-1).

The cooling system is highly efficient. It usually requires almost no work to keep it operating — just a watchful eye for leaks and an occasional check or change of coolant. This chapter explores the system part by part. Chapter 14 shows you what to do if your car overheats and how to maintain and troubleshoot the cooling system and make easy repairs. Chapter 21 helps you get out of trouble if your car overheats on the road.

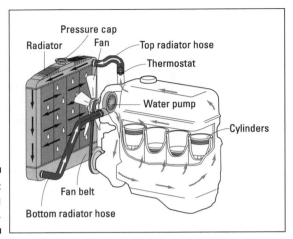

Figure 8-1:
The cooling
system.

The Radiator

When the fuel/air mixture is ignited in the cylinders, the temperature inside the engine can reach *thousands* of degrees Fahrenheit. It takes only *half* that heat to melt iron, and your engine would be a useless lump of metal in about 20 minutes if your vehicle couldn't keep things cool. Naturally, the liquid (coolant and water) that circulates around the cylinders in the engine block gets very hot, and so it's continually circulated back to the radiator, where it cools off before heading back to the scene of the action.

The radiator is designed to cool the liquid quickly by passing it over a large cooling surface. The liquid enters the radiator through the *top radiator hose,* which is usually connected to (you guessed it) the *top* of the radiator (refer to Figure 8-1). As the liquid descends, it runs through channels in the radiator, which are cooled by air rushing in through *cooling fins* between the channels. When the liquid has cooled, it leaves the radiator through the *bottom radiator hose* (surprise!). This hose usually has a spring inside it to prevent it from collapsing when the water pump draws coolant from the radiator. (If it collapses anyway, Chapter 14 has instructions for replacing it.)

Additional hoses

There are also smaller-diameter hoses also leading from your engine to the heater core (see the end of this chapter). Some vehicles have a small bypass hose near the thermostat as well (see "The Thermostat," later in this chapter). These hoses are an important part of the cooling system, as they are designed to carry the liquid in it from one component to another.

Coolant/Antifreeze

To keep the water in the cooling system from boiling or freezing, the water is mixed with coolant/antifreeze (which, in the interest of brevity, I just call "coolant").

Most coolants contain about 95 percent *ethylene glycol,* a chemical that stops water from freezing or boiling, even in extreme temperatures. (Ethylene glycol is toxic; there are nontoxic coolants that contain *propylene glycol* instead. See the sidebar "Keeping coolant out of the mouths of babes and small animals" in Chapter 14.) In addition to the ethylene glycol, coolant also contains rust, corrosion, and foaming inhibitors, so coolant does more than just keep the water in the system in a liquid state: It also helps to prevent the formation of rust on the metal surfaces of the engine and the radiator, lubricates the water pump, and keeps the liquid from foaming as it circulates through the system. Since the early 1960s, auto manufacturers have designed the cooling systems of most vehicles for a 50/50 mixture of ethylene glycol and water, which is still generally considered the proper proportion of coolant to water for the cooling system of most vehicles. (I usually refer to the coolant and water mixture as "liquid" in the rest of this chapter.)

Today's engines require specially formulated coolants that are safe for aluminum components. Also, some manufacturers are using a new coolant called Dex-cool that can last about twice as long as other coolants.

If your cooling system is operating properly, you shouldn't have to keep adding liquid to it. Chapter 3 shows you how to check the level and condition of the liquid in the cooling system, and Chapter 14 shows you how to add liquid or flush the system and replace the liquid in it.

The coolant recovery system

A coolant recovery system is just a clear plastic container with two little hoses coming out of the cap (see Figure 8-2). One hose leads to the radiator, and the other serves as an overflow pipe for the container. The container holds an extra supply of water and coolant, in case the system loses any.

When your cooling system heats up and starts to overflow, the liquid pours back into the recovery container instead of pouring out of the radiator overflow pipe and onto the ground. When the system cools off, the pressure drops and the liquid is drawn out of the container and back into the radiator. This process not only saves you coolant, but it also protects animals and children from sampling puddles of the toxic stuff.

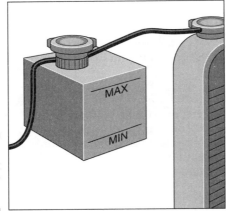

Figure 8-2:
A coolant
recovery
system.

Some of today's vehicles have *pressurized* reservoirs. In these cases, you find the radiator pressure cap on the reservoir and not on the radiator.

Most recovery systems are considered "sealed" because you can check whether your coolant needs changing — and add water and coolant — by opening the cap on the container. You can also check the level of liquid in the system by seeing whether it reaches the fill level shown on the side of the container. (For instructions on adding liquid to a sealed system safely, see "Using a coolant reservoir system" in Chapter 14.)

The radiator pressure cap

To further retard the boiling point of the liquid in the cooling system, the entire system is placed under pressure. This pressure generally runs between 7 and 16 pounds per square inch (psi). As the pressure increases, the boiling point rises as well. This combination of pressure plus coolant gives the liquid in your cooling system the capability to resist boiling at temperatures that can rise as high as 250 degrees Fahrenheit or more in some new vehicles.

To keep the lid on the pressure in the system, and to provide a convenient place to add water and coolant, each radiator has a removable radiator pressure cap on either its radiator filler hole or its coolant recovery system.

The pressure cap has two valves: a pressure valve and a vacuum valve. The pressure valve maintains a precise amount of pressure on the liquid in the system. The vacuum valve allows the liquid to travel back into the radiator from the recovery reservoir when the engine cools down.

If you have no coolant recovery system

Today, most vehicles come with coolant recovery systems. If your vehicle lacks such a system and it overheats, you'll often notice liquid pouring out from under the car — especially if you're using the air conditioner on a very hot day. This liquid — which is usually colored and sometimes has white foam on it — is the water/coolant mixture pouring out of the overflow pipe on your radiator. Because this liquid is toxic to small children and animals, be sure to clean up thoroughly, following the instructions in Chapter 14.

When your engine heats up, the pressure in its system rises. If this pressure exceeds the level of pressure that your radiator cap is built to withstand and you don't have a recovery system, the liquid in the system bypasses the radiator cap and escapes through an overflow pipe located near the fill hole. This pipe provides a safe way for your vehicle to "let off steam." Of course, if this kind of overflow occurs often, your car loses enough water and coolant to substantially lower the level in the cooling system. You have to keep adding water, and eventually, the level of coolant protection is inadequate. To prevent this problem, you can buy and install a coolant recovery kit yourself by following the instructions in "Using a coolant recovery system" in Chapter 14.

Pressure caps are relatively inexpensive, but if you have a cap that isn't working properly, or if you have the wrong type of cap, you'll be amazed at the amount of trouble it can cause. For example, if the gasket (rubber ring) inside the cap isn't working, the pressure in the system will escape, allowing the liquid to boil at a lower temperature. A modern cooling system that's been designed to operate normally at temperatures over 212 degrees Fahrenheit, and that is filled with liquid and in perfect condition, will still continually boil over if the radiator cap isn't operating efficiently. That boiling liquid will be forced into the overflow system, and your vehicle's engine will overheat. This can cause an inconvenient highway breakdown and possible danger to your engine.

If your vehicle overheats on the highway, Chapter 21 can get you cooled down safely. The section "If Your Car Is a Chronic Hothead" in Chapter 14 offers remedies for other overheating problems.

Although most vehicles come equipped with a *safety* pressure cap, which features a little lever that releases the pressure before you remove the cap, some older vehicles have a cap that lacks this feature. If you have one of these caps, replace it with a safety pressure cap immediately. Doing so can keep you from burning yourself if you have to remove the cap while there's still some pressure in the system.

The Fan

Air rushing through the radiator cools things off when you are driving merrily down the freeway, but a fresh supply of air won't be moving through the radiator fins when the vehicle is standing still or crawling its way through heavy traffic. For this purpose, a **fan** is located behind the radiator, positioned so that it can draw air through the radiator (refer to Figure 8-1). Today, most fans have a plastic shroud that funnels air through the radiator. And some sports cars have air dams that help force the air up through the radiator from below.

Originally, a **fan belt** drove the fan as long as the engine was running. Now, *fan clutches* on many vehicles automatically limit the fan's movement at speeds over 25 mph. Because the air rushing past them allows these fans to simply "coast" at high speeds, the engine doesn't have to work as hard or burn as much fuel to supply the power that the fans would normally consume. Most cars with **transverse engines** have electric fans, some of which continue to run for a short while after the engine is shut off. Chapter 14 has instructions for adjusting and replacing fan belts and other accessory belts.

The Water Pump

The **water pump** (see Figures 8-1 and 8-3) draws the liquid from the radiator through the *bottom* radiator hose and sends it to the engine, where it circulates through **water jackets** located around the **combustion chambers** in the cylinders and other hot spots. An **accessory belt** drives some water pumps, while some **overhead cam** engines drive the water pump with the **timing belt**.

If the timing belt drives your water pump, the water pump will be difficult to see unless you remove the plastic timing belt cover.

Figure 8-3:
A water pump.

The Thermostat

The thermostat is the only part of the cooling system that does *not* cool things off. Instead, it helps the liquid in the cooling system warm up the engine quickly. Here's how — and why — it does this:

The thermostat is a small, metal, heat-sensitive valve (see Figure 8-4) that's usually located where the upper radiator hose meets the top of the engine. (On a few vehicles, you find the thermostat where the bottom hose joins the engine. Your owner's manual should tell you where yours is.) When it senses hot liquid, the thermostat allows the liquid to pass through. But when the thermostat senses that the liquid is cold (like when you first start your car in the morning), it shuts and doesn't allow the liquid to circulate through the radiator (refer to Figure 8-1). As a result, the liquid stays in the engine, where it gets hot as the engine warms up, and in turn, the increasing heat of the liquid helps the engine to warm up more quickly. As a result, the vehicle runs more efficiently and burns less fuel.

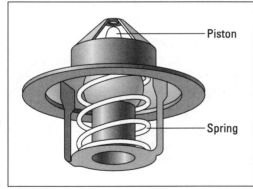

Figure 8-4:
A thermo-
stat.

Piston

Spring

The Heater Core

The heater core is located inside the vehicle between the instrument panel and the firewall. It looks like a miniature radiator minus the fill neck and cap. The purpose of the heater core is to provide heat for the passenger compartment. The same liquid that the water pump circulates throughout the engine also circulates through the heater core when the engine is operating. When you get chilly, you can direct air across the heater core and heat the interior of your vehicle by turning on the inside fan. Because the heater core is relatively "passive," it usually doesn't need attention (unless it breaks).

That's all you need to know about the parts involved in the cooling system and how they work. Of course, some vehicles have more complicated systems, or variations on the theme, such as two fans run by electric thermostats that aren't connected to the water pump at all. These go on independently and draw air in to cool the engine when necessary. But in general, if you understand the way the basic cooling system works, you should have little trouble handling the one in your vehicle. Chapter 14 provides instructions for troubleshooting, maintaining, and making simple repairs.

Air Conditioning

Air conditioning is fast becoming standard equipment, rather than an option, on most vehicles. It uses *refrigerant* to remove the heat from the air (rather than cooling it) and a blower to send the cool air into the passenger compartment.

Until 1992, a refrigerant called CFC-12 (commonly called Freon) was standard on most vehicles. When it was found to contribute to the depletion of the ozone layer, CFC-12 was phased out and replaced by R-134a. Production of CFC-12 ceased at the end of 1995, and, although the stuff can be recycled, supplies may be limited.

If your vehicle was built before 1992, you may have trouble getting Freon if you need to replace the air conditioner's refrigerant. Conversions to an alternative refrigerant (R-134a) are expensive, so think about this fact before buying a pre-1992 used vehicle or undertaking expensive repairs on one you already own.

Chapter 14 has suggestions on extending the life of your air conditioner and tips on servicing it and finding out what it would cost to convert from CFC-12 Freon to R-134a refrigerant.

Chapter 9

Take the Drive Train: Understanding Transmissions without Losing Your Mind

● ●

In This Chapter

▶ What a transmission does

▶ What the drive train is

▶ How a manual transmission works

▶ How an automatic transmission works

▶ How a transfer case works

● ●

*T*he transmission system in your car is probably its most complex system in terms of automotive mechanics. But take heart; you don't have to be a mechanical genius to understand it (or I wouldn't be writing about it!). For starters, think of the transmission as a communication system that takes messages from you about whether you want to go forward or backward — and at what speed — and passes them on to the wheels.

Transmission systems vary from one vehicle to another. With a manual transmission (sometimes called a *standard* transmission), you shift into the proper gear at the proper time *yourself*; with an automatic transmission, the shifting is done *for* you. But the result is the same: Whether you have an automatic or a manual transmission, the transmission transmits power from the engine and directs it to the wheels. But it doesn't do the job alone, it's part of a system that has several components, commonly known as the drive train.

This chapter takes you for a ride on the drive train. By the end of the line, the transmission and its related parts should no longer be a mystery and Chapter 17, which deals with maintaining and troubleshooting the transmission, should easily become familiar territory.

All *aboooard!*

The Drive Train

When your vehicle changes direction from forward to reverse, the rear wheels (or the front wheels on cars with front-wheel drive) don't just have to be told which way to rotate. They must also know how fast to turn, and they must be supplied with extra power for starting, climbing hills, and pulling heavy loads. All these things are accomplished via the drive train. By knowing what each part does and how it relates to the other parts of the drive train, you can trace the flow of power from the engine to the wheels.

Here's an interesting way to look at how the drive train functions: Imagine that you are the captain of a ship. You have a lovely set of engines down in the engine room that manufactures power to move your ship. You are up on the bridge, surveying the blue ocean with your binoculars, when suddenly you see an iceberg dead ahead. Instead of running down to the engine room and personally reversing the propellers so that the ship will move backward, you pick up the intercom and call the engine room, saying, "This is the captain speaking. Reverse engines!" The person in the engine room hears you and does what's necessary. The ship is saved.

In a car, with a crew of one, you're still at the wheel giving orders. But you're giving them to a vehicle that can't hear you. You need a piece of machinery to communicate with other machines. In this case, that piece is your gearshift. By moving the gearshift with your hand, you can tell the transmission what to do. Then the transmission tells the wheels via the driveshaft.

With the aid of the drive train, you can not only tell your wheels to go forward or backward, but you can tell them how fast to go as well. When you step on the accelerator, you compel the engine to produce power, but that power has to get to the wheels in the proper way for the wheels to respond most efficiently. There are ways to convey that extra power to the wheels by controlling how fast they turn in relation to the engine's speed when you're going up a hill, pulling a heavy load, or just trying to overcome inertia and get the car started. So your transmission has more than just forward and reverse gears; it has low and high gears, too. Some transmissions have as many as six forward gears to control power and speed efficiently. (I won't even talk about those huge semis with 14 and more forward gears!) In all cases, the *lower* gears provide *more power* at *lower speeds*. The *higher* gears provide *less power* but allow the vehicle to move at *higher speeds* because the wheels can turn faster in these gears at any engine speed.

How Power Flows through the Drive Train

You can more clearly visualize how power flows through the drive train by following the flow of power through it. Figure 9-1 shows all the components as they are located on a vehicle with **rear-wheel drive.** If your vehicle has front-wheel drive, Figure 9-2 shows you the way the power flows through a transaxle. The principles and parts are pretty much the same in each type of drive train:

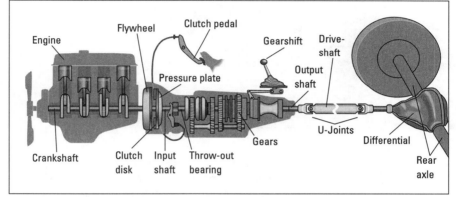

Figure 9-1:
The drive train in a vehicle with rear-wheel drive.

1. The running engine produces power that causes the crankshaft to turn at a particular rate of speed. The faster the engine runs, the more power it produces and the faster the crankshaft turns.

2. At the rear end of the crankshaft is the engine flywheel. This disk-shaped plate turns at the same rate, and in the same direction, as the crankshaft.

3. Facing the flywheel is the first part of the clutch. This disk-shaped plate is called a clutch disk. When you are *not* stepping on the clutch pedal, this disk is forced against the flywheel (see Step 4). A coating of friction material causes the two plates to adhere to each other, which forces them to turn at the same speed.

4. Next to the clutch disk is the clutch pressure plate. This mechanism forces the clutch disk against the flywheel or allows it to move away from the flywheel when it is time to change gears. Here's how it does that:

   • When you step on the clutch pedal to disengage the clutch and disconnect the engine from the transmission, a clutch *release arm* forces a throwout bearing into the pressure plate's *release levers.* As a result, the pressure on the clutch disk is released, and the disk can turn independently of the flywheel.

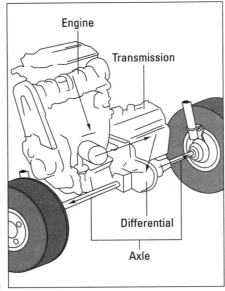

Figure 9-2:
The flow of
power
through a
transaxle.

Engine

Transmission

Differential

Axle

- After you move the gearshift to the proper gear, you release the clutch pedal. This movement causes springs in the pressure plate to force the disk against the flywheel again, and both the disk and the flywheel resume spinning together at a new speed.

  In this way, the clutch disk can catch up with an engine that is turning faster — or more slowly — than before and can transmit its motion to the transmission.

5. On the clutch side of the flywheel, the drive train continues, but its name changes. It is not called the crankshaft anymore; it is now called the transmission input shaft because it carries the power via the turning shaft *into* the transmission. It rotates at the same speed and in the same direction as all the parts I've covered up to now.

6. Inside the transmission is a group of gears of varying sizes. These gears can move together and apart, in various combinations, to determine how fast and with how much power the car's wheels will turn, and in which direction.

7. The next part of the drive train emerges from the other side of the transmission, with another new name. This time it is called the *transmission output shaft* because it transmits the power that the transmission is putting *out* to the driveshaft.

8. The driveshaft of a rear-wheel-drive vehicle with a conventional engine has a *U-joint* (short for universal joint) at either end. The U-joints enable the driveshaft to move freely without affecting the more rigid transmission shaft at one end, and to absorb the vertical movement of the rear axle and wheels at its other end.

On cars with transverse engines, you can find the U-joints where each axle joins the transaxle and where each connects with the car's drive wheels. Called constant velocity (CV) joints, they can, like other U-joints, turn and move in any direction — up, down, and from side to side.

9. The differential (see Figure 9-3) is another box of gears that takes the movement of the spinning driveshaft through a 90-degree angle to the axle that turns the drive wheels. It also allows each side of the axle to rotate at a different speed. This ability is necessary because, when you go around a sharp curve, the outside wheel travels farther than the inside wheel and has to move more quickly than the inside wheel, just like the ice skater at the end of a snap-the-whip line.

10. The differential also provides the drive wheels with extra power by using its gears to convert every three revolutions of the driveshaft into one revolution of the drive wheels, which is called a 3:1 gear ratio. On front-wheel-drive cars, the differential is located inside the transmission; that's why it's called a trans*axle* assembly.

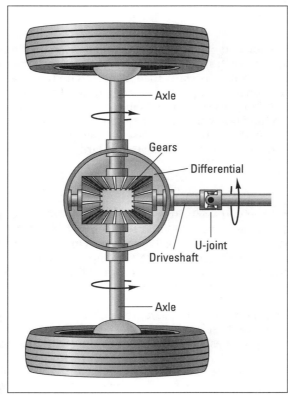

Figure 9-3:
The differential causes the axle and the rear wheels to move at right angles to the spinning driveshaft.

Chapter 17 includes information about drive train repair and maintenance.

Manual Transmissions

Whether your car has an automatic transmission or a manual (sometimes called *standard*) transmission, you should understand how a manual transmission works. The principles involved are fairly simple, and an automatic transmission does basically the same things, just without a manual clutch and with less manual shifting.

What a manual transmission consists of

This section takes a look at each major part of a manual transmission. I covered most of them in the drive train section earlier in this chapter. This section should put them into closer perspective.

The gearshift

The gearshift can be located on the steering column or on the floor in front of, or between, the front seat(s). Older cars designed for the general market used to have shifts with three forward speeds located on the steering column (very old cars had a two-foot gearshift located in front of the driver). Then sportier models with four forward speeds emerged. The gearshift in these cars was located on the floor, which gave rise to the term "four on the floor." Today, most vehicles with manual transmissions have floor shifts with five forward speeds. And some sports cars have standard gearboxes with six forward speeds.

The clutch

You use the clutch when you start, stop, and shift gears. In each case, you step on the clutch pedal with your left foot to disengage the clutch disk from the flywheel so that the engine's crankshaft can turn independently of the transmission's input shaft. Otherwise, if you attempted to shift gears without using the clutch, the gears in the transmission would rotate at different speeds and would clash and break their teeth.

The clutch consists of several major parts, each of which is listed here (refer to Figure 9-1 to see where these parts are). The section "Taking Care of Your Clutch" in Chapter 17 provides instructions for dealing with many of them.

✓ **The clutch pedal** is located on the floor of the car to the left of the brake pedal. The clutch pedal is connected to the clutch release lever via linkage. Sometimes a cable is used; most newer cars use hydraulic components.

✔ **The clutch disk,** as you saw in the earlier drive train section, moves back and forth to connect and disconnect the engine from the transmission.

✔ **The clutch pressure plate** clamps the clutch disk against the engine's flywheel when the clutch pedal is not applied. The pressure plate releases its force and pulls away from the clutch disk when you depress the clutch pedal.

✔ **The throw-out bearing** is linked to the clutch pedal and activates the release levers that move the pressure plate back and forth.

After you have the engine going at its new speed (or going at all), you release the clutch pedal to bring the clutch disk into contact with the flywheel again. The friction material on the clutch disk causes them to grab each other lovingly and turn at the same rate once more.

The gears

The transmission contains the gears and responds to messages from the **gearshift** and the clutch. The gears are actually metal wheels with notches on the rims that allow them to mesh with one another (see Figure 9-4). Originally, the gears in most manual transmissions were moved into and out of mesh with each other by the gearshift lever. In modern vehicles, the gears are always in mesh and only the *synchronizers* move, causing a change in power flow.

The number of gear wheels in the transmission depends on the number of forward speeds the vehicle has. An additional gear reverses the direction of power so that your car can move backward. This Reverse gear works in conjunction with the lowest gear. Because you must bring a vehicle to a stop before you back up and because you rarely want to hit high speeds in Reverse, the Low gear provides the power to overcome inertia and get the car moving again in the "wrong" direction. That's why your car usually moves backward fairly slowly but with a good deal of power.

How a manual transmission works

Generally speaking, the faster your engine runs, the more power it puts out. If you need extra power to get your car up a hill — or to overcome inertia and just get that heavy monster moving in the first place — your engine must run faster than it runs simply to maintain speed after your vehicle is on the road. Low gears supply that power by making your wheels turn at a slower rate than your engine does.

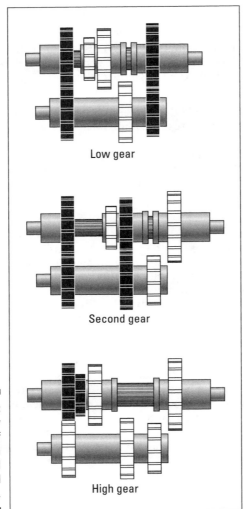

Low gear

Second gear

Figure 9-4:
Cutaway
view of
gears in a
three-speed
manual
transmission.

High gear

Figure 9-5 shows a large gear placed next to a small gear so that their teeth mesh. If the large gear has 30 teeth and the small gear has 10, the large gear turns once to every three turns of the small gear. In other words, the large gear turns only a third of the way around for every complete revolution of the small gear. The gears in your transmission work on this principle, which is called a 3:1 gear ratio. As you can see back in Figures 9-1 and 9-4, the turning drive train brings a gear into contact with other gears of different sizes. That's why the transmission input shaft that runs between the engine and the transmission turns at the same rate of speed as the engine, but the transmission output shaft that leaves the transmission and carries the power via the driveshaft and differential to the rear wheels turns at a different rate, depending on which gears in the transmission are engaged.

(If you're feeling mind-boggled, reread Steps 5 through 10 in "How the power flows through the drive train" earlier in this chapter.)

Figure 9-5:
3:1 gear ratio: A gear with 10 teeth will have rotated completely when a 30-tooth gear has traveled only a third of the way around.

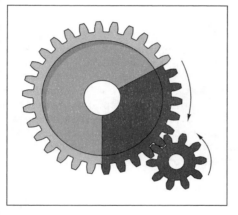

Now take a closer look at what goes on when you shift into each gear.

In Low gear, the gears in the transmission make the driveshaft (and therefore the wheels) turn *more slowly* than the engine. In fact, the driveshaft may turn only once for every four engine revolutions. All the power of the swiftly running engine is channeled into those few turns. The wheels turn more slowly, but they have more power to put into each turn, so your car can start, climb a hill, or pull a trailer. Not only does the engine run faster, but you also have the mechanical advantage of the big gear providing more leverage by turning slowly but with more force.

In Second gear, the engine turns more slowly than it did in Low, putting out less power but more speed because the wheels can turn more quickly. In this gear, the driveshaft may turn once for every two engine revolutions, or twice as fast as in Low gear.

In High gear, the gear ratio can drop to around 1:1, which means that the engine and the driveshaft turn at relatively the same rate of speed. The wheels can go very fast; yet the engine doesn't put out additional power to produce that speed. Because you've overcome inertia by the time you shift into high gear and generally have nothing more to contend with than wind resistance and the surface of the highway, you don't need much power to keep moving at a good clip after you get there.

In Fifth gear, the ratio is usually an overdrive of around 0.75:1, which means that the engine can turn *more slowly* than the output shaft's speed. You want to be at that ratio on the highway for good fuel economy. However, you do need to downshift if you want to pass someone, because you don't have much engine power with this ratio.

Automatic Transmissions

Did you know that today's automatic transmissions are computer-controlled hydraulic systems? Previous automatic transmissions were mechanically controlled. This section covers the basic features of both.

An automatic transmission works on the same basis as a manual transmission does, with a gear selector on the steering column or floor to allow you to tell the car to park, idle, go in reverse, go forward at varying speeds, or move into lower gears in certain circumstances. But instead of a manual clutch, an automatic transmission uses a torque converter and hydraulic pressure to change gears automatically.

The torque converter replaces the standard transmission's clutch. The torque converter is a fluid coupling that transfers power from the engine to the transmission input shaft. It allows for smooth transfer of power and at highway speeds can be locked up to reduce slippage and improve fuel economy.

Shifting in an automatic transmission is controlled by either a hydraulic system or an electronic system. Hydraulically controlled transmissions consist of an intricate network of valves and other components along with hydraulic pressure to control the operation of planetary gearsets (see Figure 9-6). These gearsets can be fashioned to generate three, four, or five forward speeds.

A very thin oil called transmission fluid fills the transmission system and generates hydraulic pressure. As the engine speed changes, the pump that pumps the transmission fluid to develop hydraulic pressure also changes speed. The transmission fluid responds to the changes in pressure by flowing through the transmission at different rates. When the car is moving slowly, the pressure is low, and only the low gears respond. In Drive, as the car's speed increases, so does the pressure, and higher gears are brought into play.

The hydraulic pressure drives the transmission gears by means of *friction bands* and *plates*. These bands and plates do the same thing that the clutch on a manual transmission does — they pull various gears into and out of action. When mechanics tell you that your bands need adjusting, these are the bands they're talking about. They can usually make this adjustment without taking the transmission apart.

Newer transmissions use electronically controlled solenoids to control shifting because electronic shifting is more precise than hydraulic systems.

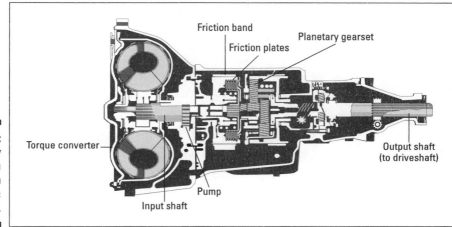

Friction band

Friction plates

Planetary gearset

Torque converter

Figure 9-6:
A cutaway
view of a
modern
automatic
transmission.

Output shaft
(to driveshaft)

Pump

Input shaft

The Transfer Case

If you own a sport-utility vehicle (SUV) that features four-wheel-drive, your drive train includes a transfer case. The transfer case mounts between the transmission and the driveshafts to control the power to the front and rear drive axles. When you switch from two- to four-wheel drive with either a dash-mounted switch or a floor-mounted shifter, a gear in the transfer case engages the front driveshaft along with the rear driveshaft so that all four wheels get power from the engine. In two-wheel drive, only the driveshaft connected to the rear wheels gets power from the engine, and the front wheels are disengaged. In four-wheel drive, the engine powers all the wheels.

Four-wheel-drive (4WD) vehicles are different from all-wheel-drive (AWD) vehicles in that AWD vehicles send power to all four wheels *all* the time. AWD vehicles usually employ a center differential to split power from the engine to the front and rear wheels.

Well, you've survived the ride on the drive train. If you're ready to deal with troubleshooting and repairing it, head for Chapter 17!

Chapter 10

It's the Brakes!

● ●

In This Chapter

▶ Understanding how a basic brake system is set up

▶ Knowing the difference between drum brakes and disc brakes

▶ Looking at the parking brake

▶ Discussing anti-lock brakes

● ●

*B*efore you relegate this book to the "guess-I'll-finish-it-later" pile and go on to learn macramé or fly-tying, take the time to educate yourself about an automotive system that most people take for granted, even though it may be the only system in your car that can kill you if you don't keep it in good repair. As you've probably guessed — especially if you read chapter titles — I'm talking about your brakes.

Brake System Basics

One reason that today's vehicles are the safest in history is that they're equipped with hydraulic brake systems designed to operate on very simple principles with a minimum of parts and maintenance. Since 1968, all vehicles are also equipped with *dual* brake systems to ensure that if one set of brakes fails, the other set will still be able to stop your car; and with a dashboard light to warn you if your front or rear brakes fail.

Figure 10-1 shows a basic brake system with a power booster, disc brakes on the front wheels, and drum brakes on the rear wheels. Your vehicle may not have power brakes or may have disc or drum brakes all around, but the principle is the same in any case.

The following sections take a look at each of the components of a brake system, starting with the first point of contact between you and your brakes and working down the line to the brakes themselves.

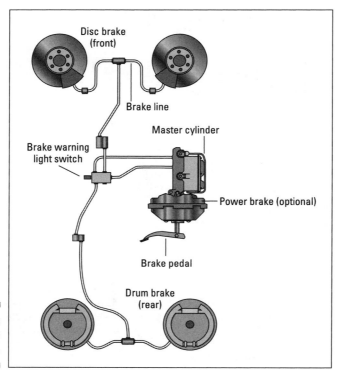

Disc brake
(front)

Brake line

Master cylinder

Brake warning
light switch

Power brake (optional)

Brake pedal

Drum brake
(rear)

Figure 10-1:
The brake
system.

The brake pedal

The brake pedal in your car is attached to a shaft that leads to the brake
master cylinder. When you step on the brake pedal, small pistons in the
master cylinder force brake fluid out of the master cylinder and into the
brake lines. I tell you how to buy the proper brake fluid and work with it
safely in "Flushing and Changing Brake Fluid" in Chapter 18.

If your brakes are working properly, the pedal should stop a couple of inches
from the floor. It should push down easily, stop firmly at its lowest point without feeling spongy, and stay put instead of sinking down slowly when you put
normal pressure on it. To check the brakes on your vehicle, see Chapter 18.

The power-brake booster

Today, most vehicles have power brakes. If your car has power brakes, a brake booster is located between the brake pedal and the master cylinder to increase the force applied to the pistons in the master cylinder so that your car can stop with less effort on your part (see Figure 10-2). The two most common types are *vacuum-assisted boosters,* which use engine vacuum and atmospheric pressure to do the job, and *hydraulic-assisted boosters* (commonly referred to as "hydro-boost units"), which use hydraulic pressure from the car's power steering to accomplish the same thing. Some vehicles with anti-lock brake systems (ABS) have a hydraulic pump to generate pressure for booster operation. (There's a section on ABS at the end of this chapter.)

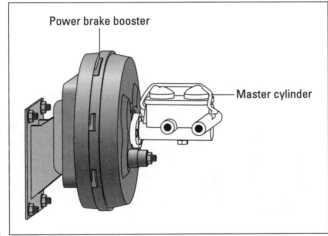

Power brake booster

Master cylinder

Figure 10-2:
The power brake booster is located near the master cylinder.

The brake master cylinder

Look under the hood of your car, up near the firewall on the driver's side. You should see either a metal box or a plastic bottle. Have you found it? This piece is the brake master cylinder (see Figures 10-3 and 10-4). It's filled with brake fluid and is connected to your brake pedal, with brake lines leading from it to the four wheels of your car. When you step on the brake pedal, fluid goes out of the master cylinder into the brake lines. When you release the pedal, the fluid flows back into the master cylinder. In Chapter 18, I show you how to open and check the master cylinder safely. This task is also part of the monthly under-the-hood check in Chapter 3.

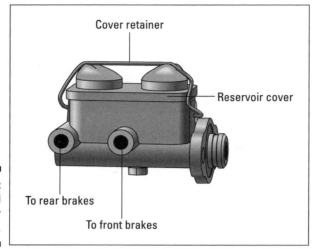

Figure 10-3:
A metal
master
cylinder.

Cover retainer

Reservoir cover

To rear brakes

To front brakes

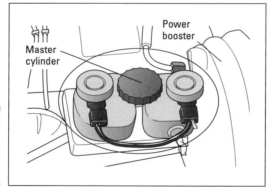

Figure 10-4:
A plastic
master
cylinder.

Master
cylinder

Power
booster

Brake lines

The brake lines run from the master cylinder, along your car's frame, to each wheel. The lines are made of steel, except for the portions that lie right near your front wheels and your rear axle. These portions of the brake line are made of rubber that is flexible enough to contend with the greater amount of movement that takes place in these areas when you steer your car.

The parts discussed thus far are common to most hydraulic brake systems. Now let's get to some of the major differences: When you press the brake pedal and force the brake fluid from the master cylinder into the brake lines, what happens next depends on the type of brakes you have. For many years, cars had drum brakes (shown in Figures 10-1 and 10-5) on all four wheels.

Dual brakes

A *dual* brake system simply means that the inside of the master cylinder is divided into *two* compartments, each filled with brake fluid. On a vehicle with rear-wheel drive, one compartment has brake lines that lead to the brakes on the front wheels; the other compartment has lines leading to the brakes at the rear wheels (refer to Figure 10-3). If a leak or a block develops in one set of lines, the fluid in that compartment is lost or useless. But the other compartment and set of brakes can still stop your car. It may not stop smoothly, but it will stop, and in such a case,

that's all that counts! This simple modification has saved countless lives.

Most front-wheel-drive vehicles have a diagonally split hydraulic brake system that ties the right-front wheel with the left-rear wheel and the left-front wheel with the right-rear wheel. That's because the front brakes on front-wheel-drive vehicles do almost 90 percent of the braking. By diagonally splitting the hydraulic system, you always have one front brake and one rear brake operating in the event of a hydraulic failure. (Refer to Figure 10-4.)

Later models had drum brakes on the rear wheels and disc brakes (refer to Figures 10-1 and 10-8) on the front wheels. Today, many vehicles have four-wheel disc brakes, and most have *power-assisted* drum or disc brakes. Anti-lock brake systems (ABS) have also become popular.

To confuse you completely, since 1963, most brakes are *self-adjusting,* but a couple of real oldies with *manually adjusted* brakes are still around. (Chapter 18 shows you diehards who still have manually adjusted brakes how to deal with them. You're lucky I'm a classic-car nut!)

Your owner's manual can tell you what kind(s) of brakes you have on your vehicle, in case you don't already know, but seeing for yourself is more fun. The following sections cover each type of brakes in detail.

Drum Brakes

Drum brakes, shown in Figure 10-5, are the oldest type of brakes still on the road. Their main advantage is that they require less hydraulic pressure to stop your car, because the brake shoes tend to screw themselves into the brake drums after the pistons in the wheel cylinders push them there. Chapter 18 shows you how to open a drum brake and check its condition. The following sections get you acquainted with what's inside drum brakes and how they work.

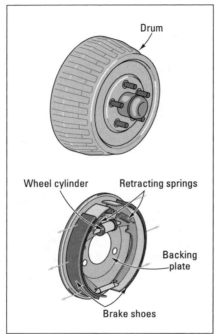

Drum

Wheel cylinder   Retracting springs

Backing
plate

Figure 10-5:
Anatomy
of a
drum
brake.

Brake shoes

Brake drums

Brake drums are hollow steel cylinders located in back of each wheel (refer to Figure 10-5). Because the *lug bolts* that go through them are the same as the ones that go through the wheels of your car, they turn when the wheels turn. If you keep your brakes in good condition and replace your brake linings before they become too worn, your brake drums should last for the life of your vehicle. If drums become worn, they can be "reground" or "turned" to a smooth surface — unless they are worn more than .060 of an inch. In that case, the drums must be replaced. Chapter 18 shows you how to inspect your brake drums and get a fair deal if they need work.

Wheel cylinders

As you can see in Figure 10-6, wheel cylinders are small but powerful mechanisms located inside each **brake drum** on the **brake backing plate.** Figure 10-7 shows how the wheel cylinders work.

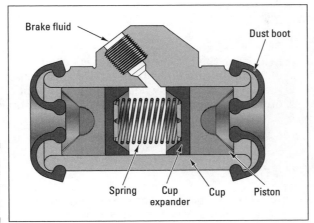

Figure 10-6:
Anatomy of a wheel cylinder.

The brake fluid that's forced through the brake lines by the piston in the master cylinder goes into the wheel cylinders. The fluid then activates the two small pistons located inside each wheel cylinder by forcing them farther apart (see Figure 10-7). The pistons emerge from either end of the wheel cylinder and push against the brake shoes.

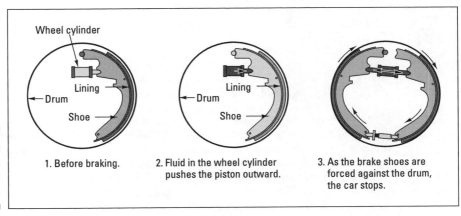

Figure 10-7:
A drum brake in action.

1. Before braking.

2. Fluid in the wheel cylinder pushes the piston outward.

3. As the brake shoes are forced against the drum, the car stops.

Seals inside the wheel cylinder, called _cups,_ keep the brake fluid from leaking out. _Dust boots_ on each end of the wheel cylinder prevent dirt and dust from entering and fouling the cylinder.

Brake shoes

As you can see in Figures 10-5 and 10-6, **brake shoes** are curved pieces of metal that stop the car when the pistons in the wheel cylinders push them against the inside of the brake drum. The brake shoes are attached to a set of springs that draw them back into place when you take your foot off the brake pedal. Chapter 18 provides tips on getting the best deal if your brake shoes have to be replaced.

Brake linings

Either bonded or riveted to the brake shoes are curved **brake linings** of tough, very heat-resistant material. As you can see in Figure 10-6, when the brake shoes are forced against the insides of the brake drum, the linings create friction, which causes the brake drum to stop turning. This in turn forces the wheels to stop turning, which stops the car.

The brake linings on the front wheel brakes have a larger surface than those on the rear wheels because the front wheels bear most of the pressure of stopping — the weight shifts from the rear to the front when you brake. However, on each set of brake linings, on any given wheel, the lining toward the rear of the car is larger and often is a different color.

You should check your brake linings for wear every 10,000 to 20,000 miles. Chapter 18 shows you how.

Adjusting devices

At the bottom of the brake backing plate is either a *manual adjusting wheel* or a *self-adjusting device.* These are used to adjust the distance between the surface of the brake lining and the inside of the brake drum when you step on the brake pedal. As your brake linings become worn, the distance increases, and this adjustment compensates for that. If you didn't have this gadget and your linings became very worn, eventually the brake shoes wouldn't reach the inside of the drum and your car wouldn't stop. You can get a close look at various types of adjusting devices in Chapter 18.

Disc Brakes

Disc brakes are composed of a flat steel disc — you knew that, right? — sandwiched between a pair of calipers (see Figure 10-8). These calipers contain one or more pistons that force the brake fluid in the brake lines into the disc. Between the disc (sometimes called a *rotor*) and the pistons are brake pads, which operate in the same way that brake shoes do: They grab the disc with their rough friction linings and force the disc to stop turning, which in turn forces the wheel to stop turning and the car to stop moving. The effect is the same as on a bicycle when the brakes grab the wheel directly to stop it from turning. Chapter 18 tells you how to inspect and troubleshoot disc brakes.

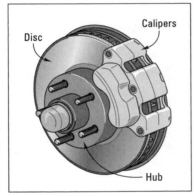

Figure 10-8: A typical disc brake.

Disc brakes have advantages and disadvantages. Because they operate in the open air (instead of inside brake drums), they're less prone to overheating. They're also affected less by water because the leading edge of each brake pad scrapes the water away before it can get between the pads and the disc. (When drum brakes get wet, the brake linings may not grab the brake drum satisfactorily, and sometimes the car won't stop.) Disadvantages include the difficulty of attaching a parking brake to the rear disc brakes and the fact that disc brakes usually need to be power-assisted. In the past, some manufacturers compromise by producing vehicles with disc brakes on the front wheels and drum brakes on the rear wheels, as shown earlier in Figure 10-1. Today, nearly all vehicles have four-wheel disc brakes, with the parking brake integrated into the rear discs.

The Parking Brake

The parking brake, or *emergency brake*, is usually attached to a car's rear wheels. On vehicles with drum brakes, the parking brake is usually attached with cables to the rear brakes. These are called *integral* parking brakes (see Figure 10-9). You can easily adjust the cables, which run underneath the car, by turning a screw that controls the tension on the cable. Chapter 18 provides instructions on how to do so.

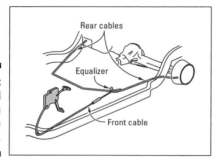

Figure 10-9:
An integral parking brake system.

On other vehicles with drum brakes, different devices do the same job. Some parking brakes are linked to the transmission, and rather than activating the rear brakes, they stop the driveshaft from turning the rear wheels. On these brakes, shown in Figure 10-10, the band and lining are attached to a drum on the transmission. When you pull the lever, the band squeezes the lining against the drum, and the driveshaft stops turning. When a transmission-type parking brake doesn't seem to be performing properly, have a professional check it.

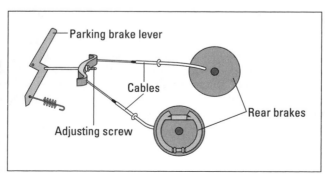

Figure 10-10:
A transmission-type parking brake system.

If you can't find a typical parking brake linkage under your vehicle, you may have transmission-type parking brakes, or you may have rear disc brakes on your car. Rear-wheel disc brakes incorporate a parking brake that works like a mini-drum brake (see Figure 10-11).

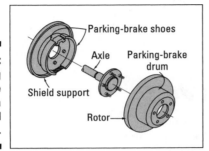

Figure 10-11:
A parking brake system on a rear-wheel disc brake.

Anti-Lock Braking Systems (ABS)

Anti-lock braking systems (ABS) are designed to prevent skidding and enable you to keep steering control of your vehicle until you can stop safely. This system also often shortens the distance your car takes to stop and can prevent the tire damage that would result if you had to bring the car to a stop with the wheels locked.

ABS comes in two types. Some light trucks and vans have a *two-wheel* anti-lock braking system on the rear wheels that maintains directional stability. Although the front wheels can still lock up, the vehicle will continue to move in a straight line. With just enough pressure applied to the brake pedal, the driver can control the steering.

You find *four-wheel* anti-lock braking systems on other light trucks and cars. These prevent all four wheels from locking up, which enables you to maintain steerability in emergency stopping situations. If no impending lockup occurs, the ABS stays in standby mode.

How ABS works

Here's how an anti-lock brake system operates: A microprocessor, called an *anti-lock brake computer,* monitors the speed of each wheel with an electronic component called a *speed sensor.* When you apply firm pressure to the brake pedal, the system triggers electronic solenoids to trap or release hydraulic pressure to each wheel independently, thousands of times faster than if you pumped the brake pedal as you would with ordinary brakes. You can usually hear this happening and feel the brake pedal pulsing when the system energizes. While the system is working, it's important to keep your foot pressed firmly on the pedal until the car stops.

If the anti-lock system has a problem, an amber light on the dashboard goes on, and normal braking without anti-lock takes over. So if your amber anti-lock light illuminates, remember that you still have normal brakes. Just pump them and steer in the proper direction as though you'd never head of ABS. And be sure to get the ABS fixed as soon as possible!

What ABS doesn't do

ABS cannot prevent all skids, nor does it always stop your car in a shorter distance. Although ABS does help you maintain steering, your vehicle may not turn as quickly on a slippery road as it would on dry pavement. A combination of excessive speed, sharp turns, and slamming on the brakes can still throw an ABS-equipped vehicle into a skid. On roads covered with loose gravel or freshly fallen snow, the locked wheels of a vehicle without ABS can build up a wedge of gravel or snow and stop faster that an ABS-equipped vehicle. Therefore, it's important to keep a safe distance between your vehicle and the one in front of you, and to try to maintain a constant speed rather than jamming on the brakes at the last minute.

Driving with ABS

Do *not* pump your brake pedal if your vehicle has anti-lock brakes. Instead, use firm pressure on the brake pedal, keep steering, and let the microprocessor do the work for you.

If your car has anti-lock brakes, it's a good idea to know what they feel like when they are operating normally. Find an empty parking lot on a rainy or snowy day and slam on the brakes, noticing how your vehicle responds. Keep your foot firmly on the pedal and get a feel for steering while they are operating. Then you'll know what to expect in a panicky situation. Chapter 18 shows you how to check your anti-lock braking system; a professional must do adjustments and repairs.

Chapter 11

Steering and Suspension Systems Smooth the Way

In This Chapter

▶ Understanding how the steering system works

▶ Looking at the various types of suspension systems

---

*E*xcept for the steering wheel, you probably consider the steering and suspension systems located under your vehicle to be unknown territory, and, up until now, you've probably been content to leave it that way. But these systems are the unsung heroes that smooth out the driving process and keep you headed exactly where you want to go. This chapter can help you get a good idea of what type of steering and suspension your vehicle possesses so that you can deal intelligently with a technician if something goes wrong. And you can lengthen your vehicle's life significantly by using the instructions in Chapter 16 to lubricate the parts of those systems that require it.

The Steering System

The steering system consists of a series of linkages and gears that link the driver to the wheels. Two types of steering systems are in use today: *rack-and-pinion* and *parallelogram*.

The older parallelogram linkage system is still found on some cars and trucks. The parallelogram includes a frame-mounted steering gearbox, pitman arm, relay rod, idler arm, and inner and outer tie rod-ends. The parallelogram system has the most grease fittings. The rack-and-pinion system eliminates the pitman arm, relay rod, and idler arm.

The steering linkage

The steering linkage is the part of the steering system that connects the steering wheel to the front wheels (see Figure 11-1). When you turn your steering wheel, the steering linkage causes your front wheels to respond by moving in the proper direction.

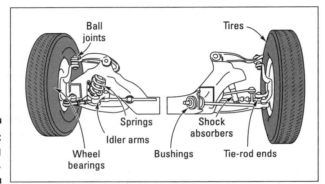

Figure 11-1:
The steering linkage.

Tie-rod ends

Along the steering linkage, wherever two parts meet, is a type of ball socket assembly called a tie-rod end that's sometimes filled with grease. On some vehicles, the grease can be replenished; others have sealed ends; and some have an internal rubber bushing that requires no grease at all. As the two parts of the linkage move against each other, the grease in these tie-rod ends cushions them. This keeps them moving freely and prevents friction that would wear them away.

Ball joints

Ball joints are important parts of the steering systems on all vehicles. A ball joint is a ball socket assembly that attaches the steering knuckle to the suspension system. The ball joint allows for pivotal and rotational movement of the wheel as it moves up and down and is steered left to right (see Figure 11-2).

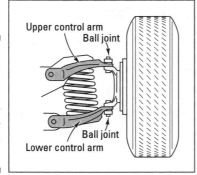

The steering linkage actually connects to the wheels, which are held in place by a spindle that goes through the wheel and is attached to upper and lower control arms (refer to Figure 11-2). The control arms allow the wheels to turn in any direction. To keep things moving freely, ball joints are located at the points on the control arms where the movement takes place.

Most ball joints and tie-rod ends are filled with grease to cut down on friction and keep the parts they protect from wearing away prematurely. Some vehicles have *lifetime lubrication systems* that are designed to operate for the life of the vehicle without the need for additional lubrication. Others need to be replenished with grease periodically.

Chapter 16 shows you how to lubricate the ball joints and tie rod ends on vehicles that require it. It also helps you determine whether you should lubricate the tie-rod ends and ball joints on your particular vehicle.

The Suspension System

Underneath your vehicle are the main elements of the suspension system, which supports the vehicle and keeps the passenger compartment relatively stable on bumpy roads. This section gives you a general overview of the basic parts of the suspension system; you can find instructions for lubricating the parts that require lubrication in Chapter 16.

Types of suspension systems

Most cars have independent front suspension systems. In that type of system, each wheel is attached separately and can move independent of the others. Two common arrangements are *double-wishbone* suspensions and *MacPherson strut* suspensions:

> ✔ **Double-wishbone suspension:** Also known as *short-long arm suspensions*, these systems use a short upper control arm and a longer lower control arm that hold the wheel to the frame. The control arms allow the wheel to move up and down, kind of like a hinge allows a door to swing open and closed. There are rubber bushings at the inboard end of the control arms, and a ball joint at the outboard end of the control arm allows the wheel to rotate and pivot. (See Figure 11-3.)

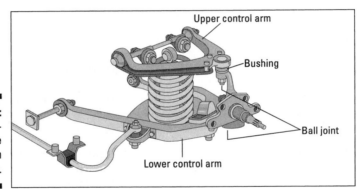

Figure 11-3:
A double-wishbone suspension system.

> ✔ **MacPherson strut suspension:** There are two types of strut suspensions: *conventional* and *modified* (see Figures 11-4 and 11-5). Conventional struts have the coil spring wrapped around the strut cartridge, and modified strut suspensions have a remotely mounted spring. Strut suspensions use no upper control arm. The upper strut mount is what holds the wheel in place.

Some cars also have independent rear suspensions, hence the term *four-wheel independent suspension*. Older rear-wheel-drive cars and most of today's trucks use a dependent-type rear suspension that incorporates the rear drive-axle assembly.

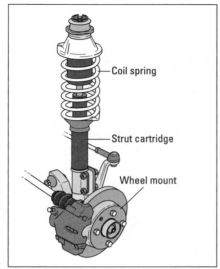

Figure 11-4:
Conventional
strut
suspension.

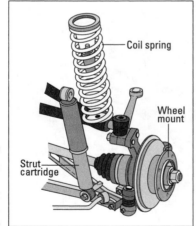

Figure 11-5:
Modified
strut
suspension.

Control arms

Control arms are sometimes referred to as *A arms, A frames, I arms,* or *links* (refer to Figure 11-3). Ever hear the term *multi-link suspension?* That means that more than one link is holding the wheel to the frame or body.

Stabilizer bars

Most vehicles have a *front* stabilizer bar with associated linkage that is designed to prevent the car from leaning when it corners (see Figure 11-6). These stabilizers (or *anti-sway bars*) also improve high-speed stability. Some cars also include a *rear* stabilizer bar. The stabilizer connects one side of the suspension to the other through the frame. As your car begins to dip on one side, the stabilizer bar restricts that side's movement, depending on the diameter of the bar. Larger-diameter stabilizers restrict more than smaller ones do.

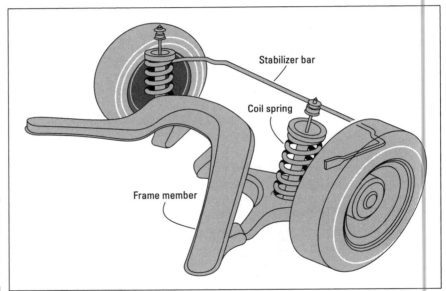

Figure 11-6:
Typical
stabilizer
bar and
linkage.

Springs

Springs are the core of the suspension system. Various types of springs are used to absorb the bumps and keep your car at its proper trim height. These can be coil springs, leaf springs, torsion bars, or air springs (see Figure 11-7). Most cars use either coil or leaf springs; sport-utility vehicles use coil springs, torsion bars, or leaf springs. You'll find computer-controlled air springs on select luxury cars, such as Chrysler New Yorkers, Lincoln Continentals, and some Cadillacs.

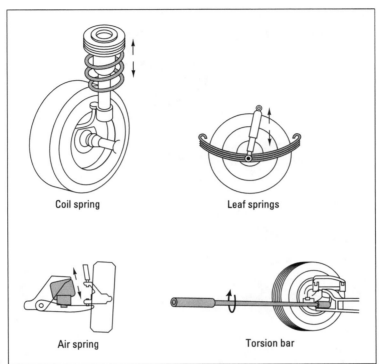

Coil spring   Leaf springs

Figure 11-7:
Coil springs,
leaf springs,
torsion bars,
and air
springs.

Air spring   Torsion bar

✔ **Leaf springs** are usually made up of several relatively thin metal plates, called *leaves,* piled one on top of the other. The reason for using these layers instead of one thick metal bar is that, as a bar bends, the top of the bar has to stretch a little. Unlike a single, thick bar, which, if bent too far, would split from the top down, leaf springs are more flexible — each leaf bends independently, and the leaves can slide on one another instead of breaking (see Figure 11-8).

Each end of a set of leaf springs is attached to the *frame* at the rear of the car with fittings that allow the springs to bend and move freely. These fittings usually have rubber bushings that allow the fittings to bend and twist freely; they also absorb some of the vibration and prevent it from reaching the passenger compartment. See Chapter 16 for details on leaf springs and how to care for them.

Some vehicles, such as the Chevrolet Corvette, utilize fiber-composite (fiberglass) leaf springs.

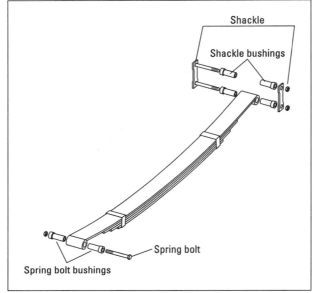

Shackle

Shackle bushings

Spring bolt

Spring bolt bushings

Figure 11-8:
Leaf springs
bend but do
not break
because
they can
slide flexibly
on one
another.

✔ **Coil springs** look like old-fashioned bed springs. They're usually found at the front of the car, although they can be at both the front and the rear. Coil springs are typically used with strut-type suspensions, too. Figure 11-7 shows one type of coil spring; Figure 16-7 shows front and rear springs. You can find instructions for lubricating them in Chapter 16. At the front end, coil springs help cushion the bumps, vibrations, and steering movements. At the rear, they're suspended between control arms that have rubber bushings.

✔ **Torsion bars** (refer to Figures 11-7 and 16-9) are used mainly in sport-utility vehicles and pre-1980 Chrysler products. They are located at the front of the vehicle, connected to the lower control arms. They twist to accommodate differences in the load that the car may be carrying, allowing the front wheels to move up and down freely. Think of torsion bars as coil springs that didn't get wound into a spiral.

✔ **Air springs** are usually found on luxury vehicles. A rubber air spring can be filled with the right amount of compressed air to control the ride and maintain the proper height. With this type of system, a computer monitors the ride height and signals an onboard air compressor to pump more air into the air springs whenever weight is added to the vehicle. When the weight is removed, the computer turns on an exhaust solenoid to let air out of the air springs (refer to Figures 11-7 and 16-10).

Usually, there's nothing to lubricate with air springs. But check with the dealer to find out whether it's okay to apply a rubber conditioner to the air bags to prevent them from wearing out prematurely.

Shocks and struts

Shock absorbers (see Figure 11-9) and *MacPherson struts* (see Figure 11-10) do most of the work of protecting the passenger compartment from bumps. One or the other is located near each wheel. The way they cut down on vertical movement is interesting. When a wheel hits a bump, it tends to keep bouncing up and down long after the bump has been left behind unless the movement is controlled. The bouncing effect is due to the inflated rubber tire on the wheel, and also to the fact that a coil spring that is either pulled or compressed doesn't just snap back into its former shape but keeps moving up and down for some time afterward. Shock absorbers and struts allow the springs to compress freely and to return or rebound slowly — like the door check on a storm door that opens quickly and easily but closes gently.

Figure 11-9:
Standard
shock
absorbers.

Figure 11-10:
MacPherson
strut.

Many vehicles feature MacPherson strut suspension. A MacPherson strut does a little more than shock absorbers do: Both shocks and struts control the ride, but a strut is also a structural member of the suspension system.

Part III

Keeping Your Car in Good Condition, System by System

The 5th Wave   By Rich Tennant

"I don't know about your oil, but the goulash you're cooking in your crankcase looks done."

In this part . . .

*E*very vehicle needs regular maintenance to keep it running smoothly. And at some point, your vehicle *will* need to be repaired. After all, cars and trucks are machines, and machines don't last forever. This part helps you fix the minor (and most common) stuff and helps you recognize the problems you need to take to a professional service facility. Like Part II, it's organized by system so that you can find what you're looking for easily.

Chapter 12

Keeping Your Electrical System in Tune

● ●

In This Chapter

▶ Determining when your vehicle requires a tune-up

▶ Knowing whether you can tune your car yourself

▶ Gathering the tools you need

▶ Obtaining and deciphering the specifications for your vehicle

▶ Reading, gapping, and reinstalling spark plugs

▶ Servicing a non-electronic distributor

▶ Checking and adjusting dwell and timing

▶ Replacing fuses

▶ Adjusting, aligning, and replacing headlights

● ●

Most vehicles on the road today have *electronic* ignition systems that are built to go for years between tune-ups. These systems need no major servicing until something goes wrong, and then they usually require a technician's expertise and electronic equipment. The good news for you lucky people who own one of these modern marvels is that — except the final section, "Fixing Electrical Gadgets That Are on the Blink" — the only sections of this chapter that need concern you are those that deal with checking, reading, and reinstalling spark plugs. The symbols 🏍 and ⓕ will alert you to sections that pertain to you. The bad news is that when the time comes to tune or repair your vehicle's sophisticated electronic system, the bills will probably be expensive.

For those of you who have older vehicles with *non*-electronic ignition systems that need regular tune-ups, the good news is that this may be the last book that still provides *easy* instructions for tuning your car yourself. This chapter tells you how frequently you should do it, what parts you need, how to make sure that you get the right ones, and how to do the main tasks associated with servicing your distributor and adjusting dwell and timing. You'll find this little symbol ⓕ in the margin next to sections that apply only to these older vehicles.

If you have an old-style non-electronic distributor that needs to be serviced on a regular basis, you can do it yourself for a fraction of what it would cost to have a service facility do it for you. (Don't worry; most of the parts involved are easy to adjust and replace.) And there are several additional good reasons to tune your car yourself: First, you can afford to tune your vehicle more often. This saves you even more money because a well-tuned car lasts longer than one that isn't. Second, a well-tuned car is a gas saver. You not only spend less money for fuel, but your vehicle produces less air pollution, too. Finally, if you tune your car yourself, you know whether it's been done properly, and you can adjust it yourself for peak performance.

 Before you read this chapter or attempt *any* of the work in it, be sure to read Chapter 5, which describes the different types of electrical systems on your car: the starting, charging, and ignition systems. It introduces you to their principal parts, tells you what each one does, and shows you what they look like and where to find them on your vehicle. If you try to work without that data, you'll be flying blind in dangerous territory!

Also, be sure to read the sections in Chapter 1 called "Safety Rules" and "How to Take Anything Apart — and Get It Back Together Again" before you undertake any electrical work.

All set? Great! Tackle ignition tune-ups first, and then get on to easy stuff like replacing fuses and adjusting, replacing, and aligning headlights.

How Often You Should Tune Your Car

Tune-up intervals vary from one vehicle to another. Most older cars should be tuned every 10,000 to 12,000 miles or every year, whichever comes first. Newer cars with electronic ignition and fuel injection systems are scheduled to go from 25,000 miles to as many as 100,000 miles without needing a major tune-up.

See your owner's manual for recommended tune-up intervals, but be aware that even if it says that the vehicle doesn't require *scheduled* tune-ups very often, it's in your best interest to check periodically that it's working at peak efficiency. If you do a lot of stop-and-go driving or pull heavy loads (like a camper or boat), your ignition system may need to be tuned more often, no matter what type of system it is.

Here are some of the symptoms that tell you that your ignition system probably needs to be tuned or adjusted:

✔ **The car stalls a lot.** The spark plugs may be fouled or worn, the gap may need adjusting, or the idle speed or an electronic sensor may need to be adjusted. Stalling can also be caused by problems with the fuel system (see Chapter 13). If you're having trouble pinpointing the cause, you can help your automotive technician diagnose the problem if you're aware of whether the engine stalls when it's hot, cold, or when the air conditioner is on.

✔ **The car gets harder to start.** The problem can be in the starting system or can be due to an electronic component, such as the starting sensor or the ignition system's computer. It could also lie in the fuel system, so check that out, too.

What You Need to Do the Work in This Chapter

When it's time to change your spark plugs and/or tune your car, have the items you need for each task assembled and handy before you begin. You probably already have some of these items. If you're buying tools, Chapter 2 describes them and provides tips on buying good ones. Everything should be easy to find at reputable hardware and auto supply stores.

Before you go shopping, see the sections of this chapter called "Buying the right parts for your car" and "Understanding tune-up specifications." They can help you avoid what is probably the most annoying part of any automotive job: disabling your car to work on it only to find that you have to drive back to the store to exchange the stuff they sold you in error!

It's a good idea to stick with parts from the same manufacturer as those that your vehicle originally came with. That brand may be listed in a service manual for your vehicle. If you don't have a service manual, tell the sales clerk at the auto parts store that you want OEM (Original Equipment Manufacturer) parts.

When you go to buy parts, keep in mind that most professional mechanics get discounts at auto parts stores. See if you can get a discount by telling them that you're installing the parts yourself. It can't hurt to try. Even if you don't get a price break, you're still ahead of the game because you don't have to pay labor charges.

If you have an *electronic* or *distributorless* ignition system, almost the only work you'll need to do is to check and reinstall your spark plugs. Ignore the items on the following list that have just this symbol ⊘ in the margin next to them. They apply only to tuning up *non*-electronic ignition systems.

Here's a list of the things you may need:

- **An old blanket or mattress pad or a padded car protector to place over the fender where you'll be working to protect it from scratches:** Commercial car protectors often come with handy pockets that hold tools and little parts while you work. You can make such a pocket yourself by pinning up the bottom edge of your folded blanket or pad — or you can forget about it completely if you don't mind rummaging in your tool kit a lot.

- **Work clothes:** Wear something that you won't mind getting stained with grease, oil, and other stuff.

- **Hand cleaner:** Chapter 2 has suggestions for the best type to buy.

- **A work light (or flashlight, at least).**

- **A new set of spark plugs:** Buy one for each cylinder in your engine. Never change just a few plugs; it's all or nothing for even engine performance. If you're feeling especially wealthy, buy an extra plug in case you get home and find that one of them is defective, or in case you accidentally ruin one by dropping and cracking it or by cross-threading it when you install it. If you don't use it, keep it in your trunk compartment tool kit for emergencies. Spark plugs don't get stale. And don't be shocked if you're told that you need eight spark plugs for your 4-cylinder engine. Some engines require two spark plugs per cylinder.

- **Anti-seize compound and silicone lubricant:** The threads of the spark plugs should be lightly coated with anti-seize lubricant before you install them in the engine. Also apply silicone lubricant to the spark plug wire boots to prevent them from sticking to the porcelain part of the spark plug.

- **Spark plug starter:** Some spark plugs are difficult to reach by hand, which can make installation tough. Special spark plug starters are available, or you can use an old spark plug wire boot or a piece of vacuum hose to make your own.

- **A wire or taper feeler gauge:** For gapping spark plugs (see Chapter 2).

- **A flat feeler gauge:** For gapping points (see Chapter 2).

- **Spark plug wires (if equipped):** If you have an older vehicle, check to see whether the spark plug wires (also known as *ignition cables*) are brittle, cracked, or frayed. If so, it's easy to replace them by following the instructions later in this chapter. Some newer vehicles have no spark plug wires, though. So don't be surprised if you ask for them at the parts store and they say that none are available for your vehicle.

- **Distributor cap (if equipped):** Distributor caps usually last about 50,000 miles on vehicles with electronic ignition systems. If your cap needs replacing, stick with a name brand like AC Delco (for GM), Mopar or Champion (for Chrysler), Motorcraft (for Ford), and so on. The cheap ones usually don't last very long.

✔ **Distributor rotor (if equipped):** Distributor rotors should be replaced whenever the distributor cap is replaced. Again, stick with a good name brand.

✔ **Points and condenser (if equipped) and distributor cam lubricant:** Vehicles from the 1970s and earlier usually have contact points and a condenser inside the distributor, which need to be replaced periodically. They may be sold separately or as a kit designed for your vehicle's make, model, and year. Check to see whether a little capsule of cam lubricant is in the package with the points. If it isn't, buy a small tube — it's cheap. Without the lubricant, the new points won't last very long.

✔ **Standard and Phillips screwdrivers:** In assorted sizes. You can find pictures of both types in Chapter 2.

✔ **A screwholder:** This tool is optional, but excellent for working in a small space like a distributor. Because it holds onto the screw until you release it, a screwholder cuts down on the chances of your dropping the screw into the works. It makes it easier to operate in the relatively tight distributor area because you don't have to cram your fingers in to hold onto the screw. (See Chapter 2 for a picture of a screwholder.)

✔ **A small set of basic socket wrenches that includes a ratchet handle and a spark plug socket:** Chapter 2 tells you what these look like and how to buy them.

✔ **Combination wrenches:** You can buy only the sizes you need to work on your distributor, but a small set of basic sizes is useful for a variety of home and automotive tasks. You can see how to buy and use combination wrenches in (you guessed it) Chapter 2.

✔ **A tach/dwell meter:** This dual-purpose gadget (refer to Figures 12-42 through 12-44) not only has a dwell meter for measuring your point gap, but it also has a tachometer for measuring the revolutions per minute (rpm) of your engine, a function that's extremely valuable if you need to adjust your carburetor so that it idles properly. If you're going to buy a tach/dwell meter, look for one that has both high and low ranges on the tachometer, which can give you a more precise reading. (Because you won't need this very often, you may want to borrow one.)

Don't let the lack of a dwell meter keep you from tuning your car! This chapter tells you how to do the job quite well with feeler gauges. I recommend a dwell meter because it's more accurate and can also help you adjust your carburetor (if your vehicle has one), but you can definitely live without one.

✔ **A timing light:** A timing light is a specialized piece of equipment that you use to check ignition timing on vehicles with non-electronic ignitions (refer to Figure 12-45). Because you won't need this tool very often, think about borrowing one from someone in your neighborhood who works on an older vehicle or has an old timing light.

If you decide to buy a timing light, keep in mind that, generally, the more you pay, the brighter the light is. Neon lights are the cheapest, but because they operate off the spark plug circuit and use minimal voltage, they may not produce enough light for you to see clearly unless you work in almost total darkness. Xenon lights cost more but provide more light. I suggest that you buy a cheap light, try it out, return it, and buy the next more expensive one until you get what you need.

When you look for a timing light, be sure that the cord is long enough and that the clamps are properly insulated so that you can grab them easily without getting shocked. The light should go on and off with a strobe effect when the clamps are properly affixed. When you shine the light at the timing marks on the moving crankshaft pulley of your engine, this strobe effect makes the marks appear to stand still so that you can see whether you have tuned your car properly. I go into the proper way to use this gadget and explain what timing really means later in this chapter.

Buying the right parts for your car

To buy the proper spark plugs and parts for a basic tune-up, you must know your vehicle's specifications (or "specs," as they're often called). To obtain the specs for your particular vehicle, you need the following information.

All this information should be in your owner's manual, and most of it is also printed on metal tags or decals located inside your hood. You can usually find these in front of the radiator, inside the fenders, on the inside of the hood — anywhere the auto manufacturer thinks you'll find them. I know of one car that has its decal inside the lid of the glove compartment. These ID tags also give a lot of other information about where the vehicle was made, what kind of paint it has, and so on, but don't worry about that information right now.

- **The make of the vehicle** (for example, Ford or Honda).
- **The model** (Taurus, Accord, and so on).
- **The model year** (for example, 1988 or 1999).
- **The number and type of cylinders in the engine** (4, 6, 8, V-4, V-6, or V-8).
- **Whether the vehicle has an automatic or a manual (standard) transmission.**
- **The engine displacement:** How much room there is in each cylinder when the piston is at its lowest point. (For example, a 300-cubic inch 6-cylinder engine has a displacement of 50 cubic inches in each cylinder.) The bigger the displacement, the more fuel and air the cylinders in the engine hold.

Engines on older cars may be listed in cubic inches, such as 302, 350, 454, and so on. Newer cars may be listed in liters (1.8, 2.3, 5.9) or cubic centimeters (2200, 3400, 3800).

✔ **The kind of fuel system:** If your engine has a carburetor, you need to know how many **carburetor barrels** it has. It may be a 1-barrel, 2-barrel, or 4-barrel carburetor. ("Barrel" may be abbreviated as "bbl" on some specifications.) If your engine is fuel-injected, you may need to know whether your car has *throttle body* injection or *multi-port* injection. (Chapter 6 makes sense of this stuff.)

✔ **Whether the vehicle has air conditioning.** It's necessary to take this into account when buying certain parts, but not usually spark plugs or distributor tune-up parts.

Understanding tune-up specifications

Your owner's manual may have specifications for everything you need for a basic tune-up. If you don't have an owner's manual, or if yours lacks the necessary data, you can go to an auto supply store and use a general "Tune-Up Specification Guide" (called a "spec sheet" for short). These guides are either in pamphlet form or printed on large sheets that are displayed near the parts section of the store (see Figure 12-1). If you can't find a spec sheet at the store, ask a salesperson to show it to you.

Don't ask what part you should buy because you have a very good chance of getting the wrong one. First look up the specifications yourself, and then ask for the part by number. If you're unsure, have the salesperson double-check it for you.

I include a Specifications Record at the end of this book to provide a place for keeping the part numbers and specifications of the parts you should replace at regular intervals on three vehicles. Photocopy it, enter the information listed in the preceding section, and take it with you to the auto parts store. I also include a Maintenance Record at the end of the book to help you keep track of what you check and change during your tune-ups and monthly checks. While you're at it, make copies of this one, too, so that you have one for each vehicle and each new year.

1967 Make and Model	Dist. Rotation	Dwell	Contact Gap	Spark Plug Gap	Firing Order	Ign. Timing B.T.C. @RPM
Chrysler (Neg. Grd.) (INCLUDES IMPERIAL)						
383 Cu. In. V8 Eng. (2 bbl.)	CC	30	.016	.035	3A	12°@550
• 383 Cu. In. V8 Eng. (2 bbl.)	CC	30	.016	.035	3A	5°@600[52]
383 Cu. In. V8 Eng. (4 bbl.)	CC	30	.016	.035	3A	12°@500
• 383 Cu. In. V8 Eng. (4 bbl.)	CC	30	.016	.035	3A	5°@500[52]
440 Cu. In. V8 Eng.	CC	30	.016	.035	3A	12°@650
• 440 Cu. In. V8 Eng.	CC	30	.016	.035	3A	5°@650[52]
Dodge (Neg. Grd.) (INCLUDES CHARGER, CORONET, DART)						
170 Cu. In. 6 Cyl. Eng.	C	42	.020	.035	5	5°@550
• 170 Cu. In. 6 Cyl. Eng.	C	42	.020	.035	5	5°ATDC@650
225 Cu. In. 6 Cyl. Eng.	C	42	.020	.035	5	5°@550
• 225 Cu. In. 6 Cyl. Eng.	C	42	.020	.035	5	TDC@650
273 Cu. In. V8 Eng. (2 bbl.)	C	30	.016	.035	3A	5°@500[56]
• 273 Cu. In. V8 Eng. (2 bbl.)	C	30	.016	.035	3A	5°ATDC@650
Lincoln (Neg. Grd.)						
462 Cu. In. V8 Eng.	CC	30	.017	.034	8C	10°@475
• 462 Cu. In. V8 Eng.	CC	30	.017	.034	8C	10°@500
Ford (Neg. Grd.) (INCLUDES BRONCO, FAIRLANE, FALCOLN, MUSTANG, THUNDERBIRD)						
170 Cu. In. 6 Cyl. Eng.	C	40	.025	.035	5	6°@550[6]
• 170 Cu. In. 6 Cyl. Eng.	C	40	.025	.035	5	5°@550
200 Cu. In. 6 Cyl. Eng.	C	40	.025	.035	5	6°@525[56]
200 Cu. In. 6 Cyl. Eng.	C	40	.025	.035	5	4°@500[52]
240 Cu. In. 6 Cyl. Eng.	C	40	.025	.035	5	6°@550[6]
• 240 Cu. In. 6 Cyl. Eng.	C	40	.025	.035	5	5°@550
289 Cu. In. V8 Eng. (2 bbl.)	CC	29	.017	.035	8C	6°@475
• 289 Cu. In. V8 Eng. (2 bbl.)	CC	29	.017	.035	8C	TDC@550
289 Cu. In. V8 Eng. (4 bbl.)	CC	29	.017	.035	8C	6°@525
• 289 Cu. In. V8 Eng. (4 bbl.)	CC	29	.017	.035	8C	TDC@550
Oldsmobile (Neg. Grd.) (INCLUDES F85, TORONADO)						
250 Cu. In. 6 Cyl. Eng.	C	32	.019	.035	5	4°@500
• 250 Cu. In. 6 Cyl. Eng.	C	32	.019	.035	5	4°@500
330 Cu. In. V8 Eng.	CC	30	.016	.030	3A	8°@850
• 330 Cu. In. V8 Eng.	CC	30	.016	.030	3A	7°@850

Figure 12-1:
A sample specifications guide (or spec sheet).

The following steps explain the proper way to use a specification sheet to obtain the right parts for your vehicle:

1. **Armed with your Specifications Record containing the information about your vehicle, look up your vehicle by make and model under the proper year on the spec sheet at the store.**

   For my first car, Tweety Bird, I looked under 1967, then under Ford, then under Mustang, then under "200 cu. in. 6 Cyl. Eng. (1 bbl.)" — which means that Tweety had an engine displacement of 200 cubic inches, a 6-cylinder engine, and a single-barrel carburetor.

2. **Write down the following information from the spec sheet at the store in the appropriate columns on your Specifications Record:**

   If you're just changing spark plugs, here's all you need:

   - **Spark plug gap:** The proper space there should be between the center and side electrodes of each spark plug.

   - **The part number for the spark plugs designed for your vehicle.**

   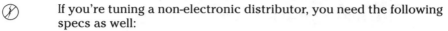

   If you're tuning a non-electronic distributor, you need the following specs as well:

   - **Dwell:** This number refers to the place on the dwell meter that the needle should point to if your points are correctly gapped. It's given in degrees.

   - **Point gap:** The proper gap for your points. (Surprise!)

   - **Firing order:** You need to know the firing order to help you locate your #1 plug, which you must know to check your timing.

   - **Ignition timing:** This number, given in degrees, refers to the proper timing mark on your crankshaft pulley (I'll help you find it), and the number after "@" indicates at how many rpm to check your timing on your dwell meter/tachometer. (It's not as complicated as it sounds.)

3. **Jot down the proper part numbers given for your vehicle's points, condenser, distributor cap, and rotor on your Specifications Record.**

   The points and condenser are sometimes packaged together as a tune-up kit. You may not need to replace the cap and rotor now, but the data will be handy when you do.

Changing Your Spark Plugs

How often you replace spark plugs depends on the type of plugs you have. You may have 30,000-mile plugs, or — if the plugs have platinum tips — they may be good for up to 100,000 miles. (For detailed information about what spark plugs do, see Chapter 5.)

Finding your spark plugs

Of course, before you can change your spark plugs, you have to find them. Look for a set of thick wires (or thin cables) that enter your engine block in neat rows — on both sides if you have a V-6 or V-8 engine, or on one side if you have a straight 4- or 6-cylinder engine (also called an in-line engine). These spark-plug wires run from the distributor (or ignition coil) to the spark plugs.

Some engines, like General Motors' 2.3-liter Quad-four, have no spark plug wires, and you can't see the spark plugs until you remove the aluminum cover that's bolted to the top of that engine.

Before you take care of your spark plugs, you must understand what the terms cylinder sequence and firing order mean.

Cylinder sequence

The cylinder sequence of an engine is the order in which the cylinders of the engine are numbered. This sequence varies from one type of vehicle to another, depending on whether it has front-wheel drive or rear-wheel drive and whether the vehicle has a "straight" (sometimes called "in-line") engine, a V-type engine, or a transverse engine. Here are cylinder sequences for all of these:

✓ **In all U.S.-made straight 4- and 6-cylinder vehicles with rear-wheel drive, the cylinder nearest the front of the car is called the #1 cylinder.** The numbering for the rest of the cylinders (#2, #3, #4, and so on) runs in sequence back toward the firewall at the rear of the engine compartment (see Figures 12-2 and 12-3).

Some foreign-built cars reverse the cylinder sequence. The #1 cylinder is at the rear, near the firewall. If you have a foreign car and no owner's manual, ask your local dealer where your #1 cylinder is.

Figure 12-2:
The cylinder sequence and firing order of a straight 4-cylinder engine.

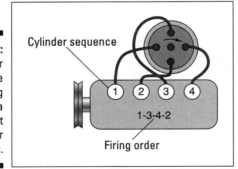

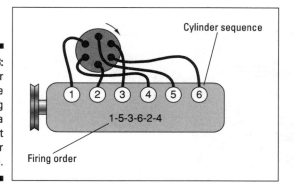

Figure 12-3:
The cylinder
sequence
and firing
order of a
straight
6-cylinder
engine.

✓ **Vehicles with front-wheel drive have transverse engines, usually combined with the transmission into a single unit called a transaxle.** On these engines, the cylinders run from one side of the car toward the other, with the #1 cylinder on the passenger side of the vehicle. (See Figure 12-4.)

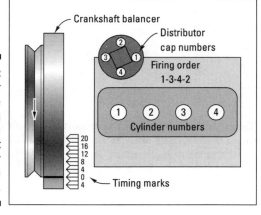

Figure 12-4:
The cylinder
sequence
and firing
order of a
straight
4-cylinder
transverse
engine.

✓ **V-8 engines are not as easy. Most Ford V-8s with rear-wheel drive have the #1 cylinder in the front on the passenger side of the car.** Then, #2, #3, and #4 follow it toward the rear firewall. The #5 cylinder is up front on the driver's side, with #6, #7, and #8 in sequence going toward the rear (see Figure 12-5).

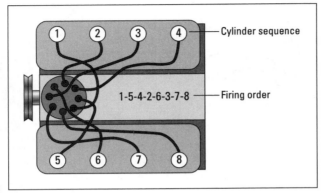

Figure 12-5:
The cylinder sequence and firing order of a Ford V-8 engine.

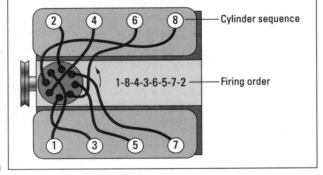

Figure 12-6:
The cylinder sequence and firing order of many other V-8 engines.

✔ **On most other vehicles with rear-wheel drive and V-8 engines, the #1 cylinder is up front on the driver's side, with #3, #5, and #7 proceeding toward the rear of the vehicle.** Then #2 is up front on the passenger side, with #4, #6, and #8 following. (See Figure 12-6.)

✔ **V-6 engines are similar to V-8s.** The three odd-numbered plugs are on one side, and the three even-numbered plugs are on the other side, with the lowest-numbered plugs usually up near the radiator.

✔ **Front-wheel drive vehicles with transverse V-type engines have the #1 cylinder up front on the driver's side, with the odd-numbered cylinders proceeding toward the rear, and #2 up front on the passenger side, with the even-numbered cylinders following (see Figures 12-7 and 12-8).**

No matter what the engine configuration, the #1 spark plug is always the spark plug in your #1 cylinder.

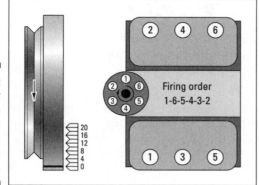

Figure 12-7: The cylinder sequence and firing order of a transverse V-6 engine.

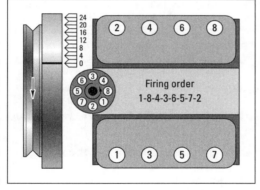

Figure 12-8: The cylinder sequence and firing order of a transverse V-8 engine.

Firing order

Don't confuse cylinder sequence with firing order. Although your engine may have its cylinders in simple numerical sequence, if the cylinders were fired in that order, the engine would rock violently as first the cylinders on one side (or toward the front) fired in rapid succession, and then the other cylinders did likewise. To avoid this, the firing order is carefully arranged to distribute the shock of combustion evenly throughout the engine.

The cylinders fire in very swift sequence, and the result is a fairly stable engine. A typical firing order for a Ford V-8 engine (with cylinders #1 to #4 on one side and cylinders #5 to #8 on the other) would be #1, #5, #4, #2, #6, #3, #7, #8. The firing order is printed inside each of the engines shown in Figures 12-2 through 12-8. Trace the path of combustion back and forth throughout each of these engines so you can see how the shock of combustion is distributed to avoid rocking the engine. Remember, the whole thing happens very rapidly.

Removing the spark plugs

To maintain the proper firing order, each spark-plug wire must go from the proper terminal on your distributor cap to the proper spark plug, so before you remove anything, label each wire with its proper number in the cylinder sequence.

To label your wires, place a piece of masking tape or a clothespin on the spark plug wire near the boot that covers the tip of each plug. Put the proper cylinder number on each one. If you also label the boot where each wire enters the distributor cap terminal, you'll never be unsure about hooking things up properly. (Of course, if you make it a habit to remove the wire from only one plug at a time and to put it back before you remove another, you won't ever get into trouble — unless another wire comes off accidentally.)

One way to royally confuse yourself and make the relatively simple task of changing spark plugs into a nightmare is to pull all your spark plugs out at one time. To keep your sanity and to avoid turning this job into an all-weekend project, work on one spark plug at a time: Remove it, inspect it, clean it, and, if it's salvageable, gap it. Then replace it — *before you move on to the next spark plug.*

After you label the wires, follow these steps to remove each spark plug:

1. **Gently grasp a spark plug wire by the boot, where it connects to the spark plug.**

   Never yank on the wire itself (you can damage the wiring); just grasp the boot, twist it, and pull it straight out so that you can pull it off the plug. The shiny thing sticking out of the engine block is the *terminal* of the spark plug. Figure 12-10, later in this chapter, shows you all the parts of a spark plug, including the terminal.

2. **Use a nice soft rag or a small paint brush to clean around the area where the spark plug enters the block — or you can blow the dirt away with a soda straw.**

   Doing so keeps loose junk from falling down the hole into the cylinder when the plug is removed.

3. **Find your spark plug socket (the big one with the rubber lining) and place it down over the spark plug; exert some pressure while turning it slightly to be sure that it's all the way down.**

   Like everything else in auto repair, don't be afraid to use some strength. But do it in an even, controlled manner. If you bang or jerk things, you can damage them, but you'll never get anywhere if you tippy-toe around.

4. Pick up your ratchet handle and stick the square end into the square hole in the spark-plug socket.

If you can work more comfortably by adding a couple of extensions between the handle and the socket so that you can move the handle freely from side to side without hitting anything, go ahead. You add them in the same way you added the socket to the handle. (If you have trouble with getting the plug loose, see the "Dealing with difficult plugs" section, which follows, for encouragement.)

The little knob on the back of the ratchet handle makes the ratchet turn the socket either clockwise or counterclockwise) You can tell which way the handle will turn the plug by listening to the clicks that the handle makes when you move it in one direction. If it clicks when you move it to the right, it will turn the socket counterclockwise when you move it, silently, to the left. If the clicks are audible on the leftward swing, it will move the socket clockwise on the rightward swing. Every screw, nut, bolt, and so on that you encounter should loosen counterclockwise and tighten clockwise. If your ratchet clicks in the wrong direction, just move that little knob to reverse the direction. Figure 12-9 shows you the proper way to use a socket wrench, and the sidebar "Breaking loose old plugs and misconceptions" tells you how to handle difficult plugs.

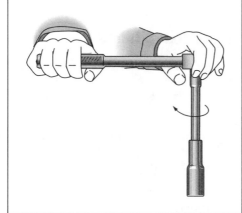

Figure 12-9:
Using a
socket
wrench.

5. Loosen the spark plug by turning it *counterclockwise*. When the ratchet turns freely, finish the job by removing the ratchet handle and turning the socket by hand until the plug is free from the engine.

After you've removed the spark plug from the engine, remove the plug from the socket. But don't go on to the next plug until you've read the plug (see the section "Reading your spark plugs" and Table 12-1) and gapped and replaced it, following the instructions later in this chapter.

Breaking loose old plugs — and misconceptions

You may have some difficulty loosening the spark plugs for the first time. Grease, sludge, and other junk may have caused the plugs to stick in place, especially if it's been a long time since they were changed.

To get the proper leverage, place your free hand over the head of the wrench, grasping the head firmly, and pull the handle as hard as you can, hitting it gently with the palm of your hand to get it going. (See Figure 12-9.) If you can't budge it, don't feel like a weakling. At first I thought I had trouble because I was female, but the biggest man in my first auto class had problems loosening the plugs on my car. The general opinion is that strength depends less on the size or sex of

the individual and more on the way in which you have been taught to focus your strength in your hands or on the tool you are using. I now approach hard-to-move objects with the proper tool and the conviction that I can move anything by pouring all my strength down my arms and into my hands. It works! Also, the longer the handle, the more leverage it gives you.

You'll feel better knowing that after you've installed your new plugs by hand, it will be a lot easier to get them loose the next time. So persevere. I've never met a plug that didn't give up and come out, eventually. The section called "Dealing with difficult plugs" gives you additional tips.

Dealing with difficult plugs

With all the stuff crammed under the hoods of vehicles, it can be hard to get at some spark plugs and, even when you can reach them easily, they may be difficult to remove. This section provides tips on extracting your spark plugs with a minimum of hassle.

Almost every vehicle has at least one plug that's a miserable thing to reach. If you have one, save it for last. Then you can work on it with the satisfaction of knowing that, when you get the darn thing finished, you will have finished the job.

If you find that one or more plugs are blocked by an air conditioner or some other part, try using various ratchet handle extensions to get around the problem. There are *universal* extensions that allow the ratchet handle to be held at odd angles; *T-bar* handles for better leverage; and *offset* handles for hard-to-reach places. (See Chapter 2 for examples.)

On some vehicles, you can't get at the plugs until you remove other parts that are in the way. On some transverse engines, you have to remove the top engine mount bolts by the radiator so that you can tilt the engine forward to replace the rear spark plugs. And on other engines, it may be easier to get to some spark plugs from underneath or through the wheel well area.

On some small cars equipped with optional big engines, you have to hoist the entire engine out of the car to reach at least one plug. If you have one of these beasts, I bet that when you finally get that plug out, you'll find that it's never been replaced during all the professional tune-ups you've paid for. And you've paid even more because that one funky plug probably not only increased your fuel consumption but also added to air pollution. Both you and your car should be glad to get rid of it!

If you absolutely cannot reach the offending plug, you can always drive to your service station and humbly ask them to change just that one plug. They won't like it, but it *is* a last resort. If you get to that point, you'll probably be glad to pay to have it done. But do try very hard first. If you can't get to the plug in the ordinary way, go under, over, around, or through gaps in the thing that's blocking it. Or get someone to help you move what's in the way (but be sure that you can get it back in place correctly). Use your imagination; it's the only hard part of the job. And you won't have to do it again for a long time.

If you're lucky enough to own a car without air conditioning, power steering, power brakes, and so on, chances are much greater that all your plugs will be easy to get at. Think it over next time you're tempted to buy a vehicle with all the "extras." Those "extras" tend to block the things you want to work on, and they often go wrong themselves. Some, like air conditioning if you live in a hot climate, are worth it. Others, like power brakes on a small car, are not.

Reading your spark plugs

You can actually *read* your spark plugs for valuable "clues" about how your engine is operating. To read your spark plugs, follow these steps:

1. **When the first spark plug is out of the engine, remove the plug from the spark plug socket and take a look at it.**

   Compare the deposits on the plug to the conditions shown in Table 12-1. Figure 12-10 can help you to identify the various parts of a plug mentioned in the table.

2. **Check the plug's shell, insulator, and gaskets for signs of cracking or chipping.**

3. **Look at the plug's *firing end* (the end of your plug that was inside the cylinder).**

   The hook at the top is the *side* electrode (refer to Figure 12-10). The bump right under its tip is called the *center* electrode. The spark comes up the center of the plug and jumps the gap between these two electrodes. This gap *must* be a particular distance across for your engine to run efficiently.

Table 12-1 **What Your Old Spark Plugs Tell You about Your Car**

Condition	Clues	Probable Causes	Remedies
Normal plug	Brown or grayish-tan deposit on side electrode	Everything's fine.	Just clean and regap the plug.
Carbon-fouled plug	Black, dry, fluffy soot on insulator tip and electrodes	Overly rich fuel/air mixture; malfunctioning choke; dirty air filter; or just too much driving at low speeds, or standing and idling for a long time.	Switch to "hotter" plugs. (The higher the plug number, the hotter the plug.)
Oil-fouled plug	Wet, black, oily deposits on insulator tip and electrodes	Oil may be leaking into cylinders past worn pistons or poorly adjusted or worn valves.	Clean and regap the plug or replace it, but find out where the leak is coming from.
Burnt plug	Blisters on insulator tip, melted electrodes, burnt stuff	Engine overheating; gap too wide; wrong or loose plugs; overly lean fuel/air mixture; incorrect timing.	Replace the plug.
Worn plug	Severely eroded or worn electrodes	Plug has been in there too long.	Replace the plug.

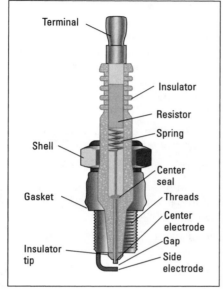

Figure 12-10: The anatomy of a spark plug.

4. **Take your *wire* or *taper* feeler gauge and locate the proper wire (if your spark-plug gap specifications say .035, look for this number near one of the wires on the gauge). Then slip that gauge wire between the two electrodes on your old plug.**

Figure 12-11 shows why you should never use a *flat* feeler gauge for this purpose. The reading will be inaccurate.

Figure 12-11: Why you can't use a flat feeler gauge on an old spark plug.

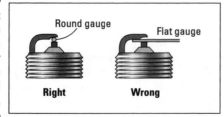

The gauge wire probably has a lot of room to wiggle around in. This may be because your old plug has worn down its center electrode, causing a gap that is too large. If the gauge goes in and out with a lot of room on either side, the gap is too large. If the gauge can't fit between the center and side electrodes, the gap is too small, which means that the spark plug is not burning the fuel/air mixture efficiently.

5. **Look at the little center electrode bump again and use Table 12-1 to judge its condition.**

   Is it nice and cylindrical, like the center electrodes on your new spark plugs? Has the electrode's flat top worn down to a rounded lump? Or has it worn down on only one side? Chances are it's pretty worn because it's old. When the center electrode wears down, the gap becomes too large. When you do your tune-ups yourself, you'll probably check your plugs more often and replace them before they get too worn to operate efficiently.

6. **Clean the plug. Then either gap it or replace it with a new one, following the instructions in the next two sections.**

   To clean a plug, gently scrub the gunk and goo away with a wire brush.

   Keep in mind that although you don't need to clean new spark plugs, you *do* need to gap them. Some plugs are sold "pregapped," but I'd check them with a feeler gauge anyway.

7. **Repeat the entire process for each additional plug, *working on only one at a time.***

   A good way to keep track of which plug belongs in which cylinder is to use an egg carton as a container and put the plugs into the carton's depressions in numerical order as you remove them from the engine.

Either replace *all* the plugs with new ones or clean and reinstall *all* the old ones. Don't mix plugs in varying states of wear. If you do, your engine won't operate efficiently. If you find that a few of your old plugs aren't too worn and are in fairly good shape, but you need to replace the others, clean and regap the salvageable plugs and store them in your trunk compartment tool kit for emergencies.

Sometimes you can cure a problem — such as carbon-fouled plugs — by going to a hotter- or cooler-burning plug. You can identify these by the plug number. The higher the number, the hotter the plug. Never go more than one step hotter or cooler at a time.

If your plugs indicate that something is seriously wrong with the way your engine is running, ask a professional mechanic for an opinion. If you're told that it requires extensive or expensive work, get a second opinion at another service facility without telling the technicians that you went to the first place. This is a good policy to follow whenever major repair work is suggested. We wisely get second opinions when doctors tell us we need major surgery; why not give your vehicle the same thorough attention before incurring a major expense?

Gapping your spark plugs

As I mentioned in the preceding section, the space, or *gap*, between the center and side electrodes needs to be a particular distance across; otherwise, your plugs don't fire efficiently. Adjusting the distance between the two electrodes is called *gapping* your spark plugs.

Gap new as well as old spark plugs, even if the package says that the new plugs are "pre-gapped." To avoid problems, work on only one plug at a time, in cylinder sequence order.

The following steps explain how to gap your spark plugs:

1. **If you're regapping a used plug, make sure that it's clean. If you're using a new plug, it should be clean and new-looking, with the tip of the side electrode centered over the center electrode.**

   There should be no cracks or bubbles in the porcelain insulator, and the threads should be unbroken.

2. **Take your feeler gauge, select the proper wire, and run it between the electrodes (see Figure 12-12).**

   If the wire doesn't go through or if it goes through too easily, without touching the electrodes, you need to adjust the distance between the electrodes.

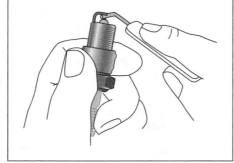

Figure 12-12:
Gapping a plug with a wire gauge.

3. **Adjust the gap as necessary.**

   If the wire didn't go through, the gap is too narrow. Hook the part of the feeler gauge that is used for bending electrodes under the side electrode and tug *very gently* to widen the gap.

   If the wire goes through too easily, without touching the electrodes, the gap is wide. Press the side electrode against a clean, mar-proof surface, *very gently*, until it's *slightly* bent down toward the center electrode.

4. **Run the gauge through the gap again.**

5. **Repeat Steps 3 and 4 until the gap is *just right*.**

   You want the gauge wire to go through fairly easily, just catching the electrodes as it passes. The wire should just "hang" in the gap but go through with a little guidance.

If you keep getting the gap too narrow or too wide, don't feel bad. Everyone I know goes through the "too large-too small-too large" bit a couple of times for each plug, especially the perfectionists.

After you're done gapping your spark plug, it's time to insert it in the engine. The next section has the details.

Installing a spark plug

To insert a spark plug into the engine, follow these steps:

1. **Clean the spark plug hole in the cylinder block with a clean, lint-free cloth.**

   Wipe *away* from the hole; don't shove any dirt into it.

2. **Lightly coat the threads of the spark plug with anti-seize compound, *being careful not to get any on the center or side electrodes*.**

3. **Carefully begin threading the spark plug into the engine by hand, turning it *clockwise*.**

   This is called "seating the plug." You have to do it by hand, or you run the risk of starting the plug crooked and ruining the threads on the plug or threads in the engine.

   If you have trouble holding onto the plug, you can buy a *spark plug starter* and fit it over the plug, or you can use an old spark plug wire boot or a piece of vacuum hose to make your own.

4. **After you engage the plug by hand, turn it at least two full turns before utilizing the spark plug socket and ratchet.**

5. **Slip the spark plug socket over the spark plug, attach the ratchet handle, and continue turning the plug clockwise until you meet resistance.**

   Don't overtighten the plug (you can crack the porcelain); just get it in nice and tight with no wiggle. The plug should stick a little when you try to loosen it, but you should be able to loosen it again without straining yourself. Tighten and loosen the first plug once or twice to get the proper feel of the thing.

If you have a torque wrench, you can look in the manual for the proper setting and use it *after* you seat the plug by hand. Then try to loosen the plug by hand. This gives you the proper feel for how tight it should be. Most do-it-yourselfers tend to replace plugs without torque wrenches because torque wrenches are difficult to work with in the small space between the block and the other parts of the vehicle.

6. **Inspect the entire length of the spark plug wire before attaching its boot to the plug. If the wire is cracked, brittle, or frayed or is saturated with oil, replace it.**

7. **Before you attach the boot to the spark plug, apply some silicone lubricant to the inside of the boot; then push the boot over the exposed terminal of the new plug and press it firmly into place.**

   You've just cleaned, gapped, and installed your first spark plug. Don't you feel terrific? Now you have only three, five, or seven more to do, depending on your engine.

8. **Repeat the steps to remove, read, gap, and install each spark plug.**

   It's at times like these that owners of 4-cylinder cars have the edge on those who drive those big, expensive 8-cylinder monsters.

When you're done, start your engine to prove to yourself that everything still works. Then wash your hands with hand cleaner. If you've had a hard time with a hard-to-reach plug, get some rest before taking on additional work. Next time, the job should be a breeze.

Servicing Your Distributor

 Most cars built after 1975 have electronic ignition systems that require no regular servicing. Some have no distributors at all. All testing and servicing of these systems should be left to trained professionals because they are easily damaged if hooked up improperly, and they employ high voltage that can also damage *you.*

 If your car has an electronic ignition system, the only work you can do is to replace the distributor cap and rotor if they become damaged. However, even if you have a distributorless system, don't forget to read and change your spark plugs and check that your cables and connections haven't become corroded or detached. I'd do so at least twice a year, or whenever your vehicle stops running smoothly or your fuel consumption suddenly increases.

If you aren't sure whether your vehicle has one of the older non-electronic distributors that must be manually serviced, note that older distributors have one thin wire on the side, whereas the electronic ones have two wires or more. If you're still not certain, check your owner's manual or service manual, or call the service department at a dealership that represents your car's manufacturer.

⑦ If you have a distributor that does need servicing, check the items in the section called "What You Need to Do the Work in This Chapter," paying special attention to the parts and tools preceded by the ⑦ symbol.

Get to the scene of the action

The distributor gets voltage from the ignition coil and distributes it to each spark plug in turn. To accomplish this, the distributor contains a set of points, a rotor, and a condenser. Servicing your distributor involves cleaning and checking these parts and replacing them if necessary. Of course, to get to the scene of the action, you have to remove some stuff that's in the way. But don't panic: The following sections take you step by step through the entire process.

⑦ ① Although you can jump to any of the following sections to get specific information, I recommend that you read Chapter 6 before going any further. It will help you find your distributor and familiarize you with what each part looks like and does. Then return here and work your way through the rest of the sections in succession, using the ⑦ and ① symbols to identify work that you can do on your particular system.

If you go step by step, you can do everything you need to in the most efficient order, thereby increasing the chances of your vehicle starting the first time you try it after the work is done.

Remove your distributor cap

⑦ ① The distributor cap is the first thing to go. To remove it, follow these steps:

1. **Find your distributor.**

   If you're still not sure where to find it, Chapter 6 provides a description of the distributor — where it is, what it does, and what it contains.

2. **Use a long-handled screwdriver to loosen the distributor cap.**

   Most caps are held in place by either screws (see Figure 12-13) or clips (see Figure 12-14).

3. **Now that your distributor cap is free, remove it *without removing any of the wires that are attached to the cap*. Place it to one side and take a look inside your distributor (see Figure 12-15).**

   Does the stuff in there look like the replacement parts you bought? Look at the structure of the rotor (and the points and condenser, when you get to them). They should be similar, although some parts may be made of plastic instead of metal. If they look different, you've got the wrong parts. Go back to the auto parts store and start over. (You may not collect $200, but at least you won't go to jail.)

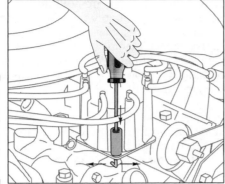

Figure 12-13:
Removing a distributor cap with screw clamps.

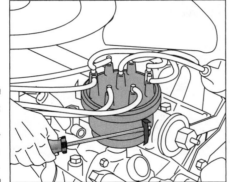

Figure 12-14:
Removing a distributor cap with clips.

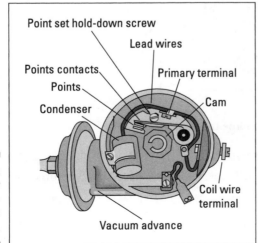

Figure 12-15:
The anatomy of a non-electronic distributor.

Point set hold-down screw

Lead wires

Points contacts

Primary terminal

Points

Cam

Condenser

Coil wire terminal

Vacuum advance

If, when you look inside your distributor cap, you do not find the parts in the illustrations in the following sections, you probably have an **electronic ignition** system and can consider yourself pretty lucky. As I mentioned earlier, you don't have to deal with adjusting or replacing traditional points and condensers. All you have to do is check and change your spark plugs now and then and check for a defective distributor cap or rotor if your engine starts running roughly or stops running completely.

Because there are many types of electronic ignition systems, and adjustments usually require expensive tools and specialized expertise compared to conventional ignitions, I strongly advise you to rely on a good automotive technician if neither the cap nor the rotor appears damaged.

Remove the rotor

Sitting on top of everything else inside the distributor is the rotor. Rotors vary in size from small plastic gizmos that simply lift off the distributor shaft, to big round plastic plates that have two screws to remove (Figure 12-16 shows different kinds of rotors).

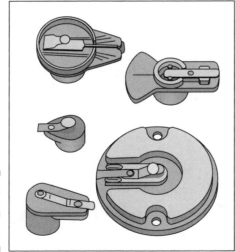

Figure 12-16:
Various
types of
rotors.

To remove your rotor, follow these steps:

1. **Before you remove your rotor, move it on its shaft.**

   Does it move easily? If not, you really need this tune-up badly!

2. **Remove the rotor from the shaft.**

   To remove a small rotor, just lift it straight up off the distributor shaft (see Figure 12-17). To remove a large rotor, you need to unscrew the two screws and lift the rotor off the distributor shaft (see Figure 12-18).

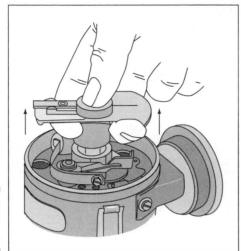

Figure 12-17:
Removing a small rotor.

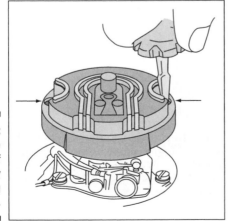

Figure 12-18:
You release this type of rotor by removing the screws.

3. **Take a close look at the old rotor to see how it fits onto the shaft so that you can put the new one in properly later on.**

All rotors go on in only one way: They either have a square-pin-in-square-hole/round-pin-in-round-hole arrangement, or they're notched or shaped so that they fit on the shaft pointing in only one direction. Still, it's a good habit to take a long look at anything you remove before you remove it, because you tend to forget how it's situated, and sometimes you have to make a choice. Don't be afraid to draw pictures if you aren't sure you'll remember how something fit together.

4. **Look at the metal contacts that conduct current to the spark plug terminals.**

   If the rotor contacts are corroded, broken, or cracked, you really need a new one! In any case, plan to use the new one after you're through working on the rest of the distributor.

5. **Set the old rotor aside.**

Under the rotor on some vehicles, you may find something called the *centrifugal advance* (see Figure 12-19). Its function is rather complicated, it has nothing to do with this minor tune-up, and it hardly ever breaks. Just leave it where it is and forget it.

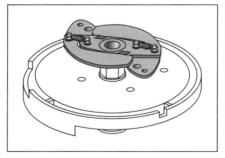

Figure 12-19:
A
centrifugal
advance.

Remove the static shield

On some vehicles, you may find a *static shield*, shown in Figure 12-20, which you have to remove before you can change your points and condenser. The static shield's purpose is to prevent radio interference. Sometimes the working of the electrical system in your car produces strange noises on the car radio. This gizmo prevents that.

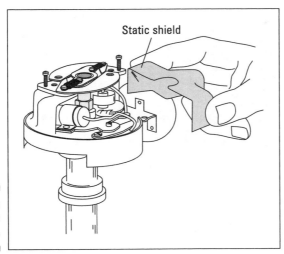

Figure 12-20:
The static
shield.

The static shield isn't hard to remove, but when you finish working on your distributor, be careful to put the shield back exactly the way it was. If you can't get it back properly, don't worry — your car will run perfectly without it, so just put the pieces in a paper bag and drive to your friendly service station. They'll put it back for you (although you may have to take a little kidding).

Remove and replace the condenser

Under the rotor (and possibly the static shield) are the points and condenser. Before you remove the condenser, look at the two little wires, one leading to the points and the other to the condenser, that join together — usually with some sort of little screw and washer arrangement (refer to Figure 12-13).

Take a good look at how the wires (sometimes called *leads*) fit together in the gadget that holds them (called the primary terminal). The main purpose of the primary terminal is to prevent the clips at the ends of these wires from touching the floor of the distributor, which is called the breaker plate. If they touch the breaker plate, they short out and the car doesn't start.

Now follow these steps:

1. **Take a closer look at how the wires connect.**

   Are the little clips at the ends of the wires touching each other? Or are they separated with something? Does the screw that holds them in place touch them? Or is there something in between? Figures 12-21, 12-22, 12-23, and 12-24 show how to disconnect several types of primary terminal arrangements.

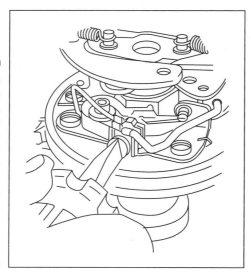

Figure 12-21:
On some distributors, the wires must be loosened from the primary terminal, as shown, before you can remove them.

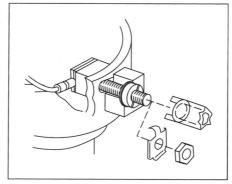

Figure 12-22:
On another type of distributor, you must use a special tool to remove the primary terminal nut and release the contact spring and lead wires.

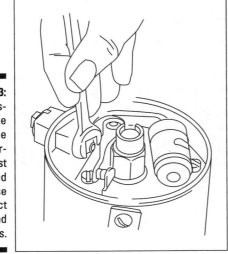

Figure 12-23:
On other distributors, the nut on the primary terminal must be loosened to release the contact spring and lead wires.

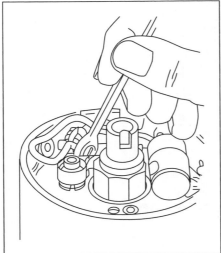

Figure 12-24:
Still another distributor has its wires attached as shown. You remove these by loosening the nut at the primary terminal.

Even if you think that you can remember exactly how the wires are connected, draw a picture of them *before* you remove them!

2. **When you have a picture of how they are attached, disconnect the wires.**

   Put the screws or other parts that came off on a clean surface so that you'll know where they are when you need them later.

3. **Push the condenser (that little cylinder in there) through the ring that holds it, and then put it near the screws that you removed in Step 2.**

   Some condensers are attached to the clips that hold them, and you have to remove them, clip and all. Figures 12-25, 12-26, and 12-27 show a few of the most common setups.

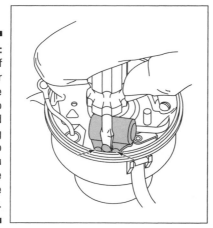

Figure 12-25: This type of condenser has one screw to remove and two locating bumps to help you position the new one securely.

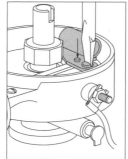

Figure 12-26: Other condensers have a locating hole in the mounting bracket.

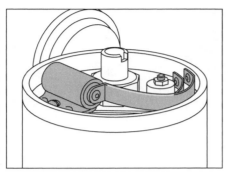

Figure 12-27: Some condensers are connected to the primary terminal by a copper strap that must be released before they can be removed.

4. **Use a clean, lint-free rag to wipe around the breaker plate where the condenser was resting. Then take the new condenser and slide it in where the old one was.**

   If there's a new clip in the tune-up kit but you were able to slide your old condenser out without removing the old clip, forget the new clip as long as the old one seems to be in good condition and doesn't wiggle around.

Congratulations! You just replaced your condenser. On to the points!

Remove and replace the points

The points on your vehicle may look a bit different from the ones in Figure 12-28, but they work the same way. Here's a rundown of some basic types of points that you may encounter:

✔ Some points are made in a single unit; others consist of two halves that fit together. Some Chrysler products have dual sets of points, but these are no more difficult to install or change.

✔ Some foreign cars have little springs that come out separately from the points. If you have points like these, be sure to hold your free hand over the distributor when you loosen the points, or it will spring out and get lost.

✔ Some points have two screws that fit into slots in the points — these can be loosened, and the points will slide out. Others have a screw to hold the points down and another screw to adjust them.

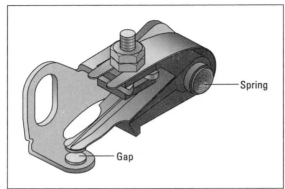

Figure 12-28:
A set of
points.

Before you remove your old set of points, compare them to the new set of points you just bought. If they don't look exactly alike, return them for the proper kind.

Once you know which kind of points you have, do the following:

1. **Take your screwdriver and open up the points in your distributor so that you can see between them.**

   Are the contacts rough where they meet? This is usually the result of normal wear and tear. If they're badly burned or pitted, the points should be replaced.

   If the points are relatively new, excessive wear can be a sign that something is improperly adjusted or malfunctioning. Excessively worn points or burned points usually result from either poor adjustment when they were installed (this means that they were incorrectly gapped) or a bad condenser, or the accidental introduction of oil or cam lubricant between the point contacts.

   Because used points are impossible to read accurately with a feeler gauge (Figure 12-29 shows you why), you won't be able to tell if this is a case of poor adjustment. But if your olds points look badly burned or worn, be sure to check your new points after about 1,000 miles of driving, and if these look bad, too, ask your mechanic for an opinion.

2. **Remove the old points by removing the screw or screws that hold them in place (see Figure 12-30).**

If you have slotted points, simply loosen the screw and slide the points out.

This is a good time to use a screwholder. It holds the screw until you release it, so you don't have to cram your fingers into the distributor to hold onto the screw.

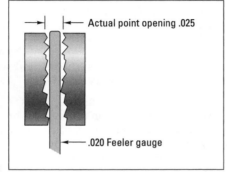

Figure 12-29: Why you can't get an accurate gap reading on old points.

Actual point opening .025

.020 Feeler gauge

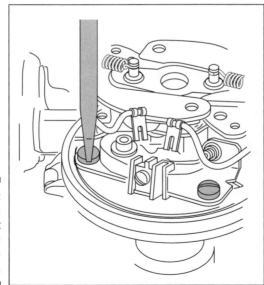

Figure 12-30: Remove the screws that hold the points in place.

3. **Put your old points aside, and use the clean rag that you used to clean around under the condenser to wipe the rest of the breaker plate (the floor of your distributor).**

Before installing the new points, you need to do another little job.

Lubricate your distributor

Lubricating your distributor is something that seems inconsequential but is really very important because it can increase the life of your points. In the package with your new points, there may be a little capsule of cam lubricant. If there isn't any, you can buy a tube of it very cheaply. Then follow these steps:

1. **Take a *little bit* of cam lubricant on your index finger and wipe it around the sides of the cam wheel (see Figure 12-31).**

Use the lubricant *very* sparingly. You don't want lumps, just a nice greasy finish on the cam wheel *only.* If you don't lubricate this wheel, your points could burn out very quickly. If you use too much, the stuff flies around inside the distributor when the wheel spins and fouls things up or causes your points to burn. Because your points open and close very fast (at around 12,000 times a minute when you drive a V-8 engine at 60 mph), you can see why the lubricant is necessary and why it tends to fly around if you're too generous. You want just enough to make your cam wheel lobes slide easily past the points.

Figure 12-31:
Place only a *small* amount of lubricant on the cam wheel, or it will fly around and burn the points.

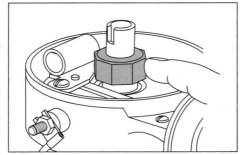

2. **Look at the top of the distributor shaft, where the rotor was sitting. If there's a wick inside it, place a few drops of light engine oil on the wick in the shaft, as shown in Figure 12-32.**

   If you don't have the proper kind of oil, forget it this time and pick some up in time for the next tune-up.

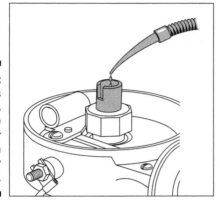

Figure 12-32:
If a wick is present, lubricate the distributor shaft with just a *few* drops of oil.

Install the new points

After the distributor is properly lubricated (see the preceding section), you're ready to install your new points. Follow these simple steps:

1. **Pick up the new points and gently rub the two contact tips together.**

   Points usually come from the factory with some kind of coating on them, and this coating can keep the spark from going across the gap. Gently rubbing the tips together removes this coating.

   Don't use cloth, paper, or a file to remove this coating — the lint or tiny filings will foul the points. A little rub is all they need.

2. **Install the new points where the old ones were (see Figures 12-33 and 12-34), but** *don't tighten down the screws that hold them in place until you have adjusted the gap.*

   Sometimes it's easier to connect the lead wires that come from the points and the condenser *before* you replace the points in the distributor.

3. **Be sure that the clips on both wires touch each other but do not touch any other metal.** They're designed to go back to back so they fit snugly into the clip on the primary terminal. Refer to Figures 12-21 through 12-24 to see the different types of configurations and the way to reassemble yours.

If you don't see your configuration in these illustrations — and you neglected to make a drawing of the way yours was — use your imagination. If you get it wrong, your car simply won't start until you get it right. Nothing else will happen, so don't worry. Just fit the wire clips together and put them in the clip so that they're not touching anything metal (this includes the side of the clip, if it's made of metal, and the distributor base). As I said earlier, this can be done either before or after you get the points in place, whichever is easier.

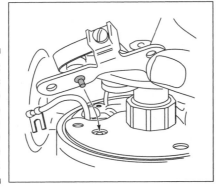

Figure 12-33: Some points have a knob that fits into a locating hole on the floor of the distributor.

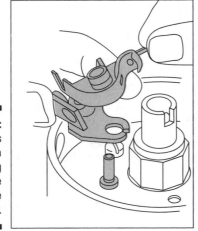

Figure 12-34: Other points fit over a locating post on the floor of the distributor.

Adjust your points

Now it's time to adjust your point gap (also called "gapping your points"). Before you can adjust the point gap, the little rubbing block that protrudes from the side of the points nearest the cam wheel must rest on the highest point of one of the cam lobes. This forces the points open to their widest gap — and that's the gap you're going to adjust:

1. **If the rubbing block isn't resting on the point of the cam lobe, use your ignition key to "bump" your starter until the cam wheel turns to the correct position (see Figures 12-35 and 12-36).**

Figure 12-35:
The rubbing block causes the points to open when it is pushed up by the highest point on the cam lobe.

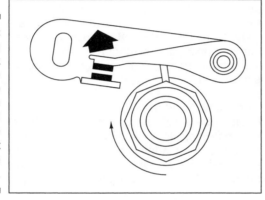

Figure 12-36:
Crank the engine with the starting motor until the point rubbing block is on the peak of the cam lobe. This brings the points to their widest gap.

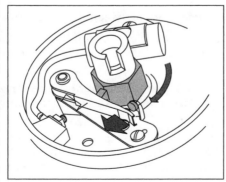

If you have difficulty doing this, run a chalk mark down the side of the distributor and onto the base, or whatever it's sitting on. (This line will help you later to get it back the way it was.) Then turn to the section called "Adjust your timing," later in this chapter, to see how to locate the distributor hold-down clamp. Loosen it and turn the distributor until the rubbing block is resting on the point of the cam lobe and the points are wide open.

2. **Look at your specifications for the proper point gap; then take your** *flat* **feeler gauge and select the correct blade.**

3. **Slide the blade of the feeler gauge between the points and note how narrow or wide the opening is.**

   Is the gap too small to let the blade in? If you left it like that, your car would be hard — or impossible — to start, and your points would get burnt and pitted. Is the gap so wide that the gauge doesn't touch both surfaces as it goes in and out? This results in a weak spark and poor engine performance at high speeds. So if your gap is either too wide or too small, it needs adjusting.

There are three basic kinds of point-adjusting set-ups. Some cars have an *adjusting screw* (in addition to the screw or screws that hold the points in place). Other cars have an *adjusting slot*. Still others have a little *window* in the distributor cap that allows you to adjust the points without removing the distributor cap. Look at Figures 12-37, 12-38, and 12-39 to determine which one your vehicle has and then follow the appropriate set of steps:

If you have an adjusting *screw,* see Figure 12-37 and follow these steps:

1. **Loosen the screw or screws that hold the points in place.**

2. **Turn the off-center adjusting screw.**

3. **Place the correct feeler gauge blade between the point contacts.**

   The contacts should still be at their widest gap. If they aren't, follow Step 1 at the beginning of the "Adjust the points" section to turn the distributor until they are.

4. **Turn the adjusting screw (see Figure 12-37) until the feeler gauge blade can slip in and out between the contacts, just touching them as it slides.**

   There should be a minuscule grab as the blade goes through, but it should go through easily. If you aren't sure, try the next thicker and thinner blades. If the gap is correct, neither should work properly.

5. **When you get the gap just right, tighten the screws that hold your points in place (*not* the adjusting screw) and recheck with the gap with the gauge.**

6. **If you've moved the distributor, put it back where it was, with the chalk marks lined up.**

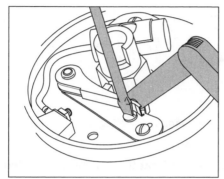

Figure 12-37:
Adjusting
screw-type
points.

If you have an adjusting *slot,* see Figure 12-38 and follow these steps:

1. **Loosen the locking screw or screws that hold the points in place.**

2. **Make sure that the points are at their widest gap.**

   If they aren't, follow Step 1 at the beginning of the "Adjust the points" section to move the distributor until they are. Then insert the tip of your screwdriver into the adjusting slot and, by moving it one way or the other, open the gap so that the correct feeler gauge blade can slip in.

3. **Insert the correct feeler gauge blade and, using your screwdriver in the adjusting slot, adjust the contacts to allow the blade to slide in and out between the contacts, just touching them as it slides.**

   The blade should just touch both contacts as it moves, but it should move easily, with just a little bit of grab as it goes by. If you aren't sure, try the next thicker and thinner feeler gauge blades. If the gap is correct, neither should work properly.

4. **Tighten the screws that hold the points in place and then recheck the gap with the gauge.**

5. **If you moved the distributor, put it back the way it was, with the chalk marks lined up.**

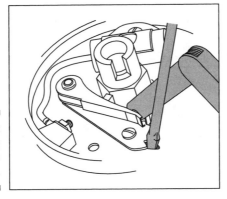

Figure 12-38:
Adjusting
slot-type
points.

If you have an *external adjustment window,* see Figure 12-39 and follow these steps:

1. **Reassemble your distributor and put the distributor cap back on.**

   You can find instructions for doing so in the next section under "Replace the static shield" and "Replace the rotor."

   Your points probably won't need adjusting because they come preset from the factory. They should need adjusting only if your car won't start.

   • **If your car won't start,** first make sure that you've hooked the wires from the points and the condenser together so that they don't touch any metal parts except each other. (See Step 3 of the section called "Install new points" for details.)

   • **If your points *do* need adjusting,** follow the rest of these steps.

2. **Use a hex wrench (an Allen wrench shaped to fit into hexagonal holes) to turn the adjusting nut behind the sliding window in the distributor cap, as shown Figure 12-39.**

   If a little hex wrench came with the points, use it. If not, you'll have to get your own.

3. **Start your car and leave the engine running with the emergency brake on and the car in either Park or Neutral. Turn the nut clockwise until the engine starts to falter. Then turn the screw *half a turn* counterclockwise, remove the wrench, and close the window.**

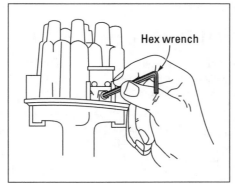

Hex wrench

Figure 12-39:
Adjusting
points with
an external
adjustment
window.

Get it all together again

 Once you've replaced the condenser, replaced and adjusted your points, and put those pesky little lead wires safely back in their clip, it's just a matter of putting everything back the way it was before you started servicing the distributor. Relax; you're in the home stretch. The next sections will see you safely to the winner's circle.

Replace the static shield

If you have a static shield, put it back now, before you replace the rotor. For details, refer to "Remove the static shield" and Figure 12-20 in the earlier section called "Getting to the scene of the action."

Replace the rotor

Now it's time to install the new rotor you purchased.

 Be sure to put the new rotor back exactly the way the old one went (the previous section called "Remove the rotor" may refresh your memory). All rotors fit properly one way only, and it's easy to check the position of yours. Once it's back on the shaft, just turn the rotor to see whether it settles back into place easily. If you can turn it in more than one direction, you haven't replaced it properly.

Check the distributor cap

Take the time to clean and check your distributor cap thoroughly. If it's defective, replace it:

Replacing a distributor cap is easy

If your old cap is damaged, buy a new distributor cap for your vehicle's make, model, and year at the parts department of your dealership or an auto supply store. Make sure that it looks *exactly* like the old one. The wires attached to the old cap snap in and out of it. You should have no trouble moving the wires from one cap to the other if you hold the two caps side by side, in the same direction, noting the position of the locating lugs or slots (see the accompanying figure).

Then just pull the wires off the old cap *one at a time* and insert them in the new cap in the *correct order.*

Each wire must be placed on the tower on the new cap that's in the same relative position as the tower on the old cap, or your car won't run properly. Be sure to push each wire to the bottom of its tower and then push the rubber boot onto it securely.

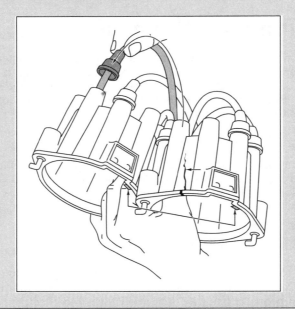

1. **Pick up the distributor cap (don't let any wires come off) and take a look inside it. Wipe the inside clean with a lint-free rag.**

   Do you see any cracks in the cap when you hold it up and shine a light through it? If you do, you can buy another cap very cheaply. Follow the instructions in the sidebar called "Replacing a distributor cap is easy."

2. **Look at the inside of your cap where the wires enter it. Push gently on each wire where it enters its "tower," and make sure that it's in tightly.**

Are the insides of the towers clean? Each little metal thing you see inside the cap is an electrode that transfers electricity to the rotor; you don't want these electrodes to be too fouled to conduct the electricity.

3. **If the electrodes look dirty, scrape them with a small screwdriver to remove the carbon.**

If the electrodes are burnt or very dirty, you may need to replace your wires. If you feel that you can do the job accurately, connecting each wire to the proper tower on the cap and the proper spark plug, *one at a time,* fine. If not, you're probably better off having someone with more experience replace the wires for you.

4. **When you're satisfied that all is well, replace your distributor cap.**

Figures 12-40 and 12-41 show you the two steps necessary to replace different types of caps.

5. **Start your engine to see whether you've got everything right.**

If your car starts right up, great! You're ready to move on to the section called, "Checking and adjusting your work." If the car won't start, don't panic; the instructions in the next section will soon set things right.

Figure 12-40:
Some distributor caps have either a locating lug that fits into a slot in the cap spring hanger *(left),* or a groove or slot in the cap that fits over a boss on the distributor housing *(right).*

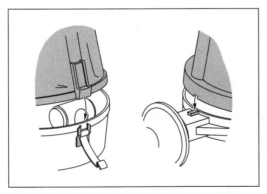

Figure 12-41:
Fasten the
cap to the
housing
either by
pressing on
the center
of the cap
spring,
forcing the
spring over
the mount-
ing lugs on
the cap
(left), or by
pressing
down on the
screw and
turning it
until the
clamp is
under the
slot on the
bottom of
the housing
(right).

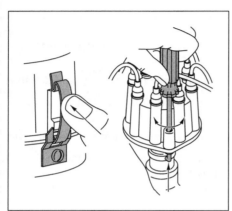

Restart your car

If your car doesn't start (this isn't unusual), the answer to one of these troubleshooting questions will solve your problem:

- ✔ **Is your vehicle still in Park or Neutral?** It won't start in any other gear.

- ✔ **Is your distributor cap on correctly?** If it isn't, put it on properly. If it is, remove it so that you can look inside and answer the other questions in this list.

- ✔ **Are the lead wires from the condenser and the points correctly replaced and tightened down?** (Refer to Figure 12-13.) If they're touching anything metal except each other, the spark is grounding out instead of passing through the points while they're closed.

- ✔ **Are your points properly gapped?** Check them again with the proper feeler gauge blade. Sometimes they move back together when you tighten them down after adjusting them.

Run a bit of *very clean,* lint-free cloth between them — maybe something got in there and is preventing the spark from going across. Do the points close completely? They must open and close to work.

✔ **Did you accidentally disconnect any other wires while you were working?** Reattach them.

After you correct the problem, put your distributor cap back again and start the engine. It should start this time. Don't panic if you still have trouble — almost everyone does the first time. But you ran the engine after you changed the spark plugs, so if there is a problem, it has to be in the distributor, right?

If you still can't get the car started, remove the new condenser and put the old one back in. Maybe the new one is defective. This could also be true of the points or rotor. If you keep trying and still have no luck, the worst that can happen is that your friendly mechanic will have to get you out of the hole. So how bad can it be?

Check your distributor with a dwell meter

After you start your car following a tune-up, it's time to check the dwell — assuming that you bought or borrowed a dwell meter. (You'll also want to check your vehicle's timing, following the instructions at the end of this chapter.)

The difference between the cost of doing this tune-up *once* yourself and paying to have it done for you is probably more than the cost of a dwell meter *plus* a timing light.

A dwell meter (see "What You Need to Do the Work in This Chapter" for a description of this and other tools) is a handy gadget for determining whether your points are properly gapped and whether your distributor is operating properly.

A dwell meter checks the distance that your distributor shaft rotates when your points are closed — which is the same as saying that it measures how long the points stay closed (or "dwell together"). This distance is called the *cam angle,* and, like all angles, it's measured in degrees.

Hooking up a dwell meter

The first thing you have to do when you check the dwell is to hook up the dwell meter to the distributor. The following shows how to hook up two of the most popular types of dwell meters.

To hook up a dwell meter with *two* clips (see Figure 12-42):

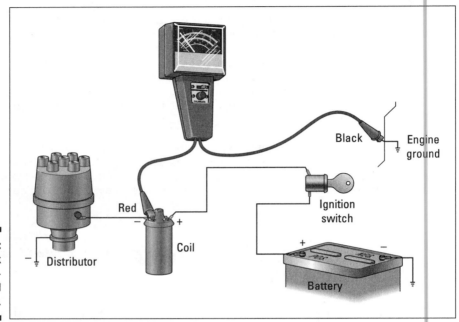

Figure 12-42:
How to hook
up a two-
clip dwell
meter.

1. **With the engine shut off, find the little wire on the side of the coil that connects at its other end to the distributor and hook the *red* clip to the clamp that holds that wire in place.**

2. **Hook the *black* clip to "ground."**

   "Ground" can be anything on the vehicle that's made of metal, through which electricity can pass back to the battery. In this case, ground can be any part of the metal frame of the car, but the best ground is an *unpainted* pipe or bolt bolted directly to the engine. (Not too near the carburetor, please! You don't want a stray spark setting off the fuel in the carburetor.)

To hook up a dwell meter with *three* clips (see Figure 12-43):

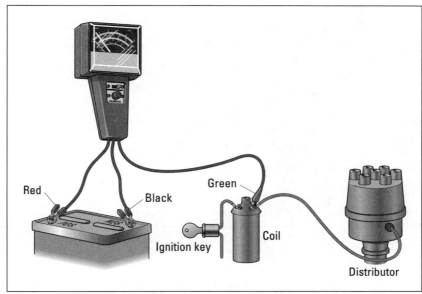

Figure 12-43:
How to
hook up a
three-clip
dwell meter.

1. Connect the *red* clip to the *positive* terminal of the battery.

2. Connect the *black* clip to the *negative* terminal of the battery.

3. Connect the *green* clip to the clamp that holds the little wire on the
   side of the coil that connects at its other end to the distributor.

Some Ford cars have an insulated slip-on terminal on the wire leading from
the distributor to the ignition coil. If you have a Ford with this configuration,
lift the slip-on terminal and slide the Ford adapter clip in place (see Figure
12-44); then push the terminal down. Attach the Green clip to the adapter
clip, as shown in Figure 12-44.

Don't allow the Ford adapter clip to touch any other metallic part of the coil
case or the engine.

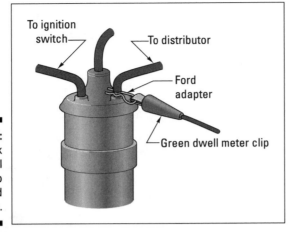

To ignition switch—

—To distributor

— Ford adapter

—Green dwell meter clip

Figure 12-44:
How to hook up a dwell meter to some Ford cars.

Checking dwell

After your dwell meter is hooked up, follow these steps to check the dwell:

1. **If your dwell meter has one, turn the *calibrated* knob to set it.**

2. **Turn the proper knob to the number of cylinders that your vehicle has.**

3. **Start the engine and let it idle, with the emergency brake on and the gearshift in Park or Neutral.**

4. **Look at the line on the dwell meter that has the same number of cylinders as your vehicle has, and see where the needle is pointing.**

   Is the needle pointing to the correct figure listed under "Dwell" on your specifications sheet? It can be plus or minus 2 degrees. For example, if your spec sheet shows a dwell of 38 degrees, a dwell anywhere between 36 and 40 degrees is fine. If the dwell is further off than that, you have to readjust your points, as explained in the next step.

5. **Depending on whether you have a distributor with an external adjusting window (refer to Figure 12-39) or the kind of points that adjust with an adjusting screw or slot (Figures 12-37 and 12-38, respectively), do the following:**

   • **If you have a distributor with an external adjusting window:** Let the engine idle and keep the dwell meter in place. Then open the little window in the side of the distributor cap (it slides up) and turn the adjustment screw with the hex wrench until the needle on the dwell meter points to the correct number.

- **If you have the kind of points that adjust with an adjusting screw or slot:** Shut off the engine, remove the distributor cap again, and readjust your points to the correct gap with your flat feeler gauge by following the instructions in the section "Adjust your points." When you've got it right, put everything back and check the dwell again. Sorry, but that's life. . . .

If the dwell is too low, the gap is too large, and vice versa.

When the dwell is correct, it's time to check your timing, which is the topic of the next section. If you have a *tach/dwell* meter (a dwell meter with a tachometer built in), there's one additional thing that you can do.

If you have a tach/dwell meter, turn the knob to set it to the tachometer readings. Some tach/dwell meters have both Hi and Lo readings; if yours does, you can choose either line. Start your engine and let the car idle. After it warms up a bit, check the tachometer to see at how many rpm (revolutions per minute) the car is idling. Try to keep the tach/dwell hooked up while you check your timing, but if it's too difficult to clip both the tach/dwell and the timing light to the battery terminals, disconnect the tach/dwell and keep it handy.

Check your timing with a timing light

Did you get a timing light? If you plan to check your timing, I hope you did. I've heard of a variety of ways to check your timing without one, but none of them has proven very accurate, and many turned out to be impossible. So beg or borrow one if you don't want to buy one. The section "What You Need to Do the Work in This Chapter" tells you all about them.

As a last resort, if you have no timing light, you can drive down to your local service facility after you've done your tune-up and ask them to check your timing for you, but be prepared to deal with the consequences. Instead of using a timing light, the technicians will probably hook your car to an electronic diagnostic machine in order to give you an answer, so be sure to ask beforehand if there's a charge for this service. If there is, ask whether the charge covers adjusting the timing for you, if it's necessary. If they're willing to check your timing for nothing and your timing is off, they'll probably charge to adjust it for you. And if you tell them that you want to fix it yourself, you'd better plan to go somewhere else for a timing check when you're through. Once you've exhausted all the garages in the neighborhood, you'll probably have to go out and borrow or buy a timing light anyway!

To check your timing, follow these steps:

1. **Read the instructions that came with the light.**

Reading the instructions is a good idea with any piece of new equipment.

2. **Hook up your timing light as suggested in those instructions.**

   Most lights have three clips on them. If you have no instructions, the ones in this book will work for most timing lights with three clips (see Figure 12-45).

3. **If you haven't already turned your engine off, do so.**

4. **Clamp the big *red* clip to the *positive* terminal of your car battery, as shown in Figure 12-45.**

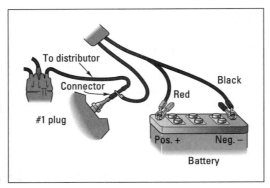

Figure 12-45:
Hooking up a three-clip timing light.

5. **Clamp the big *black* clip on the *negative* terminal of the battery.**

   Make sure that the battery terminals are clean enough to allow current to pass through them. If they look *very* funky, scrape the clip around on them a little, or wash off the junk with a clean rag dipped in water and baking soda.

   Try not to get the stuff from the battery terminals on your hands — it has acid in it. If you do get it on your hands, just wash them off with water; it won't burn holes in you right away.

6. **Attach the third clip (the one with the thickest insulation) to your #1 spark plug.**

   To find out where the #1 plug is on your vehicle, refer to Figures 12-2 through 12-8.

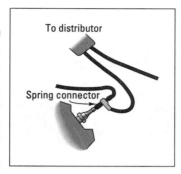

Figure 12-46:
Using a spring connector to attach the third clip to the #1 spark plug.

To distributor

Spring connector

There are three ways to place the clip:

- You can remove the **boot** from the spark plug, put the clip on the terminal end of the plug that sticks out of the engine, and replace the boot so that it fits snugly and allows the current to pass through from the wire to the plug (refer to Figure 12-45).

- You can use a small metal spring or clip that fits over the terminal end of the plug, leaving a gap between the boot and the plug on which to clip the third clip from the timing light (refer to Figure 12-46).

- If your #1 spark plug is hard to get at, you can attach the third clip to the distributor terminal tower where the wire from the #1 plug enters the distributor cap. Just trace the wire from the plug to the distributor, remove the boot from the distributor cap terminal, add a metal extension (usually supplied with the light), replace the boot, and clamp the clip to the extension (see Figure 12-47).

7. **With your engine still shut off, try to pull up on your fan belt with one hand to tighten it, and turn the fan with the other hand to rotate the wheel that has the fan belt hooked around it (the lower wheel).**

   This wheel, called the crankshaft pulley (or the harmonic balance wheel), probably has your timing marks on it (see Figures 12-48 and 12-49). On some vehicles, the timing marks are located elsewhere, so if you can't find yours on the crankshaft pulley, consult your owner's manual or service manual for their location, or call the service department at your dealership.

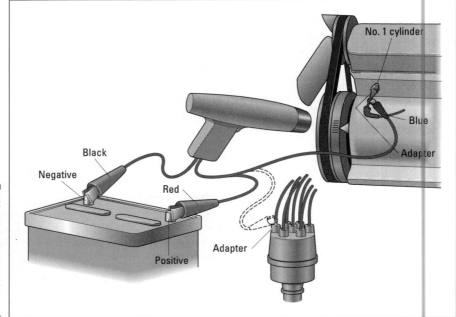

Figure 12-47:
Attaching the third clip to the #1 spark plug or the #1 distributor terminal.

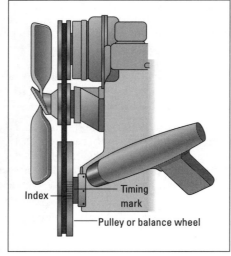

Figure 12-48:
Timing marks on the crankshaft pulley of a vehicle.

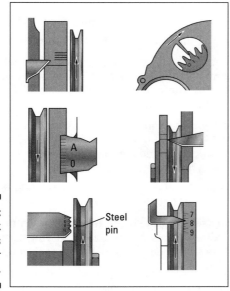

Figure 12-49:
Timing mark
locations
on other
vehicles.

Steel pin

If you can't move the fan by hand, remove the big wire from the center of your distributor cap and lay it on an unpainted metal part (not the carburetor!) to ground it. Then turn the key in the ignition to "bump" the starter without starting the engine. Doing so turns the crankshaft pulley, and as the pulley turns, a set of lines should come into view. These are your timing marks. A pointer attached to the engine block usually points to these marks. To set your timing, you have to get the pointer to point to the correct timing mark while the engine is running. Figures 12-48 and 12-49 show where the timing marks may be on your vehicle.

8. Look at your spec sheet to see what your timing *degree* should be.

The spec sheet (refer to Figure 12-1) will say something like "10°@550," which means that you want to line the pointer up with the 10° timing mark when the engine is idling at 550 rpm.

The spec sheet may say something about BTDC or ATDC. This simply means that your timing marks will have a line labeled 0, with marks above and below it. The 0 is top dead center (TDC). Depending on the direction that the wheel rotates, the lines that come into view before the 0 (or TDC mark) are "before top dead center" (BTDC), and the ones that appear after TDC are "after top dead center" (ATDC). In case you're curious, "top dead center" is the point at which the piston reaches its highest point in the cylinder and compression is greatest. (How's that for cocktail party chatter?)

9. **Once you find the timing marks and know which mark to set your timing at, use a piece of chalk to make that mark stand out.**

   You can also chalk the tip of the pointer to make it more visible.

10. **Attached to the side of your distributor is a round gizmo called a vacuum advance. Disconnect the little rubber hose that comes from it, and put a piece of tape on the end of the hose — or stick a screw in it — to seal it off (see Figure 12-50).**

   Some vehicles have distributors *without* vacuum advance mechanisms. If you have one of those vehicles, you may need to disconnect a special electrical connector. Consult a service manual or call your dealership if your vehicle has no vacuum advance.

11. **Start your engine, making sure that your emergency brake is on and that you're in Park or Neutral. Let the car warm up.**

12. **If your tach/dwell meter is still hooked up, look at the "rpm" line to see whether the car is idling at the proper speed. If you have no tach/dwell, check the idle speed on the dashboard tachometer.**

   If your car isn't idling at the proper speed, you have to adjust your idle. Adjusting the idle is a simple matter of turning one screw, so don't be dismayed. You can find instructions for doing this in the section called "Adjusting idle speed screws" in Chapter 13.

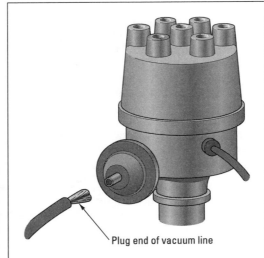

Figure 12-50:
Disconnecting the vacuum advance.

Plug end of vacuum line

13. **Aim the timing light at the timing marks and press the button on the light.**

The fact that the light is hooked to your #1 cylinder spark plug means that current passes through the light every time your #1 plug "fires." This makes the light go on and off with a strobe effect. As a result, the timing marks appear to be standing still, although the crankshaft pulley is actually turning rapidly. Fascinating, isn't it?

14. **Note to which timing mark the pointer is pointing.**

Is it pointing to the correct mark? If it isn't, you must adjust your timing — the focus of the next section.

Adjusting your timing

If you need to adjust your timing, follow these steps:

1. **On the base of the distributor shaft, below the distributor, is a nut called the distributor hold-down clamp.**

Use a combination wrench to loosen this nut so that the distributor can turn a bit on the shaft when you grasp the vacuum advance and move it back and forth.

If you have trouble reaching the hold-down clamp, a distributor wrench can make it easier (refer to Figure 2-5 in Chapter 2).

2. **Move the distributor *a little bit* on the shaft; then shine your timing light at the timing marks again to see whether you got it right.**

Is the pointer closer to the right mark? Is it farther away? If it's farther away, you have moved the distributor in the wrong direction. Go back and move it the other way. Every time you move the distributor, go back and check again with the timing light.

3. **Repeat Step 2 until the pointer is pointing to the correct timing mark.**

If your idle speed changes, adjust your idle to specifications and recheck your timing. Then tighten the distributor hold-down clamp again, *making sure that you don't move the distributor when you do so.* Check again with the light. Are the timing marks dead on? Good! (You can be off a little bit without causing trouble, but be as accurate as you can without driving yourself crazy.) You now have your car timed perfectly, which leads to much better engine performance and fuel consumption — and cuts down on air pollution.

4. **Shut off your engine and disconnect the timing light and the tach/dwell meter.**

If you've used a metal extension on your #1 plug, be sure to remove and put the boot back on the plug.

Well, you've changed your spark plugs, serviced your distributor, and checked your dwell, idle, and timing. You just completed a basic tune-up! If you had a little trouble, would it have been worth big bucks to avoid it? Probably not. (As I write this book, the cost of tune-ups seems to be going up daily.) Plus, by doing the job yourself, you *know* that all the work has been done and done properly. Congratulations!

Fixing Electrical Gadgets That Are on the Blink

Periodically, you need to fix electrical doodads and gizmos that are on the blink. Maybe your stereo quits working, your turn signals don't blink, a headlight burns out, or something else goes wrong. When these small but inconvenient problems arise, you can usually fix them yourself, easily and with very little expense. This section shows you how.

Your battery should be checked and maintained regularly. You can find instructions in Chapter 3 for dealing with it as part of your monthly under-the-hood check.

Changing fuses

A fuse box is easy to recognize (see Figure 12-51), and replacing burnt-out fuses is a fairly simple matter. If your stereo, clock, map light, turn signal, or other electrical appliances stop working, chances are that a fuse has blown. Changing a fuse is much cheaper than paying for a new clock or for repairs that you don't need, even if you chicken out and have an automotive technician do it, so take a few minutes to find your fuse box. It's usually located under the dashboard — often behind a panel — or in the engine compartment. Your owner's manual can help you locate it.

Before you open or work on your fuse box, be sure the key in the ignition is turned to "Off."

To fix a blown fuse, look for a fuse that's black inside or no longer has its filaments intact (see Figure 12-52). Unless you have a blade-type fuse with prongs, take a bobby pin or paper clip, bend it, and use it to pull out the bad fuse. Then press a new fuse into place. When you've replaced all the burnt-out fuses, try your stereo or clock again. If it still doesn't work, then worry about having it repaired or replaced.

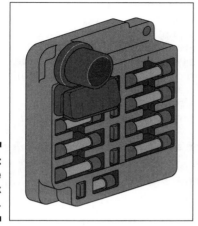

Figure 12-51:
Automotive
fuse box
and fuses.

Figure 12-52:
A good fuse
(top) and a
burnt-out
fuse.

Replacing and adjusting headlights

Today's vehicles feature many kinds of illumination: headlights, taillights, directional signals, and fog lights make it easier for you to see and be seen; overhead lights, map lights, lit glove compartments, and illuminated mirrors on sun visors all require attention periodically. In this section, I deal primarily with headlights. If you experience problems with other lights, it's usually just a matter of removing the face plate and changing the bulb, or changing the fuse associated with the light. If that doesn't do the trick, seek professional help.

There's one exception: If any of your directional signals stop flashing, or you can no longer hear clicking inside the car when they're supposed to be on, the signals themselves may not be malfunctioning. Directional signals also serve as troubleshooting tools to alert you to other lights that may not be working properly. For this reason, you can find information about directional signals in Chapter 20.

It doesn't hurt to wash the outside of your headlights and taillights occasionally; clean lights provide better visibility at night. If you still have trouble seeing at night (and you've been getting enough vitamin A), check to make sure that both of your headlights are shining straight ahead rather than at the side of the road or into the eyes of other drivers. If they appear to be out of alignment, check out the section called "Checking headlight alignment," later in this chapter.

Here are some other headlight problems and how to deal with them:

- ✔ **If one of your headlights won't work on low but does work on high,** you have to replace the bulb.

- ✔ **If a light doesn't work on either high or low beam,** you probably have a bad connection in the wiring.

Before attempting to replace or adjust your headlights, you need to know whether you have the old-style sealed-beam units or the newer halogen headlights.

Replacing halogen headlights

Since around 1980, most vehicles have come with halogen headlights. Although they are twice as powerful as sealed-beam units and enable a driver to see 20 percent farther, they require less power to operate.

To replace a bulb on a halogen headlight, use Figure 12-53 as a guide while you take the following steps:

1. **Open the hood and unplug the electrical connector that plugs into the lock ring.**

2. **Unscrew the bulb-retaining ring (if your unit has one) or the bulb assembly to expose the socket.**

3. **Remove the old bulb and install the replacement.**

    Do not touch the glass bulb! Natural oils from the skin on your fingers will create a hotspot that will cause the bulb to burn out prematurely. Instead, handle the bulb by its plastic base, or the metallic tip if it has one.

4. **Replace the unit and the retaining ring or bulb assembly and replug the connector.**

If you need to adjust the alignment of a halogen headlight, it has two adjusting screws, as shown in Figure 12-54.

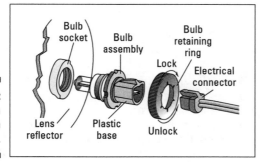

Figure 12-53:
Replacing a halogen bulb.

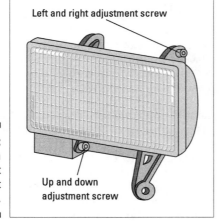

Figure 12-54:
Halogen headlight adjustment screws.

Replacing sealed-beam headlights

Older vehicles have sealed-beam units, which are relatively easy to deal with. If one of your headlights ceases to shine, first consult your owner's manual to see whether it contains instructions for replacing the bulb. If it doesn't, the following should get you through the job with a minimum of hassle:

1. **Make sure that the key in the ignition is turned to "Off" before you open the unit.**

2. **Carefully turn the correct screws to loosen the plate that holds the unit in place.**

   The plate has six screws; three loosen the plate, and the other three align the headlights by adjusting the angle of the bulb. If you turn the wrong screws, your headlights go out of alignment, so check your owner's manual for details.

3. **Remove the bulb and insert the new one in its place.**

   Be sure to put the new bulb into its locking slots with the unit number at the *top*.

Checking headlight alignment

If you managed to goof up your headlight adjusting screws, or if you just aren't sure whether your headlights are properly adjusted, there's an easy check that you can do. When you're driving on a fairly straight road at night, check to see whether your headlights appear to be shining straight ahead and are low enough to illuminate enough of the road in front of you to enable you to stop safely if an obstruction appears. Be sure to check your headlights on both high and low beams.

You can also have headlights checked out and adjusted professionally. Auto repair facilities often have headlight-aiming equipment to check and set your headlights in accordance with state laws. Some are certified Motor Vehicle Bureau inspection stations. Note, though, that if you go to a repair facility that does MVB inspections just to see whether your headlights are aimed properly, you'll have to pay them for checking the lights and for an inspection certificate *whether or not they have to adjust your lights.*

A cheaper way to check out headlight adjustment is to look for a highway patrol station near your home. They either have the equipment to check your headlights for you, or they can tell you where their current highway checkpoints are, so you can check them yourself. Of course, if the highway patrol finds that your headlights aren't in focus or find anything wrong with your car's emissions, you have to get the trouble fixed within a stipulated period or face a fine. (Be positive about this; it's to your benefit to correct a situation that can cause an accident or pollute the environment.)

If you can fix the problem yourself by turning the adjustment screws shown back in Figure 12-54, go back to the checkpoint afterward for an okay.

Be sure to get a certificate saying that the lights have been adjusted and meet the proper standards. This certificate is usually part of the price.

Checking other electronic devices

If you have trouble with your defroster, heater, anti-theft devices, or stereo system, get professional help. Later, if you turn into a confirmed do-it-yourselfer, you can find books that deal with these repairs.

Do not attempt to work on your air conditioner under any circumstances. It contains refrigerant under pressure that can blind you if it escapes. For service or repairs, head to the dealership or to an air-conditioning specialist.

Chapter 13

Keeping Your Fuel System in Tune

● ●

In This Chapter

▶ Checking and replacing your fuel and air filters

▶ Checking your fuel pump, PCV valve, and accelerator pump

▶ Adjusting your idle speed, idle mixture, and choke

▶ Installing a new or rebuilt carburetor

▶ Knowing what jobs to pass off to professionals and protecting yourself from overzealous mechanics

● ●

*F*uel system problems may occur for a variety of reasons. Some remedies, such as replacing a fuel filter, are relatively inexpensive. Others, such as replacing a fuel pump, are costly. Mechanics often try the more expensive solutions first and work backwards to the cheaper ones. You end up paying for all the time, labor, and parts involved. You can avoid this by using the easy instructions in this chapter to check things out before heading for professional help. If you can do the job yourself, great! If you can't, you may save time and money anyway by being able to communicate better with your technician and by suggesting that the less-expensive possible solutions be pursued first. At the very least, *try* to do the simple adjustments and maintenance tasks (such as changing the air filter) yourself. Doing so will cost you little in time and money and may prevent major repair bills.

If your vehicle has fuel injection, you can skip the entire "Tuning Your Carburetor" section of this chapter. Just be sure to have your car checked periodically to ensure that it's performing well.

If your vehicle has a carburetor, it requires periodic tune-ups to keep it operating at peak efficiency. The "Tuning Your Carburetor" section of this chapter provides instructions for making most of these adjustments.

If you're not sure whether your vehicle is fuel-injected or carbureted, refer to your owner's manual or call the dealership and tell them the make, model, and year.

Regardless of what kind of fuel system your car has, it probably still requires the other basic maintenance (such as changing air and fuel filters) mentioned in this chapter. All the work is under-the-hood stuff, so you won't need to jack up your vehicle, and you probably won't have to indulge in any acrobatics to reach the scene of the action.

Before you undertake any work in this chapter, be sure to read (or reread) Chapter 6. If you understand *where* the part you're dealing with fits into the system and *what* it does, you'll have a clearer idea of *why* the work you're doing is necessary and *how* it needs to be accomplished. This not only makes the job easier and more pleasant, but it also helps you locate each part and understand how it functions. Also check out "Safety Rules" and "How to Take Anything Apart — and Get It Back Together Again" in Chapter 1. Believe me, the aggravation you can prevent is well worth the time!

Filters on all vehicles should be replaced on a regular basis according to your owner's manual or the intervals suggested in this book. However, if your vehicle isn't starting right up in the morning, idling without conking out at stoplights, or producing readings within the acceptable range on a tach/dwell meter or on the electronic analyzer at your service station, it probably needs the work outlined in this chapter.

Replacing Your Air Filter

If you unscrew the wing nut on the lid of your air cleaner and undo any other devices that hold it down, you'll find the air filter inside. Figure 13-1 shows a round air cleaner and filter; some vehicles have square ones instead. Most vehicles come with pleated-paper filters that can be replaced for a few dollars. Replacing these filters is easy: You simply buy a new one for your vehicle's make, model, and year, lift out the old one, and drop in the new one. A few older vehicles have permanent air filters, which you need to clean according to the instructions in your owner's manual.

Checking your air filter

To see whether your air filter needs to be replaced, just lift it out (it isn't fastened down) and hold it up to the sun or to a strong light. Can you see the light streaming through it? If not, try dropping it *lightly,* bottom side down, on a hard surface. Doing so should jar some dirt loose. (Don't blow through the filter — you can foul it up that way.) If the filter is still too dirty to see through after you've dropped it a few times, you need a new one.

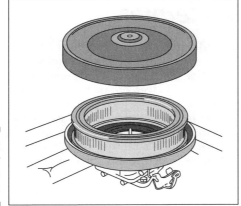

Figure 13-1:
The air filter
is inside the
air cleaner.

Because the air filter extracts dirt and dust particles from the air, you should change it at least once a year or every 20,000 miles, whichever comes first — unless yours gets very dirty before then. If you do most of your driving in a dusty or sandy area, you may need to replace your air filter every 5,000 miles, or less. If a road trip takes you to such an area, it's a good idea to check the air filter after you return.

Buying an air filter

When buying an air filter, keep the following points in mind:

- ✔ **Look for well-known, quality-brand filters; you can often get them quite cheaply at discount stores.** Unknown brands sell for very little, but they aren't always of good quality, and if your air filter lets a lot of junk get into your carburetor, you may find that a cheap filter is very costly in the long run.

- ✔ **If you need help determining which air filter is the one you need, go to your local auto supply store or to the parts department at your dealership.** Give them your vehicle's make, model, and year.

- ✔ **Make sure that the filter you get matches your old filter in size and shape.** If it doesn't, you've been sold the wrong filter for your car. To save yourself a trip back to the auto supply store, check the filter you purchase against your current filter while you're still in the parking lot.

Removing Your Air Cleaner

To change the air filter, you need only to detach and lift the lid on your air cleaner. But you have to *remove* the air cleaner to view and access a carburetor or other stuff under the cleaner. To do so, just unscrew the wing nut and other hold-down devices as though you were going to replace the air filter, and then lift the *entire* air cleaner up and off. If it refuses to budge, look for additional clamps or screws that may be holding it in place. If you have to disconnect any hoses in order to free the air cleaner, just disconnect the ends that connect to the air cleaner, and make sure that you remember exactly where they were attached. (If more than one hose is involved, draw a sketch before you detach anything.)

You can run your engine with the air cleaner off, but never drive around like that. The amount of dirt that gets into your engine determines the life of your vehicle. This dirt creates the kind of wear that causes engines to break down.

Replacing Your Fuel Filter

It's important to get in the habit of changing your fuel filter every time you tune your vehicle, especially if you tend to ride around with an almost-empty fuel tank. (See the sidebar "Why you should keep your fuel tank full" to find out why.) If your vehicle starts to run roughly right after you fill it up with gas, contaminants in the fuel may have plugged up the filter. In any case, a fuel filter is usually inexpensive and easy to replace. The first thing you have to do is find it.

Why you should keep your fuel tank full

Because the space in the fuel tank above the fuel level is filled with air, and because air contains quite a bit of water vapor, the water in the air tends to condense on the sides of the fuel tank and elsewhere on cool mornings. This water vapor can rust the insides of your fuel tank, it can mix with the fuel, and it can act in a variety of pesky ways to keep your car from operating efficiently. If you keep your fuel tank well-filled, there's less room for air and therefore less water vapor hanging around. This is an excellent reason for *not* driving around until your fuel gauge reads "Empty."

Another reason for making those extra trips to the gas station is that the rust formed by the water vapor in the air tends to sink to the bottom of the fuel tank. These sediments can do no harm as long as they're happily sloshing around in the bottom of the tank. But if you let the fuel level in the tank get too low, the fuel that gets fed to your engine could be like the last bit of coffee in the bottom of the pot — full of sediment that tends to stick in the throat. Some fuel tanks have filters to prevent this, but the filters can get choked up if you consistently drive on an empty tank.

Locating your fuel filter

Your owner's manual should show you where your fuel filter is. If it doesn't, consult a service manual for your vehicle's make, model, and year (you can usually find these manuals at your local library) or ask someone in the service department at your dealership.

- ✔ **If your engine is fuel-injected,** your fuel filter is located somewhere in the high-pressure line, either by the fuel tank or near the engine.

- ✔ **If your engine is carbureted,** your fuel filter is located in the fuel line between the fuel pump and the carburetor. Most fuel filters on carbureted engines are close to the carburetor. And some (like those in General Motors vehicles) have a fuel filter inside the carburetor inlet. To get to these fuel filters, you have to remove the air cleaner that sits on top of the carburetor. Doing so is easy if you follow the instructions in "Removing Your Air Cleaner," earlier in this chapter.

Externally mounted fuel filters consist of a little metal or plastic cylinder with an internal pleated paper filter element like the one shown in Figure 13-2.

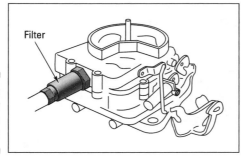

Figure 13-2:
A fuel filter near a carburetor.

On some vehicles, the fuel filter is held in place by metal clamps on either side of it, either in the fuel line or in the carburetor inlet fitting. This is called an *in-line* filter. Some vehicles have the fuel filter inside the carburetor or fuel pump, but getting at these *integral* filters is no more difficult. (In-line and integral filters are illustrated in Figure 13-3.) Some fuel filters on fuel-injected engines require special tools to disconnect the fuel lines.

Don't use a drop light with an incandescent bulb when changing a fuel filter. Fuel that drips on the bulb can cause it to break and start a fire. Use a flashlight if you need to shed some light on the subject.

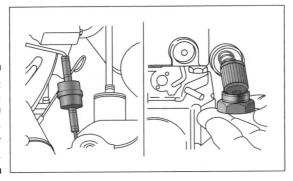

Figure 13-3:
An in-line filter *(left)* and an integral filter *(right)*.

Replacing fuel filters on carbureted engines

To replace your fuel filter, buy a new one at the auto supply store (on the basis of your vehicle's make, model, and year — plus type of carburetor, in some cases). Again, go for well-known brands at discount prices. Take a look at Figure 13-4, and buy new gear-type clamps, too, if yours look old, rusty, brittle, or are the wire-ring type. The filter and the new clamps should cost only a few dollars.

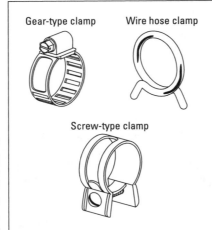

Figure 13-4:
Various types of hose clamps.

Here's how to replace the fuel filter on a vehicle with a carbureted engine:

1. **Unfasten the clamps that hold the filter in place.**

2. **Slip the old filter out and the new one in.**

There's usually an arrow on the filter to show you which way it goes, but take a good look at the way the old one is pointing before you remove it.

3. **Replace the clamps.**

   If you get the clamps on nice and tight (without cutting or shutting off circulation in the hose), you won't have any leaks or trouble.

Changing fuel filters on fuel-injected engines

This job is more complicated than replacing the fuel filter on a carbureted car. You need to disable the fuel pump to relieve the pressure on the lines and the fuel lines may be secured to the filter with clamps, threaded fittings, or special quick-connect fittings. If the lines have threaded fittings, you need a special flare-nut line wrench. If the lines have special quick-connect fittings, you may need to purchase special tools to disconnect them. Ask the clerk at an auto parts store or the service department at your dealership which type of filter your vehicle has. If doing this infrequent job requires purchasing special tools, it's probably cheaper to have it done by a technician. If not, the following instructions will guide you through the job:

1. **Relieve the pressure in the fuel line before disconnecting the line.**

   To do so, you have to disable the electric fuel pump *before* you start the engine. To disable the fuel pump, do the following:

   1. With the engine off, remove the fuel pump fuse from the fuse box (your owner's manual should show you where it is), following the instructions in Chapter 12.

   2. Make sure that the emergency brake is on and that the car is in Park or Neutral, and then start the engine. It won't run very long after you start it up, but the pressure in the lines will be reduced.

   3. Turn off the engine.

   With the fuel pump disabled, you're ready to disconnect the fuel lines from the filter.

2. **Look at the new filter before installing it.**

   You should see an arrow stamped on the filter that shows in which direction the fuel flows through it.

3. **Put the new filter on with the arrow facing *toward* the engine.**

4. **Replace the fuse for the fuel pump in the fuse box.**

5. **Make sure that the emergency brake is on and that the vehicle is in Park or Neutral, and then start the engine and check for leaks around the filter.**

Checking Your Fuel Pump

If your engine doesn't seem to be getting enough (or any) fuel, the problem can be caused by many reasons — a blocked fuel line or fuel filter or a faulty fuel pump, fuel injector, or carburetor. Before you allow anyone to talk you into replacing your fuel pump, check it yourself to see whether it really is the culprit. An easy way to do so is to unhook the hose that carries the fuel from the fuel pump to the fuel injectors or carburetor at the end farthest from the pump, and stick it in a clean can. Then, with the emergency brake on and the car in Park or Neutral, have someone use the ignition key to crank the engine while you see whether fuel comes out of the hose. If it does, your fuel pump is doing its job, and the trouble is farther up the line.

Be sure to shut off the engine before the fuel overflows the can, and be careful not to spill the gasoline — it can ignite easily.

If your fuel pump *does* need replacing, a rebuilt one is often as good as a new one, and a lot less expensive. If you're feeling adventurous, some manufacturers supply rebuild kits. You can take your pump apart with a screwdriver and rebuild it yourself, following the directions on the kit. If that idea doesn't enchant you, ask your service facility to locate and install a rebuilt fuel pump. It should be guaranteed for at least three months.

Checking and Servicing Your PCV Valve

If your engine has been idling roughly, you may want to check the PCV valve (shown in Figure 13-5) before you make other adjustments.

Figure 13-5:
A PCV valve.

When your vehicle is running, a certain amount of fuel and exhaust gases find their way past the piston rings and into the crankcase. Originally, these fumes were simply dispelled into the air through a tube, because if they were left to accumulate, they would foul the oil in the crankcase. Since the early 1960s, a method called *positive crankcase ventilation* (PCV) has been in general use. This is much more efficient and desirable: Instead of allowing exhaust fumes to pollute the air, the method reroutes them back to the intake manifold so that they can be reburned in the cylinders along with the rest of the fuel/air mixture. PCV also increases fuel economy, because the engine can run on the fuel in the exhaust fumes as well as on the regular fuel/air mixture.

Not every vehicle has a PCV valve, but most do. If yours has one, check the PCV valve every time you do a tune-up to make sure that it isn't clogged with sludge from the contaminants in the exhaust fumes. If it ceases to function, the fuel/air mixture that has been adjusted to take these fumes into consideration will go out of balance, and your vehicle won't operate as efficiently. Most car manufacturers suggest that you clean and replace PCV valves after about 12,000 miles of driving.

Locating your PCV valve

To locate your PCV valve, use these tips:

   ✔ **On fuel-injected engines,** the PCV valve may be located in the intake manifold or inside the valve cover (see Figure 13-6).

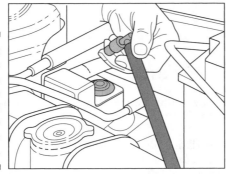
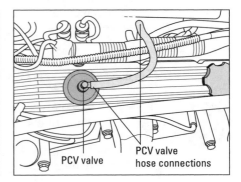

Figure 13-6: PCV valves located in the intake manifold and inside the valve cover.

PCV valve

PCV valve hose connections

   ✔ **If your engine is carbureted,** look for a ⅜-inch diameter hose that leads from the bottom area of the carburetor to the top of the valve cover or to the oil filler hole (see Figure 13-7). If your engine has *both,* you want the hose that does *not* lead to the oil filler hole.

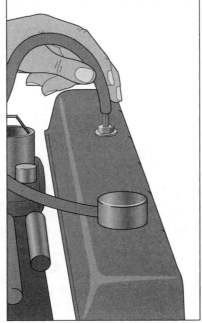

Figure 13-7:
A PCV valve located on the valve cover, with the hose that leads to it removed.

Some PCV valves screw into the base of the carburetor; some push into a rubber grommet in the valve cover at the end of the hose that leads from there to the carburetor; and still others screw or push into the oil filler cap or tube. If you can't find yours, consult your owner's manual or dealership.

Checking your PCV valve

There are several ways to check whether your PCV valve is functioning properly. Pick the one that seems easiest for you:

- ✔ **Method 1:** With the engine idling, pinch the hose hard to shut off any air that may be going through it, *but don't puncture the hose.* If the PCV valve is operating, the idle speed should drop perceptibly; you'll be able to *hear* the change.

- ✔ **Method 2:** Remove the PCV valve from the valve cover, with the hose still attached, and place your finger over the open end of it (see Figure 13-8). If it's working well, you will feel strong suction.

- ✔ **Method 3:** Remove the oil filler cap from the valve cover and place a stiff piece of paper over the opening. If your PCV valve is working properly, the paper should be sucked against the hole within seconds.

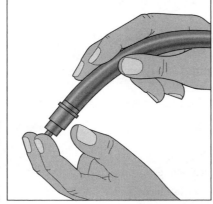

Figure 13-8:
One way to
check your
PCV valve.

Checking the PCV valve hose

While you have the PCV valve off, check the hose by removing it and blowing through it. If the hose is dry, brittle, soft and spongy, or full of sludge or hard deposits, replace it. When everything is shipshape once more, reassemble the hose and valve and put them back on.

Cleaning your PCV valve

If your PCV valve isn't working and you have the kind that comes apart, you can clean it yourself by taking it apart and immersing it in carburetor cleaner or PCV solvent, if you can get some cheaply. Lacquer thinner and fuel oil can also do the job. There should be no gummy deposits or discoloration on a clean valve. If your PCV valve must be replaced, buy a new one, remove the old valve, and insert the new one in its place.

Tuning Your Carburetor

Carburetors on 1970s and later vehicles require very few adjustments because of tighter emissions regulations. If you have a carburetor that's older than that (see Figure 13-9), you can do several things to keep it in tune:

✓ Adjust the idle speed screw to keep the vehicle idling at the proper number of revolutions per minute (rpm).

✓ Readjust the automatic choke if your vehicle doesn't start properly in the morning.

✔ Adjust the idle stop solenoid to prevent dieseling when you shut the engine off.

✔ Check and clean your PCV valve or, if necessary, replace it. (See the instructions earlier in this chapter.)

✔ Determine whether more radical surgery is in order.

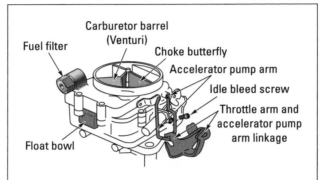

Figure 13-9:
A typical
carburetor.

You can find out how to do all these things in the following pages.

If your carburetor doesn't respond to any of the adjustments in this chapter and is still causing your vehicle to stall, accelerate improperly, burn enormous quantities of gasoline, and so on; *and* if the inside of your carburetor looks foul and gunky, you may want to have it rebuilt. I'd leave the job to a professional because the darn things have so many nuts, screws, washers, and gizmos that remembering where everything goes when it's time to reassemble the carburetor can be very difficult.

An easier — and probably cheaper — way to deal with the problem yourself is to *replace* the carburetor with a new or rebuilt model, following the instructions later in this chapter.

Checking your accelerator pump

If your vehicle hesitates when you step on the gas pedal, your accelerator pump may not be working properly. Here's how the accelerator pump causes your car to speed up when you step on the gas pedal: When you step on the pedal, a rod connecting the pedal to a little lever, called the *accelerator pump arm*, which is located on the outside of the carburetor, pushes on a little piston

inside the carburetor, which squirts a little extra fuel into the carburetor venturi. (See Figure 13-10.) That extra fuel creates a richer fuel/air mixture, which
provides the extra power for acceleration. If your accelerator pump isn't
working properly, your carburetor probably needs to be rebuilt or replaced.

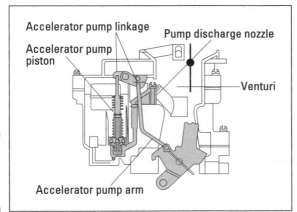

Figure 13-10:
Accelerator
pump
system.

To check your accelerator pump, with the engine off, remove the air cleaner
(following the instructions earlier in this chapter) so that you can see the carburetor. Then have someone step on the gas pedal while you watch the
accelerator pump arm to see how freely it moves. (The arm is the *little* lever,
not the big one; that's the throttle.) If the lever doesn't move, try pushing it
with your finger. If it still doesn't move, it may be caught on something. Try
bending it *a little* to clear the obstruction.

If the accelerator pump arm moves freely when someone steps on the gas
pedal, take a look down the carburetor barrel to see whether fuel is squirting
in when the accelerator pump arm moves. If there's no fuel action, the carburetor probably needs to be rebuilt (which involves taking it apart, cleaning it,
and replacing various parts) or replaced. If you need a new carburetor, you
may be just as well off getting a cheaper, rebuilt one. The sections "Installing
a New or Rebuilt Carburetor" and "What to Do When All Else Fails," later in
this chapter, provide your alternatives.

Adjusting your accelerator pump arm

Some accelerator pumps have more than one hole where the arm hooks up,
to enable you to adjust the arm. Adjusting for a shorter stroke (so that the
arm moves a shorter distance) gives you a leaner mixture of fuel and air; a
longer stroke gives you a richer one. If your accelerator pump arm is moving

when the gas pedal is stepped on, and fuel is squirting into the venturi when the arm is pushed, but you're still having acceleration problems, try adjusting the arm for a longer stroke.

Checking your idle speed

Follow these steps to check the speed at which your engine idles. If it's idling too fast or too slow, the next section has instructions for adjusting the mechanisms that control it:

1. **Hook a tach/dwell meter to the distributor.**

   See the section "Checking your distributor with a dwell meter" in Chapter 12 for details. (A plain tachometer will do, but a dwell meter without a tachometer is useless here.)

2. **Remove the air cleaner, following the instructions given earlier in this chapter.**

3. **With the emergency brake on and the car in Park or Neutral, start the car and let it run until the engine is hot and the butterfly valve on the choke is fully open.**

4. **When the engine is hot enough, turn the knob on the tach/dwell meter to "tach" and look on the rpm line of the meter to see at how many rpm your car is idling.**

5. **Check that rpm reading against the specifications in your owner's manual or a service manual for your vehicle's make, model, and year to see whether the car is idling at the proper rpm.**

   If your car isn't idling at the proper speed, you have to adjust your idle. Adjusting the idle is a simple matter, as explained in the following section.

Adjusting idle speed

Before you adjust your idle speed, you need to determine whether your vehicle has an idle speed screw or an idle air bleed screw, and whether it has an idle stop solenoid. If the figures in this section don't help you determine this (Figure 13-11 shows common idle speed screws, and Figure 13-12 shows an idle stop solenoid), either call and ask the service department at your dealership or consult a service manual for your vehicle's make, model, and year.

Adjusting idle speed screws

If your vehicle has an idle speed screw, follow these steps to adjust it:

1. **Check your owner's manual to see whether the idle speed should be adjusted with the air cleaner off or on the carburetor.**

   Most cars are adjusted with the air cleaner off. If there's a hose that goes from the carburetor to the air cleaner, plug the hose with a clean, lint-free rag after you remove the air cleaner.

2. **Adjust the idle.**

   If you have an idle speed screw (see Figure 13-11): Use a screwdriver to turn the screw until the needle on the tach/dwell meter rests on the proper number of rpm. Turning the screw _inward_ (clockwise) _increases_ idle speed; turning it _outward_ (counterclockwise) _decreases_ it.

   If you have an idle air bleed screw instead of an idle speed screw: Do exactly the same thing to adjust it. However, in this case, you turn the screw _clockwise_ to _decrease_ idle speed, and turn it _counterclockwise_ to _increase_ idle speed.

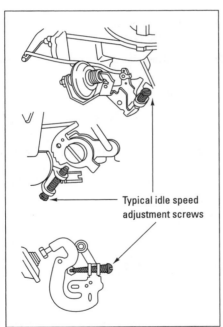

Typical idle speed
adjustment screws

Figure 13-11: Typical idle speed adjustment screws.

Adjusting an idle stop solenoid

If you have an idle stop solenoid (sometimes located on the outside of the carburetor, as shown on Figure 13-12), you'll probably find a tag somewhere under the hood of your vehicle that gives you special instructions for adjusting it.

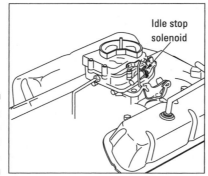

Idle stop
solenoid

Figure 13-12:
The idle
stop
solenoid.

If you can't find your instructions, and your owner's manual either isn't helpful or is too difficult to follow, and you've already hooked up your tach/dwell meter, then do the following:

1. **Adjust the nut on the end of the solenoid until your car is idling at the proper number of rpm (at least 700 rpm is usual).**

2. **Disconnect the little wire that runs from the end of the solenoid to whatever it leads to.**

   This causes your idle speed to drop.

3. **Adjust your idle speed screw or idle air bleed screw, following the instructions in the preceding section.**

   Your owner's manual usually indicates that this last adjustment is at a lower number of rpm. This is called *shutdown idle speed,* and it is the reduced speed that allows your engine to stop running when you shut off the ignition.

4. **Reconnect the little wire.**

Checking and adjusting the fuel/air mixture

The easy way to check whether the fuel/air mixture is too rich or too lean is to run your finger around the end of the inside of your tailpipe (when the engine is cold, please). If a black, *sooty* deposit comes off on your finger, your fuel/air mixture is too rich. If the deposit is *greasy* or *shiny,* you're burning oil. A vehicle that's running too lean runs poorly only when it's cold. In either case, you'll find instructions for adjusting the idle mixture screw(s) and the choke in the following sections. If the adjustments you make don't help, you'll have to seek professional service.

Adjusting the idle mixture screw(s)

If checking your fuel/air mixture shows that it needs to be adjusted or your engine isn't idling smoothly now that you've corrected its idle *speed,* the idle mixture screw (or screws) on your carburetor can do just that. (Figure 13-13 shows common locations for idle mixture screws.)

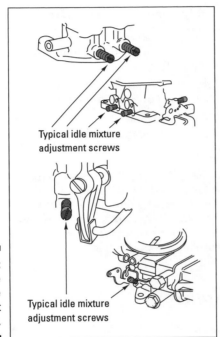

Typical idle mixture adjustment screws

Typical idle mixture adjustment screws

Figure 13-13:
Typical idle mixture adjustment screws.

Because of federal and state smog standards, on vehicles built since 1981 idle mixture screws have been covered by metal plugs or by plastic limiter caps, which either don't allow you to adjust the screws or limit adjustments to around a quarter of a turn. These limitations were added to keep you from adjusting for a too-rich mixture that would result in an increase in the exhaust emissions that pollute the air.

If your carburetor has limiter caps, leave them alone. The idle mixture screws were preset at the factory and are probably set properly. If you have problems that nothing else seems to cure, have a mechanic take a look.

If your engine has a single-barrel carburetor with no cap on the idle mixture screw, use your owner's manual or service manual to locate the screw, and then follow these steps to adjust the idle mixture screws.

Some engines are adjusted according to special instructions provided on a tag or decal under the hood. These tags can be almost anywhere, usually on the cylinder head cover or on the air cleaner lid or up front on the frame. If you have such a tag, follow the instructions on it instead of the following steps:

1. **With the car at idle speed, turn the idle mixture screw *inward* until the engine starts to falter. Then turn it back the other way, about half a turn.**

2. **If the engine is idling roughly, continue to turn the screw *outward* until the engine smoothes out.**

   If you turn the screw too far outward, the too-rich fuel/air mixture will cause the engine to run roughly again.

   If you use a tach/dwell meter, you'll know that the engine is properly set when it returns to the highest idle speed after its initial drop when you turned the screw inward.

   Two- and four-barrel carburetors have more than one screw. Adjust these screws one at a time.

On Tweety Bird, my 1967 Mustang, I adjusted the screws to make the mixture as lean as possible, to see how far I could cut down on fuel without affecting the smoothness of the idle. If you have an older model with adjustable screws, you may want to try the same thing. However, write down exactly how many times you turned the screw so that you can set it back the way it was if leaning the fuel/air mixture affects performance.

Checking your choke

If you have trouble getting your vehicle to start in the morning, the choke may not be working properly. If you want to see whether the choke on your vehicle is working, read the section about the choke in Chapter 6 to see where it's located and what it does, and then do the following:

1. **Take the air cleaner off some morning, *before* you start your engine.**

   See the earlier section "Removing Your Air Cleaner" for instructions.

2. **Look down the carburetor barrel at the choke, as shown in Figure 13-14.**

   Does the butterfly valve seem to be closed?

3. **If the butterfly valve isn't closed, step on the gas pedal a couple of times before you start the car; the valve should close.**

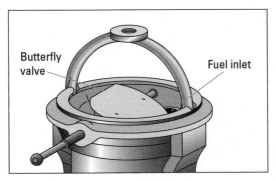

Figure 13-14:
When you look down the carburetor barrel, you can see the butterfly valve.

Butterfly valve

Fuel inlet

If your car has a *manual* choke (as opposed to an automatic choke), see whether the butterfly valve opens and closes when someone pushes the choke knob on the dashboard in and out.

Don't let anyone start or accelerate the car while you're looking down the carburetor. It could backfire.

4. **With the emergency brake on and the gearshift in Park or Neutral, start the engine and let it run for a few minutes.**

   By the time the car has warmed up, the butterfly should open so that you can see past it, down the barrel of the carburetor.

5. **If the butterfly valve refuses to open or close, try wiggling it with your finger.**

The valve may simply be stuck because of dirt or poor lubrication. If wiggling it with your finger doesn't work, squirt a little carburetor cleaner or automatic choke cleaner on the moving parts. Then wipe them dry and put a drop of oil on them. If this doesn't work, the next sections tell you how to adjust your choke properly.

Adjusting an automatic choke

Before you can adjust your choke, you need to know what type it is. Figure 13-15 shows a thermostatic spring choke, and Figure 13-17 shows a thermostatic coil choke. Check which one more closely resembles the one on your vehicle. If you're not sure, consult the choke specifications in your owner's manual. If the information isn't there, try a service manual for your vehicle's make, model, and year, or call the service department at the dealership and ask them what type of choke your vehicle has, and what the proper setting is. Then follow the instructions that pertain to your type of choke.

Adjusting a thermostatic spring choke

Many cars have a thermostatic spring choke (see Figure 13-15). Some are riveted in place and can only be overhauled by a mechanic, but if you have an older car and have trouble starting it in the morning, you may be able to adjust yours.

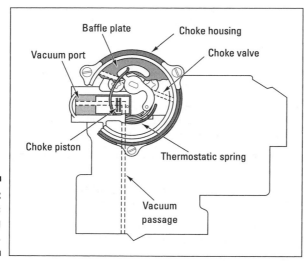

Figure 13-15:
Thermostatic
spring
choke.

Before you fiddle with the choke, check the specifications for your automatic choke and see whether it's properly set (if the proper notch on the carburetor housing is opposite the indicator on the plastic cap shown in Figure 13-16).

If the choke is properly set and the valve doesn't close, try adjusting the thermostatic spring choke to a richer setting. If the choke is *not* properly set, adjust it to the proper setting. To accomplish either of these tasks, follow these steps:

1. **Loosen the three screws that keep the plastic cap in place (see Figure 13-16).**

2. **Turn the cap until the notch on it lines up with the proper mark on the carburetor housing.**

   On the back of the cap are the words *Lean* and *Rich* with arrows to indicate direction (refer again to Figure 13-16). Your specifications may read "one notch Lean," in which case you turn the cap until the indicator lines up with the first mark on the Lean side of the carburetor housing.

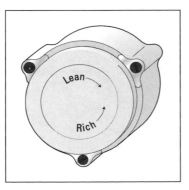

Figure 13-16:
The three screws you need to loosen when you adjust a thermostatic spring choke.

If your cap was already set at the specified mark, just turn the cap one notch to the richer side and see how that works the next morning.

3. If you car still doesn't start properly, try setting the cap one more notch richer.

These chokes are generally set on the lean side, so they often run better cold when set a notch richer. Never adjust more than one notch at a time.

4. When you're done, tighten down the three screws.

Adjusting a thermostatic coil choke

If you have a thermostatic coil choke (shown in Figure 13-17), it has a rod leading from the top of the carburetor near the butterfly valve to a small box mounted not far away, usually on top of the exhaust manifold.

Unless it's been tinkered with since the vehicle came from the factory, an automatic choke of this type stays set properly until it breaks down. If you think that your choke isn't working properly — either because the butterfly won't close when the car is cold or won't open when it warms up, or because you can't get the car started properly in the morning — get a new one for a couple of dollars. You can install it yourself if you want to.

Other types of automatic chokes exist, but these should be adjusted by a professional. If you have one of these and your choke doesn't seem to be working properly, ask your technician to look at it.

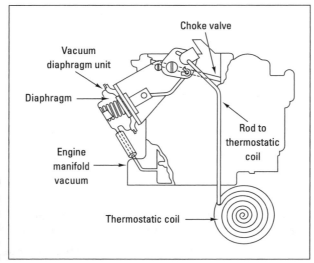

Figure 13-17:
The
thermostatic
coil choke.

Making Float Level Adjustments

If the float in your float bowl is set improperly, you may find that your vehicle hesitates or stalls when you accelerate, or it may be hard to start. Because the float level is preset, it would be incorrect only if someone had tampered with it since the carburetor was installed. If you suspect that this is your problem, then have a professional look at it. If the mechanic finds that the float level is correct, chances are that the tiny passages in the carburetor have become plugged with dirt. An overhaul (dismantling and cleaning your carburetor and resetting the float level to the manufacturer's specifications) can correct this problem, but it may be cheaper simply to replace the carburetor with a rebuilt one. You can find instructions for installing a new or rebuilt carburetor in the next section.

Installing a New or Rebuilt Carburetor

Why throw money away when you have inexpensive solutions to explore? Make sure that you have checked and properly adjusted all the gizmos mentioned previously in this chapter before you let anyone talk you into a new carburetor or any other expensive major repair.

If you're told that your carburetor needs to be replaced, get another opinion (without telling the second service facility that you've been to the first one). You can probably get a rebuilt carburetor for your vehicle at a much lower price than a new one would cost — they usually work just as well and should be guaranteed for 30 days. Ask whoever is going to do the work to find a rebuilt one, if possible. Or call an auto wrecker and provide the information in Step 1. Then either bring it to your mechanic or install it yourself, with the help of a knowledgeable friend or an auto shop instructor. It's easier than overhauling one!

Don't try this yourself unless you have someone at your elbow who has done it before.

To install a new or rebuilt carburetor, follow these steps:

1. **Go down to the local auto parts store or call an auto wrecker and ask for a rebuilt carburetor for your vehicle.**

   Give them the make, model, and year of the vehicle; the size of the engine; how many cylinders it has; and so on. If your carburetor still has a metal tag on it, bring the tag along; the tag has all the information that the salespeople need to know.

   Check out a couple of sources by telephone, using the Yellow Pages. Prices can differ drastically from one place to another. Ask for a *mechanic's discount,* because you're going to do the job yourself. (Who knows — you may get it!) Or ask whether they'll accept your old carburetor in exchange for a discount or core charge.

   Before you go any further, take a gander at the section "How to Take Anything Apart — and Get It Back Together Again" in Chapter 1. It will help you do this job with a minimum of hassle. Also, get yourself a couple of clean, lint-free rags and a few resealable plastic bags. You're going to need them.

2. **Detach the throttle arm and choke linkages (all the things that attach the moving parts of your old carburetor to other parts of your vehicle), and all the pipes, hoses, and other gizmos that connect your old carburetor to your vehicle.**

   Just detach the ends that join the carburetor. Leave the other ends attached to the car so that all you need to do is rehook them to your new carburetor.

   Be sure to remember, or draw, the way they were attached. If you think that you'll have trouble remembering in what order these things should be replaced, write little numbers on the drawing next to each thing you disconnect as you disconnect it.

4. **Remove the carburetor hold-down nuts that fasten the base of your old carburetor to the top of your engine, and lift the old carburetor out of your vehicle.**

There will be fuel in the float bowl of the old carburetor and in other parts of it, so handle it carefully and dispose of the old fuel before setting the old carburetor aside. If fuel spills out, wipe it up — and for heaven's sake, *don't smoke while you do this job!* Pour the fuel into a clean glass container and pour it back into your fuel tank. Don't forget to wash the container thoroughly before you use it again, or discard it! Put fuel-contaminated rags or sponges in a resealable plastic bag so that you can take it to a toxic waste recycling center, or ask your friendly mechanics to send it along when they dispose of their toxic stuff.

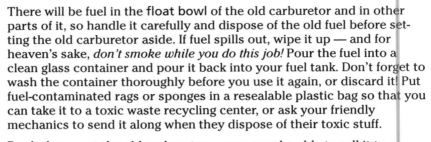

Don't throw out the old carburetor — you may be able to sell it to a place that can rebuild it and sell it again. Seal it up immediately in a plastic bag so that it doesn't leak fuel on anything.

4. **Compare the gasket from the new carburetor to the one under your old carburetor.**

When you get the carburetor, there will be a gasket with it. The gasket goes between the carburetor and the thing it sits on. The new gasket should be the same as the old gasket; if not, you have the wrong carburetor. I know this is a heck of a time to find this out, but at least you'll save yourself the trouble of installing the wrong carburetor!

5. **Remove the old gasket and clean the surfaces where the old gasket lay. If necessary, draw a picture so that you'll remember how it went.**

If the old gasket is stuck to the car, be sure to keep the pieces of the old gasket from falling down the intake manifold while you remove it. (You can stuff a clean, lint-free rag into the top of the hole while you get the junk off — just don't forget to remove the rag before you put on the new gasket!)

6. **Lay the new gasket in place, making sure that it goes on the same way the old one did.**

Never use anything to cement the new gasket in place. Just place it where it belongs. The weight of the carburetor holds it in place.

7. **Place the new carburetor on the gasket, and replace the carburetor hold-down nuts.**

Don't overtighten these — or any other bolts — you don't want to break them or crush the gasket. Have an experienced friend check it over when you're through, or ask your friendly auto mechanic to check it for you. It's impossible to *tell* someone how tight or loose to make a bolt; you have to *feel* it for yourself. And only experience can bring that sense of tightening something properly.

8. **Reattach the linkages, pipes, hoses, and so on in the *reverse* order in which you took them off.**

The idle mixture screws and idle speed screws on the new carburetor should be preset by the manufacturer. If you installed a rebuilt one and it doesn't function properly, you may have to adjust them yourself. You can find instructions on how to do so earlier in this chapter.

Have someone with experience check your work when you're through, *before* you head for the freeway.

Checking the Compression in Your Cylinders

If your vehicle has been running roughly or seems to be losing power, it's possible that there is a lack of pressure in one or more of the cylinders. If there isn't enough pressure, the fuel/air mixture won't explode. If there's less pressure than there should be, the mixture won't explode as efficiently. If one or more cylinders has a good deal less pressure than the others, the car won't run evenly.

Now, why wouldn't there be enough pressure? Because something is letting the pressure escape from the cylinder. Where can it go? Basically, two places: either out through one of the valve openings — because the valve is improperly adjusted or so worn that it doesn't close properly — or down past the rings on the piston. These rings prevent the pressure at the top of the cylinders from escaping and the oil that lubricates the engine from entering the cylinders. When the rings get worn, oil gets in and pressure gets out.

To determine whether this is the case in your vehicle, you need to check the compression in the cylinders. For this job, you need a compression gauge (see Figure 13-18). This device tests the amount of pressure that the piston exerts on the fuel/air mixture before the spark plug fires the mixture. Your compression gauge can tell you whether your cylinder is firing efficiently and whether your rings or valves are worn or out of adjustment. These gauges don't cost much, and using them doesn't take much time or effort. Some gauges screw into the spark plug opening, and others have to be held in place.

Checking compression is easier if you have someone to assist you, especially if your gauge needs to be held in place (see Figure 13-19).

Here's how to use a compression gauge:

1. **Unless you want to buy or borrow a remote starter switch, have someone sit in the driver's seat with the engine off, the gearshift in Park or Neutral, and the emergency brake on.**

2. **On non–General Motors vehicles, pull the big wire that leads to the coil from the center of the distributor cap and lean the metal connector against a metal surface *as far away from the spark plugs as possible*.**

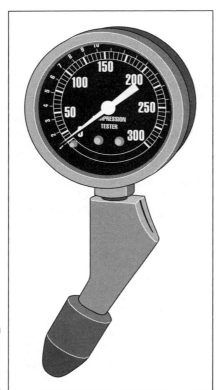

Figure 13-18:
A compres-
sion gauge.

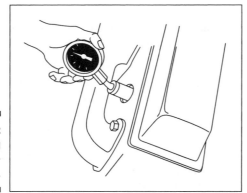

Figure 13-19:
Checking
compres-
sion.

Note that on some General Motors vehicles, the coil is built right into the distributor cap. There are two plugs on the side of the cap. One plug has three wires leading to it; the other has one wire. Pull this second plug and get it out of the way.

On vehicles with distributorless ignitions, disconnect the electrical connector at the ignition module. If you're not sure what to disconnect, ask a mechanic.

3. **Before you remove them, label the boots that connect each spark plug wire to a spark plug so that you can remember which plug each boot was attached to.**

If you get them mixed up, you can really screw up your engine.

4. **Remove all the spark plugs and lay them down in a clean place.**

Keep them in order or label them; you need to return each one to the cylinder it was in originally.

5. **Have your friend turn the ignition key until the engine cranks over about half a dozen times.**

The car won't run because the ignition has been disabled.

6. **If your car has a manual choke, open it. If it has an automatic choke, prop it open with a screwdriver.**

If you're not sure which type of choke you have, read the section "Checking and adjusting your choke" in this chapter.

7. **Insert the compression gauge into the hole in the engine where the first spark plug screwed into the cylinder (refer to Figure 3-19).**

8. **Ask your friend to crank the engine about five times.**

Be sure to keep the gauge plug firmly inserted while the engine is cranking.

9. **Look at the gauge and write down the reading. Then go on to the next cylinder.**

Don't forget to reset the gauge and crank the engine each time.

10. **After you've done this to each cylinder, look at the readings.**

The highest and lowest should not vary by more than 15 percent. If one or more of the cylinders reads way below the rest, use a trigger-type oil can to send a good squirt of motor oil down the spark plug opening, and retest the compression with the gauge. If the reading stays the same, the valves either are worn (and letting pressure escape) or are out of adjustment.

If the reading rises dramatically after you insert the oil, you probably need new rings on the piston in that cylinder. If the pressure is less than 100 psi, the cylinder definitely isn't mechanically sound.

After you know what's wrong, you have to decide whether the problem is worth correcting. If your vehicle was on its way out anyway, it's time to get rid of it. If it's otherwise in good shape, you may want to have the engine rebuilt or replaced with a new or remanufactured one.

11. **Replace each spark plug in the cylinder it came from.**

   Make sure that the ignition is off before you reconnect the spark plug wires, and be sure to put the correct spark plug wire boot back on each plug.

What to Do When All Else Fails

If you make all the adjustments in this chapter and your vehicle still isn't idling properly, isn't starting up in the morning without a hassle, or is hesitating or stalling at corners or when you accelerate sharply, then you need extra help. *But* you don't want to seek help like a lamb being led to the slaughter!

If you want to drive into a service facility like someone who knows the score and is prepared to judge intelligently whether the proposed remedies are necessary, here's what to do:

1. **Ask the people at your service facility to put your vehicle on their electronic analyzer and test your ignition system, in case that's the culprit.**

2. **Ask them to test your exhaust to see whether you're running on a fuel/air mixture that's too lean or too rich.**

3. **After they identify the problem, get a second opinion if the remedy they suggest is costly or seems overly drastic.**

   Also, remember to request a rebuilt carburetor if you need to have your old one replaced.

You've just finished some of the most difficult jobs in this book! If you've given your vehicle a complete tune-up (including both the ignition system, covered in Chapter 12, and the fuel system, covered in this chapter), everything else about caring for your car should be a breeze. Relax and enjoy yourself — you're practically a professional! And if you've "chickened out," take heart: The rest of this book has lots of things you can do to save money and keep your vehicle running well.

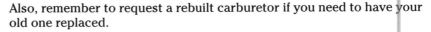

Chapter 14

Keeping Your Car from Getting Heartburn

• •

In This Chapter

▶ Dealing with overheating problems

▶ Checking and adding coolant and water to your cooling system

▶ Removing a radiator cap safely

▶ Installing and using a coolant recovery system

▶ Determining whether your coolant needs to be flushed and changed

▶ Flushing your cooling system and changing your coolant

▶ Finding and repairing leaks

▶ Replacing hoses and hose clamps

▶ Replacing a water pump

▶ Adjusting and replacing accessory belts

▶ Replacing a thermostat

▶ Considering other options to reduce chronic overheating

• •

*E*very vehicle has a cooling system to help it run efficiently and prevent it from overheating. Keeping it operating properly usually requires no work — just an occasional check or change of coolant and a watchful eye for leaks.

Chapter 8 takes a close look at the parts of the cooling system. If you haven't read that chapter, please review it before undertaking any of the work in this chapter.

This chapter discusses the things you can do to help your vehicle keep its cool under normal circumstances. It tells you how to prevent overheating by checking and replacing the liquid in the system, how to flush the system and change the coolant, and how to deal with other common causes of overheating: a malfunctioning radiator pressure cap or thermostat, deteriorated hoses, and coolant leaks.

Overcoming Overheating

The first sign of overheating is when the temperature gauge needle pushes its way into the ominous red zone, or the "Check Engine" or "Temperature" light on the dashboard glows a sinister scarlet. Left alone, the liquid in the radiator eventually boils over, and steam rolls out from under the hood.

If you ignore the problem, your vehicle eventually loses power, your engine grinds to a halt, and you end up with a giant repair bill. If you take action at the first indication of a problem, you can probably avoid this doomsday scenario. Even if you end up needing major repairs, at least you'll know that you explored all the cheaper options first.

Addressing occasional overheating

Almost every vehicle overheats occasionally. Usually, the cause of the problem is nothing more than being stuck in stop-and-go traffic on an excruciatingly hot day. If this happens to you while you're on the road, the section called "If Your Vehicle Overheats" in Chapter 21 tells you what to do.

Dealing with a chronic hothead

If your vehicle overheats often and constantly loses liquid, the problem may be caused by a leak — or leaks — in your cooling system (see "Finding and Repairing Coolant Leaks" later in this chapter). If your vehicle overheats in normal weather and traffic, you may need to replace the thermostat, adjust the fan belts, or check the water pump. You can deal with most of these problems cheaply and easily by following the instructions in later sections of this chapter.

Identifying other causes of overheating

Some overheating problems aren't related to the cooling system at all. Other circumstances that can cause a vehicle to overheat include lack of oil, a blown head gasket, and transmission problems. If the cooling system seems to be in good order after you check it and do the maintenance work in this chapter, investigate these possibilities:

✔ **Late timing:** If you haven't tuned and timed your engine recently, late timing may be causing it to overheat by making the spark plugs fire the fuel/air mixture *after* the piston moves back down from the top of its stroke. When the spark plugs fire too late to allow all the gases to burn properly, more heat burdens your cooling system. Late timing alone doesn't cause a car to overheat by more than a few degrees, but coupled with other problems, it can bring the engine temperature to a critical point. The remedy is simple: Just check your timing and adjust it by following the instructions in Chapter 12.

✔ **Plugged radiator:** Some radiators get so plugged up with rust, sediment, or small insects that even cleaning and flushing them doesn't get all the junk out. Because plugged passages cut down on the system's liquid circulation, the system can't cool efficiently. The remedy is to have a radiator specialist remove and steam clean the radiator.

✔ **Slipping fan belt:** Check the fan belt or accessory belt that drives the water pump to be sure that there's no more than about ½ inch of give. If the belt is looser than that, it may not be driving the pump properly, and that can impair circulation and overheat the cooling system. If your fan belt seems loose or very frayed, replace it according to the instructions in "Adjusting and Replacing Accessory Belts" later in this chapter.

✔ **Collapsing bottom radiator hose:** Occasionally, a bottom radiator hose begins to collapse under the vacuum that the water pump creates, and the impaired circulation causes overheating. Here's how to check the hose:

If your car starts to overheat, park safely and open the hood *without shutting off the engine*. Make sure that the car is in Park with the parking brake on. Then take a look at the bottom hose (be careful not to get your hair or clothing caught in the fan or the fan belt) and see whether the hose has collapsed. If it has, replace it. You can find instructions for replacing hoses later in this chapter.

✔ **Low oil level:** If you still can't find the cause of overheating, check your oil dipstick. A vehicle that's low on oil tends to overheat because the oil removes from 75 to 80 percent of the "waste heat" in your engine (in addition to doing its other job of cushioning the moving engine parts).

If you're 1 quart low in oil and your vehicle holds 5 quarts, the oil can carry away 20 percent less heat (the oil cools off in the crankcase). See Chapter 3 for instructions on checking the oil level and adding oil.

Under normal circumstances, you can prevent overheating by checking the level of liquid in the system and maintaining it properly. The next sections tell you how to do so.

Checking and Adding Liquid to Your Cooling System

One of the quickest, easiest, and least expensive tasks you can perform to keep your cooling system cool is to check the fluid level in the system and add water and coolant, if necessary. Before you attempt to do anything to your cooling system, be aware of two important safety rules:

> *Never remove the cap from a radiator when the engine is hot.*
>
> *Never add cold water to a hot engine!*

Removing a pressure cap safely

Before you can do anything involving your cooling system, you need to know how to remove the **pressure cap** safely. There's almost no reason to remove the pressure cap from the radiator or coolant recovery system reservoir while the engine is still warm. Because it's hard to tell just how hot things are inside the engine, follow these guidelines when removing a pressure cap:

Never **remove the cap from a radiator or reservoir when the engine is hot.** If your car overheats on the freeway, get to the side of the road, shut off the engine, and then wait 15 to 20 minutes for things to cool down. You can lift the hood to help the heat escape, *but leave the pressure cap alone.* Because adding cold water to a hot engine is automotive suicide, you have no reason to get the cap off until the engine cools down. *Keep your cool until your car regains its own!* Chapter 21 has more tips about overheating on the road.

To open the pressure cap safely, follow these steps:

1. **If your car has a safety pressure cap, lift the lever on the safety cap to allow the pressure to escape; then turn the cap counterclockwise to remove it.**

   To keep from burning your hand, place a cloth over the cap after you raise the lever (see Figure 14-1).

   If your car *doesn't* have a safety cap, place a cloth over the cap and turn it counterclockwise to its first stop.

   Turning to the first stop allows some of the pressure to escape, but if you see liquid or a great deal of steam escaping, retighten the cap and wait for things to cool down. If not, continue turning the cap counterclockwise to remove it.

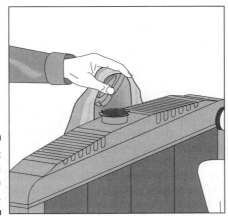

Figure 14-1:
Removing a
radiator cap
safely.

2. *Tilt* the cap as you remove it so that the opening points *away* from you (and anyone else nearby) — again, see Figure 14-1.

This way, if there's still enough heat and pressure to spray hot stuff around, it lands on the engine or inside the hood, where it can do no harm. *Be particularly sure to follow this procedure if you don't have a safety cap.*

Of course, if the engine is completely cold, you face no risk at all, so try to do routine peeking into your radiator in the morning before you warm up the car. Get into the habit of checking your coolant level at least once a month (as part of the under-the-hood check in Chapter 3).

Adding liquid to any type of cooling system

Some vehicles have coolant recovery systems, and others require you to add liquid directly to the radiator. The following cautions apply no matter which type of vehicle you have.

Never add cold water to a hot engine!

Adding cold water to an engine that's hot can crack the engine block because the hot metal contracts sharply when the cold water hits it. If you *must* add water to an engine that's still *warm,* always do so with the engine running. This way, the cold water joins the stream of hot water that's circulating through the system, rather than falling all at once into the system when you start the engine again.

Under normal conditions, a 50/50 mix of water and coolant is preferred for most vehicles. If the temperature is extremely hot or cold, a higher proportion of coolant/antifreeze may be necessary. (See "Determining whether your coolant needs changing" later in this chapter.)

Don't overfill the system!

If you do overfill the system, the extra liquid gets hot, expands, and flows out of the overflow pipe. Because coolant is toxic, it can harm animals, who love its sweet taste (see "Keeping coolant out of the mouths of babes and small animals" later in this chapter).

If you don't have coolant on hand and you just need to add a little liquid, plain old tap water will do. But try to maintain a good coolant level by adding a similar amount of straight coolant the next time you add liquid to the system.

Several types of coolant are on the market. If your vehicle has an aluminum engine, make sure that the coolant container specifies that it's safe for aluminum engines. If you have extended-life coolant in the system, only add extended-life coolant to it.

Checking and adding liquid to a coolant recovery system

If your vehicle *lacks* a coolant recovery system, installing one is a good idea (see the sidebar "Installing a coolant recovery kit" later in this chapter). Until then, skip this section and follow the instructions in the section "Checking and adding liquid to a radiator."

Most vehicles have a coolant recovery system that makes opening the radiator unnecessary. Figure 14-2 shows you what a coolant recovery system looks like.

Most cooling systems with coolant recovery systems are considered "sealed" because the safety pressure cap is on the recovery reservoir rather than on the radiator. On these systems, check the level of liquid, check whether the coolant needs changing, and add water and coolant by opening the cap on the reservoir rather than opening the cap on the radiator.

With a system of this type, if you have to open the cap on the radiator for any reason, make sure to fill the radiator to the top before replacing the cap. This "bleeds" the system by forcing any air that may have gotten into the system into the reservoir and out through its overflow pipe when the car heats up.

1. **Check the liquid level.**

   Look at the *outside* of the reservoir to see where the level of the liquid in it lies relative to the "Max" and "Min" lines embossed on the side. (Refer to Figure 14-2.)

Installing a coolant recovery kit

If you have an older vehicle that lacks a coolant recovery system, you can buy a coolant recovery kit and install it yourself. Installing such a kit is simple: You usually just attach the bracket that holds the plastic container to the frame of your vehicle under the hood so that the bottle sits slightly lower than the overflow pipe from your radiator. Then one of the hoses from the container is usually connected to the radiator overflow pipe. You then replace your original radiator cap with the cap that comes in the kit. And that's it!

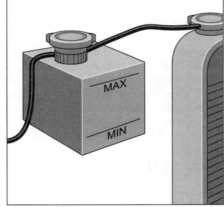

Figure 14-2:
A coolant recovery reservoir.

2. **If the level is low, add equal parts coolant and water to the reservoir.**

   Follow the instructions earlier in this chapter to remove the pressure cap on the reservoir safely and add equal parts coolant and water until the level reaches the "Max" line on the side of the container.

Checking and adding liquid to a radiator

If you don't have a coolant recovery system, you have to add liquid directly to the radiator. Here's how:

1. **Open the radiator cap, following the instructions in the preceding section.**

2. **Take a peek down the radiator fill hole to see how high the liquid level is inside.**

   If you're unsure about what the liquid level should be, just make sure that it covers the radiator tubes that are visible when you look down the hole or reaches to within a couple of inches below the cap.

3. **Add water and coolant as necessary.**

   Be sure to follow the tips given earlier in this chapter for adding liquid safely to any type of system.

4. **When you finish, replace the cap by screwing it on, clockwise. (If you have a safety pressure cap, push the lever down again.)**

Radiator safety caps cost very little, so if you don't have one, buy one! Almost every service station stocks them, but they're cheaper in auto supply stores. Check your owner's manual for the amount of pounds per square inch of pressure in your system and look for the proper number of psi on the new cap. These safety caps are well worth the money.

My own mysterious car problems were eliminated by a new safety cap. I got off with only $40 in unnecessary repairs before it occurred to me to change the cap. But I know someone who paid hundreds of dollars for radiator rebuilding and a new water pump, plus other unnecessary heartaches and expenses before discovering that all he needed was a new cap that cost less than $10!

Flushing Your System and Changing Your Coolant

You should do three things to keep your cooling system in good shape:

- ✔ Check for leaks.
- ✔ Replace worn hoses before they split.
- ✔ Flush the system and change the coolant at least once a year or every 20,000 miles, whichever comes first, unless your vehicle has the new extended-life coolant that lasts for five years.

I discuss the leak situation and how to change hoses later in this chapter. This section covers the proper way to flush your system and change the coolant in it.

There are pros and cons to doing this job yourself. The difference in cost is tremendous: If you do it yourself, all you need to buy is a jug of coolant, which sells for less than $10. A professional job can cost as much as five times more. Remember, not only does your service station expect to make a profit on the coolant (they bought it and stocked it, didn't they?), but they also charge for labor and recycling the coolant. In the "good old days," flushing the system and changing the coolant yourself was easy. You just hooked a garden hose to a little tee in the heater hose, opened the radiator cap, and let the coolant and water flow through the system until it was clean. However, times have changed.

Coolant is highly toxic, especially to small animals, who love its sweet taste. If a dog or cat drinks the stuff, it will probably die. To protect your pets and the animals in your area, see "Keeping coolant out of the mouths of babes and small animals" later in this chapter.

Because of the need to keep the used coolant out of the environment, flushing and changing coolant has become more complicated. Service stations in most states must either meet stringent disposal requirements or purchase a machine that cleans the coolant as it flows out of the vehicle, adds a shot of the chemicals that have been depleted by use, and puts the coolant back into your system. The good news is that this recycled coolant is every bit as good as the stuff you buy at the auto supply store.

Although professionals may have installed a flushing "tee" in one of the heater hoses, please don't try to use it yourself. Without the recycling process, the coolant that leaves your system endangers the environment. Instead, follow the instructions in "Flushing the system," later in this chapter, to do the job safely.

Determining whether your coolant needs changing

You should definitely change your coolant in two situations. The first is if you haven't changed it in a year or in the past 20,000 miles. The second is if your car has been losing liquid in the system for some time and overheats easily. If you've frequently added plain water to your cooling system, you've probably significantly lowered the proportion of coolant to less than half the required 50/50 mixture.

Even if neither of the above is true, you may still need a change. Here are a couple of things to consider to ascertain whether you should do the job:

 ✔ **The quality of the liquid in the system:** Unscrew the radiator cap and look in. Is the liquid inside clear? Or is stuff floating around in it? Does it look rusty? Coolant can be red in color, so don't mistake coolant for rust. (Rusty water has particles floating around in it.) Coolant can also be green, greenish yellow, or blue. The new extended-life coolant is orange and reminds me of orange Kool-Aid.

Don't mix extended-life coolant with any other type of coolant. Doing so shortens its life expectancy.

✔ **How frequently you add water and how much you add:** If you've been adding plain water every couple of days or weeks, your coolant protection level is probably low.

Checking is especially important if you haven't changed the coolant recently or if you've been adding a lot of plain water. Little testers (see Figure 14-3) that are cheap and easy to use tell you whether the protection level of the coolant in your system is adequate. The instructions are on the package. They usually involve drawing a bit of liquid out of the radiator into the tester. Then little balls or a float in the tester tell you whether you need to add coolant. While you're at it, also check the liquid in the tester or reservoir for rust. Or you can buy test strips that do the same thing by changing color.

✔ **What kind of climate you live in:** If the temperature gets very cold in the winter or very hot in the summer, be sure that you have enough coolant/antifreeze in your system before extreme weather sets in. In most areas, a 50/50 solution is recommended for year-round use. If the weather turns *extremely* cold, you can add a slightly higher proportion of antifreeze without hurting your cooling system.

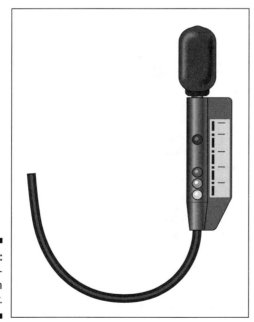

Figure 14-3:
A coolant-
protection
level tester.

Never exceed a 70/30 mixture of antifreeze to water. Freeze protection actually worsens with too much antifreeze and not enough water. If the weather is extremely hot, exceeding the recommended proportions of water and coolant won't help prevent your vehicle from overheating; it may actually cause it to overheat more rapidly.

✔ **How often you use your car's air conditioner:** Although the air conditioner does a fine job of keeping the interior of the car cool, it raises your engine's temperature. So be sure to have a 50/50 mix during the months when you use your air conditioner most often.

If, during a pre-summer check, you find that the level of coolant is very low or its protection level is weak, it may be a good time to flush your cooling system. If you don't flush the system then, make sure to check the level again at the end of autumn to see whether you should flush it before the cold weather sets in.

Determining how much coolant you need

You can consult your owner's manual, the back of the coolant jug, or the charts that coolant manufacturers supply for the number of quarts that your cooling system holds. Divide that number by two and buy that amount of coolant. Adding an equal amount of water gives you a 50/50 water/coolant mixture, which is fine for everything but extremely cold weather.

If your vehicle has an aluminum engine, make sure that the coolant is marked "Safe for use on aluminum engines." If the old coolant is extended-life coolant, replace it with the same stuff.

Flushing the system

If your owner's manual has instructions for draining the liquid from the cooling system, follow them. (This option is better than following the instructions in this section, because air is less likely to be trapped in the system after you finish the job.)

If you don't have a manual or it lacks such instructions, follow these steps to flush your cooling system and change the coolant without endangering the environment:

1. **Park the vehicle in a safe place, away from children and small animals.**

   Make sure that the engine is cold, the ignition is off, and the parking brake is on.

2. **Place a bucket that can hold at least 2 gallons under the drain valve at the bottom of the radiator.**

3. **Open the drain valve and allow the liquid to drain into the bucket.**

   Do *not* allow the liquid to drain onto the ground or into a storm drain or sewer.

4. **Close the drain valve.**

5. **Pour the liquid into a container with a tight-fitting lid, labeling it clearly as "antifreeze" or "coolant" and storing it away from kids and pets until you can dispose of it safely.**

6. **Open the radiator cap and fill the radiator with water.**

7. **Run the engine with the heater on high for about ten minutes.**

   Keep an eye on the temperature gauge to make sure that the engine doesn't overheat.

8. **Allow the engine to cool and then drain the water out of the system into the bucket again.**

   Pour that water into a closed container for disposal.

9. **Refill the system with water and coolant.**

   See "Determining how much coolant you need," earlier in this chapter. The liquid should reach the "Max" line on the coolant recovery reservoir. If it doesn't, add equal parts water and coolant until it does.

10. **Replace the pressure cap and run the engine with the heater on high until the temperature gauge reads in the normal range.**

    This step disperses the water and coolant evenly throughout the system.

11. **Shut off the engine and allow it to cool.**

12. **Clean up any spills, dispose of coolant and contaminated rags, and store the unused coolant safely.**

    (See "Keeping coolant out of the mouths of babes and small animals" later in this chapter.)

13. **After you've driven for a few days, check the liquid level again, adding equal parts water and coolant if the level is low.**

You can buy products for cleaning the cooling system during the flushing process. These products remove rust and sediment that flushing with plain water can't. If your cooling system has been cleaned regularly and you want to clean it yourself, buy a well-known brand and follow the instructions on the package carefully.

Be aware that using a cleaner on a system that has years of built-up rust and sediment can free so much of the stuff that you run the risk of clogging your radiator or thermostat, or possibly loosening the deposits that have prevented the system from leaking. If your vehicle's cooling system hasn't been cleaned for a couple of years, have the system flushed, cleaned, and refilled professionally.

Keeping coolant out of the mouths of babes and small animals

 Anyone who has raised kids through the crawling and toddling stages knows that they tend pick up the most revolting stuff off the ground and put it into their mouths. Because coolant looks and tastes good, a puddle of the stuff can be hazardous. That goes double for thirsty cats, dogs, and wildlife. Most coolant contains ethylene glycol, which is poisonous when swallowed. According to the EPA (Environmental Protection Agency), this chemical causes depression, followed by respiratory and cardiac failure, kidney damage, and brain damage.

 Although no coolant is completely nontoxic, some coolants on the market contain propylene glycol instead of ethylene glycol to reduce their toxicity. At least one (Prestone LowTox) has received the Seal of Approval from the ASPCA (American Society for the Prevention of Cruelty to Animals). However, even if you use this type of coolant, be sure to follow the instructions in this section.

Take these steps to protect your pets and small children from accidentally drinking coolant:

1. **Make it a habit to check under your vehicle for coolant leaks.**

   If you find a puddle of colored liquid below the under-the-hood area — and it isn't oily — it's probably coolant.

2. **Clean up the spill thoroughly.**

   Sop up *all* of it with kitty litter or absorbent rags, and then hose down the area thoroughly until the surface is clean.

3. **Dispose of the contaminated rags or kitty litter safely by placing it in a plastic bag, sealing it, and putting it in the trash.**

4. **Store unused coolant safely.**

   The jugs have childproof lids, but you should still store them out of reach and away from heat, which can release toxic fumes.

5. **Store used coolant safely until disposal.**

   Pour the used coolant into a container with a screw-on cap, label the container as "coolant" or "antifreeze," and place it well out of the reach of kids and pets until you can dispose of it, following the instructions in Step 6.

   Don't use containers that formerly contained beverages. They are too easily mistaken, and the sweet taste of the coolant can compound the error.

6. **Dispose of used coolant safely.**

   The most environmentally safe method is to take the coolant to a recycling center that handles toxic waste or bring it to a place that specifically recycles used coolant.

   Some auto supply stores accept used coolant as a public service. Call the major stores in your area to see whether they do so. If not, try a service station. They can either run the coolant through their recycling machine or include it in the batch they send out for safe disposal.

   The EPA (Environmental Protection Agency) advises, "If your home is connected to a sanitary or municipal sewer system, household quantities of antifreeze can be flushed down the drain *with plenty of water.*" The EPA warns that antifreeze can overwhelm the organisms in your septic system, damaging the system, and suggests that if your wastewater goes into a septic tank, you should dispose of antifreeze in a sanitary sewer system. The organization cautions, "Do not pour antifreeze into storm sewer openings, sinkholes, or abandoned wells."

   If your engine boils over, be sure to clean up the spill wherever you are. Wild animals are just as vulnerable to being poisoned by coolant as domestic pets are.

Finding Leaks in the Cooling System

In addition to keeping the water and coolant level where it needs to be, you can prevent trouble by keeping an eye out for leaks and replacing old or damaged hoses. Figure 14-4 shows the common trouble spots in the cooling system — the places where you should check for coolant leaks.

The following sections give you a few pointers on what types of coolant leaks to look for, and the section "Repairing Leaks in the Cooling System" tells you what to do if you find them.

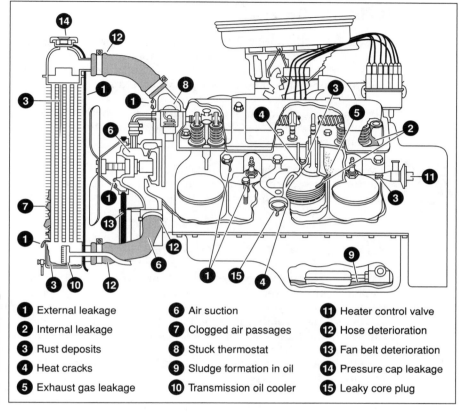

Figure 14-4:
Where to
check for
leaks and
other
problems.

1. External leakage
2. Internal leakage
3. Rust deposits
4. Heat cracks
5. Exhaust gas leakage

6. Air suction
7. Clogged air passages
8. Stuck thermostat
9. Sludge formation in oil
10. Transmission oil cooler

11. Heater control valve
12. Hose deterioration
13. Fan belt deterioration
14. Pressure cap leakage
15. Leaky core plug

Look under the car

Look under your vehicle in the morning to see whether any liquid is on the
ground under it. If you see liquid, stick your finger in it and smell it. If it's
coolant (green, red, blue, orange, or rust colored), look around the parts of
the car that are over the puddle and feel around for wetness.

If you're not sure what the stuff that's leaking out of your vehicle is, see
Chapter 20 for an easy way to locate, troubleshoot, and deal with leaks of all
types, including oil, transmission fluid, and brake fluid.

Check the radiator

Look around your radiator for whitish deposits or rust-colored stains. These indicate old leaks that have dried. They may not be all that old; water tends to evaporate quickly on a hot radiator. If you find any, the "Radiator leaks" section later in this chapter tells you what to do.

Also check the front end of the radiator to see whether the surface is befouled with dirt, leaves, and bugs. If so, remove them with a brush and a garden hose.

If your radiator catches a lot of debris, you can attach a piece of nylon window screen over the front surface with twist-ties to trap the stuff and keep it from getting stuck between the radiator fins.

Check the radiator cap

If you don't have a safety **pressure cap**, or if your vehicle overheats easily, the cheapest possible remedy is to buy a new safety cap or replace the rubber **gasket** in the cap you have. If you aren't sure, ask a mechanic to pressure-test your cap to see whether it's functioning properly. If you need a new one, give the salesperson the make, model, and year of your vehicle and check the pressure limits (psi) on the new cap against your owner's manual to make sure that you're buying the proper cap for the amount of pressure in your cooling system.

Never let a service station you don't normally frequent hook you into buying a new radiator cap unless you make them pressure-test your old cap. You may want to have them test the new cap, as well. I've been sold a faulty new cap to replace a faulty old one!

Check the hoses

Regularly check all the hoses under the hood of your vehicle, whether or not you've been having trouble. For instant panic, there's nothing like having a hose burst while you're driving. If it's a radiator hose, the resulting shower of steam is frightening at best and dangerous at worst. If a vacuum hose goes, the sudden loss of vacuum can stop your car in the midst of traffic. Checking your hoses and replacing the funky ones *before* they leak can save your nerves and your pocketbook in the long run.

If you find a hose that's soft and squishy, bulgy, hard or brittle, cracked, leaking, or marked with a whitish deposit where stuff has leaked and dried, replace it immediately, *before* it breaks. I show you how to do that in the section "Leaky hoses" later in this chapter.

If you find a hose that is collapsed when the engine is cold but springs back when you remove the radiator pressure cap, the cap or coolant recovery system — not the hose — is at fault.

While you're at it, check the hose clamps that secure the hoses and tighten any that appear loose. Replace those that are rusty, corroded, or impossible to remove without special tools with screw-type hose clamps (see "Buying hose clamps" later in this chapter).

Repairing Leaks in the Cooling System

When you find a leak, you must decide whether you can handle it yourself or whether you must see a professional. The following sections give you a few pointers to help you decide.

Radiator leaks

If the radiator is leaking badly, see a reliable radiator repair shop (doctors aren't the only specialists, you know). Most service stations just remove the radiator and send it to radiator specialists, so you may as well go directly to the specialist yourself and discuss the matter in person. If you're on good terms with your local garage, the mechanics there may be willing to steer you to a good radiator shop.

A word about sealer

If you find a leak in your radiator or engine block — and if the leak is just a small one (a couple of drops a day, with no need to add water more frequently than once a week) — you may want to try a sealer, or *stop-leak,* as it's sometimes called, before you head for a repair shop.

You add sealer to the liquid in your cooling system. It circulates around with the water and coolant, and when it finds a hole where a leak is occurring, it plugs it up.

You can purchase several kinds of sealers. The trick is to choose the one that does the best job without gumming up the cooling system. Ask for advice at the auto supply store. It's especially important that the sealer be compatible with your coolant (the label should tell you). Sealers are usually added through the radiator fill hole. Some coolants have a sealer built in, but these are rarely strong enough to deal with established leaks. If you try a sealer and the leaks recur in a couple of days, get professional help.

On the other hand, if the leaks occur in any of the hoses, replacing the hoses yourself is quite simple.

At the radiator shop, ask the radiator specialists what they intend to do and request a written estimate *before* they do the work. If the estimate seems very high, call another radiator shop (use the Yellow Pages), tell them what needs to be done, and ask them for an estimate.

Leaky hoses

If you followed the instructions in "Check the hoses" earlier in this chapter and found one that's leaking or deteriorated, replacing it is usually pretty easy and inexpensive, with two caveats:

- ✔ **Make sure that both ends of the hose are accessible:** Some heater hoses disappear through the firewall and under the dashboard. I'd much rather pay a mechanic than hang upside down in a cramped space until I can locate and replace one of these hoses.

- ✔ **Never attempt to replace a hose connected to your air conditioner:** Air conditioners and their hoses contain refrigerant under pressure that can blind you. If you have *any* problems with your air conditioner or its hoses, seek professional help.

Buying the right hose

So much for the scary stuff. Before you can replace a hose, you need to go to an auto supply store and buy the proper type, diameter, and length for your vehicle.

If possible, check the new hose that you buy against your old hose before removing the old one from the radiator. If the hose does not seem to be the same size as your old one, take it back. If you have another way of getting to the auto supply store, just remove the hose, following the instructions later in this section, and take it with you so that the auto supply store can match it.

If you must drive your car, here's how find the right hose without a sample on hand:

- ✔ **If it's a *top* radiator hose:** *Don't* get a radiator hose that has wire inside it. Radiator hoses have to bend to fit properly between the radiator and whatever they lead to. Some hoses are straight tubes, with wire coiled inside the rubber casing. These are called *universal* hoses; they're designed to bend to fit many cars. Often, the wire breaks or works its way through the top covering of the hose, causing the hose to leak. The kind of hose to look for is called a *preformed* hose, shown in Figure 14-5, which is made with the proper bend already in it and no wire inside the rubber.

Figure 14-5:
A preformed radiator hose.

The hose should be squeezable — another reason that you don't want a top radiator hose with wire inside. This way, if you have problems with your cooling system, you can squeeze the hose to see whether the system is operating under pressure. A dangerously pressurized hose that's hard to squeeze warns you not to remove the radiator cap until the car cools down and the pressure is reduced.

✔ **If it's a *bottom* radiator hose:** The hose *must* have a wire coil inside it to help it keep its shape and withstand the vacuum caused by the water pump drawing water out of the radiator. In this case, look for a hose with a wire coil insert inside it (see Figure 14-6).

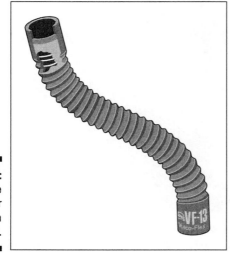

Figure 14-6:
A flexible radiator hose with a wire insert.

✔ **If it's any other kind of hose:** Either drag the salesperson out to the parking lot to see which hose it is, or provide all the following information to help the person determine the type and size of the hose you need:

- **The make, model, and year of your vehicle:** The supply store may also need to know the size and type of your engine and whether the vehicle has air-conditioning.

    Make a photocopy of the Specifications Record at the back of this book for each of your vehicles and enter the following information on it. Then take it to the auto supply store whenever you have to buy parts.

- **The *type* of hose, if you know it:** For example, a heater hose or vacuum hose.

- **What it *connects* to:** For example, the hose that runs between the carburetor and the fuel pump.

- **The diameter, color, and length of the hose:** Most hoses are sold by their *inside* diameter (see Figure 14-7), so you may have to disconnect one end of the hose, measure its inside diameter, and reconnect it in order to drive to the store.

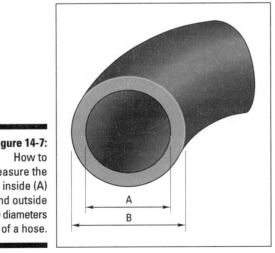

Figure 14-7:
How to measure the inside (A) and outside (B) diameters of a hose.

Buying and replacing hose clamps

Don't forget to buy new hose clamps. They should be large enough to fit the *outside* diameter of the hose.

Clamps are so inexpensive that you should make it a habit to replace them whenever you change a hose. If you are changing a hose that was secured with *wire* hose clamps or *screw*-type clamps, replace them with *gear*-type clamps.

Figure 14-8 shows all three types of clamps. Here's how to deal with each kind:

- **Wire hose clamps:** I hate these clamps. To deal with them, you need a special tool called *wire hose clamp pliers* that has a slit inside each of its jaws for gripping the ends of the clamps. Instead of buying one, either find something to pinch the wire ends together so that you can slip them off the hose, or bust them loose any way you can — use a saw, if necessary; you're going to throw them out anyway.

- **Screw-type clamps:** These clamps don't loosen easily, so they're often found on radiator hoses and the like to keep them in place. Unscrew the screw and remove it. Then slip your screwdriver under the clamp and loosen it. To avoid the hassle of reinserting the screw, replace with *gear-type clamps*.

- **Gear-type clamps:** These clamps are my favorites. Just use a screwdriver to turn the screw counterclockwise to loosen the clamp, slip the clamp over the hose, slip the end of the new hose in place, and turn the screw clockwise to tighten the clamp. Easy!

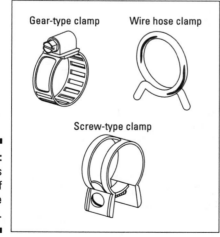

Figure 14-8:
Various types of hose clamps.

It's impossible to tell someone in a book how tight or loose a clamp should be. If the clamp is so tight that it appears to be cutting into the hose, loosen it. If you can hear or see air or liquid escaping from the ends of the hose, the clamp should be tighter. Give the hose a tug to see whether it's secure, and check it again after you've run the engine to make sure that it isn't leaking.

Replacing hoses

The basic process of changing a hose is quite simple (see Figure 14-9), but there are differences depending on the type of hose you're replacing:

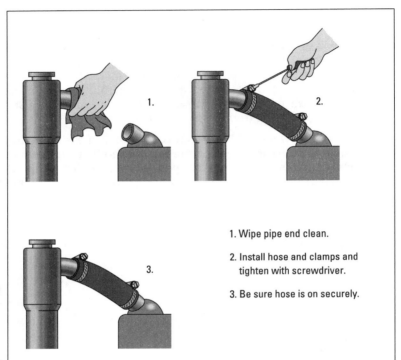

1. Wipe pipe end clean.

2. Install hose and clamps and tighten with screwdriver.

3. Be sure hose is on securely.

Figure 14-9: How to install a hose.

✔ **If the hose is a vacuum hose:** You'll find literally *nothing* in it. Just loosen the clamps, remove the hose, slide the new clamps on the new hose, slip the ends of the hose over whatever they connect to, and tighten the clamps.

✔ **If the hose is a fuel hose:** When the engine is shut off, most of the fuel flows back to the fuel tank. So you need only to stick the first end of the hose you remove into a *clean* can and allow whatever fuel remains in the hose to drain into it. When you finish the job, pour the fuel in the can back into your gas tank. (If you've managed to contaminate the fuel, put it into a container with a tight-fitting lid and take it to a toxic waste disposal center.)

Obviously, you're *not* going to smoke while you do this job! Also, if any fuel leaks onto the ground, clean it up thoroughly and dispose of the rags immediately so that they won't be a fire hazard.

✔ **If the hose contains liquid under pressure:** To prevent leaks, some manuals suggest putting a water-resistant sealant on the ends of the fittings to which the hose connects. Because these sealants tend to make the hoses difficult to remove when you need to replace them again, I suggest that you try it without sealant first. In most cases, if the hose is the right one and the clamps are on tight enough, you should be able to get by without it. If the hose leaks, you can always go back and use the sealant as recommended.

✔ **If the hose is a radiator or heater hose:** You'll need a bucket or pan that holds at least 2 gallons of liquid to catch the coolant and water that will run out of the system.

Never allow coolant to drain onto the ground. If you don't know why, see "Keeping coolant out of the mouths of babes and small animals" earlier in this chapter.

If you haven't flushed your cooling system and replaced the coolant in the past year, do so at the same time you replace the hose. (See "Flushing Your System and Changing Your Coolant" earlier in this chapter for instructions.)

Some newer engines have cooling systems that need to be bled (see Step 9 in the following list). If your engine falls in this category, the cooling system will contain special bleeder screws. If you're not sure what type of system your vehicle has, check the owner's manual or ask a mechanic *before* you undertake this job.

Now follow these steps:

1. **Remove the radiator cap and place the bucket or drain pan under the radiator drain valve (called the *petcock*).**

2. **Open the drain valve, allow the coolant to drain into the container, and then close the petcock.**

3. **Remove the clamps at both ends of the hose.**

   As I say in "Buying and replacing hose clamps" earlier in this chapter, you're going to replace those clamps, so cut them off if necessary. (If you haven't read that section, do so before going any further.)

4. **Carefully twist the hose to remove it and use the container to catch the liquid that drains from it.**

   Be gentle. If you're not careful, you could damage the radiator.

5. **Clean the fittings that the new hose will attach to and install new clamps over the hose (refer to Figure 14-9).**

6. **Install the new hose, attaching and clamping one end in place before you tackle the other end.**

   Make sure that the hose won't interfere with any moving parts and that the clamps are tight. (The section "Buying and replacing hose clamps" tells you how to install them.)

7. **If the coolant that you drained is fairly new and your container was clean, pour the liquid back into the system; otherwise, refill the system with a 50/50 mix of fresh coolant and water.**

   If you're replacing the coolant, see "Keeping coolant out of the mouths of babes and small animals" for instructions on disposing of it safely.

8. **Start the engine and add more water and coolant as the level in the radiator drops.**

   Make sure that the **parking brake** is on and that the car is in Neutral or Park before you start it up.

   Don't fill the radiator to the top of the neck until the thermostat opens. When you see coolant passing through the radiator tubes and the upper hose is hot, you know that the thermostat has opened. Then it's okay to top off the radiator.

9. **Replace the radiator cap.**

   If your engine is the type that needs to be bled, do so now, following the instructions in the owner's manual or service manual for your vehicle.

10. **Run the engine and double-check that the clamps are nice and tight so that no liquid leaks out.**

Leaks in the engine-block core plugs

On the sides of the engine block are little circular depressions called core plugs, or *freeze plugs*. (Refer to Figure 14-4.) These plug the holes where the sand was removed when the engine block was cast. If you see leaks or rusty streaks leading away from the core plugs on your engine block, or signs that leaks from them have dried, and you've been losing liquid lately, you may need to have the core plugs replaced. Your best bet is to seek professional help on this one. If replacing them is a high-ticket item, get a second opinion.

Internal leaks

Sometimes a leak right under the cylinder head can be the result of an ill-fitting gasket or the fact that the bolts that hold the cylinder head on the engine block are too loose or too tight. If you try to tighten these bolts yourself, you may damage the gasket, so the best thing to do is to get professional help here. If a mechanic only has to tighten the bolts, the cost is minimal.

Even if the gasket needs replacing and you can't do the job yourself, you're still ahead if you go to a professional with a good idea of what's wrong and what it'll take to correct the problem. (Don't *tell* the technician what to do; *ask* whether it would be wise to try tightening the bolts instead of replacing the gasket immediately.)

With today's aluminum cylinder heads, it's quite possible that your cylinder head may have small cracks that are allowing coolant to leak internally. If this is the case, usually you'll notice thick, white smoke from the **tailpipe** and/or engine oil that looks like a mocha milkshake. Also, vehicles with **automatic transmissions** have a transmission cooler inside the radiator that can leak. When it leaks, coolant mixes with the **transmission fluid**, making your transmission fluid look like a strawberry milkshake. Both problems require professional help.

Leaky water pump

Often, a **water pump** that's about to break down sends out noisy warning signals and then starts to leak before it goes completely. You can check your pump either by shaking the **fan belt** pulley — *when the engine is shut off* — to make the pump rattle, or by removing the fan belt that drives the water pump, and running the engine to see whether the noise stops. If it does, the water pump is the noisy culprit.

On some **overhead cam** engines, the water pump is behind the timing cover and is driven by the **timing belt**, making inspection difficult. Leave those to a professional.

If the pump is leaking in the front where it rotates with the belt, you must replace it (the next section tells you how). If the leak is around the **gasket** that lies between the water pump and the engine, you may be able to stop it by tightening the bolts that hold the water pump in place. If tightening the bolts doesn't do the job, then you probably need a new pump.

Replacing a water pump is a lot easier than fixing one. If a **rebuilt** or remanufactured pump is available for your vehicle, you may be able to get one for about half the price of a new one. Be sure to ask for a 90-day written **guarantee**. Because you have to pay labor charges to have the pump installed by a mechanic, if you replace yours yourself, you're still way ahead of the deal whether you buy a rebuilt pump or a new one.

If the work seems like too much of a challenge, by all means have a professional do it for you. But call around for prices on a rebuilt water pump first, and bring the rebuilt pump to the mechanic. Make sure that the pump is designed for your vehicle's make, model, and year, comes with a gasket that matches the old one, and has at least a three-month warranty.

If you want to do the job yourself, follow these steps:

1. **Remove the radiator pressure cap and place a clean 2- or 3-gallon container under the radiator.**

2. **Open the drain valve (petcock) on your radiator and then let the rest of the stuff drain out when you remove the pump.**

   All the fluid doesn't have to go, but most of it will.

3. **Remove the fan (if applicable) and the fan belts by following the instructions later in this chapter.**

4. **Disconnect the hoses that lead to and from the pump.**

   Consult the sections on hoses and hose clamps earlier in this chapter. If the hose clamps look funky or brittle, replace them with new ones of the gear type shown earlier in Figure 14-8.

5. **Remove any brackets or components that are blocking access to the water pump, and unscrew the bolts that hold the water pump in place.**

   Be sure to lay down everything you've removed in the order in which you removed it, with each part facing the same direction as it was on the car. This way, you can put everything back in reverse order, with no guessing about which end was up or which bolt went where. Chapter 1 has instructions for taking anything apart and getting it back together again.

6. **Remove the pump and its gasket.**

   Scrape the spot clean and finish off the job with some sandpaper. Use an adhesive/sealant to attach the new gasket to the water pump. Allow the sealant to dry before installing the pump.

7. **Replace the pump, bolts, hoses, fan, and fan belt, and then fill the system with a 50/50 mixture of water and coolant.**

   If the liquid you drained from the system was clean, and you changed the coolant less than a year ago, you can reuse it. If not, save yourself money and labor by flushing the system at the same time, following the instructions earlier in this chapter.

8. **Replace the radiator cap and bleed the air out of the system, if necessary.**

   Your owner's manual should tell you whether bleeding a system is necessary, and how to do so.

9. **Run the engine while you check for leaks.**

Pressure-testing the cooling system

If you can't locate the source of a leak and your vehicle is losing liquid from the cooling system on a regular basis, drive to your service station and ask the attendants to test the pressure in your cooling system. They'll probably use a cooling system pressure tester to do so. The tool is inexpensive, and the test involves very little time or labor, so a friendly technician may do the test for nothing. While you're at it, have the technician pressure-test the radiator pressure cap as well.

If you have an old vehicle that hasn't had its cooling system serviced or rebuilt in a long time, pressure-testing the system may dislodge the deposits that are sealing the weak spots, causing the system to leak. Ask the technician whether testing the system is worth the risk.

Adjusting and Replacing Accessory Belts

Chapter 3 tells you how to check accessory belts. Whether or not you can adjust or replace a belt yourself depends on the type of belt(s) you have.

Serpentine multi-accessory belts

On most modern vehicles, a single, long, flat belt called a serpentine multi-accessory drive belt (see Figure 14-10) drives all the engine accessories. This belt winds its way around every accessory pulley, and on the way winds tightly around a "tensioner" pulley that keeps the belt to the correct tension. In cases where it is possible to adjust the tensioner, you usually find something that indicates the correct tension.

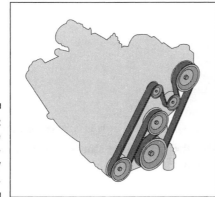

Figure 14-10: Serpentine multi-accessory drive belt.

Figuring out whether a belt is at the right tension isn't easy just by looking at it, but if the belt is loose, you'll hear squeaky noises when you accelerate sharply. (With the hood up and the emergency brake on, have a friend accelerate the engine while you listen. Be sure to keep your hair and clothing away from the belt.) If the belt squeaks, have a professional replace both the belt and the tensioner because, in many cases, radiators and air conditioning condensers may have to be removed to allow access to the belt, and it may be difficult to remove it and insert a new one.

Other accessory belts

If you find that you need to adjust or tighten an accessory belt that drives only one component, follow the instructions in this section.

Adjusting accessory belts

1. **Determine which belt is loose and what component (alternator, air conditioning compressor, power steering pump, or idler pulley) must be loosened to tighten the tension on that belt.**

2. **Loosen the nuts or bolts that secure the part that the loose belt goes around.**

   These are called either pivot bolts, because they allow the part to pivot back and forth, or securing nuts, because they keep the part in place. (I guess it's a matter of perspective.)

   Figure 14-11 shows the alternator pivot bolt being loosened. Look for a similar bolt attached to the part driven by the belt you're adjusting.

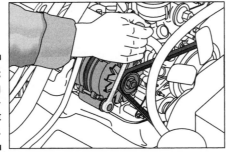

Figure 14-11:
Loosening the alterna-tor pivot bolt.

3. **Carefully pull back that part so that the belt is drawn tighter.**

4. **Tighten the nut or bolt with the adjustable slot first, followed by the pivot nut or securing bolt (see Figure 14-12).**

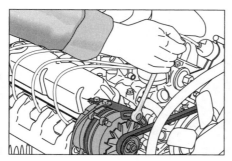

Figure 14-12:
Tightening
the adjust-
ment bolt.

5. **Check the belt after about 100 miles of driving to see whether it has loosened again.**

Replacing accessory belts

To replace a belt that drives a single component, go to the auto parts store with the year, make, and model of your car and buy the belt you need. Take the old belt with you if you can. The new one should look exactly like it. Then follow these instructions:

1. **Loosen the part driven by the belt by loosening the pivot bolt or securing nut (refer to Figure 14-11).**

2. **Loosen the adjustment bolt or securing nut (refer to Figure 14-12).**

3. **To loosen the belt, move the part by grasping the belt and pulling sharply upward (see Figure 14-13).**

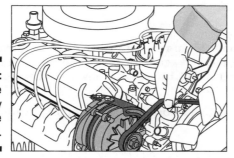

Figure 14-13:
Move the
part by
pulling the
belt upward.

If the belt is broken or missing, use a hammer handle to move the part that the belt needs to go around.

Use the hammer handle carefully to avoid applying pressure to parts that could be damaged.

4. **Remove the old belt by slipping it off the pulleys (see Figure 14-14).**

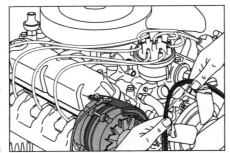

Figure 14-14:
Remove the
old belt.

To install the new belt, reverse the process.

5. **Pull the part by hand until the belt is snug; then use a hammer handle to apply leverage until the belt has less than ½ inch of "play." Tighten the adjustment bolt or securing nut (see Figure 14-15). Tighten the pivot bolt or securing nut (refer to Figure 14-11).**

Figure 14-15:
Tightening
the adjust-
ment bolt.

6. **Run the engine for about 15 minutes at varying speeds, turn the engine off, and check the belt again for the proper amount of tension (see Figure 14-16). After about 100 miles of driving, check the belt again.**

New belts stretch. If a belt has more than ½ inch of play, readjust the tension.

All the belt-driven accessories on your vehicle have similar methods of belt adjustment, so follow the procedure described above for all of them. If you find that one belt needs replacement and you have to remove and replace others to get to the defective one, replacing them all with new belts is a good idea.

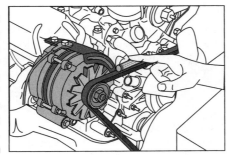

Figure 14-16:
Check the belt after running the engine for 15 minutes and again at 100 miles.

Keep old belts or spare belts in the trunk of your car for emergencies. If replacing one yourself doesn't seem worth the effort, many service stations can adjust or replace belts, but they may not have the specific belt you need.

Replacing Your Thermostat

If your vehicle has been overheating or doesn't warm up properly, and none of the things in the preceding section is the problem, you may need to replace your thermostat. This little gizmo simply stays closed and keeps the liquid in the engine block until the engine heats up. Although a simple device, it can malfunction.

If the thermostat sticks in the *open* position, it doesn't keep the liquid in the engine long enough, and you have trouble getting your car warmed up. If the thermostat sticks *shut,* the liquid isn't allowed to get to the radiator, and overheating results.

Because replacing the thermostat is quite simple and thermostats are quite inexpensive, you may want to try this task before you take more drastic measures:

1. **Locate your thermostat, if you haven't already done so.**

   Most thermostats are located where the top radiator hose joins the engine, so these steps deal with this type. If your thermostat is in the bottom radiator hose, the principle is the same.

2. **Get a new one.**

   Supply the usual information (vehicle make, model, year, and so on) to the auto supply store. If you've done other work on your vehicle, you should be an old hand by now.

3. **Unscrew the clamp that holds the end of the radiator hose where your thermostat is located.**

4. Pull off the hose.

Some liquid will escape, so have a *clean* 2-gallon container handy to catch it, and return it to the radiator when you finish the job. Or you can consider this a golden opportunity to flush your cooling system and change the coolant by following the instructions earlier in this chapter.

5. Remove the bolts that hold the thermostat housing in place, and lift out the old thermostat.

There's a gasket around it — get that off, too. Scrape off any pieces of gasket that may be stuck, but be sure not to let these pieces fall into the hole.

6. Lay the new gasket in place.

If the new gasket doesn't match the old one, you probably have the wrong thermostat.

7. Drop in the new thermostat, making sure to place the spring side *down* (see Figure 14-17); then replace the bolts.

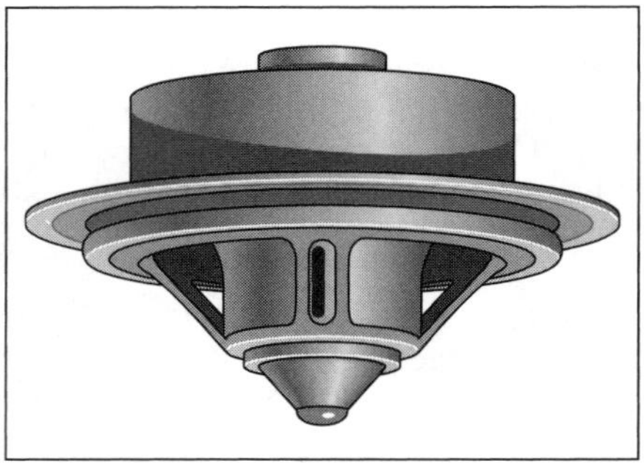

Figure 14-17:
Thermostats are replaced spring side down.

8. Replace the hose and screw down the hose clamp.

Screw it down tight, but not tight enough to cut into the hose.

9. Replace whatever liquid ran out of the hose by pouring it out of the container and into the radiator fill hole.

Servicing Air Conditioners

Most people tend to run the air conditioner in their vehicles until it breaks. However, air conditioners should be serviced professionally each year for some good reasons.

Because air conditioners contain refrigerant under pressure, which can injure or blind you if it escapes, do not attempt to work on the air conditioner or its hoses yourself.

If your vehicle was built prior to 1992, the air conditioner contains a refrigerant called Freon (CFC-12). Because Freon contributes to the breakdown of the ozone layer, manufacturers ceased production in 1995. Newer vehicles use an environmentally acceptable refrigerant called R-134a.

If you have a pre-1992 vehicle and your air conditioner breaks down, you may find that Freon is hard to obtain. Your options are to either run without air conditioning or have the air conditioner converted so that it can use R-134a.

To find out the cost to convert a vehicle's air conditioner from Freon to R-134a, consult the auto manufacturer or an authorized dealership or service facility, or call the EPA Stratospheric Ozone Information Hotline at 800-296-1996 between 10 a.m. and 4 p.m. EST. You can also find information about ozone on the Web at www.epa.gov/docs/ozone/index.html.

Troubleshooting your air conditioner

Be alert to signs that your vehicle's air conditioner may be in trouble:

- The air it puts out isn't as cold as it used to be.
- A funny smell is coming from the vents.
- The air conditioner's drive belts, compressor, or blower are noisier.
- You hear a rhythmic clicking noise under the hood when you turn on the air conditioner or defroster.
- The defroster no longer defogs the windshield effectively.
- You find water on the floor of the passenger compartment.
- The cooling fan keeps cycling on and off.

What an air conditioner inspection should include

When having the air conditioner in your vehicle inspected and serviced, be sure that the service people do the following:

- Check and adjust or replace the belts that drive the air conditioner.
- Check and clean the fins on the radiator and air conditioner condenser.
- Check all the air conditioner hoses to make sure that they're open and in good condition.
- Check the vacuum control lines.
- Check all the electrical connections.
- Check the compressor hardware.
- Check the duct outlet temperature.
- Make sure that system pressures meet specifications.
- Test the low-pressure cut-out switch.
- Check afterward for leaks.

If All Else Fails

If your car is a chronic overheater and none of the remedies in this chapter cures it, consider replacing its radiator with one that has a greater cooling capacity or installing a separate cooling device where the trouble occurs. (For example, devices are sold to cool transmission systems.) Often, these coolers are sold as part of a **trailer-towing package**, because most cars aren't designed to tow or carry very heavy loads for long periods of time, and the resulting strain causes them to overheat.

Again, a professional you can trust is the proper person to consult if you think that you may need these extras. Chapter 22 shows you how to choose repair facilities that are honest and competent, and tells you what to do if you're dissatisfied with their service.

Chapter 15

Changing Your Oil

*W*hen people think about the good life, they tend to think in terms of freedom from pressure, discomfort, and friction. If your car could talk, it would probably agree. When you consider that the temperature in your vehicle's combustion chambers can get as high as 4,500 degrees Fahrenheit, with high pressures, the shock of combustion, and many metal parts rubbing and grinding against one another, you can see that a vehicle that is *not* adequately protected against heat and friction will swiftly come to an untimely death. Luckily, this kind of protection is cheap and easy to ensure. It's a simple matter of providing sufficient lubrication to keep things running smoothly and then making sure that your vehicle gets regular attention.

Changing the oil is the most essential thing you can do to give your car a long and happy life. This chapter tells you how to choose the right kind of oil for your vehicle, how frequently you should change the oil for maximum performance, and how to do the job quickly and easily.

How Oil Benefits Your Vehicle

To choose the proper kind of oil, you should know what that oil is expected to do. When your car is at rest, the oil slops around quietly in a container located at the bottom of the crankcase, just below the engine (see Figure 15-1). This container is called the oil pan. When the car is running, oil is pumped by an oil pump through holes and channels in the engine, where the oil helps cool and clean the engine and provides a nice, slippery cushion that keeps moving parts from grinding one another into oblivion. The following sections explain in greater detail how oil benefits your vehicle.

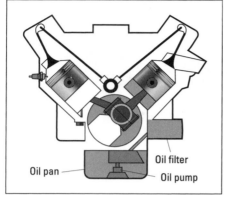

Figure 15-1:
Oil is filtered
as it
circulates
through the
engine.

Oil cools the engine

Because the oil pan is located below the engine, where the air that rushes past the moving car can cool it, the oil picks up some of the heat as it travels around inside the engine and then cools off when it circulates through the oil pan. Although this isn't enough to keep most engines sufficiently cool without a cooling system, it helps.

Oil keeps your engine clean

Most engine oils contain some detergent, which helps flush out the muck that accumulates inside your engine. Not only does detergent remove and dissolve this old sludge; it also helps prevent new gobs of the stuff from forming. Believe me, you have no idea of the meaning of any of those yucky words until you've looked into the engine of a vehicle that has not had its oil changed often enough. Masses of black slimy stuff, hunks of undefinable vileness, and pebble-like particles cling to everything. It's hard to see how these engines function at all. Even more depressing are the all-too-visible signs of wear on steel parts that have been eroded away by this ugly stuff. If your car hasn't had its oil changed in at least 6,000 miles, you can consider the growls coming out of its engine to be cries of pain!

Oil cuts down on friction

By far the most important thing that the oil in your engine does is to form a cushion between moving parts to help them slide past one another easily. This cuts down friction, which in turn dramatically reduces the heat and wear that friction can cause.

Figure 15-2 shows you how oil cuts down on friction. As you can see, each piston is attached to a connecting rod. Each connecting rod has a hole in it with a bearing that the crankshaft fits through. This makes the crankshaft and the connecting rod operate together. Now take a closer look at that hole in the enlarged portion of the figure. Notice that there's a space around the hole that's always filled with oil. When the engine is running, the oil pressure forms a cushion that keeps the connecting rod bearings from ever touching the crankshaft. Instead, each moves on its cushion of oil to prevent friction and wear, which is important because the rod exerts 4,000 pounds of pressure every time it moves down. This arrangement has additional benefits: If the bearings wear, they can be replaced for much less money than it would cost to replace the connecting rod or the crankshaft. This same principle applies to other moving parts in your car.

Oil retards corrosion

Oil also retards corrosion in your engine by enveloping the particles of water and acid that are present. These particles, plus the solid particles that the oil holds in suspension, turn oil black and thin it out. You must change the oil regularly to get rid of this stuff before it can build up to the point where the oil can't do its job properly.

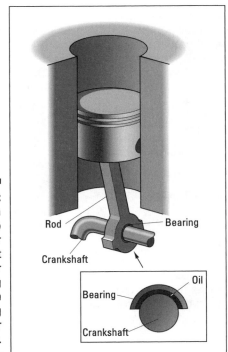

Figure 15-2:
Oil forms a cushion to keep your crankshaft and your connecting rod from wearing each other away.

How changing the oil can save you gas

An engine that's keeping its cool, and operating with less effort, uses less fuel. So if you change your oil on a regular basis, you can cut fuel consumption, which, in turn, reduces air pollution.

Such a deal! (See the section called "How to Change Your Oil Yourself," later in this chapter, for instructions on how to do this easy job.)

What You Should Know about Oil

Various types of oil are on the market, each designed for a particular purpose. This section helps you choose the proper type of oil for your vehicle by explaining the significance of the oil **additives**, viscosity ratings, and classification codes that you'll encounter at auto parts stores and service stations.

Oil additives

To help the oil keep your engine cool, calm, collected — and clean and corrosion-free — refiners blend in various additives, which can account for as much as 25 percent of the cost of the oil. (Don't confuse these with the aftermarket additives sold at auto supply stores, described in the sidebar called "Using aftermarket additives: Should you or shouldn't you?")

Additives help oil in the following ways:

- ✔ To pour better in cold weather
- ✔ To prevent corrosion of the metal parts of the engine
- ✔ To cut down on friction between moving parts
- ✔ To prevent foaming at high temperatures

Viscosity ratings

Oil is rated and identified by its **viscosity** (its capability to flow). In cold weather, oil thickens and becomes less able to flow through the engine. In hot weather, oil thins out, and although it flows well enough, it may become so thin that it can't prevent friction.

Using aftermarket additives: Should you or shouldn't you?

You can buy three basic types of aftermarket additives in auto parts stores, each of which is designed to augment the additives in the oil itself (discussed in the "Oil additives" section earlier in this chapter). The first type thickens the oil. The second type loosens junk and dissolves gummy deposits. The third type acts as a friction lubricant to make the oil "tougher" under high extremes of temperature and usage.

Remember that most oils that don't advertise the presence of additives already have most of this stuff in them, and no amount of additional additives can improve the performance of oil unless the oil you started with was of the best grade. If you buy a well-known brand, you get all the protection you need in these categories if your engine is in reasonably good shape. If you use API-rated oil of the proper weight and classification and change it often, I'd leave the rest of the additives on the store shelves. They may provide *temporary relief* if the engine is disintegrating, but they're not a *cure* for a worn-down, filthy, miserable old engine.

Two types of oil are on the market: *single-viscosity* oil and *multi-viscosity* oil. (These are also called *single-weight* and *multi-weight*.) Automakers rate oil viscosity according to the temperature range expected over the oil change period. The lower the number, the thinner the oil and the more easily it flows. In 10W-40 oil, for example, the two numbers mean that it's a multi-viscosity or multi-weight oil that's effective over a range of temperatures. The first number, 10, is an index that refers to how the oil flows at low temperatures. The second number, 40, refers to how it flows at high temperatures. The W designation means that the oil can be used in winter.

To decide which viscosity to choose, look in your owner's manual for an oil viscosity chart. Just select the range of temperatures in any location where you plan to spend a good deal of time driving, and look on the chart for the multigrade oil recommended for that area. If you don't have an owner's manual, check with your dealer.

Oil classification codes

The oil industry has adopted a symbol to certify that a particular motor oil meets the latest industry requirements for protection against deposits, wear, oxidation, and corrosion. This symbol on oil container labels (see Figure 15-3) means that the oil meets American Petroleum Institute (API) service requirements identified by classification codes. The symbol also means that the oil meets the Energy Conserving II requirements (it improves fuel economy by reducing engine friction). All tested oils carry the symbol. Oils without the symbol may not perform as well.

The codes for vehicles with gasoline engines started with SA in the early 1960s. As engines became more demanding and oil improved, the codes progressed over the years from SB up to SJ (the best oil available in 1999). You can use this oil (and any future grades that come along) in a vehicle of any age to make the engine run and feel better. All the major brands of engine oil with the API symbol are equally good.

A CF (or higher) designation means that the oil has been tested for use in diesel engines and is the latest, most advanced oil for diesels.

Figure 15-3:
The API
symbol.

How to Choose Oil for Your Vehicle

If all the preceding variables have you wondering how you're going to choose the right oil for your vehicle, ask yourself the following questions:

- **What kind of oil have you been using?** If you have an old vehicle that's been running on single-weight oil for most of its life, it's built up quite a bit of sludge because some single-weight oils don't have detergent in them. If you suddenly switch to a multi-viscosity oil, the detergent in it will free all that gook in your engine, and the gook will start to slosh around and really foul things up. It's better to let sleeping gook lie unless you want to invest in having your engine cleaned. The engine would have to be taken apart and put back together again, and you could start trouble where none existed before. If your car is running well, don't switch to another oil. Stick with the same old stuff you've been using.

- **How old is the oil in your car? How many miles have you driven it?** If your car has been logging a great many miles and has been running on 30- or 40-weight oil, multi-weight oil is not going to be consistently thick enough to lubricate the worn engine parts, which have become smaller while wearing down, leaving wider spaces between them. To keep the oil thick enough to fill these gaps, switch to heavier single-weight oil as your car gets older and starts to run more roughly or to burn up oil more quickly. If you've been running on 30-weight oil, switch to 40-weight, at least during the summer, when oil tends to thin out. The manual for Tweety Bird (my faithful 1967 Mustang) called for 10W-40 oil, but when she had more than 80,000 miles to her credit, I put her on straight 40-weight oil. There's even 50-weight oil for the real oldies!

✔ **What kind of oil does your owner's manual recommend? Is your vehicle still under warranty?** Be sure to use whatever weight of oil the owner's manual recommends; the manufacturer knows what's best for each vehicle it produces. Using something other than the recommended oil may invalidate the warranty on a new vehicle.

✔ **Do you live where it's very cold? Hot? Is it mountainous? Are there sharp changes in temperature where you live or where you're going?** Multi-weight oils cover a range of temperatures. Consult a viscosity chart to be sure that the oil you use will flow properly under extreme conditions.

Whenever you buy oil, look for major brands, such as Pennzoil, Quaker State, and Valvoline, or check *Consumer Reports*. Good brands of oil are often on sale in supermarkets and at auto supply stores, so if you want to save money and you spot a sale, buy a case and stash it away.

No matter how crazy about recycling you are, *never* put recycled oil in your precious car. You don't know where that stuff has been.

Synthetic oil

A lot of claims have been made about synthetic oils, such as longer intervals between oil changes, less wear on engine parts, and being able to operate at higher engine temperatures. The longer interval claim has yet to be proven, though; in fact, one synthetic oil manufacturer that claimed a 20,000-mile oil change interval for its oil has retracted that claim and now suggests that its oil be changed at the normal frequency for mineral-based oils.

A *Consumer Reports* test found no difference in engine wear between those vehicles that had mineral oils in their engines and those that had synthetic oils in their engines. There's no doubt, however, that synthetic oils perform better than mineral oils at high temperatures. So if your engine works very hard in a hot climate, pulling a trailer or climbing steep hills, synthetic oil may be right for you. Just be forewarned that synthetic oil is expensive, costing three times as much as mineral-based oil.

A compromise between synthetic and mineral oil has been developed. This blend of mineral and synthetic oil sells for less than synthetic oil and more than mineral oil.

What to do when no amount or type of oil can help

If your vehicle has a worn, clanking workhorse engine, investigate the following alternatives:

- **Find out how much it would cost to rebuild the engine.** The price will depend on how many parts have to be replaced and how much work is involved. Prepare to pay up to $2,000 or more for this service. Is the car worth it?

- **Buy a new engine or a good rebuilt one and have it installed.** This option is even more expensive. I'd do it only for a classic car.

If rebuilding or replacing the engine will cost more than the vehicle's blue book value, it's not worthwhile (unless Old Faithful has sentimental value because your first-born was conceived in the backseat).

- **Put Old Faithful out of its misery.** Both of you will be happier in the long run. Either sell it to a wrecker, who will resell some of its parts and recycle the rest, or donate it to a charity and take a tax deduction for its blue book value.

How Often You Should Change Your Oil

Dirty oil just doesn't do the job as well as fresh oil does. The additives boil out, contaminants form in the crankcase and eat metal parts, and water collects over time and forms sludge. The oil holds more and more abrasive particles of metal suspended in it, and these particles wear away the parts of the engine that the oil is supposed to protect. That's why you want to change your oil at regular, reasonable intervals. But what is a reasonable amount of time — or mileage — between oil changes?

All oil looks pretty black within a couple of days after an oil change, so the only way to avoid running on oil that's so dirty that it becomes a liability is to keep a record of when it was last changed and to change it frequently — as often as every 1,000 miles, if necessary. By changing your oil frequently, you may get *twice* the mileage out of an otherwise good engine.

Some manufacturers suggest that oil be changed every 7,500 miles or more, but they're the people who get to sell you a new car if your old one wears out prematurely. Although new vehicles can run longer on the same oil than older ones, to be on the safe side, I change oil every 3,000 miles or every three months, whichever comes first. If you're a freeway driver who goes on a lot of long journeys at high speeds, you can probably extend the oil change interval, but I wouldn't go longer than 5,000 miles between changes.

If you do a lot of stop-and-go driving in city or rush-hour traffic, change your oil as often as every 1,000 miles. Your engine rarely gets hot enough to evaporate the water that forms in the crankcase and builds up sludge in the engine.

Some auto repair experts believe that it's more accurate to determine how often you should change your oil by the number of cold starts your engine experiences than by the number of miles it's driven. So if you make a lot of short trips each day and leave the car parked long enough to have your engine cool down between them, you may want to take this into consideration when you're deciding how often to change your oil.

How to Change Your Oil Yourself

Changing oil is easy. In fact, unless your oil filter and/or oil drain plug is impossible to reach, you have good reasons to change your oil and oil filter yourself. It's cheaper, you know that the job's being done right, and it requires little time or effort. (During one of my TV guest appearances, Regis Philbin changed the oil in a car in five minutes, and he didn't get a spot on his Italian silk suit!) All you have to do is unscrew a plug and a filter, let the oil drain out, replace the filter and plug, and pour in some new oil.

If you have a professional do it for you, you have to telephone the shop to make an appointment, drive the car in, either wait for it or find a ride home and back again to pick it up, and then wait until they make up your bill — which takes much longer. If you go to one of those quickie oil change places, you don't know what viscosity of oil they've used, whether they really changed the filter, and whether the drain plug was secured properly. (If you don't think that's a problem, check out the "tragic tale" sidebar!) Most important, once you see how inexpensive and easy it is, you'll change your oil as often as necessary rather than adding visits to the service station to your procrastination list!

 If you can't reach the oil filter or drain plug without having to crawl under your vehicle, or if you want to chicken out of the job for any other reason, most shops have low-priced oil and lube specials now and then. Just be sure that they use high-quality oil and that they change the oil filter, too.

Get your supplies together

Before you start the job, assemble the following items:

✔ **Oil:** Check your owner's manual to find the proper oil recommended for your car and how many quarts you need. (As a general rule, most vehicles require 5 to 6 quarts of oil, but you don't want to risk overfilling it.) If you have no manual, call a local dealer who sells your vehicle make and model and ask someone in the service department. Or find the information in an auto repair manual for your vehicle's make, model, and year at the library.

A tragic tale

Before I stopped being an automotive "dummy," my family car resided for its first 35,000 miles in a garage, where professional mechanics looked after it. Whenever they said that the car needed the oil changed, I scheduled the work promptly. Yet when I took the engine apart in an adult-education automotive class, I found that the mechanics had never changed the oil! This lack of proper lubrication had led to big trouble: The dirty old oil had formed big, black pebbles, and the camshaft had practically worn away! When this happens, either you opt for major and expensive surgery or you get rid of the vehicle. As I sadly watched my dear Macho-Mobile vanish into the sunset, the major question in my mind was, "How did this happen?"

The answer, unfortunately, was that I'd depended on someone else for lubrication reminders and had trusted someone else to do the job properly. Not only had I been paying at least twice as much as it would have cost to do the job myself, but I ended up paying to replace a car that could have gone almost twice as far if it had been lubricated properly.

If this sad story inspires you to undertake your own lubrication work, then dear old M-M will not have been towed away in vain. Besides, paying someone a lot of money to do something that you can do yourself in a couple of minutes is just plain silly. And if you can unscrew the top of a bottle, you can change your oil without any trouble.

✔ **An oil filter:** Under the hood of your car, sticking out of the engine, is what looks like a tin can screwed into your engine block. This is your oil filter (see Figure 15-4). As the oil circulates from the oil pan through your engine, it passes through this filter, which cleans the oil and removes some of the particles of metal and dirt. You should change the oil filter every time you change your oil, especially if you're going to do so less frequently than every 3,000 miles. Oil filters sell for very little at auto supply stores; at a service station, you'll pay more. Make sure to get the right filter for your car's make and model.

You may wonder what happens if your oil filter gets totally clogged and no more oil can pass through it. Your friendly auto designers have saved your bacon by installing a pressure relief valve that pops open, allowing the oil to bypass the filter so that the engine isn't starved of oil. Of course, all the dirt and metal particles then circulate through your precious bearings and onto your cylinder walls until you change your clogged filter.

Check the price of an oil filter at your dealer's parts department. If it's within a dollar or two of the auto parts store price, buy it. It's probably a better filter. (Some of the auto parts store filters are very cheaply made, and they fail occasionally.)

Figure 15-4:
An oil filter.

✔ **An oil filter wrench (optional):** Most oil filters screw on and off. If your old filter hasn't been changed in a long time, you may need an oil filter wrench, shown in Figure 15-5, to unscrew your filter (but always tighten the new one by hand to avoid crushing the seal).

✔ **An adjustable wrench:** Use this tool to unscrew the oil drain plug. If you're not sure what an adjustable wrench is, see Chapter 2.

✔ **An oil drain plug gasket:** This piece of equipment is inexpensive, and it's wise to buy one in case the one on your car needs replacing. If you buy your oil filter from a dealer, a new gasket may be in the package.

Some vehicles don't have drain plug gaskets, relying instead on a tapered metal-to-metal contact to prevent oil leakage. Don't try to use a gasket on one of these. It won't work, and you may end up with your new oil in a pool on the floor.

✔ **Something to catch the oil:** Find an old basin that's low enough to fit under your car without your having to jack up the car, and large enough to hold all the old oil — usually about 5 quarts. Line the basin with a large plastic garbage bag, opened so that it can catch the oil, leaving the basin clean.

You can also buy a container made especially for holding old oil. These containers are reusable, but you have to wash them out and find a place to keep them.

✔ **A funnel (optional):** Oil is sold in containers that have narrow necks to facilitate pouring the oil into the engine. If you're still worried about your aim, use a funnel to prevent messy spills.

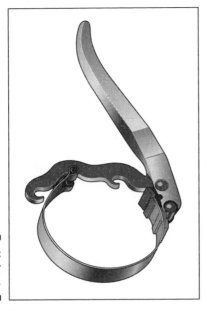

Figure 15-5:
An oil filter
wrench.

> ✔ **Rags:** You should also have a clean, lint-free rag for wiping your oil dip-stick and a dirty, old, thick rag that you don't mind throwing away. You can use paper towels to clean up spills and tools, but you don't want to risk bits of paper getting into your engine.
>
> ✔ **A work light:** A work light helps you see better underneath the vehicle, and a flashlight can be awkward if you have to hold it between your teeth!

Do the job systematically

Always use a *system* when you do an oil change: Do each part of the job in order, and don't change that order from job to job. This may sound unduly restrictive if you like to improvise, but if you ignore this advice, you may find that you've added the new oil before replacing the oil drain plug or changing the filter. In either case, you wind up with your brand-new oil all over the ground and not enough oil in the engine to drive to the store for more. Also, the *minute* you replace the oil drain plug, *always* tighten it completely and put in the new oil. That way, you won't forget to put in the new oil. (Don't laugh; people have done that and have ruined their engines in a couple of miles.)

If you're not going to have to jack up your car to change your oil, either park it on level ground or in such a way that the oil drain plug is at the lower end of the oil pan. If you do have to jack up your car, read Chapter 1 to be sure that you do so *safely.* Block the wheels, use jack stands, and don't jack the car up too high, or the oil may not drain out of the oil pan completely. If you can, jack up the car so that the oil drain plug is at the lower end of the oil pan.

In any case, be sure your gearshift is in Park or Neutral with the emergency brake on before you work on it. Place all the stuff you're going to use within easy reach so that you don't have to jump up and run around to the other side of the vehicle in the middle of the job. Now follow these easy steps to change your oil and oil filter:

1. **Warm up your engine for two or three minutes so that the gook gets churned up and can flow out of the engine easily.**

   You *don't* want the engine so hot that you burn yourself. When it is slightly warm, shut off the engine.

2. **Use a light to look under your car. You should be able to see and reach a large nut or plug located under the oil pan at the bottom of the engine. (See Figure 15-6.)**

   This is the oil drain plug. It unscrews with the aid of an adjustable wrench. If the plug is too hot to touch comfortably, let the car cool off for a while longer.

   If you can't reach your oil drain plug easily and you still want to do this job yourself, you'll have to either crawl under your car to reach the plug or jack up the car.

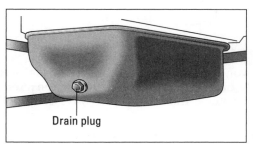

Figure 15-6:
The drain plug is located at the bottom of your oil pan.

Drain plug

3. **Push the basin with the plastic bag opened inside it (or the oil-change container) under the oil drain plug so that it can catch the oil.**

   The oil may not come down vertically to start with; it may come out sideways from the direction the drain plug is facing. Allow for that when you place the drain pan.

4. **Use your adjustable wrench to unscrew the oil drain plug until it's *almost* ready to come out. Then protect your hand with the dirty rag or some paper towels and give the plug a last quick turn by hand to release it. Pull your hand away quickly so that you don't get oil all over yourself.**

If the plug falls into the container, you can retrieve it later. The oil now drains out of your engine into the container (remember the gasket, if you're going to reuse it). While the oil drains, get out from under the car and take a look under the hood.

5. Remove the cap from the oil filler hole at the top of your engine.

This large cap is easy to recognize: It lifts or screws right off, revealing a largish hole.

6. Unscrew the oil filter, using an oil filter wrench if you can't do it by hand.

The oil filter looks like a tin can that's screwed onto the outside of your engine (see Figure 15-7). Like most other things you find on a car, the oil filter unscrews if you twist it counterclockwise. The old filter will have oil in it, so be careful not to dump it on anything when you remove it. If any remnants of the rubber seal from the old filter remain on your engine, remove them.

Figure 15-7:
The oil filter is screwed to the side of your engine.

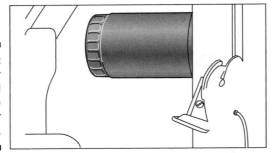

On some vehicles, you can easily reach the oil filter by leaning under the hood. Unfortunately, other car manufacturers place the filter so that it must be reached from under the car. If your vehicle is one of these, you will have to get under it.

7. Empty the oil from the filter into the drain pan.

Once the filter has drained *completely,* wrap it in newspaper and set it aside to take to a recycling center with your old oil. The Steel Recycling Institute says that if all the oil filters sold in the U.S. each year were recycled, we'd recover enough to build 16 stadiums the size of Atlanta's Olympic Stadium!

In many locales, putting oil filters into a landfill is against the law, so don't just throw away the old oil filter unless you check first to be sure that you won't be breaking the law. You can call the Used Filter Recycling Hotline at 800-99-FILTER.

8. While the old oil drains out of the engine, open a new bottle of oil.

9. **Dip a finger in the new oil and moisten the gasket on the top of the new oil filter. Then screw the new filter into the engine where the old one was.**

   Follow directions on the filter, or turn it gently until it "seats" and then turn it another three-quarter turn.

   Unless the filter manufacturer specifically recommends it, or there isn't enough space to get your hand into, don't use an oil filter wrench to *tighten* the filter. It should fit tightly, but you don't want to crush the gasket, or the filter will leak.

10. **Reach under the car again and use your dirty rag to wipe around the place where the oil drain plug goes.**

11. **Replace the oil drain plug and use an adjustable wrench to tighten it. If your vehicle uses an oil drain plug gasket, make sure that the old one has been removed and lay a new gasket on the pan before you replace the plug.**

12. **After you install the oil filter and replace the oil drain plug, use a funnel — or just good aim — to pour all but 1 quart of the fresh oil into the oil filler hole (see Figure 15-8).**

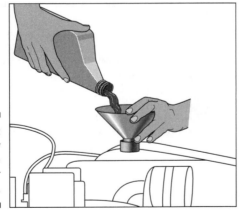

Figure 15-8:
Pouring new oil down the oil filter hole.

13. **Replace the oil filler cap and run the engine for 30 to 60 seconds while you check for leaks from the oil drain plug and around the filter.**

   The oil pressure light on your dashboard should go out in 10 or 15 seconds (or if your car has an oil pressure gauge, the needle should move off of "Low"). Don't rev up your engine during this period. Your oil pressure is low to zero while the light is on, until your oil filter fills up. If the light doesn't go out, check under the car and around the engine for leaks. Running the engine circulates oil into the new oil filter, and because filters hold from a half to a full quart of oil, you want to be sure that your filter is full to get an accurate reading on the oil dipstick.

14. **Shut off the engine and wait five to ten minutes for the oil to settle into the oil pan. Then remove the oil dipstick, wipe it with a clean, lint-free rag, and shove it back in. Pull it out again and check it.**

    Keep adding oil a little at a time and checking the stick until you reach the "Full" line on the dipstick. (Refer to Figure 3-10 in Chapter 3 to see what an oil dipstick looks like.)

15. **Remove the drain pan from under the vehicle, drive around the block a couple of times, let the oil settle down again, and recheck the dipstick and the dashboard indicator.**

Remember, *never* keep running an engine or drive a vehicle that tells you its oil pressure is low. Because oil not only lubricates but also helps cool the engine, you can ruin your engine if you drive even a short distance with insufficient oil or with a defective oil pump.

Use the Maintenance Record at the back of this book to record the vehicle mileage and date of the oil change. On the Specification Record at the back of this book, note the oil filter make and part number and the weight and number of quarts of oil you needed. These records not only keep track of when you need to change the oil again but also help you find the right parts quickly next time. They may even increase the price of your vehicle (if you ever decide to sell it) by giving the buyer confidence that the engine has been looked after.

Although this process takes 15 steps to explain, it shouldn't take more than 15 minutes to accomplish, once you buy the necessary stuff. When you see how easy changing the oil is, you'll tend to change your oil more frequently, and your car will ride better, last longer, burn less fuel, and cause less air pollution. You'll feel pretty happy with yourself, too!

If you're really feeling good about the oil change and you've got the car jacked up anyway, you may want to consider doing a lube job now. See Chapter 16 for details.

Recycle your old oil

Never dump oil onto the ground, throw it out with your regular garbage, or flush it down a drain. It's a major toxic pollutant that needs to be treated accordingly. So what do you do with your old oil? Use the funnel to pour it into one or more *clean* disposable containers with tight-fitting (preferably screw-on) lids — the bottles the new oil came in or old, *washed* soda bottles work well.

Many auto parts stores and some service stations accept old oil for recycling. If you don't have one close by, look in your phone book for the nearest oil recycling center or toxic waste disposal center. You can also bring the old oil filter along. Be sure not to contaminate the oil by mixing it with another substance or putting it into a dirty container, or recycling centers may not accept it.

Chapter 16

Lubrication Extends the Life of Your Vehicle

• •

In This Chapter

▶ Understanding what a lube job entails

▶ What you need to lube your vehicle

▶ Lubricating the steering linkage

▶ Lubricating the suspension system

• •

*J*ust as the inside of your engine needs lubrication (via oil, as explained in Chapter 15), other parts of your vehicle need lubrication as well. A lube job involves applying lubricants (various kinds of grease and oil) to some of the moving parts under your vehicle and to some of the rubber parts to keep them supple.

Your transmission fluid, power steering fluid, and brake fluid are lubricants, too. (See the monthly under-the-hood check in Chapter 3 about checking these fluids if you haven't already done so.)

The parts of your vehicle that need periodic lubrication can include the steering linkage, transmission shift linkage, clutch linkage, parking brake cables, differential, and driveshaft universal joint fittings.

Because some of these are hard to find and hard to reach, most require a special kind of lubricant. Because you can get into trouble if you don't deal with them properly, I suggest that, once or twice a year, you take your vehicle to the dealership or to a good independent repair facility. Have them lubricate *everything* that needs it — including the distributor, if your vehicle has one. The rest of the time, just lubricate the things that I point out in this chapter, and you'll be way ahead of the game.

What *do* you lubricate when you do a lube job? What tools do you need? And how to you do it? This chapter answers all these questions.

What a Lube Job Involves

Grease fittings are those places on your vehicle that hold lubricants to protect moving parts from one another. They must be kept packed with grease to keep the components they protect moving freely without friction. Naturally, these are usually the parts that move the most, except for those inside your engine (which are lubricated with oil).

Think about your vehicle and take a look at Figure 16-1. Where does most of the movement take place when you drive (not counting any kids in the backseat)? Well, the front wheels turn on **wheel bearings**, and they can change direction when you steer because of the **steering linkage** between the steering wheel and the front wheels. Your vehicle moves up and down on its **suspension system** and **shock absorbers**, which keep it level, even when the wheels are bobbing up and down on rough stretches of road.

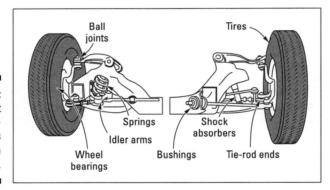

Figure 16-1:
Where most of the movement takes place when you drive.

Ball joints   Tires

Springs   Shock absorbers

Idler arms

Wheel bearings   Bushings   Tie-rod ends

All these areas can have **grease fittings** (sometimes called **lubrication points** or just *lube points*), and replacing or replenishing the grease in them is called a *lube job, grease job,* or *chassis lube,* depending on who's doing the talking. To keep your vehicle young and healthy, lubricate the parts that need it every 3,000 miles.

Before you undertake any of the work in this chapter, be sure to review Chapter 11, which tells you all about the steering and suspension systems and describes the grease fittings, where most of the work is done. It's much easier to do a job when you understand what the parts you're working on do and how they relate to one another.

The Tools You Need to Do a Lube Job

Here's what you need to lubricate your vehicle:

- ✓ **A decent grease gun:** Borrow one at first; if you hate the job, you won't have made a big investment. If you can't borrow one, buy a cheap one. You can always pass it on to a friend who's just getting into auto maintenance and then buy yourself a super one if you plan to do the job repeatedly. Most grease guns come with a couple of adapters to fit the grease fittings on your car and an extender for hard-to-reach places. If your gun doesn't have these, you can get an adapter or an extender for a couple of dollars if you need one. (You may not. Some grease guns are fitted to take grease cartridges, which save you the time and mess of loading them.)

- ✓ **The proper kind of grease:** The following sections explain what kind of grease you need for each type of job. Another way to find out is to consult your owner's manual, your service manual, or a salesperson at an auto supply store. They have manuals that tell all.

Lubricating the Steering System

As Chapter 11 explains, every vehicle has ball joints and tie-rod ends that contain grease to protect the moving parts of the steering and suspension systems from rubbing against one another. Without this grease, the friction would cause the parts to wear away.

On some vehicles, all or some of these grease fittings are designed for *lifetime lubrication,* which means that the grease is pumped in and sealed so that it can't get out. Because this kind of sealed system also prevents dirt, air, and water from getting *in,* these lifetime lubrication systems seem to last pretty well, and you don't have to lubricate them yourself, ever. Of course, if they break down, installing a whole new part is a bit more expensive, but they don't break down very often.

If your owner's manual tells you that your vehicle has one of these systems, be happy, skip the rest of this section, and go on to "Lubricating the Suspension System." If your vehicle doesn't have lifetime lubrication, take a close look at the ball joints that are the scene of the action for most lube jobs.

Anatomy of a ball joint

Each ball joint has two basic parts: a rubber, ball-shaped **boot** and a little metal nozzle called a **zerk fitting** (see Figures 16-2 and 16-3). The boot holds the grease, and the zerk fitting lets the grease into the boot and keeps it from getting out again.

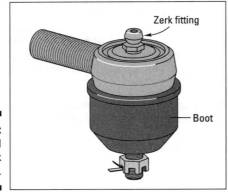

Figure 16-2: A tie-rod end zerk fitting.

Zerk fitting

Boot

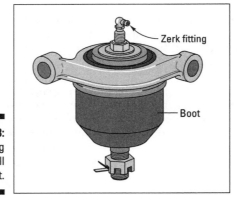

Figure 16-3: A zerk fitting on a ball joint.

Zerk fitting

Boot

✔ Most ball joints are sealed in the sense that the only place for the grease to go in and out of the joint is through the zerk fitting. If you fill this type of joint too full, the boot will burst and have to be replaced or lubricated more frequently.

✔ Other ball joints are designed to allow the grease to escape so that the new grease you insert pushes the old grease out the other end. Check under your vehicle to see which type of ball joints you have. If you aren't sure whether those gooey ball joints are sealed ones that have burst or the kind that are supposed to have a back door, your auto dealer can tell you.

✔ Here's another way to tell what kind of ball joint your vehicle has: If only *one* of the ball joints has a mound of grease coming out of it when you put the new grease in, it's probably a sealed joint that has burst. If they all tend to leak grease when you add more, they're probably supposed to do so.

Some vehicles come with *plugs* on the ball joints instead of zerk fittings. You can replace the plugs with zerk fittings by unscrewing the plugs and screwing in the fittings. The fittings then become permanent fixtures on the ball joints, and you can throw the plugs away (or save them for a rainy day).

Finding the lube points

Now that you know what the ball joints are, what they do, and how they work, you're probably thinking, "Fine! But how do I find the ball joints on *my* vehicle?" Here's where to look:

✔ **Before you go down to the service station, try to find the ball joints yourself by looking under the front end of your vehicle.** Trace the bar that runs from one front wheel to the other. Grease fittings are usually found at the base and top of the arms that attach your wheels to the **steering linkage** (these are the **steering knuckles**) and at the center of the steering linkage where the tie rods meet the center. Some cars have as many as eight or ten of these fittings. Others have none. Most have four to six. See Figure 16-4 for a few of places you can expect to find grease fittings on your car.

Some vehicles with independent rear suspensions have grease fittings at the rear wheels, too. And some trucks have grease fittings along the driveshaft.

Figure 16-4:
Some of the places to look for grease fittings on your car.

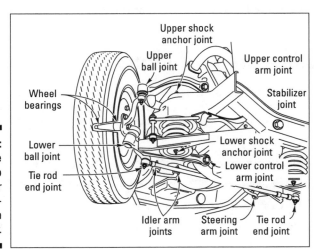

✔ **Look in the owner's manual.** Some (but not many) of the more enlightened owner's manuals tell you.

✔ **Look in the service manual.** The service manual for your vehicle's make, model, and year tells you the location and nature of each lubrication point (or grease fitting or ball joint or whatever they're called in your book). You can find one at your local library or buy one at an auto parts store or at your local dealership.

It's a good idea to own a copy of the service manual for your vehicle, even if you just lend it to the independent shops that work on your car. There's no way that they can keep a copy of every service manual, and access to specific instructions for servicing and repairing your particular vehicle can significantly cut the time — and therefore the cost — involved in doing a job.

✔ **Look in the lubrication manual.** Every service station has a lubrication manual that's published by one of the major oil companies each year. These manuals show every lube point and grease fitting for every vehicle manufactured during the year of publication. Your service station probably has the last couple of years' manuals on hand. If you don't have a service manual, ask to see the lube manual if you're having trouble locating the lube points on your vehicle.

✔ **Ask a professional.** If you really have trouble finding your ball joints and you're unwilling to throw yourself at the mercy of a service station just for a look at the lube manual, give in and take the car in for a lube job someplace where they'll let you hang around and ask questions. Casually ask for a look at the lube manual or ask them to point out the lube points that they're going to work on. Say, "How many lube points does this model have?" They're usually happy to show you and answer your questions. People who work on cars love to talk shop (and most of them never suspect that "civilians" are secretly planning to do the work themselves next time). If you get a real talkative technician, you've found a gold mine; be sure to ask about the rest of the job, too.

Lubricating the ball joints

Lubing ball joints is really as simple as wiping the zerk fitting, fitting the grease gun onto it (use an adapter if you need one), and *gently* squeezing a *little* grease into the joint. The following takes you step-by-step through the procedure:

1. **Find out how many lube points your car has and where they are.**

   See the preceding section, "Finding the lube points," for help.

2. **Wipe off the first zerk fitting and try to fit your gun to it.**

   Does it fit? If not, you may need an adapter. Can you reach it? If not, you may need an extender.

3. **Load your grease gun with grease.**

   The kind of grease you want is called *suspension* lube grease.

4. **Place the grease gun to the fitting and *gently* squeeze a little bit of grease into it (see Figure 16-5).**

   Never add so much grease that the ball is tightly packed. There should be plenty of give when you squeeze the sides of the ball. If the joint looks too hard and full, squeeze some grease out if you have the kind of fitting that has a back door. If you have a sealed joint, just add enough grease to fill it out a little. If the joint looks full before you start, don't add any grease at all; just go on to the next joint.

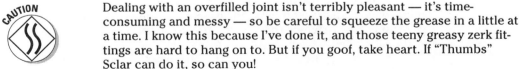

Figure 16-5:
A grease gun with adapter and a zerk fitting.

5. **Repeat Steps 2 through 4 until you have serviced all the joints.**

6. **If you overfill a sealed joint, take an ignition wrench of the proper tiny size and unscrew the zerk fitting (counterclockwise). Squeeze out the excess grease and replace the fitting.**

   (If you don't know what an ignition wrench is, see Chapter 2.)

   Dealing with an overfilled joint isn't terribly pleasant — it's time-consuming and messy — so be careful to squeeze the grease in a little at a time. I know this because I've done it, and those teeny greasy zerk fittings are hard to hang on to. But if you goof, take heart. If "Thumbs" Sclar can do it, so can you!

7. **If one or more of your ball joints boots has burst, have it (or them) replaced *immediately*.**

   The parts that these joints protect get a lot of action, and you can be in for a very expensive job (or risk losing your ability to steer) after a very short trip on a nonfunctioning ball joint.

When you buy a new vehicle, ask the service manager if there are any trouble spots on the model that may benefit from having grease fittings inserted. I had several installed on my new truck for very little money. If you have a persistent squeak, you may want to find out whether having a grease fitting installed in the area will quiet things down.

Lubricating the Suspension System

The suspension system technically includes the **steering linkage**, but in my mind, it's easier to deal with these things in terms of the functions they perform. Therefore, try to see the **steering linkage** as being concerned with the *horizontal* directions in which the car can go (left and right) and the suspension system as being concerned with the *vertical* movement (up and down) of the car as it travels over the road.

The following sections detail how to lubricate parts of your suspension system. (If the suspension system itself gets out of whack, get a professional to diagnose and deal with the trouble.)

Lubricating the springs

Various types of springs are used to absorb bumps and keep your vehicle level on turns. These can be **coil springs, leaf springs, torsion bars,** or **air springs.** Some cars have leaf springs at the rear wheels and coil springs at the front wheels. Some luxury cars, full-size trucks, and buses have air suspension systems. For more detailed information about each type of spring, see Chapter 11. The following list explains what you need to lubricate and how to do it, depending on the type of spring that you have:

✔ **Leaf springs:** Each end of a set of leaf springs is attached to the frame at the rear of the car with fittings that enable the springs to bend and move freely. These fittings usually have rubber **bushings** that enable the fittings to bend and twist freely and also absorb some of the vibration and prevent it from reaching the passenger compartment (see Figure 16-6). If your leaf springs have more than one leaf per side, called *multiple leaf springs,* there may be a piece of plastic between the leaves. That plastic, called a *slipper,* can be lubed with suspension grease to prevent noise as the leaves slide over one another during jounce and rebound.

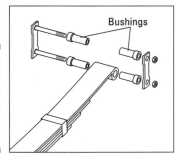

Figure 16-6:
Leaf springs
have rubber
bushings to
cushion
them.

✔ **Coil springs:** These look like old-fashioned bed springs. They're usually found at the front of the car, although they can be at both the front and the rear. (Figures 16-7 and 16-8 show where the ball joints and bushings are on coil springs.) Sometimes these coil springs have rubber cushions at the top and bottom. If the coil springs are making noise, you can lube them with grease where they sit at the top and bottom. Use spray-on grease from an aerosol-type dispenser.

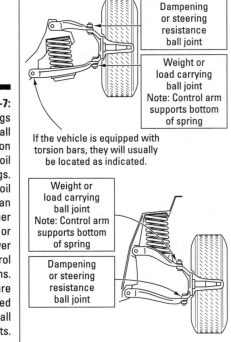

Figure 16-7:
Bushings
and ball
joints on
front coil
springs.
Front coil
springs can
sit on either
the upper or
the lower
control
arms.
They are
cushioned
by ball
joints.

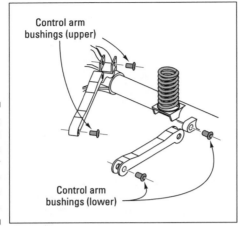

Figure 16-8:
Rear coil springs have rubber bushings to cushion them.

- ✔ **Torsion bars:** These are a popular type of spring used on the fronts of many sport-utility vehicles and trucks. They usually run parallel to the frame and are attached to the **control arm** at one end and the *cross member* at the other end (see Figure 16-9). Torsion bar springs require no lubrication. Most are adjustable, meaning that if your vehicle is sitting too high or low, you can make an adjustment by turning an adjusting bolt.

- ✔ **Air springs:** These are filled with the right amount of compressed air to control the ride and maintain the proper height. A computer monitors the ride height and signals an on-board air compressor to pump more air into the air springs whenever weight is added to the vehicle. When the weight is removed, the computer turns on an exhaust **solenoid** to let air out of the air springs (see Figure 16-10). Usually, there's nothing to lubricate with air springs. But check with the dealer to find out whether it's okay to apply a rubber conditioner to the air bags to prevent them from wearing out prematurely.

Taking care of the stabilizers

Stabilizers keep the passenger part of the vehicle from swaying and lurching on sharp curves and turns and when the wheels are traveling over uneven ground (a better solution than the legendary mountain goat that had shorter legs on one side than on the other for traveling along slopes!). There are various kinds of stabilizers, but all you need to know is that you can lubricate the rubber parts yourself.

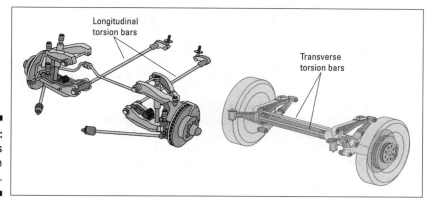

Figure 16-9:
Torsion bars provide stability.

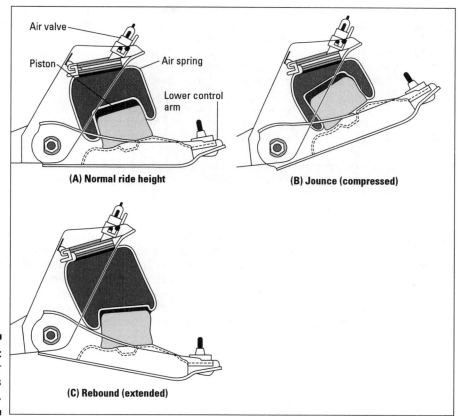

Figure 16-10:
How air springs work.

Dealing with shocks and struts

Located near each wheel, shock absorbers do most of the work of protecting the passenger compartment from bumps. Chapter 11 provides details about shock absorbers that are worth reviewing before you read this section.

Many vehicles are equipped with MacPherson strut suspension instead of conventional shocks. This simplified and improved system takes up less space and is well worth having. The downside is that because MacPherson struts are surrounded by, and assembled with, the suspension springs, they're always under spring pressure and therefore *must* be replaced professionally. You may be taking your life in your hands if you tamper with them. (Chapter 11 has information and illustrations of MacPherson and other strut systems.)

You can tell whether your vehicle needs new shock absorbers by leaning heavily on a fender or placing your weight on a bumper and then releasing it suddenly, watching to see whether the vehicle returns slowly to its original position. If it continues to bob up and down, you need new shocks. Another way is to stop fairly short. If your car dips up and down a couple of times before coming to rest, you need new shocks.

Bad shock absorbers increase tire wear and can cause you to lose control of the steering if you go over bumps and dips at high speeds. If any of these things seems to be happening to you, have your shocks replaced.

Although replacing *standard* shock absorbers isn't hard, the job can be brutal if you have to jack up your vehicle and crawl under it. Unless you can replace them under supervision on the lift at an auto class, I strongly recommend having a professional do it for you.

To save money, buy the shocks yourself and pay a professional to install them. The store will know what type of suspension system your vehicle has and what kind of shocks it needs. Within limits, you do have a choice: "Heavy-duty" shocks provide a slightly harder ride; other shocks may not do as well with the entire family and two Great Danes in the car, but give a softer ride. Some shocks even provide automatic level control for vehicles that carry loads ranging from very heavy to almost weightless. Suit yourself.

Chapter 17

What to Do If Your Transmission Stops Running Smoothly

· ·

In This Chapter

▶ Troubleshooting transmission problems

▶ Maintaining your drivetrain

▶ Caring for your clutch and knowing what to expect when it needs work

▶ Understanding what's necessary for common transmission repairs

▶ Protecting yourself from being ripped off on transmission work

· ·

Your vehicle's transmission is probably its most complex system. This system's primary job is to take instructions from you (via the **gearshift**) and send those instructions to the wheels so that your vehicle can move forward and backward at varying speeds with maximum efficiency.

It's always easier to maintain, troubleshoot, or repair something if you really understand what the parts you're working on do and how they relate to one another. So if you haven't read Chapter 9, please read it before going on with this chapter. I'll wait. . . .

Because most of the parts related to your transmission are difficult to get at and require special tools and a hoist (unless you really love lying prone under a car with oil dripping in your face), you really can't do much to repair your transmission yourself. However, you have no reason to feel helpless, because there are lots of things you *can* do:

✔ You can troubleshoot problems and make minor repairs and adjustments yourself.

✔ If you drive a manual transmission, you can do preventive maintenance on your clutch.

✔ You can cultivate driving techniques that extend the life of your transmission by not subjecting it to unnecessary strain.

> ✔ If, despite all your care and attention, you run into transmission problems anyway, you can learn to protect yourself from unnecessary or shoddy transmission work.

This chapter tells you how to do all these things.

Troubleshooting Your Transmission

A low transmission fluid level or a malfunctioning, inexpensive gizmo may cause the same symptoms as a faulty transmission. Who knows how many unsuspecting customers have paid big bucks to rebuild or replace transmissions when they could have corrected the problems themselves with very little money or effort? This section shows you how to troubleshoot your transmission and try the cheapest remedies before paying professionals to do major surgery.

If you have to take the problem to a specialist, read the sections in this chapter on dealing with professionals before going to one for a diagnosis. If you're lucky, your transmission may need only a simple adjustment. If you're not so lucky, your transmission may need to be rebuilt or replaced. But in any event, you'll know that you're getting the proper service.

Those low-transmission-fluid blues

If your automatic transmission seems to be acting up — by hesitating when you change gears, or by shifting with a "clunk" — first check your transmission dipstick. Your transmission fluid may be low or dirty, or it may have dried. Chapter 3 tells you how to find and check your transmission dipstick and how to buy the proper kind of transmission fluid for your vehicle. It's a good idea to check this fluid fairly often anyway as part of your regular under-the-hood check. A good many "band jobs" have been bought and paid for when a quart of transmission fluid would have solved the problem for pennies. Before emptying your wallet, check your transmission fluid level and try the following remedies:

> ✔ **If your fluid level is low,** with the emergency brake on and the gearshift in Neutral or Park, use a funnel to add a teeny bit of fluid at a time down the dipstick hole until the fluid level just reaches the "Full" line on the stick.

> *Do not fill beyond the line;* driving with too much transmission fluid can damage your transmission. If the level is low again in a couple of days, look under the car for a leak around the transmission; you may need to replace a seal.

✔ **If your fluid level is fine but your transmission isn't working well** — or if your fluid keeps disappearing and no leaks are evident — you probably need transmission work.

✔ **If your transmission fluid looks or smells burned or dirty,** you may want to consider having the fluid, filter, and pan gasket changed.

Transmissions should be serviced every 20,000 to 25,000 miles, but if your vehicle has more than 100,000 miles on it and the transmission fluid has never been changed, don't change it unless there are really serious reasons for doing so. The old transmission fluid has formed a deposit around the front transmission seal. If this fluid is totally replaced with fresh fluid, the new stuff can dissolve the deposit, and the old seal may start to leak. In this case, I'd add just enough new fluid to bring the level up to the "Full" mark on the dipstick or as close to it as possible. Then, when the poor, neglected beast dies, have the transmission rebuilt (unless the rest of the car is dying, too). This does *not* mean that you shouldn't have the transmission *serviced*. Because you'll probably lose only 3 quarts in the process of servicing, replacing the lost fluid shouldn't disturb the seals.

If you have an all-wheel-drive or four-wheel-drive vehicle, don't forget to check the fluid level in the transfer case, too.

The malfunctioning vacuum modulator caper

Many older vehicles with automatic transmissions have an inexpensive device called a vacuum modulator. When the vacuum modulator goes bad, the car tends to stay in low gear all the time or shift with a bang — especially into lower gears. These little devils can suck up transmission fluid and burn it, causing white or gray smoke to emerge from the tailpipe as you shift gears. If your car has a vacuum modulator and it's easy to reach, it's worth the gamble to replace it *before* you consider more costly remedies. You usually only have to unscrew the old one to replace it. To be clear about the work involved, consult a service manual for your vehicle's make, model, and year at your local library.

Keeping Your Drive Train Running Smoothly

Your manual or automatic transmission system will work better and live longer if you have the U-joints in your drive train checked and replaced with new ones if they're loose, and if you have your differential lubricated at regular intervals. Even if you're now lubricating your steering linkage and suspension system yourself (as I describe in Chapter 16), you should still take your car to a service station to have *everything* lubricated at least once a year.

Check to see whether your rear end (sorry, that's the way they refer to the differential) needs lubrication. Here's how:

1. **Find the inspection plug in the differential (that's the gear box between the two rear wheels of the vehicle).**

2. **Remove the plug.**

   You can usually remove it by putting the square end of a ½-inch drive ratchet into the square hole in the plug.

3. **If fluid drips out when you remove the plug, you're okay. If nothing comes out, add differential/manual transmission grease until it's full.**

   If your vehicle has a limited slip or positraction rear end (very few do), it requires special fluid. Check the specifications in your owner's manual or call your dealer to find out for sure.

Checking the grease level on a manual transmission is the same as checking the differential on a vehicle with an automatic transmission. You just locate the inspection plug, remove it, and see what comes out. If nothing does, you use the same differential/manual transmission grease to fill it up again. (On vehicles with automatic transmissions, the transmission dipstick does this job for you, and automatic transmission fluid instead of gear grease is used.)

Taking Care of Your Clutch

Many newer vehicles with manual transmissions have self-adjusting clutches that require no adjustment, but if you have an older model, you can cut down on the wear on your clutch disk — Chapter 9 tells you what these parts are — by keeping your clutch pedal properly adjusted.

Your clutch pedal should move down ¾ inch to 1 inch without effort and then require a good deal more effort to travel the rest of the way down to the floor. This free pedal play ensures that when you release the pedal, the clutch disk is fully engaged. Too much free pedal play is not good, either, because too much pedal travel is used up doing nothing: There's not enough movement left at the bottom of its travel to compress the clutch springs and allow the engine flywheel and the clutch disk to separate. With this excessive pedal play, the gears clash whenever you shift into First or Reverse from a stopped position.

If there's no free pedal play on your clutch pedal, another problem can occur, even if there's enough play to allow the clutch disk to engage. In this case, the throwout bearing, which responds to pressure on the clutch pedal by causing the disk to disengage, may go on spinning. If the throwout bearing is allowed to revolve constantly in this way, it will wear out, which makes getting into or out of gear difficult.

Don't ride the clutch. Riding it can wear out the throwout bearing, too. You can tell that something is wrong because the bearing makes whirring, whining sounds. If the sounds disappear when you release the clutch pedal and resume when you step on it, you have a bad throwout bearing. If you think that you have one, or if your clutch misbehaves in other ways, go to a reliable mechanic and have the clutch checked out.

Your clutch can be good for 5,000 to 50,000 miles. This wide variation depends on the type of vehicle, the way you drive it, and how much maintenance it receives. The clutch may last for as many as 100,000 miles, or it may break down after only 10,000. If you have a clutch disk replaced, have the pressure plate and the flywheel checked at that time to be sure that they aren't badly worn. Here's what should probably be done in each case:

- ✔ **If the flywheel is worn,** have a professional resurface it. This procedure involves grinding it down to a new, flat surface and then polishing it to a mirror-like finish. If you fail to have this work done, the worn flywheel can wear out the facing of the new clutch disk very quickly. And if you've already had the disk replaced, chances are that it managed to score the flywheel by the time you recognized the trouble signs and had the disk attended to.

- ✔ **If the pressure plate is excessively worn, scored, or glazed,** you should replace it. If you replace it with a rebuilt unit, you can turn in your old one and receive credit for a core charge.

- ✔ **If the springs on the pressure plate become loose,** have them replaced.

Because excessive wear on any part of your clutch results in wear on the other parts, it's generally a good idea to have the clutch assembly, levers, clutch disk, and throwout bearings checked and, if necessary, replaced at the same time. You can also have the *pilot bearing* (located where the crankshaft meets the flywheel) checked then, too, which saves you money on labor charges by eliminating the necessity of getting into your clutch and putting it back together a second time.

To save yourself from paying for unnecessary R&R (which means removal and repair, not rest and relaxation!), keep this good practice in mind when dealing with other parts of your vehicle as well: If the technicians have to open your transmission, ask them to check the whole thing and replace gaskets and other parts that look as though they're about to go. If they have to open your cylinder head or get into the engine, make sure that they look for potential trouble from the rest of the stuff in there.

Don't give them *carte blanche* to replace anything they please. Tell them that you want to see the parts that are wearing *before* they proceed with any unauthorized work. But do keep in mind that a good chunk of the labor cost is associated with just taking stuff apart and putting it back together, so if the mechanics have to do R&R only once, you save money.

If your vehicle is equipped with a hydraulic clutch, don't forget to check the fluid level in the clutch master cylinder. It's just like checking the fluid in your brake master cylinder, which I discuss in Chapter 18.

Undertaking Transmission Repairs Wisely

Your first line of defense against unnecessary transmission work is to have your automatic transmission serviced periodically, according to the manufacturer's recommendations (usually around every 24,000 miles). Your second line of defense is to understand what the basic kinds of transmission work involve. Here are the various types of work that your vehicle may require and what each of them entails:

✔ **If your transmission needs *servicing:***

- The transmission fluid should be changed, if necessary.

- The bands should be adjusted, if this job can be done externally.

- The transmission filter should be replaced.

- The gasket around the transmission pan should be replaced, and the fluid it holds should be changed.

✔ **If your transmission is *leaking:***

- If the *front seal* is bad, the technician must remove your transmission to replace it, but he or she doesn't have to take the transmission apart. Front seals usually have the biggest leaks.

- If the problem is the *rear seal,* the technician must remove your driveshaft, but your transmission can stay in place.

✔ **If your transmission must be *overhauled:***

- The transmission should be removed and disassembled.

- The seals, clutches, bands, and bushings that are worn or defective should be replaced.

✔ **If your transmission must be *replaced:*** The old transmission must be removed and a new one installed. You do have an option as to whether you replace it with a used, rebuilt, or new transmission. I make the distinction between *used* and *rebuilt* because you can buy a transmission from a wrecking yard that has salvaged one designed for your vehicle's year, make, and model. This option is cheap, but risky. Or you can find a rebuilt one that has been salvaged and then completely refurbished and warranted for at least three months. These cost a bit more, but you get a chance to make sure that the thing is in good working order.

Occasionally, gearshifts may become hard to move. This problem can happen if the *gearshift linkage,* which connects the shift lever to the rods that go to the transmission, needs adjustment, lubrication, or minor repair. These repairs aren't expensive and should certainly be investigated before you let anyone talk you into major transmission work.

Front-wheel-drive vehicles have a transmission and axle assembly all in one, called a transaxle. All-wheel-drive and four-wheel-drive vehicles usually have an additional component called a transfer case. Expect to pay more for transaxle repairs and transmission repairs on vehicles with a transfer case.

As you can see, knowing what kind of transmission work is necessary can save you from paying for more work than you need. A number of other things can go wrong and seem to indicate that you need major transmission work to correct them; yet these problems often can be fixed for very little money. An unscrupulous mechanic can diagnose one of the problems as a major transmission breakdown and charge you hundreds of dollars when the real solution could be achieved for much less. (See "Those low-transmission-fluid blues" and "The malfunctioning vacuum modulator caper," earlier in this chapter, for two of these scams.)

Protecting Yourself from Being Ripped Off on Transmission Work

When your transmission needs work, you have to rely on professionals, but that doesn't mean that you have to blindly accept whatever they tell you. Transmission repairs can range from regular service, which is relatively simple and inexpensive, to highly complicated and *very* expensive rebuilds and replacements. The best way to get an accurate diagnosis and the repairs that your vehicle really needs is to follow the advice I give in this section.

For transmission repairs, take your car to a reputable transmission specialist and ask the technician to diagnose the trouble and give you an estimate of the costs. *Do not let the technician take the thing apart.* Once your transmission is in pieces, you're a sitting duck. Have the specialist drive the car, listen to it, ask you questions about its history and its symptoms, and give you his or her ideas. The technician may say, "You may just need your bands tightened, or you may need a new transmission; I can't tell until I open it up." Fine. Ask for estimates for both jobs and, if the prognosis is expensive, get additional estimates. You'd see several doctors before choosing one for major surgery, wouldn't you?

Here are some guidelines for getting the best deal on major transmission work:

✔ **Get three estimates, or more if the first three vary widely.** Discard the highest estimates. Discard a *very* low one, too: If it seems way out of line with the others, it may be a hustle. Then return to the place with the fairest price and/or the best vibes. Of course, an enthusiastic recommendation from someone you know who is fairly knowledgeable about cars is usually worth extra points when you're deciding. But I'd get at least one other estimate anyway.

✔ **After the work is underway, ask to be notified about what they find when they open it up.** Will it be a simple adjustment or a major rebuild? Get the estimated costs on the receipt, signed by you, *before* the actual work begins, and ask to be called if that estimate changes because they uncover other problems.

✔ **Ask them to save the parts they replace so that you can see what you paid for.** Consumer laws in many states hold the repair facility responsible for failing to provide a written estimate, for failing to notify the customer if the estimate increases radically because more problems have been uncovered, and for failing to turn over parts that have been replaced when you've asked that they be saved.

Now go home, cross your fingers, and wait for the operation to be over. Of course, you may still be ripped off, but you'll know that you've done everything possible to prevent it. And because you've been so canny about estimates, open about shopping around, familiar with the transmission itself (read Chapter 9), and insistent about written estimates and such, you just might scare someone who would like to cheat you into doing a good job and charging you properly for it.

If this whole thing sounds paranoid, so be it. The fact is that a few bad apples give the honest, hard-working, car-loving, competent transmission specialists a lot of competition. So go ahead and be paranoid — it can't hurt. You haven't done anything to insult the shop; you've just been careful. Chapter 22 has lots of advice about finding a good repair facility and keeping one happy, and it tells you how to get satisfaction on complaints if you get ripped off anyway.

How to keep from driving your transmission crazy

Driving your vehicle with expertise can prevent many of the most common causes of transmission failure. This involves getting into the proper gear to reduce the strain on the engine and the transmission, and not riding your clutch. A good driver with a manual transmission learns to watch the tachometer, or just "feel" the car's need for more power or more speed, and shift into the proper gear for each occasion. But many drivers with automatic transmissions just shift into Drive and go up steep hills, carry heavy loads, and bounce into jackrabbit starts, happily oblivious to the fact that even automatic transmissions have gear selectors that provide one or two lower gears for these occasions.

An automatic transmission works with gears, too. If you're in low gear, you're transmitting more power to your rear wheels, and your transmission feels the strain. If you attempt to speed in a low gear, you strain the transmission even more. On the other hand, if you attempt to climb hills in high gear, you force the car to make the effort in a gear that lacks the power for the job. The result: more strain.

To avoid unnecessary wear and tear and extend the life of your transmission, whether it's manual or automatic, use the following shifting strategies:

✔ **When you need a sudden burst of speed, use passing gear.** On vehicles with an automatic transmission, passing gear provides the same kind of increased power that downshifting a manual transmission does. You use passing gear when you're already in high gear and need an extra burst of power to pass a car or enter a freeway. If you've been traveling at less than 50 mph, the sudden flooring of the accelerator makes your car downshift automatically from High to Second, which provides more power by speeding up the engine. When you release the pedal, the car goes back to High.

✔ **Use Overdrive (or Fifth gear on a manual transmission), if you have it, when you're travelling along steadily at a high speed.** With Overdrive or Fifth, you have an extra, higher gear that allows your rear wheels to turn even faster while maintaining the same engine speed. After you're really moving, shifting into Overdrive means that you can move at the same speed while the engine turns more slowly and consumes less fuel.

✔ **Shift to higher gears as soon as your speed enters their range.** (Your owner's manual should tell you the range of speed for each gear.) There's no need to supply extra power when it's not needed. However, if traffic slows and you feel the engine straining (called *lugging*), downshift to allow the lower gears to provide more power.

✔ **When the engine is lugging, shift into a lower gear so that it can turn faster and carry you along with less strain.** After you get everything moving freely, return to a higher gear.

✔ **Use lower gears for heavy loads and steep hills.** If you come to a steep hill — or if you're carrying four kids, two dogs, and everything you'll need for a month in the country — go for the lower gears instead of trying to haul the whole mess as fast as you can. Then shift back up again to coast down the hill. This way, the power goes toward carrying the load rather than toward maintaining speed.

Chapter 18

Being a Buddy to Your Brakes and Bearings

In This Chapter

▶ Extending the life of your brakes

▶ Checking the "feel" when you press the brake

▶ Paying attention to the fluid level in the master cylinder

▶ Looking for leaks in your brake lines

▶ Checking drum and disc brakes for wear

▶ Checking and packing wheel bearings

▶ Flushing the system and changing the fluid

▶ Bleeding the air out of your brake lines

▶ Adjusting your parking brake

▶ Checking your anti-lock braking system (ABS)

As I explain in Chapter 10, all vehicles today are equipped with dual hydraulic brake systems. Many newer vehicles are also equipped with anti-lock brake systems (ABS). This chapter provides instructions for doing preventive maintenance on your brakes and doing checkups that help you to spot trouble before it occurs. If you need professional work done, this chapter also provides tips that enable you to deal on an informed basis with an auto mechanic or brake specialist.

If you haven't read Chapter 10, or if you've forgotten what you read, please go back and review it before continuing with this chapter. Chapter 10 describes hydraulic brake systems on a part-by-part basis, explains the differences between disc brakes and drum brakes and between *manual* and power brakes, and describes parking brakes and anti-lock brake systems. You must be familiar with what *should* be happening when you stop your car before you can tell whether the brakes need adjusting. And you need to be familiar with the parts involved before you can work on your brakes.

Although it's possible to do most of the work in this chapter yourself — it's not terribly complicated — I don't think that you should do *major* brake work without supervision. If you don't get things back properly, you risk losing much more than you gain! However, if, after reading this chapter, you simply can't stand the idea of having a total stranger replace your worn brake linings, you can always get yourself to a good auto repair class and do the work under an instructor's watchful eye. Auto classes generally have the hydraulic hoists, brake lathes, and other expensive equipment that you need to do a really good job. So even if you're sure that you need no further instruction after reading my enlightened and crystal-clear prose, having the equipment and the instructor's expertise available is still worth the price of enrollment.

Extending the Life of Your Brakes

Riding your brakes causes them to wear out prematurely. The excess heat can also warp disc brake rotors and brake drums.

Although being cautious is always a good policy, try to anticipate stopping situations well enough in advance to be able to slow down by releasing the pressure on your gas pedal and then using your brake pedal for that final stop. In slippery conditions — or situations that call for slowing down rather than stopping — if you have traditional brakes, pump your brake pedal to reduce speed and avoid sliding rather than jamming on your brakes and screeching to a halt.

If the road is slippery and your vehicle is equipped with an anti-lock braking system (ABS), *don't* pump the brake pedal; simply apply firm, steady pressure and keep steering.

Checking Your Brake System

Let's start by going over the brake system in your vehicle and checking each part for wear and proper performance. If it's safe for you to do the necessary work, I'll tell you how to do it. If you need professional help, I'll tell you what the work should probably entail so that you don't end up paying for more work than is necessary.

Check your brakes every 10,000 to 20,000 miles, depending on the age of your vehicle, the history of its brakes, and how much stop-and-go driving you do. If you tend to ride your brakes (keep your foot on the brake pedal when you drive), they're getting more than normal wear and should be checked more frequently.

Use extreme caution when checking vehicles with anti-lock brake systems. Some anti-lock systems are pressurized by an electric pump, and there may be more than 2,000 psi pressure in certain parts of the system!

Checking your brake pedal

If you're like most people, you're usually aware of only one part of your brake system: the brake pedal. You're so familiar with it, in fact, that you can probably tell if something's different just by the way the pedal feels when you put on the brakes. When you check your brake pedal, you simply do the same thing you do every time you drive: You step on the pedal and press it down. The only difference is that, this time, you pay attention to how the pedal feels under your foot and evaluate the sensation you get. The following steps tell you what to look for.

Note: If your vehicle is equipped with power brakes (most are), check the brake pedal with the engine running.

1. **With the car at rest, apply steady pressure to the brake pedal.**

   Does it feel spongy? If so, you probably have air in your brake lines. Correcting this problem isn't difficult; you can probably do the job yourself with the help of a friend. For instructions, see "Bleeding Your Brakes" later in this chapter.

   Does the pedal stay firm when you continue applying pressure, or does it seem to sink slowly to the floor? If the pedal sinks, your master cylinder may be defective, and that's unsafe.

2. **Drive around the block, stopping every now and then (but without driving the people behind you crazy).**

   Notice how much effort is required to bring your car to a stop. If you have ordinary *self-adjusting* brakes, the pedal should stop more than 3 inches from the floor. If you have power brakes, the pedal should stop an inch to an inch and a half from the floor. If your vehicle has power brakes and stopping it seems to take excessive effort, you may need a new power booster.

3. **If you feel that your brakes are "low" (that the pedal goes down too far before the vehicle stops properly), pump the brake pedal a couple of times as you drive around.**

   Does the pedal now stop higher up? If so, a brake adjustment is probably in order — or you may just need more brake fluid. Check the brake fluid level by following the instructions in "Checking your master cylinder," later in this chapter.

If the level of brake fluid in the master cylinder is low, buy the proper brake fluid for your vehicle (see "Flushing and Changing Brake Fluid" later in this chapter for tips) and add fluid to the "Full" line on your master cylinder. Check the fluid level in the cylinder again in a few days. If it's low, check each part of the brake system, following the instructions in this chapter, until you find the leak, or have a brake specialist find it and repair it for you.

If you find that you're *not* low on fluid and if you can't adjust them yourself, drive to your friendly service facility and ask them to adjust your brakes. After that, the pedal shouldn't travel down as far before your car stops.

Disc brakes self-adjust and should never need adjusting. Drum brakes, however, have self-adjusting mechanisms that should keep the drum brakes properly adjusted. If any of the self-adjuster components on drum brakes stick or break, the drum brakes won't adjust as they wear out, resulting in a low pedal.

4. **As you drive around, notice how your total brake system performs.**

   Ask yourself these questions:

   - **Does the vehicle travel too far before coming to a stop in city traffic?** If it does, your brakes need adjusting or you need new brake linings.

   - **Does the vehicle pull to one side when you brake?** On vehicles with front disc brakes, a stuck caliper can cause this problem. On older vehicles with front drum brakes, a wheel cylinder may be either leaking or stuck. I explain how to check disc and drum brakes in the section called "Getting at Your Brakes" later in this chapter.

   - **Does your brake pedal pulsate up and down when you stop? Does your steering wheel shake when you brake?** If so, and you have disc brakes, your front brake rotors need to be machined or replaced. A pulsating brake pedal is usually caused by excessive *lateral run-out* (mechanic-speak for wobbling from side to side), which can happen because your brakes are overheating from overuse.

   Make sure that your rear brakes are working. If not, they could be causing your front brakes to work too hard and overheat.

   - **Do your brakes squeal when you stop fairly short?** The squealing is a high-pitched noise usually caused by vibration. Squealing can occur when the brake linings are worn and need replacement, the drum or rotor needs to be machined, the front disc brake pads are loose or missing their anti-rattle clips, the hardware that attaches the brake calipers is worn, or inferior brake linings are in use.

   Totally eliminating a squeal can be difficult. When you open your brakes to check them, make sure that your rotors or drums aren't badly scored or worn and that plenty of lining material is left. Also, the brake pads on disc type brakes should fit properly into the caliper.

Some disc brake pads require special shims to eliminate squeal. If you visit your local parts store, you'll probably see a product called *Disc Brake Quiet*. This sticky spray hardens to a rubber-like material. If you use it, make sure to spray it on the *back* of the brake pads — the metal part that rests against the caliper. Never spray Disc Brake Quiet on the brake rotor or on the lining material that contacts the brake rotor.

- **Do your brakes make a grinding noise that you can feel in the pedal?** If so, stop driving immediately and have your vehicle towed home or to a repair shop. Further driving could damage the brake rotors or drums. Grinding brakes are caused by excessively worn brake linings. When the lining wears off, the metal part of the brake pad or brake shoe contacts the brake rotor or drum and can quickly ruin the rotors or drums — the most expensive parts of the brake system.

- **Does your vehicle bounce up and down when you stop short?** Your shock absorbers may need to be replaced. See Chapter 11 for information about shock absorbers.

Never put off brake work. If any of the checks in this chapter shows that you have a problem, *take care of the situation immediately*. If your brakes fail, you (and other people) may be in serious trouble. Other kinds of automotive trouble may keep your vehicle from moving — brake trouble keeps it from *stopping*. The rest — and you — may be history.

Checking your master cylinder

Brake fluid is stored in the master cylinder. When you step on the brake pedal, fluid goes from the master cylinder into the brake lines, and then, when you release the pedal, the fluid flows back into the master cylinder. Essentially, when you check your master cylinder, you're looking to make sure that you have enough brake fluid.

If your vehicle has anti-lock brakes (ABS), consult your owner's manual before checking the master cylinder. Failure to do so may result in under- or overfilling the reservoir. And remember that some anti-lock systems are under extreme pressure.

To check the brake fluid in your master cylinder, follow these steps:

1. **Open the top of your master cylinder.**

   If you have the kind with a little plastic bottle on top, just unscrew the cap (see Figure 18-1). If you have a metal one, use a screwdriver to pry the retaining clamp off the top (see Figure 18-2).

Don't let any dirt fall into the chambers when you open the lid. If your hood area is full of grime and dust, wipe the lid before you remove it.

Figure 18-1: If your cylinder has a plastic reservoir, just unscrew the cap.

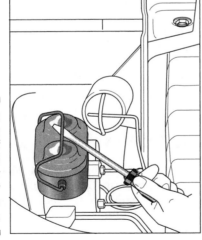

Figure 18-2: Releasing the lid of a metal master cylinder with a screwdriver.

2. **Take a look at the lid.**

   Attached to the inside surface of a metal master cylinder is a rubber diaphragm with two rubber cups (see Figure 18-3). Caps on plastic reservoirs have them, too. As the brake fluid in your master cylinder recedes (when it's forced into the brake lines), the diaphragm cups are pushed down by air that comes in through vents in the lid. The rubber cups descend and touch the surface of the remaining brake fluid, to prevent evaporation and to keep the dust and dirt out. When the fluid flows back in, the rubber cups are pushed back up.

If your brake fluid level is low, or if the rubber cups are in their descended position when you remove the lid, push them back up with your finger before you replace the lid.

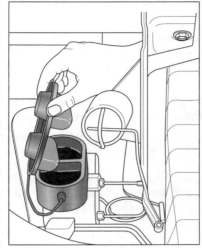

Figure 18-3:
You can see the rubber cups inside the lid of this master cylinder.

If the cups seem very gooey or can't be pushed back to their original position, the wrong brake fluid may have been used. Because some containers of power steering fluid are the same shape as brake fluid containers, there have been cases where power steering fluid was accidentally installed in the master cylinder. If this happens, everything but the steel brake lines must be rebuilt or replaced, including the master cylinder!

3. **Look inside the master cylinder.**

   The brake fluid should be up to the "Full" line on the side of the cylinder or within half an inch of the top of each chamber. If it isn't, buy brake fluid and add it to the line.

Be sure to read the "Flushing and Changing Brake Fluid" section in this chapter to ensure that you buy the proper kind. Also remember to close the master cylinder and the brake fluid container as quickly as possible so that oxygen or water vapor in the air doesn't contaminate the fluid.

A low brake fluid level may not mean anything if it's been a long time since any fluid was added, and if your car has been braking properly. If you have reason to believe that your brake fluid level has dropped because of a leak, use this chapter to check the rest of your system very carefully for leaks.

4. **If both chambers of your master cylinder are filled with brake fluid to the proper level, close the master cylinder carefully, without letting any dirt fall into it.**

If dirt gets into your master cylinder, it will travel down the brake lines. If it doesn't block the lines, the dirt will end up in your wheel cylinders and damage your brakes.

5. **Brake fluid evaporates easily, so don't stand around admiring the inside of your master cylinder. Close it quickly, and be sure that the lid is securely in place.**

   Because most master cylinders are pretty airtight, you shouldn't lose brake fluid in any quantity unless it's leaking out somewhere else. If your fluid level was low, you'll find the cause as you continue to check the system.

6. **Take a flashlight, or a work light, and look for stain marks, wetness, or gunk under the master cylinder and on the firewall near it.**

   If your master cylinder is — or has been — leaking, you'll see this evidence.

It's a good idea to check your master cylinder at least every couple of months — more often if it was low in fluid when you last checked it. This step should be part of the regular under-the-hood check that I describe in Chapter 3.

Checking your brake lines

If the fluid level in your master cylinder remains full (see the preceding section), chances are that you don't need to check for leaks in the brake lines that carry the fluid to each wheel cylinder. If, however, you find that you're losing brake fluid, or if the insides of your tires are wet and look as though something has been leaking and streaking them, it could be a leak in the wheel cylinders or the lines — or a visit from a neighbor's dog!

The easiest way to check brake lines is to put the vehicle up on a hydraulic hoist, raise it over your head, walk under it, and examine the lines as they lead from the hood area to each wheel. Leaks may be coming from holes in the lines, where the steel lines become rubber ones, or where the brake lines connect with the wheel cylinders.

If you don't have access to a hoist at the auto repair shop at your local school or at a friendly garage, you have to jack up your car, one end at a time, and get down there with a flashlight or work light to look at your lines. Before you do so, check Chapter 1 for instructions and safety tips on jacking up your car!

Do the following:

1. **Check carefully along the lines for wetness and for streaks of dried fluid.**

2. **If you see rust spots on your lines, *gently* sand them off and look for thin places under those spots that may turn into holes before too long.**

3. **Feel the rubber parts of the brake lines for signs that the rubber is becoming sticky, soft, spongy, or worn.**

Your brake lines should last the life of your car. If they look very bad, have a professional take a look at them and tell you whether they should be replaced. If the vehicle is fairly new and the brake lines look very bad, go back to the dealership and ask them to replace the lines free of charge.

4. **Look at the inner surfaces of your tires for drippy clues about leaking wheel cylinders.**

Getting at Your Brakes

The next thing to do is to check your brakes to see whether they're in good condition. This job isn't as scary as it sounds; in fact, it's quite simple — with two qualifications: First, don't fiddle with anything unless I tell you to! Second, be sure to disassemble the stuff that covers your brakes in the proper manner so that you won't have trouble reassembling it. For details on this foolproof technique, see the section in Chapter 1 called "How to Take Anything Apart — and Get It Back Together Again."

Things not to do when working on brakes

Here are a couple of "nevers" to remember when working on your brakes. Doing any of these things can cause serious damage and huge headaches:

- ✔ **Never step on your brake pedal when you have the brake drum off your brakes.** You can literally blow the brakes apart! The pistons can fly out of the ends of the wheel cylinders because the drum won't stop the brake shoes from moving outward. (If this makes no sense to you, go back and read about how wheel cylinders work in Chapter 10.)
- ✔ **Never use anything but brake fluid in your brakes.**
- ✔ **Never get oil anywhere near your brake system.** Oil blows up rubber and will destroy the master cylinder cups and the dust boots on your wheel cylinders. If it gets on your brake linings, they won't grab the brake drum.
- ✔ **Never get brake fluid on a painted surface.** Brake fluid will destroy the paint.
- ✔ **Never remove wheel cylinders or brake shoes, or tamper with the self-adjusting device on your brakes, without supervision.**

Most older vehicles have drum brakes on all wheels, but if you have a newer car, you may have disc brakes on your front wheels and drum brakes on your rear wheels or disc brakes all around. Your owner's manual should tell you what the configuration is on your vehicle. Once you know, follow the instructions in the following section(s) that deal with the type(s) of brakes on your vehicle.

When you check your brakes, check one of your front brakes first because the linings wear faster on the front brakes than on the rear ones. If the first set of brakes you look at seems to be in good condition, and if your car has been braking properly, there's probably no need to check on the other three. Just remember to check a different set the next time. However, if your brakes haven't been behaving properly, then go on checking each set until you find the culprit.

Before you start to check your brakes, scan the instructions later in this chapter (including the section on checking and packing wheel bearings) to be sure that you have the necessary tools and products on hand. When your vehicle is on up jack stands with at least one wheel off, you don't want any last-minute surprises! If you're unfamiliar with the tools you need for the job, see Chapter 2 for descriptions.

I provide separate sections for checking and reassembling drum brakes and checking disc brakes, so just read the ones that relate to the type of brakes you have. The section on checking and packing wheel bearings applies to both drum and disc brakes (but if you have disc brakes, do these jobs only under supervision at an auto class).

Checking drum brakes

As you can see in Figure 18-4, you have to remove a bunch of stuff to get to a drum brake. The steps in this section explain how to do so and what to look for when you finally get to your brakes. (*Note:* A front-wheel drive vehicle doesn't conform exactly to the following description. You can still check the brakes, but you can't repack the wheel bearings.)

Arrange to do this work in a well-ventilated area, and be very careful not to inhale the dust from the brake drum — it probably contains asbestos. If you get asbestos in your lungs, you run the risk of asbestosis and asbestos emphysema.

1. **Jack up your vehicle.**

   For instructions, see Chapter 1. Be sure to observe safety precautions with that jack!

   Brake drums are classified as either "hubbed" or "floating" (hubless). Hubbed drums have wheel bearings inside them. Floating drums simply slide over the lug nut studs that hold the wheels on the vehicle.

2. **If you have a *hubbed* drum, pry the grease cap off the end of the hub, using a pair of combination slip-joint pliers (tools shown in Chapter 2).**

   Lay the grease cap on a clean, lint-free rag.

   If you have a *floating* drum, skip Steps 3 through 7 and just slide the drum off the hub.

   You sometimes need to strike floating drums with a hammer to break them loose from the hub.

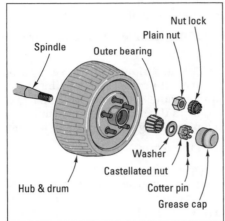

Figure 18-4: The things you have to remove to get at your drum brakes.

3. **Look at the cotter pin that sticks out of the side of the castellated nut or nut-lock-and-nut combination.**

   Notice in which direction it's lying, how its legs are bent, how it fits through the nut, and how tight it is. If necessary, make a sketch.

4. **Use a pair of needle-nose pliers to straighten the cotter pin and pull it out.**

   Put it on the rag that you're using to hold all the parts you've taken off, and lay it down in the same direction it pointed when it was in place.

5. **Slide the castellated nut or nut-lock-and-nut combination off the spindle.**

   If it's greasy, wipe it off with a lint-free rag and lay it on the rag next to the cotter pin.

6. **Grab the brake drum and pull it toward you, but *do not slide the drum off the spindle yet;* then push the drum back into place.**

   The things that are left on the spindle are the *outer* wheel bearings and washer.

7. **Carefully slide the outer bearing, with the washer in front of it, off the spindle.**

8. **Whether or not you want to repack your wheel bearings, check them now by following the instructions for inspecting and checking wheel bearings in the section called "Checking and Packing Wheel Bearings," later in this chapter. Then come back here and resume with Step 9.**

   As long as you're removing your bearings, you should check them for wear. If they're "packable," it's a good idea to repack them while you have everything apart. (All this task involves is squishing wheel-bearing grease into them, a wonderfully sensual job.)

9. **Carefully slide the drum off the spindle, with the inner bearings inside it.**

   Inhaling brake dust can make you seriously ill. For safety's sake, *never* attempt to blow away the dust with compressed air. Instead, saturate the dust completely by spraying the drum with brake parts cleaner according to the instructions on the can. Wipe the drum clean with a rag; then place the rag in a plastic bag and dispose of it immediately.

10. **Take a look at the inside of the drum.**

    You can probably see grooves on the inner walls from wear. If these grooves look unusually deep, or if you see hard spots or burned places, ask your service facility to let you watch while they check out the drums with a *micrometer* (see Figure 18-5). If the drums aren't worn past legal tolerances (0.060 of an inch), they can be *reground* (or turned) rather than replaced. A special machine called a *brake-lathe* does this job in a relatively short amount of time. It shouldn't be a major job in terms of expense. You could do it yourself at a school auto shop; most classes have the machine.

    If it looks as though the drum has to be *replaced,* ask your service facility to get you a used, *reground* drum. These are much cheaper than new ones and should be just as good, if checking with a micrometer shows that they are not too worn. If your facility can't find you one, call a couple of places listed under "Automobiles–wrecking" in the Yellow Pages and ask for used drums in good condition for your vehicle's make, model, and year.

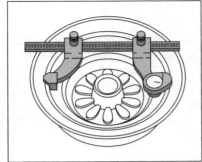

Figure 18-5:
Checking
drum wear
with a
micrometer.

Make sure that the drums look *exactly the same* as your old ones, and don't forget to specify drums for *front* or *rear* wheels. Brake drums must be replaced with drums of the same size for even braking performance. Have a professional install them for you, because the brake shoes must be adjusted to fit.

11. **Look at the rest of your brakes, which are still attached to the brake backing plate (see Figure 18-6).**

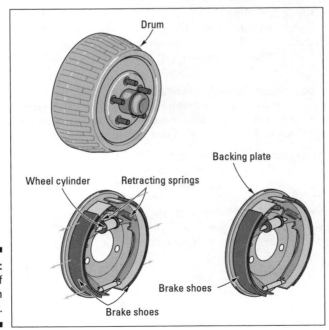

Drum

Backing plate

Wheel cylinder   Retracting springs

Brake shoes

Figure 18-6:
Anatomy of
a drum
brake.

Brake shoes

Here are the parts you should look at, what you should find, and what to do if they need to be repaired or replaced:

- **Wheel cylinders:** The wheel cylinders should show no signs of leaking brake fluid. If they're leaky, consult a brake shop.

- **Brake shoes and linings:** These should be evenly worn, with no bald spots or thin places. The brake lining should be at least 1/16 inch from the steel part of the brake shoe or 1/16 inch from any rivet on brake shoes with rivets. The linings should be firmly bonded or riveted to the brake shoes. Most brakes give from 10,000 to 20,000 miles of wear. Some last even longer. If yours have been on your car for some time, they'll have grooves in them and may be somewhat glazed.

If your brake drums have been wearing evenly and your vehicle has been braking properly, disregard the grooves and the glazing unless your linings look badly worn. If your linings are worn, have them replaced at once. This job involves replacing the brake shoes with "new" ones that have new linings on them. Always replace brake shoes in sets (four shoes for two front or rear wheels is a set) for even performance. Replacing them all at once is even better.

If your brake shoes need to be replaced, remember that almost all "new" brake shoes are really rebuilt ones. When your brake shoes are replaced, your old brake shoes are returned to a company that removes the old linings, attaches new ones, and resells the shoes. So it can't hurt to ask whether the core charge can be deducted from the price of the new shoes.

12. **Take a look at the *self-adjusting devices* on your brakes. (Figures 18-7 through 18-9 show the most common self-adjusters.) Trace the cable from the anchor pin above the wheel cylinder, around the side of the backing plate, to the adjuster at the bottom of the plate.**

Is the cable hooked up? Does it feel tight? If your brake pedal manages to apply your brakes before it gets halfway down to the floor, the adjustment is probably just fine. If not, and if the cylinders, linings, shoes, and so on, are okay, the adjusting devices may be out of whack. Making a couple of forward and reverse stops should fix them. If this approach doesn't work, you may need an adjustment at a service station. Don't attempt to fiddle with these yourself.

Figure 18-7:
Self-adjusting Delco Moraine brake: When you back up, the adjusting links and springs adjust the brakes automatically.

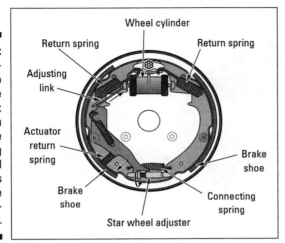

Figure 18-8:
Manually adjusted brake: You turn the star wheel adjuster by hand to adjust the brakes.

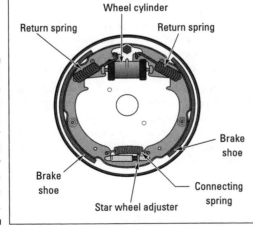

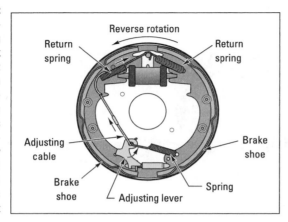

Figure 18-9:
Self-
adjusting
Bendix
brake:
When you
back up, the
adjusting
cable is
automati-
cally
tightened
and the
brakes
adjust
themselves.

Keep the following in mind for any major work your brakes may need:

✔ **Don't attempt to replace shoes, linings, or wheel cylinders yourself unless you do so under the eye of an auto shop instructor.** If you choose to go this route, the money you save more than pays for your tuition. The job is neither difficult nor complicated. It just needs supervision.

✔ **If you'd rather have the work done for you, find a reliable brake specialist rather than taking your car to the corner garage.** Try the Yellow Pages or have the mechanic at your local service station steer you to one. Call a couple of places and ask for estimates on rebuilding your brakes. Avoid the cheapest place as well as the most expensive! Chapter 22 is filled with advice on finding good service facilities and dealing with them successfully.

Reassembling drum brakes

After you finish inspecting your brakes, as I explained in the preceding section, you're ready to replace everything. Refer to Figure 18-4 to make sure that you get everything back in the proper order and direction. The following steps tell you how:

1. **As you did with the drums, saturate the dirt on the brake backing plate with brake parts cleaner; then wipe it off with a clean, *grease-free* rag and throw the rag away.**

Don't blow the dust around — it can contain asbestos and cause serious lung damage. If you'd rather not deal with it at all, just leave the grime alone.

2. **Wipe the dirt off the spindle and replace the wheel hub and brake drum on the spindle. If you have a floating drum, skip Steps 4 through 8 and slide the drum back over the lug nut studs until it contacts the hub.**

   Be gentle so that you don't unseat the grease seal.

3. **If you haven't already cleaned the inside of the drum, spray it with brake cleaner and wipe it out with a grease-free rag; then wrap the rag in a plastic bag and dispose of it immediately.**

4. **Replace the *outer* wheel bearing (smaller end first) and the washer.**

   Don't let any dirt get on these!

5. **Replace the adjusting nut by screwing it on firmly and then backing it off half a turn and retightening it "finger tight."**

   Another way to complete this step is to back the adjusting nut off one full notch (60 degrees) and, if the notch doesn't line up with the hole in the spindle, back it off just enough until it does. Then spin the wheel by hand to be sure that it turns freely. If it doesn't, loosen the nut a bit more.

6. **Insert the cotter pin into the hole in the castellated nut.**

   The cotter pin should clear the outer grooves and go all the way through. Refer to your sketch, if you made one, to make sure that it's pointing in the right direction.

7. **Bend the legs of the cotter pin back across the surface of the nut to hold it in place.**

8. **Replace the grease cap.**

9. **Follow the instructions in Chapter 1 to replace your wheel, lug nuts, and hubcap and lower the vehicle to the ground.**

Checking disc brakes

Today, most vehicles have four-wheel disc brakes. Others have disc brakes on the front wheels and drum brakes on the rear wheels.

You should check disc brakes and disc brake linings every 10,000 miles — more often if your brakes suddenly start to squeal or pull to one side, or if your brake pedal flutters when you step on it.

Before you check your brakes, go to an auto supply store or to the parts department of your dealership and ask to see a set of brake pads for your vehicle's make, model, and year. Measure the thickness of the linings on the pads so that you'll be able to tell whether the linings on your brakes are badly worn when you check them.

To check disc brakes, use Figure 18-10 for guidance and follow these steps:

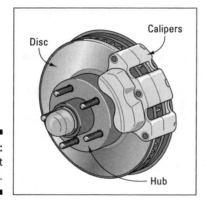

Figure 18-10:
Getting at
disc brakes.

1. **Jack up your vehicle and remove a *front* wheel.**

   You can find instructions for how to do this safely in Chapter 1.

2. **Look at the rotor, but *don't attempt to remove it from the vehicle*.**

   The brake caliper has to be removed before you can remove a disc brake rotor, and there's no need to do so. If you're working alone, just check the visible part of the rotor for heavy rust, scoring, and uneven wear. Rust generally does no damage unless the vehicle has been standing idle for a long time and the rust has really built up. If your rotor is badly scored or worn unevenly, have a professional determine whether it can be reground or it needs to be replaced.

3. **Inspect your brake caliper (the component blocking your view of the entire disc brake rotor).**

   Be careful. If the vehicle has been driven recently, the caliper will be hot. If it's cool to the touch, grasp it and gently shake it to make sure that it isn't loosely mounted and its mounting hardware isn't worn.

4. **Peek through the dust shield on the caliper and look at the brake pads inside.**

   If the linings on the brake pads look much thinner than the new ones you saw, they probably have to be replaced. If the linings have worn to the metal pads, the disc probably has to be reground as well.

5. **Follow the instructions in Chapter 1 to replace your wheel, lug nuts, and hubcap and lower the vehicle to the ground.**

   If the rotor and pads seem to be in good condition and your brake pedal doesn't flutter when you step on it, there's nothing else you need to do.

Relining, caliper maintenance, and disc grinding should be left to a professional unless you do the job under supervision at an auto class. Go to a brake specialist (use the Yellow Pages or ask a friendly mechanic to steer you to one) rather than to the corner garage for this kind of work. Call a couple of shops and ask for estimates. Choose neither the cheapest nor the most expensive. Chapter 22 is devoted to finding a good service facility and dealing with them successfully.

Checking and Packing Wheel Bearings

As you can see back in Figure 18-4, wheel bearings usually come in pairs of *inner* and *outer* bearings. They allow your wheels to turn freely over thousands of miles by cushioning the contact between the wheel and the spindle it sits on with frictionless bearings and lots of nice, gooey grease. This grease tends to pick up dust, dirt, and little particles of metal, although the bearings are protected to some extent by the hub and the brake drum or disc.

   ✔ **If you have drum brakes,** it's important to check the bearings when you check your brakes to make sure that the grease hasn't become fouled with this stuff. If it has, the particles act abrasively to wear away the very connection the bearings are designed to protect, and the result is a noisy, grinding ride. In extreme cases, you could even lose the wheel! If the bearings look cruddy, either repack them yourself or get a professional to do it.

✔ **If you have disc brakes,** you have to remove the caliper to get at the bearings. Although this task isn't terribly difficult, certain aspects of the job can create problems for a beginner. Because your brake system can kill you if it isn't assembled properly, I strongly suggest that, if you want to do it yourself, you do the job under supervision at an auto class.

Before you check your bearings, consult your owner's manual or dealer to find out whether the bearings on your vehicle are *sealed.* If they are, you can't repack them.

Usually, only the *non*-drive wheels (the front wheels on rear-wheel-drive cars and the rear wheels on front-wheel-drive cars) have repackable wheel bearings. Vehicles with front-wheel drive have sealed front bearings, but some have packable rear ones. The bearings on four-wheel-drive vehicles are quite complicated and should be repacked professionally.

If you don't want to — or shouldn't — check your bearings right now, try the process in "A quick way to tell if your bearing's wearing" at the end of this section. Then have your wheel bearings repacked when a repair facility is doing a front-end alignment or a brake job. Because they'll have the wheels off anyway, you can eliminate having to pay for duplicate labor.

Inspecting and repacking your wheel bearings

If you have disc brakes, you have to remove the caliper to get the disc off the spindle in order to get at the inner bearings. In this case, I think that you should inspect and pack them only under supervision at an auto class or under the eye of an experienced mechanic. It's not a difficult job; it's just that you may not get the calipers back on right, which could cause your brakes to malfunction.

If you have drum brakes, go right ahead and do the job yourself. Follow these steps to repack your wheel bearings:

1. **If you have drum brakes and your bearings *aren't* sealed, follow the instructions for checking drum brakes in the section called "Getting at Your Brakes," earlier in this chapter.**

   When you get to the point where you slide the outer wheel bearings off the spindle, return to this section.

2. **If you haven't already done so, carefully slide the *outer* bearing, with the washer in front of it, off the spindle.**

   As you can see in Figure 18-11, these are usually tapered *roller* bearings, not *ball* bearings.

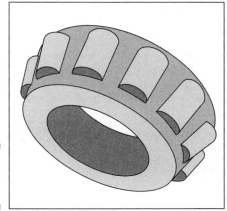

Figure 18-11:
A wheel
bearing.

3. **Take a good look at the grease in the spaces between the bearings.** *Do not wipe off the grease!*

If the grease has sparkly silver slivers or particles in it or the rollers are pitted or chipped, you must replace the bearings. If the outer bearings are damaged, the inner bearings probably are, too. In this case, either replace the bearings in an auto class under the instructor's guidance or have a repair facility do the job for you.

4. **If you *don't* intend to repack your outer bearings at this time but you want to continue your inspection, *do not* attempt to wipe any grease off them, no matter how icky they look.**

Just put them in a little plastic bag and lay them on your rag, pointing in the right direction. The bag will keep dust from getting into them. A speck of dust can wear out a bearing quickly.

If you *are* repacking your outer bearings, clean them thoroughly in solvent or kerosene with an old paintbrush.

You need to get rid of all the old grease in order to inspect the bearings properly. Also, when you repack the bearings with fresh grease, you don't want any old grease spoiling the new stuff.

5. **When the bearings are shiny clean, rinse them off with water and dry them, or use brake cleaner to remove the solvent.**

If you pack new grease over the solvent, the grease will dissolve and you'll ruin your bearings.

6. **When the bearings are clean and dry, look at the rollers for signs of wear.**

If the rollers are gouged or bluish in color, or if you can almost slip the rollers out of their place, replace the bearing and its *race,* which is pressed into the hub.

7. **To repack the outer bearing, take a gob of wheel bearing grease (which is different from most chassis-lube grease) and place it in the palm of your left hand (if you're a righty).**

You may want to invest in a pair of cheap, disposable plastic gloves for this job. However, there's something kind of nice about fresh, clean grease, and if you use gloves, you miss one of the more sensual aspects of getting intimately involved with your car. Hand cleaner gets the grease off easily, in any event.

8. **Press the bearing into the gob of grease with the heel of your other hand (see Figure 18-12).**

Doing so forces the grease into the bearing and out the other end. Make sure that you work the grease into every gap in the bearing. You want it to be nice and yucky. Now put your bearing down on your clean rag.

Figure 18-12:
How to pack bearings with your bare hands.

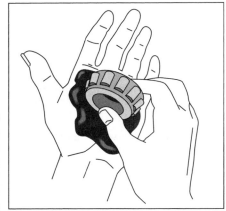

- **If you have drum brakes, you can see another set of bearings in the center hole of the drum.** These are your inner wheel bearings. At this time, you have to decide whether you're going to remove the inner bearings to check and pack them. The following will help you decide whether to remove the inner bearings:

- **You can't remove the *inner* bearing from its seat in the hub unless you have a new grease seal for it.** So if you're just checking on this expedition, leave the inner bearings alone until you're sure from the condition of the outer bearings that repacking is in order.

- **Generally speaking, if the outer bearings look okay, the inner ones are okay, too.** Just check each wheel and put everything back according to the instructions for reassembling drum brakes earlier in this chapter.

9. If you're *not* planning to repack the inner bearings, *do not* attempt to take them out of their seat in the drum. Skip Steps 10 through 13 and continue with Step 14.

   If you *are* repacking the inner bearings, slide the brake drum or disc toward you, with the inner bearings still in place, but *do not slide the drum completely off the spindle.* Instead, screw the adjusting nut back in again and pull the drum toward you and push it back.

   The adjusting nut should catch the inner bearing and its grease seal and free them from inside the hub.

10. Clean and pack the inner bearings, using the technique described in Steps 5 through 8.

11. Take a rag and wipe out the hole in the hub of the drum where the inner bearing went; then take another gob of grease and smooth it into the hole.

   Be sure that the grease fills the races inside the hub where the bearing fits. Wipe off excess grease around the outside of the hole or it will fly around when the car's in motion, possibly damaging your brakes.

12. Insert the inner bearing into the hub, with the small end first. Take the new grease seal and spread a film of grease around the sealing end (the flat, smooth side).

13. To fit the new grease seal into place properly, slide it in evenly; otherwise, it will bend or break, and you'll lose your grease.

   Use a hollow pipe or a large socket from a socket wrench set that has roughly the same diameter as the seal. With the flat, smooth side of the seal toward you, place the seal in the hub opening, and use the pipe or socket to move it into the hub gently and evenly. The new seal should end up flush with the outside of the hub or slightly inside it.

14. Return to the instructions on checking drum brakes and pick up where you left off.

You'll be glad to know that your rear wheels have no wheel bearings to pack (unless your vehicle has front-wheel drive and the manual says that you can repack the rear bearings). You do have *axle bearings,* but you must replace these if they wear out; you can't repack them. If your car is quite old and you hear a clicking or grinding noise from the vicinity of your rear wheels, have these bearings checked and replaced if necessary. Hearing worn axle bearings is easiest when you drive down an alley or a narrow driveway because the noise echoes loudly.

A quick way to tell whether your bearing's wearing

If you just want to check your bearings for wear without removing the wheels, do the following:

1. **Jack up your car and support it on safety stands.**

   If you've been checking your brakes, your car is already jacked up; if not, instructions in Chapter 1 show you how to do this task safely.

2. **Grasp each wheel at the top and bottom and attempt to rock it.**

   There should be minimal movement. Excessive play may indicate that the wheel bearing is worn and needs adjustment or replacement.

3. **Put the gearshift in Neutral if you have an automatic transmission, or take your manual transmission out of gear.**

4. **Rotate the wheel, listening for any unusual noise and feeling for any roughness as you rotate the wheel.**

   Any unusual noise or roughness may indicate that the bearing is damaged and needs to be replaced.

5. **Shift back into gear (for a manual transmission) or Park (for an automatic transmission) before lowering the vehicle to the ground.**

Flushing and Changing Brake Fluid

If, after checking your brake system, you find that you have a leak or you have to bleed your brakes (see the section "Bleeding your brakes" for more information), you'll have to restore the brake fluid in your master cylinder to its proper level. Here are some things that you should know about buying and using brake fluid:

- ✔ **Always use top-quality brake fluid from a well-known manufacturer.** Most vehicles call for either D.O.T. 3 or D.O.T. 4 fluid. Sometimes the type of fluid to use is listed on the master cylinder reservoir cover or cap.

- ✔ **Exposure to air swiftly contaminates brake fluid.** The oxygen in the air oxidizes it and lowers its boiling point. Brake fluid also has an affinity for moisture, and the water vapor in the air can combine with the brake fluid to form ice crystals that make braking difficult in cold weather. Adding water vapor-contaminated fluid to your brake system can rust the system and create acids that etch your wheel cylinders and master cylinder and foul your brakes, causing them to work poorly — or not at all. Therefore, if you're going to add brake fluid to your system, buy a small can, add the fluid to your master cylinder, and *throw the rest away,* or use it only in emergencies. The stuff if pretty cheap, and your car shouldn't need more fluid after you fix a leak. If you keep a can with only a little fluid left in it, the air that fills up the rest of the space in the can contaminates the fluid, no matter how quickly you recap it.

✔ **Keep brake fluid away from painted surfaces — *it eats paint*.** (If this stuff seems scary, remember that the same statements can be made about turpentine and nail polish remover.)

You should flush and replace the fluid in your brake system every two years. To do so, follow these steps:

1. **Use an old turkey baster, or a cheap plastic one, to remove the old, dirty fluid from the master cylinder reservoir.**

2. **Use a lint-free cloth to wipe out the reservoir, if possible.**

3. **Pour new brake fluid into the reservoir until it reaches the "Full" line, replace the cap or lid, and then follow the steps in the next section, "Bleeding Your Brakes."**

   As you bleed the brakes, the new fluid pushes the old fluid out of the system. Continue to bleed the brakes until you see clean, clear fluid exiting the bleeder screw.

Bleeding Your Brakes

For those cars with squishy-feeling brakes, the way to get the air out of the lines is to bleed the brakes. To do the job, you need either a *brake bleeder wrench* or a combination wrench that fits the bleeder nozzle on your vehicle, a can of the proper brake fluid, a clean glass jar, and a friend.

1. **Behind each of your brakes is a little nozzle called a *brake bleeder screw* (see Figure 18-13).**

   Reaching this bleeder screw may be easier if you jack up the vehicle (see Chapter 1 for instructions and safety tips). If you're going to crawl underneath, lay down an old blanket or a thick layer of newspapers first to keep from getting chilly on days when the ground is cold. If you really want to be comfortable, beg or borrow a creeper to lie on and slide around with easily. (I describe creepers in Chapter 2.)

2. **Special wrenches called *bleeder wrenches* fit the bleeder screw and can prevent rounding the screw's hex-head. Find the proper wrench or socket that fits the screw and loosen the screw.**

   Be careful not to break the screw off. If it's stuck, try spraying some penetrant around the screw. After you loosen the screw, tighten it again (but not too tight).

Figure 18-13:
A drum
brake
bleeder
screw.

Bleeder screw

3. **If you have a small piece of flexible hose that fits over the end of the bleeder screw, attach it and place the end of the hose in the jar. Then fill the jar with brake fluid to cover the end of the hose (see Figure 18-14).**

   If you don't have anything that fits, just keep the jar near the nozzle so that any fluid that squirts out lands in the jar.

4. **Have your friend pump your brake pedal a few times (see Figure 18-15).**

   If the car is jacked up, make sure that the wheels are blocked in the direction in which the car would roll, and that the car is not parked on a hill, before you let your friend get into the car with you underneath it. Leave your tires in place so the car will bounce and leave you some clearance if it falls.

Figure 18-14:
Using a bleeder hose to bleed your brakes.

Bleeder hose

Glass jar

Brake fluid

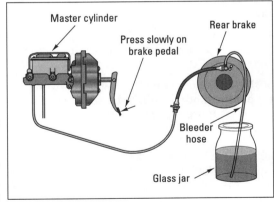

Figure 18-15:
How to bleed your brakes.

Master cylinder

Press slowly on brake pedal

Rear brake

Bleeder hose

Glass jar

5. **Have your friend say "Down" when pressing the brake pedal down and "Up" when releasing it.**

   All this "down-up" sounds like an exercise class, but what the heck!

6. **When your friend has pumped the pedal a few times and is holding the pedal *down*, open the bleeder screw.**

Brake fluid will squirt out. (Duck!) If there's air in your brake lines, air bubbles will be in the fluid. Seeing these bubbles is easiest if you're using the hose-in-the-jar method, but you can also see them without it.

7. ***Before* your friend releases the brake pedal, *tighten the bleeder screw*.**

   If you don't, air is sucked back into the brake lines when the pedal is released.

8. **Tell your friend to release the pedal, and listen for "Up." Then repeat the whole loosening and tightening sequence again and again until no more air bubbles come out with the fluid.**

9. **Open your master cylinder and add more brake fluid to the "Full" line.**

   If you neglect to do so, you run the risk of draining all the fluid out of the master cylinder and drawing air into the lines from the top. Now, that isn't fatal — it simply means that you have to go back and bleed your master cylinder until you suck the air out of that end of the system — but who needs the extra work?

   If you goof and have to bleed the master cylinder, it's the same deal as bleeding your brakes (friend and all). Just bleed it at the point where the brake lines attach to the cylinder, or at the master cylinder bleeder nozzle, if you have one (see Figure 18-16).

10. **Repeat these steps with each brake until the air is out of each brake line, remembering to add brake fluid to the master cylinder after you bleed each brake.**

11. **After you finish the job and bring the brake fluid level in the master cylinder back to "Full" for the last time, drive the vehicle around the block.**

    The brake pedal should no longer feel spongy when you depress it. If it does, check the master cylinder again to be sure that it's full and try bleeding the brakes one more time (this situation isn't unusual, and it doesn't take as long as it sounds).

If you know that no air is left in the lines and the brakes still don't feel right, you may need a new master cylinder. You should definitely consider installing it yourself — at an auto class. All it involves is disconnecting the old master cylinder (a bolt or two and the hoses leading to the brake lines), removing it without spilling brake fluid on anything painted, installing the new one, filling it with brake fluid, and bleeding it. If the job seems like too much of a hassle, have a professional do the work. You shouldn't have to pay for much labor, and if you choose a brake shop wisely, the whole deal shouldn't cost too much. Whatever you do, just be sure that, when the job is finished, they (or you) bleed the brakes and the master cylinder to get all the air out of the lines.

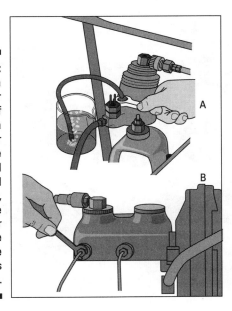

Figure 18-16:
Bleeding a
master
cylinder: If
you have a
bleeder
nozzle, use
the hose and
jar method
(A). If not,
bleed the
cylinder
at the
brake line
connections
(B).

Back in the 1970s, I had Tweety Bird's master cylinder replaced for about $60. (It would cost much more now.) Later, I helped a friend replace a master cylinder with a rebuilt one. The rebuilt master cylinder cost about half of what I'd paid for a new one, and there were no labor charges (naturally). What are your time and trouble worth to you?

Adjusting Your Parking Brake

These instructions for adjusting your parking brake work only if you have drum brakes on your *rear* wheels. If you have a manual transmission, you may have a *transmission*-type parking brake, which should be adjusted professionally and parking brakes on rear-wheel disc brakes should be left to professionals, too. Your service manual may tell you which kind you have, or you can crawl under the vehicle and see for yourself. (Chapter 10 describes both *integral* and *transmission*-type parking brakes and shows you what they look like.) Because most people have *integral* parking brakes, that's the type I deal with in this section. Figure 18-17 shows you several types of integral parking brakes.

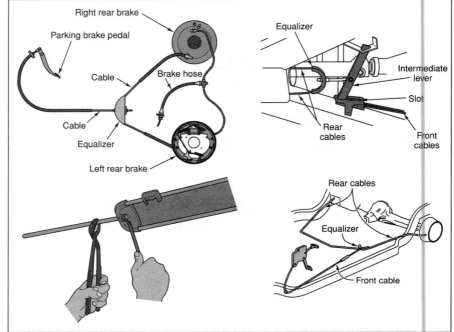

Figure 18-17:
Integral parking brakes may look different, but you adjust them all in the same way.

You shouldn't have to pull or push the parking brake handle to the most extreme level to make the brake work. (As the cables loosen up, you have to pull the handle up higher to engage the brake.)

You shouldn't be able to drive the vehicle with the parking brake on. If you can, the brake needs to be adjusted or repaired.

To adjust your parking brake, do the following:

1. **Jack up the car (a hoist would be lovely) and make sure that it's secure (see Chapter 1 for instructions). Be sure to leave your parking brake *off*.**

   You can also slide underneath with a work light if you don't want to jack the car up.

2. **Trace the thin steel cables that run from each of your rear wheels until they meet somewhere under the backseat of the car.**

   Where they meet, there should be a device (usually a bar and a screw) that controls the tension. Compare what you find with the parking brakes in Figure 18-17 to see which type you have.

3. **Turn the screw (or whatever else you have) until the cables tighten up, and then tighten the screw nuts to hold the screw in place.**

   You may have to hold the cable to keep it taut (refer to Figure 18-17).

4. **Get out from under the vehicle and test-drive it to see whether the parking brake is working.**

5. **While you're at it, pay attention to whether the parking brake warning light on your dashboard is working. If it isn't, check or replace the bulb or fuse.**

   You can find instructions for checking fuses in Chapter 12. If changing the bulb or fuse doesn't work, get someone to check the connection between the warning light and the brake; there may be a short in it.

Checking Anti-Lock Brakes

Anti-lock brake systems (ABS) vary from one vehicle to another, and most require no special maintenance. (Chapter 10 tells you how ABS brake systems work and how to operate them properly.) Manufacturers install an amber warning lamp in the instrument panel. Under normal circumstances, the amber light will go on briefly during engine startup and turn off in a short amount of time. If it goes on while you're on the road, the ABS system *isn't* working properly and your vehicle is using only the normal brake system. In this case, get the ABS repaired as soon as you can.

If you want to test the operation of your anti-lock brakes, find an empty parking lot on a rainy day. While traveling on a slippery surface at about 30 mph, firmly press the brake pedal. You should hear some clicking and feel some pulsing of the brake pedal while the vehicle comes to a stop without sliding. If the warning lamp stays on, or you suspect that the ABS isn't working properly, take your vehicle to a professional who specializes in brake systems.

Well, that's it. If you get in the habit of checking your brake system every 10,000 miles (and more frequently as they wear), you'll be able to stop worrying that they may fail you at a crucial moment. If you're a good buddy to your brakes (which involves driving properly as well as making periodic checks), they'll prove to be your best friends. After one of those breathtaking emergency stops on the freeway, I always say "Thanks, pals" and promise myself that I'll peek in again soon to check on my brakes and brake lines and make sure that they're in good shape.

Chapter 19

Checking Your Tires, Alignment, and Steering

. . . .

In This Chapter

▶ Understanding the anatomy of a tire

▶ Deciphering tire codes

▶ Choosing the right tires for your vehicle

▶ Maintaining your tires: Checking air pressure, rotating, aligning, and balancing

▶ Examining your tires for wear

. . . .

*I*f you think about tires only when it's time to buy new ones, you need to think again. The right tires in the right condition can enhance your driving experience and make it safer. In fact, your brakes and your tires have a two-way relationship: Poor braking action results in increased tire wear, but properly balanced and aligned wheels and properly inflated tires in good condition can help stop your car up to 25 percent faster!

There's also a strong correlation between tire inflation and tire wear. If your tires are underinflated, the outer treads wear out faster. If your tires are over-inflated, the centers of the tread areas go. And if the wheels get out of alignment, your tires can wear out in as little as one day of hard driving! So to get more mileage from your tires, plus better braking action and a smoother, quieter ride, you ought to know a bit about buying, checking, and maintaining the tires on your vehicle.

In this chapter, I tell you about the kinds of tires available. (You can buy different types and grades, and just as you wouldn't wear your finest shoes to the beach, you don't want to put the most expensive, long-lasting, high-speed radials on an old car that just goes back and forth to the shopping center.)

I also tell you how to check your tires and how to "read" your treads for clues about how well your car is performing — and how well you're driving. If these clues show that you need to have your wheels balanced or aligned, or your tires replaced, I provide enough information for you to be sure that the work is done the right way for the right price.

You don't have to do much (in terms of physical labor) with this chapter, so just find a comfortable place to read, relax, and enjoy. For information about how to *change* a tire, see Chapter 1.

Tire Construction

Every tire has several major parts (see Figure 19-1):

- **The tread** is the rubber part of the tire that gets most of the wear and tear. The tread patterns help the tire grip the road and resist puncturing. These patterns are also excellent indicators of tire wear. I get into reading these clues later in this chapter, in the section called "Checking your tires for wear."

- **The sidewall** is the part of the tire between the tread and the bead. The section called "The Secrets on Your Sidewalls, Revealed!" later in this chapter decodes all the useful data molded into the sidewall of a tire.

- **The bead** is a hoop of steel wire that's shaped to help hold the tire onto the rim of the wheel.

- **The casing** (or *carcass*) is the body of the tire, located beneath the tread and the sidewalls. It helps the tire keep its shape when inflated, instead of letting it blow up like a balloon. The casing is made up of various materials, called *cords.*

- **The belts** are also made up of cords, which are coated with rubber and located between the body and the tread. The type of material used for the belts, and the way it's wrapped around the bead, determine the kind of tire and its price. Originally, cotton was used for the cords, but it soon gave way to better materials, such as steel, aramid (which is harder than steel), fiberglass, polyester, rayon, and nylon. Steel-belted radials are the most popular type of tires today.

- **The tire valve** lets air into and out of a tire. The valve core prevents air from escaping. Each valve should have a valve cap to keep dirt and moisture from getting into the tire.

Until recently, tires came in a variety of constructions. There were *bias-ply* tires, which featured cords wrapped around the beads at overlapping angles. These were superseded by *bias-belted* tires, which were constructed in the same manner as bias-ply tires but featured belts of another material that wrapped around the tires' circumference, providing longer wear, puncture resistance, and more directional stability. Today, all vehicles come fitted with *radial* tires and, because all but the oldest vehicles run well with them, bias-ply and bias-belted tires are no longer readily available.

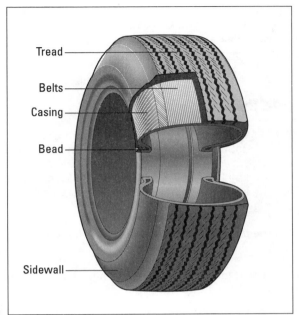

Figure 19-1:
Anatomy
of a tire.

If you have an antique or classic vehicle that requires old-style tires, you can find companies that manufacture reproductions of the original tires for your vehicle's make, model, and year.

Radial tires have become the standard because they provide better handling, especially at high speeds; they tend to grip the road more efficiently, especially when cornering; and they can deliver twice the mileage that bias-ply and belted tires did. Radial tires run cooler because they have less internal friction. (Bias and bias-belted tires had overlapping cords that translated into more internal friction and more heat when in motion.) Wear varies from 25,000 miles and up, depending on the belt material used. Top-of-the-line steel-belted radials can last from 40,000 to as many as 100,000 miles under average conditions.

To decide what type of tire is right for your vehicle, see "Tips for Buying Tires," later in this chapter.

The Secrets on Your Sidewalls, Revealed!

Many people are willing to spend extra dollars for tires with names like MACHO WILDCATS or TOUGH GUYS embossed in large white letters on the sidewalls, but did you know that a wealth of information is embossed on them in quiet little black letters that can be more valuable in the long run? And this information is *free* — if you know how to decode it. Even if you're not the inquisitive type, the data in the following sections can help you when you buy and maintain tires.

Tire size codes

Until around 1978, tire sizes were indicated by alpha-numeric codes, such as D78-14. Then, with the adoption of the metric system, the codes changed drastically. Today, the new codes are much longer and provide more information. Tire dealers are required by law to have leaflets available that explain tire grades and ratings. The leaflets also tell you which metric codes replace the old alphanumeric designations.

For example, here's the information provided by a common "P-metric" tire code, P205/75R-14:

- ✔ **P = Type of vehicle.** (In this case, P = Passenger. Other codes include LT for Light Truck and T for Temporary or spare tire.)

- ✔ **205 = Tire section width,** measured across the tread, from one sidewall to the other, in millimeters. (In this case, the tire width is 205.)

- ✔ **75 = Aspect ratio or tire series** — the ratio of the tire's sidewall height to its width. (In this case, the tire's sidewall height is 75 percent of its width.) Tires with a low series (less than 70) are referred to as *low-profile* tires and have a short sidewall.

- ✔ **R = Tire type.** (R = radial, B = bias-belted, D = diagonal or bias-ply, and E = elliptic. In this case, the tire is a radial.)

- ✔ **14 = Diameter of the wheel,** measured in inches. (In this case, the diameter is 14 inches.)

Codes may differ slightly from one tire to another. In addition to the P-metric code, there are also European metric codes, which can be as simple as 155SR13 or as complex as 185/70R14 88S, but the data they disclose is pretty much the same.

Speed ratings

Sometimes an additional letter appears between the profile and tire type, such as P205/75SR14. The additional letter S refers to a *speed rating*. The speed rating represents the safest *maximum* speed for the tire. It tells you nothing about a tire's construction, handling, or wearability, but measures the tire's ability to endure the high temperatures that high speeds create. Here's a list of what the speed rating letters mean:

✔ F = 50 mph

✔ G = 56 mph

✔ J = 62 mph

✔ K = 68 mph

✔ L = 75 mph

✔ M = 81 mph

✔ N = 87 mph

✔ P = 93 mph

✔ Q = 100 mph

✔ R = 106 mph

✔ S = 112 mph

✔ T = 118 mph

✔ U = 124 mph

✔ H = 130 mph

✔ V = 149 mph

✔ Z = 149+ mph

You may also find the speed rating listed in conjunction with the tire's *load index,* such as **97**H. In this case, the 97 is the load index, and the H is the speed rating.

If your car originally came fitted with speed-rated tires, you should replace them with speed-rated tires.

Tire quality grade codes

The Uniform Tire Quality Grading System rates tires for treadwear, traction, and temperature, but because these ratings are set by *manufacturers* and not by an objective testing service, they may not be accurate. If you want to use this information to compare various brands, consult *Uniform Tire Quality Grading,* a free consumer pamphlet published by the National Highway Traffic Safety Administration, 400 7th St. SW, Washington, DC 20590. Your dealer should also have a copy on hand.

Look for these grades on tire sidewalls or on stickers affixed to the treads. Here's what they mean:

- **Tread wear:** A comparative number grade based on carefully controlled testing conditions. In the "real world," a tire rated 200 would have twice the tread wear of one rated 100 — *if* all other wear factors were equal.

- **Traction:** This AA, A, B, or C grade represents the tire's ability to stop on wet asphalt and concrete pavement under controlled conditions (with AA being the best possible rating). The grades are based on straight-ahead braking only, not on cornering or turning. A tire with a C grade meets the government's test, while tires with B, A, and AA (in ascending order) exceed government standards.

- **Temperature:** This A, B, or C grade represents heat resistance and the tire's capability to dissipate the heat if the tire is inflated properly and not overloaded. Grade C meets U.S. minimum standards, while grades B and A exceed government standards.

DOT identification and registration

The DOT identification number on the sidewall serves as a registration number for the tire in case of a recall. This number tells where and when the tire was manufactured. Most of the data in the code isn't important for your purposes, but if you're curious, the following example tells what the various letters and numbers of a sample DOT code, DOT WOKAABC 262, mean:

- **DOT** indicates that the tire meets or exceeds U.S. Department of Transportation safety standards.

- **WO** identifies the plant where the tire was made. Because tires are made at many different plants, you don't need to know all the variations of this code. If it matters to you where your tires were made, ask the dealer.

- **KA** indicates the tire size. (In this case, the tire size is P194/75R14. Because the tire size is also on the sidewall, you don't need to know all the variations of this code, either.)

- **ABC** identifies the brand or characteristics of the tire. Instead of decoding this piece, read the brochure that describes the tire in detail.

- **262** indicates when the tire was made. (In this case, the number 262 means that the tire was made during the 26th week of 1982. Nifty, huh?)

When you buy new tires, make sure that they're properly registered. Under federal law, the dealer is required to put the tire's DOT number and the dealer's name and address on a form that is then sent to the manufacturer. Although tire outlets owned by manufacturers and certain brand-name outlets must send them in, independent tire dealers can simply fill out the forms and give them to customers to mail to the manufacturer. Unlike guarantees and warrantees, *in case of a recall, you aren't eligible to receive replacements unless your tires have been properly registered and you respond to the recall within 60 days.*

For more ideas about buying tires, see "Tips for Buying Tires," later in this chapter.

Other sidewall information

Check the sidewalls for the following safety data, too:

- ✔ **MAX LOAD:** How much weight the tire can bear safely, usually expressed in kilograms (kg) and pounds (lbs).

- ✔ **MAX PRESS:** The *maximum* air pressure the tire can safely hold, usually expressed in pounds per square inch (psi).

  MAX PRESS is *not* the pressure to maintain in your tires; you can find the manufacturer's recommended pressure for the best handling and wear on the tire decal found on the door, door pillar, console, glove box, or trunk of your vehicle.

You can find instructions for checking tire pressure, reading treads for clues, and other work that you can do on your tires in the "Caring for Your Tires" section, later in this chapter.

Tips for Buying Tires

Before you rush out and buy a set of tires, you have a couple of other things to consider. Tire wear is affected by a number of factors besides construction: the condition of the vehicle's brake system and suspension system; inflation and alignment; driving and braking techniques; driving at high speeds, which raises tire temperatures and causes them to wear prematurely; how great a load you carry; road conditions; and climate.

Here are some of the types of tires that you may want to consider:

- ✔ **Basic all-season tires** are standard equipment on most cars. The speed rating (see the "Speed rating" section earlier in the chapter) is usually S or T. If "M+S" (mud and snow) is printed on the sidewall, the tire will perform well in inclement weather without the need for snow tires.

- ✔ **Touring tires** are generally more expensive than basic all-season tires. Whether they're worth the money depends on the individual product. These tires usually are speed-rated S or T.

- ✔ **Performance tires** are designed for people who drive "aggressively." They perform better in terms of braking and cornering but are usually noisier and wear out more quickly. They are usually speed-rated H and have a wide, squatty profile.

- ✔ **Ultra-high performance tires** have both the positive and the negative aspects of performance tires to a greater degree: They go faster, brake and handle better in wet and dry conditions, but ride less comfortably and wear out even faster. They are even wider and are usually speed-rated V or Z.

- ✔ **Light-truck tires** are intended for use on light trucks and SUVs. They come in a variety of styles designed for normal conditions, driving on- or off-road, or both. The thicker treads on the off-road variety offer better traction on unpaved surfaces. Light-truck tires also vary for carrying normal, heavy, and extra-heavy loads.

- ✔ **Snow tires** may be better than all-season tires for driving in mountainous areas with heavy snowfall, but they're noisy and don't handle as well on dry roads, so use them only when necessary.

- ✔ **"Run-flat" tires** can be driven on without any air pressure inside the tire. Run-flat equipped vehicles may not even come with a jack or spare tire. (If you're driving a 1997 or newer Chevrolet Corvette or a similarly equipped new vehicle, you probably have this special type of radial tire.) The sidewalls have specially compounded inserts that prevent the tire from caving in when the tire loses air pressure. You can drive some run-flat tires up to 50 mph for 50 miles or more without further damaging the tire.

  Running on a run-flat at high speeds for a long period can damage them, so car manufacturers incorporate a warning system. For example, the Corvette has tire pressure sensors at each wheel so that the driver can be warned when one or more tires are flat. Because the driver can't feel any difference when a run-flat goes flat, a warning light illuminates on the instrument panel, signaling the driver to limit his or her driving speed and distance to avoid further damage to the tire or wheel.

Before making a decision about a particular type of tire, take a close look at your driving habits:

Are you hard on tires? If you tend to "burn rubber" when cornering, starting, and stopping, you know where that rubber comes from. A pair of cheaply made tires will wear out quickly, so buy the best quality you can afford.

Do you drive a great deal and do most of your driving on high-speed freeways? A tire with a harder surface will take longer to wear out under these conditions.

Do you drive a lot on unpaved rocky roads, carry heavy loads, or leave your car in the hot sun for long hours? You'll need higher-quality tires that have the stamina to endure these challenges.

What's the weather like in your area? Today, front-wheel drive vehicles with high-tech *all-season* tires get better traction than the old snow tires, which you had to replace when warm weather set in. However, if you drive under extreme conditions, you may want to check out tires designed for them: If it rains a lot, look for rain tires with super-wide grooves in the treads. For places with lots of snow or icy hills, look for "M+S" (mud and snow) on the sidewall.

Do you drive mostly in local stop-and-go traffic, with many turns? Softer tires with wider treads will suit you best.

How long do you intend to keep your car? Putting a pair of expensive tires on a vehicle that you intend to get rid of in 10,000 or 20,000 miles is foolish. Oh, it's possible to put well over 100,000 miles on a vehicle — especially if you maintain it properly — but if you have a relatively old vehicle with many miles on it already, and you don't intend to keep it very long, I wouldn't buy a pair of expensive mega-mile tires for it. Your car may surprise you and outlive its tires, but chances are that it won't. Similarly, it's foolish to put high-performance tires on a vehicle that will be driven mostly at normal speeds in city and highway traffic.

On the other hand, if you intend to keep your vehicle for a few years, you'll save money in the long run by opting for more expensive, longer-lasting tires than "cheapos" or tires rated for less than 40,000 miles. Cheap tires wear out more quickly and cost more in the long run if you figure in the cost of buying, mounting, and balancing that second set. What's more, if you suffer a blowout or your tires fail to grip the road, you'll pay a great deal more if your vehicle — or you — is injured.

If you drive only a couple of thousand miles a year, don't expect a pair of 40,000-mile radials to last forever. Rubber treads tend to rot eventually because of the ozone in the air, which causes cracks and hard spots in the sidewalls — a condition called ozone checking. For this reason, if you've used your tires for more than 40,000 miles, even if the treads are in good shape, have the tires checked to make sure that deteriorating rubber hasn't made them prone to blowouts and leaks.

In addition to knowing which kind of tire is best for your car and understanding the tire codes (explained in the section called "The Secrets on Your Sidewalls, Revealed!"), keep the following tips in mind when you shop for tires:

- ✔ You can find the proper tire size for your car in the owner's manual or on a sticker affixed to the vehicle. If neither exists, ask your dealer.

- ✔ Although you should never buy tires that are smaller than those specified for your vehicle, you can buy tires a size or two larger (if the car's wheel clearance allows it) for better handling or load-carrying ability. However, you should buy these larger tires in pairs and place them on the same axle. Ask your mechanic or a reputable tire or auto dealer for advice about the proper size range for your vehicle. For more advice, see "Tips for Buying Tires," later in this chapter.

- Never use two different-sized tires on the same axle.
- If you're replacing just one or two tires, put the new ones on the front for better cornering control and braking (because weight transfers to the front tires when you brake).

- If you still have bias-ply or bias-belted tires on your car, you must replace *all* of them at the same time with radials when they wear out. You can't mix different kinds of tires on the same vehicle; you should have the same type on all four wheels. The ride is so different that radial tires would throw your car out of alignment if you tried them in combination with the old-style tires.
- Remember that you have to "break in" new tires, so don't drive faster than 60 mph for the first 50 miles on a new tire or spare.
- Store tires that you aren't using in the dark, away from extreme heat and electric motors that create ozone.

Retreads: Bargains or blowouts?

Millions of tires are discarded every year, and an entire industry has developed to put them back on the road by replacing the worn tread areas with new ones. The retreading process involves grinding the tread off an otherwise sound old tire and winding a strand of uncured rubber around the tire. Then the tire is placed in a mold, where the rubber is cured under heat and pressure and the tread itself is shaped. Finally, the tire is painted.

The largest number of these "retreads" are intended for government and industrial fleets of vehicles — such as postal and fire trucks and buses — but they can be purchased for private vehicles as well. For many years, retreads had a reputation of being unreliable, and most consumers assumed that the strips of tread they saw littering the highways came from retreaded

tires that had disintegrated on the road. But today, advances in retreading have raised their quality, and the industry's Tire Retread Information Bureau claims that retreads have the same 3 percent failure rate as new tires. So if you're interested in recycling, you may be motivated to buy retreads in order to reduce the number of tires heading for landfills.

Unfortunately, the number of retread manufacturers has diminished. Of 12,000 tire retreading plants during World War II, only about 1,400 are left today. As a result, retreads may be difficult to find. It's hard to tell the good stuff from the bad, so if you buy retreads, make sure that they're from a well-known, major manufacturer, such as Fargo, which claims a failure rate of only 1.5 percent.

Caring for Your Tires

Tires don't require a great deal of maintenance, but the jobs in this section will pay off handsomely by increasing your tires' longevity, handling, and performance, as well as providing you with a more comfortable ride.

Checking tire inflation pressure

The single most important factor in caring for your tires is maintaining the correct inflation pressure. You should check your tires at least once a month and before every long trip to see that they're properly inflated. Underinflated tires wear out faster, create excessive heat, increase fuel consumption, and make the vehicle harder to handle. Overinflated tires can blow out more easily, wear out faster, and make the vehicle unstable and unsafe to handle. The section "Checking your tires for wear," later in this chapter, can help you check for signs of these problems and tells you what to do about them.

Check tire pressure in the morning before you use the car or when you've driven it less than a mile. If you drive more than that, your tires will heat up and the air will expand, so you won't get an accurate reading.

In hot weather, the pressure in your tires rises as the air in them heats up and expands, which can result in overinflation. Conversely, in cold weather, the pressure falls as the cold air contracts and your tires can end up underinflated. As you'll see in the section called "Checking your tires for wear," these conditions can cause your tires to wear unevenly and wear out prematurely.

If the weather gets very cold, it looks as though it will stay that way for some time, and you get a low reading, you may want to add a bit of air to your tires to bring the pressure back up. Generally, though, tires that are correctly inflated tend to wear properly in spite of minor weather ups and downs. Just check them regularly to keep things under control, and try not to check them under extreme temperature conditions or after you've been driving around.

Here's what you need to do to check the air pressure in your tires:

1. **Buy an accurate tire gauge at a hardware store or auto supply store.**

   Figure 19-2 shows you what a tire gauge looks like. I show you how to use one a little later in this section.

2. **Determine the proper air pressure for your tires by looking for the proper inflation pressure on the tire decal.**

   You can find the tire decal on one of the doors, door pillars, glove box, console, or trunk. Sometimes the tire decal specifies one pressure for the front tires and a different pressure for the rear tires.

Don't consult the tire's sidewall for the proper inflation pressure. The sidewall lists the *maximum* pressure that the tire is capable of handling, not the pressure that's best for performance and wear (unless you're carrying heavy loads).

3. **Remove the little cap from the tire valve that sticks out of your tire near the wheel rim.**

   You don't have to remove your hub cap to do so.

4. **Place the open, rounded end of the tire gauge against the valve so that the little pin in the gauge contacts the pin in the valve (see Figure 19-2).**

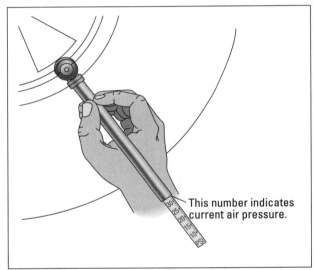

This number indicates current air pressure.

Figure 19-2:
Use a tire gauge to see whether your tires are properly inflated.

5. **Press the gauge against the valve stem.**

   You'll hear a hissing sound as air starts to escape from the tire. At this point, you'll also see a little stick emerge from the other end of the tire gauge. It emerges partway almost as soon as the air starts to hiss and stops emerging almost immediately.

6. **Without pushing the stick back in, remove the gauge from the tire valve.**

7. **Look at the stick without touching it. There are little numbers on it; pay attention to the last number showing.**

   The last number is the amount of air pressure in your tire, as shown in Figure 19-2. Does the gauge indicate the proper amount of pressure recommended on the decal?

8. **Add air if necessary.**

   If the pressure seems too low, press the gauge against the valve stem again. If it still doesn't move, you need more air. Follow the steps in "Adding air to your tires."

9. **Repeat these steps for each tire — and don't forget the spare!**

Adding air to your tires

If your tires appear to be low, note the amount that they're underinflated, drive to a local gas station, and follow these steps:

1. **Park your vehicle so that you can reach all four tires with the air hose.**

2. **Remove the cap from the tire valve on the first tire.**

3. **Use *your* tire gauge to check the air pressure in the tire and see how much it's changed so that you can add the same amount of air that the tire lacked before you drove it to the station.**

   The pressure will have increased because driving causes the tires to heat up and the air inside them to expand.

4. **Use the air hose to add air in short bursts, checking the pressure each time with *your* tire gauge.**

   The gauges on many station air hoses are inaccurate; that's why you should use your own gauge to ensure proper inflation.

5. **If you add too much air, let some out by pressing the pin on the tire valve with the back of the air hose nozzle or with the little knob on the back of the rounded end of the tire gauge.**

6. **Keep checking until you get the pressure right.**

   Don't get discouraged if you have to keep adjusting the air pressure. No one hits it on the head the first time!

Rotating your tires

People have differing points of view on tire rotation. Some say that you can get up to 20 percent more wear if you rotate your tires. Others caution against rotating them because rotation may hide the distinctive tread-wear patterns that provide the clues to poor alignment, worn shock absorbers, and defective brakes found in the "Checking your tires for wear" section, later in this chapter. If your tires seem to be wearing evenly and you haven't had any of these problems, then it's a good idea to rotate them — but check them first for signs of problems that may have arisen since the last time they were rotated.

For uniform tire wear, the tires on most vehicles should be rotated approximately every 6,000 miles, unless they show the signs of irregular wear in Table 19-1 and Figure 19-8, later in this chapter. There are a few other exceptions to this rule: Vehicles that have larger wheels and tires in the rear and vehicles that have different wheels front to back can't participate in tire rotation. And if you have unidirectional tires or tires with asymmetric tread designs, you can't rotate them in the patterns shown in Figure 19-3.

When you rotate tires, you simply move each tire from one wheel to another; for example, one configuration is to move the rear tires forward and the forward tires to the opposite rear locations (see Figure 19-3). However, where you move the tires depends on the type of tires and vehicle you have. To find out where to move the tires on your vehicle, consult your owner's manual (usually, you'll see a diagram showing how the tires should be moved), call the tire manufacturer, or ask the dealership. Of course, you can always take your vehicle to a service facility and have them rotate the tires for you.

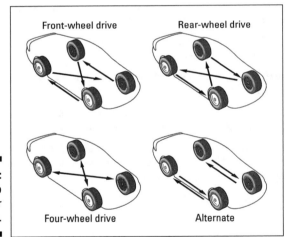

Figure 19-3:
How to
rotate your
tires.

Many shops include free tire rotation and wheel balancing in oil-change and other special service promotions, and most tire dealers include periodic tire rotation and wheel balancing in their warranties. (I explain what wheel balancing is in the next section.)

The tires on the front and rear wheels may require different air pressures. After the tires are rotated, remember to adjust the air pressure on each tire to whatever is indicated on the tire decal on your vehicle or in your owner's manual.

If you have a matching, full-sized spare, you can include it in the rotation process by starting it out in the right rear position and using the tire that would have been moved to the right rear as the spare tire until the next rotation. Do *not* include a "Temporary Use Only" spare tire (those teeny little ones) in any rotation pattern. (But you knew that, right?)

Balancing your wheels

Wheel balancing does a lot to eliminate some of the principal causes of tire wear. And an unbalanced wheel and tire can create an annoying vibration on smooth roads. Because balancing is a job that should be done with the proper equipment, and because that equipment is costly, while balancing is generally cheap, go to a service facility or tire store and have them do the job for you. Just remember that there are two kinds of wheel balancing: *static* and *dynamic*.

- **Static balancing** deals with the even distribution of weight around the axle. You can tell that you need to have your wheels statically balanced if a wheel (or more than one wheel) tends to rotate by itself when the car is jacked up. It rotates because one part of the wheel is heavier than the rest. To correct this problem, a technician finds the heavy spot and applies tire weights to the opposite side of the heavy spot to balance it out.

- **Dynamic balancing** deals with the even distribution of weight along the spindle. Wheels that aren't balanced dynamically tend to wobble and wear more quickly. Because imbalance can be detected only when the tire is rotated and centrifugal force can act, correcting dynamic balance is a relatively complex procedure. Some service stations have computerized balancers that not only balance the wheels but also locate the places where the weights are needed and decide how much weight to add.

Having your tires balanced both statically and dynamically shouldn't cost more than a few dollars.

If you plan to have your wheels balanced professionally, rotating your tires yourself beforehand is a waste of time. The technicians have to remove the tires to balance them anyway, so they may as well rotate them, too.

Aligning your wheels

A cheap and easy way to substantially improve your vehicle's handling and extend the life of your tires is to be alert to signs of misalignment and to have your wheels aligned immediately if the signs appear. This job is sometimes called front-end alignment because the front wheels get out of line most often. They get that way because of hard driving with dramatic getaway starts and screeching stops, hitting curbs hard when parking or cornering, accidents, heavy loads, frequent driving over unpaved roads or into potholes, and normal wear and tear as the car gets older. Occasionally, the rear wheels need realignment as well. Vehicles with independent rear suspensions and front-wheel drive vehicles require four-wheel alignment.

I used to think that alignment involved taking a car that had been bashed out of shape and literally pulling it back into line. Untrue. All the technicians do is adjust your wheels to make sure that they track in a nice, straight line when you drive. To do so, they use special equipment to check the following points:

✔ **Caster** has to do with the position of your steering knuckle as compared to a vertical line when viewed from the side (see Figure 19-4). If properly adjusted, it makes your wheels track in a straight line instead of weaving or shimmying at high speeds. Caster also helps return the steering wheel to a straight-ahead position after completing a turn.

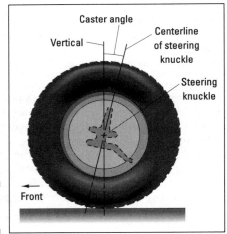

Figure 19-4:
Caster.

✔ **Camber** is the inward or outward tilt of the top of the wheels when viewed from the front/rear of the car — how "bow-legged" or "knock-kneed" they are (see Figure 19-5). If the wheels don't hang properly, your tires wear out more quickly, and your car is harder to handle.

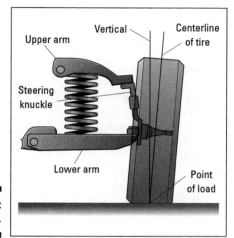

Figure 19-5:
Camber.

✔ **Toe** involves placing your tires so that they are properly positioned parallel to the frame when driving down the road. Some cars call for a little *toe-in* (tires pointing inward— see Figure 19-6), while others are set with a little *toe-out* (tires pointing outward). The result should be a nice, straight track when the car is moving quickly. On some front-wheel drive cars, the manufacturer may set the rear tires with a little toe-in and the front tires with a little toe-out so that the tires are parallel to the frame when the vehicle is in motion.

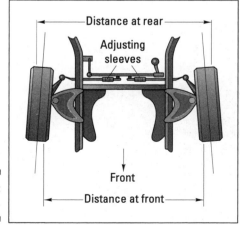

Figure 19-6:
Toe-in.

✔ **Turning radius** is the relation of one front wheel to the other on turns. If you turn to the right, the right front tire needs to turn at a slightly greater angle than the left front tire. Your car's steering arms accommodate this feat. (See Figure 19-7.) If your tires "squeal" sharply on turns, one of your car's steering arms may be your problem.

How do you know if your wheels need aligning? Look at your tires to see whether they show any of the tread-wear patterns that I discuss in "Checking your tires for wear," and pay attention to how your car steers and handles. Does it pull to one side? Does the steering feel loose and sloppy? Is your car hard to handle after a turn? If your tires show any unusual wear patterns and/or you answered yes to any of these questions, your car probably needs an alignment.

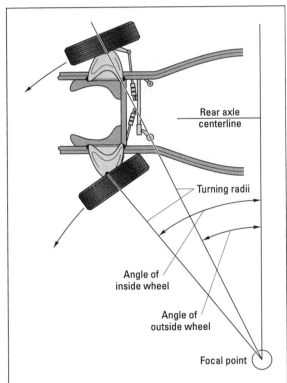

Figure 19-7:
Turning
radius.

Checking your steering

Checking your steering is easy. Just stand outside your vehicle, near the door on the driver's side. Stick your hand through the open window and move the steering wheel, with your eye on the left front tire. If you can move the steering wheel at all before the tire starts to move, then you need to have both your steering and alignment checked. There should be no "play" in the steering wheel before the signal is transmitted to the tires.

As you drive your car, be alert to signs that it isn't handling as easily as before. If the vehicle seems to have a mind of its own and begins to resist you on turns (and pulling out of turns), take a good look at your tires for signs of wear caused by misalignment.

Checking your tires for wear

You should check your tires for wear at least once a month and before and after long trips. To determine whether you need to (a) buy new tires, (b) have your wheels balanced, (c) have your wheels aligned, or (d) change your driving habits, simply read your tire treads for clues. Table 19-1 and Figure 19-8 show you what to look for.

Table 19-1	How to Read Your Treads	
Clue	*Culprit*	*Remedy*
Both edges worn	Underinflation	Add more air; check for leaks
Center treads worn	Overinflation	Let air out to manufacturer's specifications
One-sided wear	Poor alignment	Have wheels aligned
Treads worn unevenly, with bald spots, cups, or scallops	Wheel imbalance and/or poor alignment	Have wheels balanced and aligned
Erratically spaced bald spots	Wheel imbalance or worn shocks	Have wheels balanced or replace shocks
Edges of front tires only worn	Taking curves too fast	Slow down!
Saw-toothed wear pattern	Poor alignment	Have wheels aligned

(continued)

Table 19-1 *(continued)*

Clue	Culprit	Remedy
Whining, thumping, and other weird noises	Poor alignment, worn tires or shocks	Have wheels aligned or buy new tires or shocks
Squealing on curves	Poor alignment or underinflation	Check wear on treads and act accordingly

Figure 19-8: What the signs of poor tread wear mean.

Severe underinflation   Overinflation   Poor alignment   Poor alignment

Underinflated tires wear out faster, create excessive heat, increase fuel consumption, and make your car harder to handle. Overinflated tires can "blow out" more easily, wear out faster, and make the car unstable and unsafe to handle. And a new set of tires on wheels that are out of alignment can wear out completely in as little as one day of hard driving!

To determine what's causing problems with your tires, try the following:

✔ **Look for things embedded in each tire.** Do you see nails, stones, or other debris embedded in the treads? Remove them. *But* if you're going to remove a nail, first make sure that your spare tire is inflated and in usable shape.

If you hear a hissing sound when you pull a nail, push the nail back in quickly and take the tire to be fixed. If you aren't sure whether air is escaping, put some soapy water on the hole and look for the bubbles made by escaping air. If you're still not sure whether the nail may have caused a leak, check your air pressure and then check it again the next day to see whether it's lower (for help, see "Checking your air pressure," earlier in this chapter). Tires with leaks should be patched by a professional. If the leak persists, get a new tire.

✔ **Look at the sidewalls.** Check for deeply scuffed or worn areas, bulges or bubbles, small slits, or holes. Do the tires fit evenly and snugly around the wheel rims?

✔ **Look at the treads.** Most tires have tread-wear indicators built into them (see Figure 19-9). These bars of hard rubber are normally invisible but appear across treads that have been worn down to $\frac{1}{16}$ of an inch of the surface of the tire (the legal limit in most states). If these indicators appear in two or three different places, less than 120 degrees apart on the circumference of the tire, replace the tire.

If your tires don't show these indicators and you think that they may be worn below legal tolerances, place a Lincoln penny head-down in the groove between the treads. If you can see the top of Lincoln's head, your tire probably needs to be replaced.

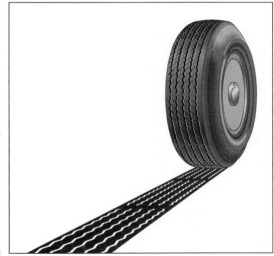

Figure 19-9: It's time for new tires when tread-wear indicators appear.

To measure tread wear more exactly, place a thin ruler into the tread and measure the distance from the base of the tread to the surface. It should be more than $\frac{1}{16}$ inch deep. (**Note:** If your front tires are more worn than your rear ones and show abnormal wear patterns, you probably need to have your wheels aligned.)

✔ **Pay attention to leaks.** If you keep losing air in your tires, have your local service station check them for leaks. Sometimes an ill-fitting rim causes a leak. The garage has a machine that can fix this problem easily.

If the garage can't find a leak, your rims fit properly, and you're still losing air, you probably have a faulty tire valve that's allowing air to escape. You can buy tire valves to replace the ones on your car. Look for the number molded into the base of the tire valves; then buy new ones that match it.

In the process of replacing the valve, you will lose most of the air from the tire, so either plan to do this job at a gas station where you can have access to an air hose, or have a mechanic replace the valve for you.

Part IV
Dealing with On-the-Road Emergencies

The 5th Wave   By Rich Tennant

GATES OF TROY

In this part . . .

Despite your best efforts, your vehicle may break down while you're on the road. Maybe it will overheat. Maybe a tire will blow. Maybe you won't know *what* the problem is, but you'll know that it sounds — or smells — bad. This part sees you through these traumas and helps you make your way out of them safely. Because some problems are beyond your capabilities as a do-it-yourselfer, I also tell you how to locate, evaluate, and work with a good automotive technician.

Chapter 20

Troubleshooting Leaks, Squeaks, Smells, and Strange Sensations

· ·

In This Chapter

▶ Recognizing the sounds of trouble

▶ Getting rid of squeaks, rattles, and vibrations

▶ Sniffing out unusual smells

▶ Deciphering smoke signals

▶ Locating and dealing with leaks

▶ Getting to the bottom of strange sensations

▶ Troubleshooting with directional signals

· ·

*A*s you work on your vehicle, you'll get to know it better. Before long, you'll become more sensitive to its signals. If something sounds funny or smells funny or just doesn't feel right, you'll soon sense it. This can help you forestall expensive repairs, because you'll be able to prevent trouble or catch it before it becomes a major problem. This chapter shows you how to use your eyes, ears, and nose to sense automotive symptoms, and how to deal with those symptoms.

The words in **special type** are defined in the Practical Glossary of Automotive Terms at the end of this book.

Sounds

You probably know how your vehicle sounds when it's running properly, and your ears can alert you to anything that sounds strange. Well, listen to your ears! If you hear a strange or different sound, pay attention to it and react accordingly.

✔ **If a fan belt or accessory belt "sings" (makes a continuous, high-pitched sound),** readjust or replace it. These belts should have at least half an inch of play and shouldn't be frayed, cracked, or glazed on the underside. Some belts tend to sing more than others. Rubbing a bit of petroleum jelly on the undersides of these belts usually quiets them down. You can find instructions for adjusting and replacing belts in Chapter 14.

Don't drive with a broken fan belt. If you carry a spare belt or an old belt in the trunk, you may be able to save yourself towing charges.

✔ **If your radiator "sings" (similar sound, different tune),** check the radiator pressure cap. The rubber gasket may be worn, and steam from the hot engine may be escaping past it. Chapter 14 tells you how to remove a radiator cap safely.

✔ **If your tires squeal on curves — and you aren't speeding —** check their inflation pressure, treads, and alignment by using the instructions in Chapter 19.

✔ **If you hear a whining or humming sounds on curves,** your wheel bearings may be wearing. Chapter 18 turns you on to the sensual thrill of repacking them with your bare hands.

✔ **If your tires "tramp" (make a weird, rhythmic sound as you drive),** check inflation, tire wear, and wheel balancing (see Chapter 18).

✔ **If you hear squealing when you step on the brake,** you've probably worn the brake pads down too far. Get them replaced immediately. Some disc brakes are naturally noisy, but if the sound gets louder, take heed.

✔ **If something ticks rhythmically while your engine idles,** shut off the engine, wait ten minutes, and then check the oil level. The hydraulic lifters that operate the valves in your engine can make these noises if you're down as little as a quart of oil. If the level is low, add oil up to the "Full" line on the dipstick and check again in a couple of days. If you have enough oil, have a mechanic check the valve adjustment if your car has adjustable valves (some don't). Faulty valves can seriously affect your car's performance and fuel consumption.

✔ **If you hear a loud knocking sound in your engine,** pull to the side of the road *immediately* and call for road service. It may be just a loose rocker arm or carbon buildup inside the engine, but if it's a loose bearing or a faulty piston, letting it go unheeded can destroy the whole engine.

Mild knocking or "pinging" may be the result of using fuel with the wrong octane rating. Check your owner's manual to see whether your vehicle needs low-octane or premium gas.

✔ **If you hear the engine running after you've turned off the ignition,** your engine is dieseling. This condition is often due to using fuel with too high an octane rating, but a tank of inferior gas or an idle speed that's set to high may also be the culprit.

✔ **If you hear rumbling noises coming from under or toward the rear of the vehicle,** the trouble could be a defective exhaust pipe, muffler, or catalytic converter; or it could be coming from a worn universal joint or some other part of the drive train. Have a service facility put the car up on a hoist and find the problem.

✔ **If you hear clunking under your vehicle, especially when you go over a bump,** check the shock absorbers and suspension system. If it's toward the rear, your tailpipe or muffler may be loose.

✔ **If you hear a whistling noise coming from under the hood,** check the hoses for vacuum leaks. If the whistling comes from *inside* the vehicle, there's probably a leak in the weather-stripping. Patch the weather-stripping according to the directions in Chapter 24.

✔ **If you hear an unlocatable sound,** get an old stethoscope from a medical supply house or ask your family doctor. As shown in Figure 20-1, take off the rubber disc and insert a piece of tubing in its place (about 1½ inches will do). Then put the plugs in your ears, run the engine, and move the tube end of the stethoscope around the hood area. The stethoscope amplifies the sound as you near the part that's causing it.

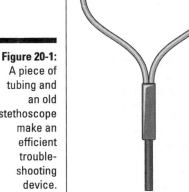

Figure 20-1:
A piece of tubing and an old stethoscope make an efficient trouble-shooting device.

A metal combination wrench works the same way. Place one end of the wrench on the bone behind your ear and, leaning over, place the other end of the wrench on the parts that seem to be the source of the noise. Be careful not to get a shock or get your hair tangled in the fan.

✔ **If your brakes squeal,** the brake linings may be glazed or worn. Some disc brake pads have built-in wear sensors that squeal when it's time to replace them. Even though some disc brakes tend to squeal under normal circumstances, it's safer to have the brakes checked, or follow the instructions in Chapter 18 and check them yourself.

✔ **If the car idles with an offbeat rhythm,** it isn't becoming creative; it's probably misfiring — one of the spark plugs or the wires that connect them to the distributor cap may be at fault. Try the following:

  • *With the engine off,* check the spark plug cables for breaks or shorts in the wiring.

  • *With the engine off,* remove the spark plugs one at a time and check whether they're clean and properly gapped. Replace any that are fouled or burned.

If that doesn't help, have a technician check the ignition system with an electronic engine analyzer. People used to check spark plugs by holding the end of the spark plug cable close to a metal surface to see whether a spark jumped across when the engine was cranked, but the high voltage in most ignition systems now makes that procedure extremely dangerous.

✔ **If the idling is rough but even and your vehicle has a carburetor,** the carburetor settings may need to be adjusted. Chapter 13 shows you how to do this yourself. If that doesn't work, you may need to replace the carburetor. Fuel-injected vehicles don't have carburetors, and a technician must check and adjust these complex electronic systems. Try checking the compression in each cylinder, following the instructions in the section of Chapter 13 called "Checking the Compression in Your Cylinders." If the engine needs to be rebuilt, you may prefer to get another engine — or another vehicle.

An easy way to see whether your car is idling evenly is to place a stiff piece of paper against the end of the tailpipe while the car is idling (with the emergency brake on, please). Doing so amplifies the sound and enables you to hear the rhythm. A misfiring cylinder comes through as a pumping or puffing sound. An even but rough idle is a clue that it's time to retune your carburetor — especially the idle mixture and idle speed screws. Chapter 13 has instructions for doing this job.

✔ **If your car sounds like a jet plane or makes some other loud, abnormal sound,** a hole in the muffler is probably the cause. Replace it immediately: Traffic cops hate noisy mufflers, and carbon monoxide hates people!

✔ **If the horn is stuck,** your vehicle is producing what may be the worst noise it can make. *Before* this happens, have someone honk your horn until you can locate it under your hood. There are usually two horns. Each has a wire leading to it. If your horn gets stuck, pull these wires to stop the noise (see Figure 20-2) — sometimes you have to pull only one. When you have the horn fixed, tell the mechanic that you pulled the wires and find out why the horn got stuck. (If you can't get at the horn wires, disconnect one battery terminal or pull the fuse that goes to the horn to stop the noise.)

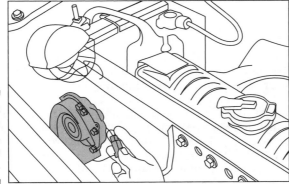

Figure 20-2:
If your horn gets stuck, pull a wire to silence it.

✔ **If your car sounds like an old taxi, especially when you drive it on a bumpy road,** it may just need lubrication (see Chapter 16). However, the problem might be worn shock absorbers or struts, suspension ball joints, or broken stabilizer links (see Chapter 11).

You may get used to the squeaks and groans, but they also indicate wear, because they're caused by parts rubbing together or moving without the proper lubrication. Obviously, action is called for. The following section may be of help.

Squeaks, Rattles, and Vibrations

If you hear suspicious rattles, squeaks, or vibrations, you may be able to save yourself some money by checking and tightening the following items before seeking professional help:

✔ **Loose screws and bolts** (Check both inside the vehicle and under the hood.)

✔ **Rearview and side mirrors**

- Dashboard knobs and trim
- Sound-system speaker grills
- Window and door cranks and locks
- Ashtray (Is it empty? Does it fit snugly?)
- Glove box (Is the door shut tight? Is anything in the glove box rattling around?)
- Hubcaps (If your vehicle has them, remove them and check inside for pebbles.)
- Outside trim
- Trunk (Is something you've stashed in there moving around?)

If none of these is the culprit, or if the noise persists, have a repair facility find the cause. Often, something inside the vehicle vibrates sympathetically because another part of the vehicle is running roughly.

Many squeaks respond well to a lube job (see Chapter 16 for details on doing one yourself). If there is a persistent squeak under the vehicle, your mechanic may be able to install an additional grease fitting in the squeaky area at a low cost. Tweety Bird and other old Mustangs of her vintage were prone to squeaks in the A-frame under the front bumper. A grease fitting on each side of the upper control arm cured the sound effects quickly and cheaply.

Smells

Ideally, other than that new-car smell, the only odors you should smell inside your vehicle should come from smelly things that you've put in it: the takeout lunch that you bought at a drive-through, the perfume that your 6-year-old squirted all over herself, your not-so-freshly groomed dog who's pressing his nose against your recently washed windows. You can get rid of persistent odors easily by using Febreze, a spray that eliminates odors rather than masking them. But if you smell any of the items in the following list, take immediate action to correct it:

- **Do you smell rubber burning under the hood?** One of your hoses may have come loose and landed on a hot part of the engine. Rescue it before it melts through.

- **Do you smell burned rubber with the hood closed?** Feel your wheels. If one is hot, a brake shoe may be dragging, or you may have left the parking brake on. If neither of these checks out, an overheated clutch may be the cause.

✔ **Do you smell oil burning?** (It has a thick, acrid odor.) First check the oil dipstick by following the directions in Chapter 3. Your oil pressure gauge may be lying, and you may be out of oil. Or your engine may be overheating, and your temperature gauge may be broken. If neither is the case, look around the engine for an oil leak that may be frying in the heat of the running engine. If the oil situation seems to be okay, check the transmission fluid dipstick. Sometimes a faulty vacuum modulator can siphon the fluid out of the transmission and feed it to the engine, where it's burned. Also, if the transmission fluid is very low, it can be burned in the transmission because the gears aren't lubricated enough and are getting very hot.

✔ **Do you smell oil or exhaust fumes in the passenger compartment?** The cause could be burned oil from the engine area — but it could also be a faulty exhaust pipe under the car that lets exhaust gases get into the vehicle through the floorboards.

Exhaust fumes are full of carbon monoxide, so if you smell oil or exhaust in the car, be sure to keep your windows open at all times and have the problem checked out as quickly as you can. We've all heard stories about people who have died on the highway from carbon monoxide or from passing out at the wheel because of it. Such stories are true.

✔ **Do you smell something sweet and steamy?** Take a look at the temperature gauge or light on your dashboard to see whether your car is overheating. Chapter 14 tells you how to cool things down.

✔ **Do you smell rotten eggs?** The smell is probably coming from the catalytic converter, which is part of the exhaust system. The converter may be malfunctioning, or you may have a problem with your engine.

✔ **Do you smell burned toast (a light, sharp odor)?** Unless you've brought breakfast with you, it may be an electrical short circuit, or the insulation on a wire may be burning. Check around under the hood. Driving is a bit risky, so either get to the nearest garage or have a technician come to you.

✔ **Do you smell gasoline?** If you just had trouble starting the car, the engine may be flooded. Wait a few minutes and try again. If the smell comes from under the hood area, check your fuel injection system or carburetor to make sure that it isn't leaking fuel. Also check your fuel pump. The gasoline will wash a clean streak across it, which can be seen with the naked eye. Then check for leaks down the fuel line all the way to the fuel tank. Also, check all the fuel lines and hoses. If they've rotted or are disconnected, you'll smell fuel vapors without seeing any leaks. Taking a look under the vehicle after it's been parked overnight may help, but remember that fuel evaporates quickly, so the clues may be stains rather than wet spots. Obviously, you don't want to smoke while you're doing this! But then you _never_ want to smoke when you're working on your car.

Gasoline ignites easily, and gasoline vapors can explode, so if you smell gasoline — and you didn't just fill your tank — find the source of the leak and have it repaired immediately. If your usual repair facility isn't close by, either drive to the closest garage and have them repair it, or call your auto club and have them deal with the leak by either fixing it on the spot or towing the vehicle to a repair facility.

Smoke

If you see smoke coming from your tailpipe, pay attention to the color for clues to what the problem is:

- ✔ **If you see white vapor on a cold morning,** disregard it if it stops after the car warms up. If it continues after the car is warm, a cracked engine block or cylinder head or a leaky head gasket may be letting water into the engine. You'll need professional help with this one.

- ✔ **If you see black smoke and you have a carburetor,** the fuel/air mixture may need to be adjusted to a leaner setting. You can find information about adjusting it in Chapter 13.

Black smoke from a vehicle with fuel injection usually requires special diagnosis and should be left to a repair facility.

You can check to see whether the fuel/air mixture is too rich by running your finger around the inside edge of the tailpipe (first make sure that it's not hot). If carbon comes off on your finger, the mixture is probably too rich.

- ✔ **If the smoke is light or dark blue,** the vehicle is burning oil, which can indicate that oil is leaking into the combustion chambers and you either need your piston rings replaced or your engine rebuilt or replaced. Remedying this situation usually costs *at least* $1,000. But it may simply mean that the oil hasn't been changed and has gotten so low and cruddy that it's smoking. If this is the case — and you're the one responsible — shame on you! Chapter 15 tells you how to change your oil quickly and easily.

- ✔ **If the smoke is light gray,** the car may be burning automatic transmission fluid. Check the transmission dipstick. Is the fluid dark and burned-looking? Does it smell burned? With luck, you may just need to change the fluid.

A faulty vacuum modulator can also suck transmission fluid into the engine, where it's burned in the cylinders and causes the same type of smoke to come out of the tailpipe. You can usually replace the vacuum modulator quite cheaply. Or the smoke may mean that your transmission is going out.

Being low on transmission fluid can cause the same symptoms as a transmission that needs servicing, repair, or replacement. To avoid paying for work that your vehicle may not need, be sure to read Chapter 17 before you see a specialist.

Leaks

Pay close attention to leaks. Running a vehicle that's drastically low on vital liquid can ruin your engine. After you find the source of the leak, the following information will help you decide whether you can handle it yourself or you need professional help.

If water is getting inside your vehicle, check the rubber **gaskets** and weather-stripping around the windows, doors, and sunroof, and refer to Chapter 24 for instructions on how to fix it.

Here's an easy way to see whether anything is leaking out from *under* your vehicle, and a few pointers to help you decide what to do about it:

1. **Park your vehicle overnight on a clean patch of pavement or a large, clean piece of white paper.**

   Either tape some sheets of paper together or buy a roll of plain white commercial wrapping paper. Newspaper is too absorbent and can change the color of the stains.

2. **Place marks on the paper to show where each of the four wheels is resting, and indicate the front and rear ends of the vehicle.**

3. **In the morning, move the vehicle and look for small puddles or traces of liquid on the ground or paper. Touch and smell each puddle or trace of liquid.**

   Here's how to decipher the evidence:

   - **If it's clear, watery, and under the air conditioner,** it's probably just normal condensation (if you've used the air conditioner recently).

   - **If it's black or dark brown, greasy, and located under the engine area,** it's probably oil. Figure out which part of the vehicle was over the spot and look for leaks around the oil-drain plug, the crankcase, and the engine.

   - **If it's red or pink and greasy and you have an automatic transmission,** it's probably transmission fluid. Check the transmission dipstick and, if the level is low, top it off with the proper transmission fluid. Then check the dipstick again in a day or two. If it's low again, have a professional check the transmission to make sure that the seals are intact.

- **If it's watery or slippery; it's green, red, blue, orange, or rust colored; and it's coming from under the radiator or engine,** it's probably coolant. To check the radiator, engine, and hoses for leaks, see "Checking For and Repairing Leaks in the Cooling System" in Chapter 14.

- **If it's oily; it's pink, red, or clear; and you find it toward the front bumper (usually on the driver's side),** it's probably power-steering fluid. Chapter 3 tells you how to check the power-steering dipstick. If the level is low, add more fluid and check again in a couple of days. If it's low again, have a mechanic check things out.

- **If it's a light-colored or clear fluid,** it may be brake fluid. Even if the leaks have dried, the stains should be visible. Depending on which part of the car was parked over the puddle or spot, check for brake fluid leaks around the master cylinder and around the brake lines. If the leak is where a wheel was standing, check down the inside surface of that wheel. If you find stains or wetness there, the brake cylinder could be leaking — or a dog could have "marked" your car!

Leaky brakes are too dangerous to leave unattended. Have a professional repair any brake fluid leaks immediately.

- **If it smells like gasoline,** it probably is! If the leak is under the hood area, check around the fuel pump and the fuel injectors — or the carburetor, if your vehicle has one. If the leak seems to be under the center of the car, check the fuel lines. If it's under the rear end, check the fuel tank. (Don't smoke while you're doing this!)

Gasoline ignites easily, and gasoline vapors can explode, so if you smell gasoline — and you haven't just filled your tank — find the source of the leak and have it repaired immediately. If your usual repair facility isn't close by, either drive to the closest garage and have them repair it, or call your auto club and have them either fix it on the spot or tow the car to a repair facility.

- **If you can't locate the source of the leak and your vehicle is losing liquid from the radiator on a regular basis,** Chapter 14 can help you find the leak and check your radiator pressure cap.

Strange Sensations

This is a catchall category for those things that just "feel funny." Use the process of elimination to check anything that may cause your vehicle to run roughly: hoses, tires, brakes, oil levels, and spark plug connections; the carburetor, cooling system, clutch, gearshift, and steering linkage. The index can steer you toward the chapters that include instructions for checking these things.

Here are a few specific sensations that you may encounter:

✔ **If steering is difficult and you have power steering,** see "Check the Power-Steering Fluid" in Chapter 3 for information about checking the dipstick in the reservoir attached to the power-steering unit to see whether there's enough power-steering fluid. If it's low again soon after you fill it, check for leaks in the hoses leading from the unit to the front wheels.

✔ **If your car starts wandering instead of running in a straight line,** the problem can be caused by worn steering components or wheels that are out of alignment. If the vehicle starts pulling to the left or right, one of the tires may be underinflated, or the front end may be out of alignment. Look for the solutions to these problems in Chapters 16 (steering) and 19.

✔ **If your car pulls to one side when you step on the brake pedal,** Chapter 18 tells you how to check your brakes.

✔ **If the engine speeds up but your car doesn't accelerate when you step on the gas pedal; if there's a delayed response (or none at all) when you shift gears; or if shifting suddenly becomes awkward or noisy,** check the transmission (see Chapter 17). If you have an automatic transmission, you may just be low on transmission fluid, or you may have a disconnected hose or plugged filter.

If you seek professional help, make sure that they check the problems that are cheapest to remedy before they decide that you need major transmission work!

Finally, I strongly suggest that you do the under-the-hood check in Chapter 3. This easy, 15-minute monthly checkup can prevent 70 percent of the problems that could cause your vehicle to break down on the highway. By checking for symptoms of trouble in advance, you can save yourself time and money that you'd otherwise have to spend for towing and repairs.

Directional Signals

Did you know that the directional signal flashers on your dashboard are designed to provide clues to malfunctions elsewhere on your vehicle? If one of your directional flashers stops flashing or stops making that ticking noise when it flashes, the light isn't necessarily out of order. The manufacturer of your vehicle has cleverly utilized these lights to tell you that a light on the outside of your vehicle isn't working.

Using the left flasher on your dashboard as an example, here are what various symptoms indicate:

- **If the left flasher on your dashboard stays on without blinking or making a noise,** get out of the vehicle and check whether your left directional signal lights are on in the front and rear. If one is out, simply replace the bulb. After you replace the bulb, your dashboard flasher should work normally again.

- **If your left rear directional signal light goes on but doesn't blink, and your left front directional signal light doesn't go on at all, but both your right directional signal lights are working perfectly,** your left front directional signal bulb is bad. After you replace it, the left *rear* light will start to blink again.

- **If *all* your directional signal lights aren't going on,** check the fuse. Chapter 12 has instructions for finding your fuse box and replacing fuses.

- **If *all* your directional signal lights go on but don't blink,** your flasher unit is bad. This unit usually plugs directly into the fuse box, so look for trouble there first. After you replace the bulb or fuse that's defective, the dashboard flashers go back to normal. Isn't that lovely?

- **If both signal lights on one side aren't going on,** check to see whether the bulbs need replacing. If they don't, the signals may not be grounded properly. Your mechanic can tell you whether this is the case.

- **If there's no light on your dashboard when you move your directional signal lever,** either the bulb on your dashboard flasher is out or the unit is malfunctioning.

- **If one signal light is flashing faster or slower than the others,** check to see whether the bulb is the proper one for your vehicle. A heavy-duty bulb will flash faster than a standard bulb. Also check for loose connections or corrosion around the socket the bulb fits into.

Be sure to replace burnt-out bulbs at once. They usually cost very little. Most service stations will replace them for the cost of the bulb. Headlights are more expensive because they have to be replaced as a unit (see Chapter 12 for instructions).

Chapter 21

What to Do If Your Car Drops Dead or Won't Start

In This Chapter

▶ Moving safely to the side of the road

▶ Figuring out what caused the problem

▶ Cooling down an overheated vehicle

▶ Dealing with a car that won't start

▶ Jump-starting your car safely

*W*hether your car dies on the road or in front of your house, it's always a time of unrivaled panic and stress. But an informed, well-organized approach to diagnosing your sick monster's ills can pay off by getting you moving again with a minimum loss of time, money, and composure. The problems involved are seldom serious, and you can usually solve them by keeping a cool head and following the instructions I provide in this chapter.

If you encounter an unfamiliar word and it's in special type, you can find its definition in the glossary.

First Things First

If you have reason to believe that your vehicle is having a problem, try to get to the right-hand shoulder of the road, especially if you're on a highway. Very often, if a vehicle is going to do its swan song while in motion, it will give you a couple of hints first. If you can recognize those hints as signs of impending disaster, you'll be able to get out of traffic before the car dies completely.

All the following symptoms are good reasons to head for the side of the road immediately, park, and check things out:

- Your vehicle experiences a sudden loss of power, or you suddenly have to floor the accelerator to maintain speed or to keep moving at all.

- A warning light has come on.

- Your car suddenly runs roughly.

- The engine is misfiring.

- You hear unfamiliar noises.

- Your car is pulling to one side.

As you pull your vehicle off the road to investigate the cause of the malfunction, keep the following safety procedures in mind:

- **Try to coast along the shoulder until you're well away from any curves in the road behind you.** Doing so pays off when you're ready to get back onto the road — because you can spot oncoming traffic before it's on your tail.

- **If the car dies right on the highway and you can't get off the road,** *don't get out of the car!* I know that sitting in a dead car with traffic piling up behind you is unnerving, but attempting to cross a high-speed freeway on foot is suicide. Most heavily traveled highways are also heavily patrolled, and a nice highway patrol officer will be along before you know it. Once the officer is on the scene, it's a simple matter of stopping traffic long enough to push your vehicle to the right-hand shoulder.

When you reach the side of the road, take these additional safety precautions:

- **Roll down the window on the driver's side, hang out a white cloth or piece of paper, and roll the window back up to secure it in place.** The cloth or paper also alerts drivers to proceed around you. If you can easily reach the passenger-side window without getting out of the car, do the same on that side. Try not to obstruct your ability to see out the windows.

- **If you know that you're going to need roadside assistance, use your cell phone to call your auto club or the highway patrol.** If you have no cell phone — and you can see an emergency call box nearby — use the call box to call for help. If no call box is handy, you're probably better off hanging a white cloth or piece of paper out the window and waiting for the highway patrol to spot you. In these days of daytime carjackings, walking along the highway alone can be dangerous.

- **To avoid being hit by a passing vehicle, don't work on your car from the left (driver's) side, unless you can do so while standing well away from the nearest traffic lane.** If you can, move the car farther off the road, and try to reach into the trouble area from the front or right side, keeping away from traffic. That goes for changing left-side tires, too.

✔ **If it's *daylight,* put on your emergency blinkers or your left-turn signal to alert oncoming traffic to the fact that your car isn't moving.** This is not a good idea at night because motorists coming up behind you may think that your vehicle is still rolling along the highway and run right into the rear end of your car. (Drunk drivers are especially prone to this sometimes fatal error.)

✔ **If it's *nighttime,* place warning lights or reflective markers about 6 feet behind the vehicle to alert traffic.** If you have neither of these, either turn on the interior lights manually or leave the *right*-hand car door open so that the interior lights stay on.

Carry a lantern, a large battery-operated light, a couple of milk cartons filled with wax and a wick, or, as a last resort, a couple of flares in the trunk for this kind of emergency.

Troubleshooting the Problem

After you're safely off the road and ready to deal with the situation, try to view what happened in dietary terms: Your vehicle lives on a mixture of air, fuel, and fire — if it won't go, it's not getting one of the following ingredients.

Air

Air is simple — and probably not the problem. Your vehicle gets its air through the air cleaner. Unless the air filter inside the air cleaner is totally clogged, your engine should be getting enough air to keep it going. Your choke or throttle may be stuck in the closed position, which could keep your car from breathing properly. To find out whether this is the problem, do the following.

Check the hoses and the PCV valve

Look at all the hoses under the hood. Have any of them become disconnected or broken? Do you hear air whistling while the car idles — if it can? One strategic lost hose can slow or stop your car. Reclamp the wanderer or tape the hole, and you'll soon be on your way. Of course, if you make a habit of checking and replacing worn hoses *before* disaster strikes (see Chapter 3), you can avoid this trouble completely.

Also check your PCV valve to make sure that it's clear and functioning. The "Checking and Servicing your PCV Valve" section in Chapter 13 can help you to do so.

For vehicles with fuel injection

1. **Make sure that the car is in Park or Neutral gear, with the emergency brake on, and that your hair, jewelry, or clothing won't get caught in anything.**

   Also check that the items you touch aren't hot enough to burn your fingers.

2. **Remove the air filter (find instructions in Chapter 6) and inspect it.**

3. **Follow the air filter's hose to the throttle body on the engine.**

   On some vehicles, the engine will stall if this hose is disconnected.

For vehicles with carburetors

1. **Make sure that the car is in Park or Neutral, with the emergency brake on, and that your hair, jewelry, or clothing won't get caught in anything.**

   Also check that the items you touch are not hot enough to burn your fingers.

2. **Remove the air cleaner (find instructions in Chapter 6) and look into the carburetor barrel, as shown in Figure 21-1.**

   Is the choke open?

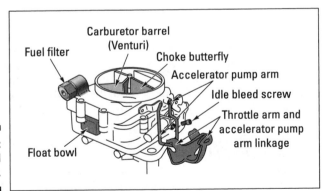

Carburetor barrel
(Venturi)

Fuel filter

Choke butterfly

Accelerator pump arm

Idle bleed screw

Throttle arm and
accelerator pump
arm linkage

Float bowl

Figure 21-1:
A typical
carburetor.

3. **Move the throttle linkage (that's the arm that makes the car rev when you push it) with your finger.**

   Does it seem to be moving freely? If so, that's not your problem.

4. **While you're looking down the throat of the carburetor, check to see whether fuel sprays in there when you move the linkage.**

   You can find instructions for doing so in the "Fuel" section, which follows.

Fuel

No matter how nervous you are, never smoke when working on a car, especially if you're dealing with the fuel system!

If the engine turns over but doesn't start running, it may not be getting fuel. The first question you need to answer is whether you're out of gas. Even if your gas gauge says that you still have some, the gauge may be on the blink. When did you last fill the tank?

If your car lost power before it died, take note of the following to see whether fuel is getting to the engine:

- **Sometimes the problem is *too much* fuel.** If you open the hood and find that everything is covered with gasoline, *don't try to start the car!* Gasoline is too flammable to monkey around with. Just hoist that white flag and get help.

- **If it's a very hot day and you've been driving in stop-and-go traffic, you may have vapor lock.** Occasionally, a vehicle gets so hot that the gasoline boils in the fuel line and forms bubbles that keep the fuel from getting to the fuel injectors or carburetor. The symptoms are easy to spot: Your engine just suddenly stops running, with no prior warning. Happily, the remedy isn't difficult: Simply open the hood, wrap a wet rag around the fuel line between the fuel pump and the fuel injectors or carburetor, and wait for things to cool down.

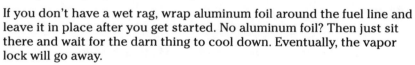

Don't try to open the radiator pressure cap or coolant reservoir to get water to wet the rag. The pressure in the overheated system can cause hot liquid to spray out and burn you.

If you don't have a wet rag, wrap aluminum foil around the fuel line and leave it in place after you get started. No aluminum foil? Then just sit there and wait for the darn thing to cool down. Eventually, the vapor lock will go away.

If neither of the above seems to be the case, try the following set of steps that applies to your vehicle.

For vehicles with fuel injection

1. **Try cranking the engine while someone sprays fuel injector cleaner into the throttle body.**

   If the engine starts and then dies, it's a fuel problem. If the engine cranks without firing, it's an ignition system or compression problem.

2. **If the engine did start with fuel injector cleaner, find out whether the fuel pump isn't pumping fuel or the computer isn't triggering the fuel injectors.**

   In either case, you're better off leaving the repairs to a professional.

For vehicles with carburetors

1. **Look down the carburetor barrel and push the accelerator pump arm.**

   Is fuel squirting into the venturi? If so, then the float bowl is full, but it still may not be getting a fresh supply of fuel when it needs it.

2. **Disconnect the fuel pump end of the hose that leads from the carburetor to the fuel pump (see Figure 21-2) and place the end of the hose in a jar or plastic bag.**

   If you don't have anything to put the hose in, forget this entire procedure. Never let gasoline run onto the ground. It's flammable and toxic to the environment. Also, be sure not to let gasoline run out of the hose onto your clothes or the engine. And if it's very hot, fan the area to disburse the fumes.

   Somewhere along that line is the fuel filter. The filter could have jammed — especially if it hasn't been changed in ages.

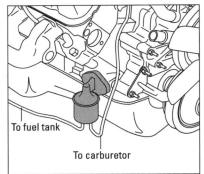

Figure 21-2:
A hose runs from the fuel pump to the carburetor.

To fuel tank

To carburetor

3. **Bump the starter and see whether gasoline squirts out of the hose.**

   If it does, then your fuel filter and fuel pump are probably all right. If nothing comes out of the hose, you probably have either a plugged fuel filter, a defective fuel pump, or a broken fuel line — or you're out of gas.

4. **Try to eliminate the fuel filter as the villain by removing it (Chapter 13 tells you how) to see whether gas comes out of the hose.**

   If you changed the filter recently, ignore this step and look under the rear end of the car to see whether fuel is leaking from a broken fuel line.

Fire

If your engine is getting enough air and fuel, you're probably having ignition system trouble. As I explain in Chapter 4, the "fire" is really electric current that's stored in the battery, replaced by the alternator, amplified by the coil and, in some vehicles, directed by a distributor to each spark plug. (Newer vehicles have distributorless ignition systems — Chapter 5 has the details.) If something along the way goes wrong and the spark fails to reach the plugs, all the air and fuel in the world won't produce combustion in the cylinders, and the vehicle won't go. Because the engine was running before it died, it's probably not the fault of the battery, solenoid, or starter, which brings you to the distributor cap — assuming that your vehicle has one. If you have a distributorless system, you'll need professional help to check it out.

Checking the distributor cap

With the engine off, check to see whether the cables that run from the distributor cap to the spark plugs are pushed down securely at each end. Check the cable that runs from the distributor cap to the coil to be sure that it, too, is secure. How about the smaller wires that come out of the coil?

Because many cars now have high-energy ignition systems that operate at 47,000 volts or higher, *pulling a distributor or spark plug cable to test for a spark is unsafe.* If your car has an electronic ignition system, the ignition module may have gone bad. If you have an electronic ignition system or a distributorless ignition system, skip the rest of the checks in this section.

If your car has a *non*-electronic ignition system, follow the instructions in Chapter 12 to remove the distributor cap and look at the points. Do they open and close when you bump the starter? If not, adjust them so that they do and try to start the car again. If there's still no action, your points could be oxidized or fouled by a bit of grease or oil. Bump the engine so that the points are closed, and insert the tip of a screwdriver, nail file, matchbook cover, or feeler gauge between them to rub the point surfaces and eliminate the oxidation or dirt. If you *still* can't get the engine to turn over, move on to the next section.

Replacing the rotor, condenser, and points

If you've kept your old rotor, points, and condenser in the trunk of your car because they were still working when you replaced them during a tune-up, you can use these parts to try to find and correct your problem. First, following instructions in Chapter 12, try replacing the rotor with the old one. If that doesn't work, replace the condenser. If that doesn't work, replace the points. Don't worry about adjusting the point gap; as long as the points open and close, the engine will run.

I've been told that the most frequent cause of engine failure on vehicles with old-style, non-electronic distributors is improper lubrication of the cam when the points were changed. Because of this, the little rubbing block gets worn down, and then, even when the block rests on the cam lobe, there's not enough surface to force the points apart. That's why, if you have a non-electronic ignition system, it's important to check your dwell every 5,000 miles and replace points at every tune-up (see Chapter 12 for instructions).

If you've checked everything out and your vehicle still won't go, you're probably going to have to wait for help. Sometimes part of your engine has given out. Sometimes it's the transmission. If that's the case, you may be saying good-bye to Old Faithful. On the bright side, you usually have plenty of warning before a car gives up the ghost. Of course, if you haven't checked and maintained your vehicle properly — if you've ignored the warnings, the knockings, the smoke from the tailpipe, the hesitations and the other symptoms I cover in Chapter 20 — well, you asked for it.

Handling a Vehicle That Overheats on a Hot Day

Even the happiest, most beautifully tuned vehicle overheats occasionally. If you find yourself in stop-and-go traffic on an extremely hot day, chances are that your car's dashboard temperature indicator will rise or a warning light will come on. Here's how to help your vehicle regain its cool:

- ✔ **At the first sign of overheating, shut off your air conditioner and open your windows.** Doing so decreases the load on the engine and helps it cool off.

- ✔ **If you continue to overheat, turn on the heater and blower.** Doing so transfers the heat from the engine to the interior of the car. (This does wonders for your overheated engine but very little for you!)

- ✔ **If you're stopped in traffic and the temperature gauge is rising, shift into Neutral and rev the engine a little.** Doing so makes the water pump and the fan speed up, which draws more liquid and air through the radiator. The increased air and liquid circulation helps cool things off.

- ✔ **Try not to ride your brakes.** Crawl along slowly, on little more than an idle, rather than moving up and then braking repeatedly. Brake drag increases the load on the engine and makes it heat up. If traffic is crawling, move up only when the gap between you and the vehicle in front of you gets too wide.

✔ **If you think that your vehicle is about to boil over, drive to the side of the road, open the hood, and sit there until things cool off.** Remember, _don't open the radiator cap_ under these circumstances, and if your engine has boiled over, _don't add water_ until the engine is quite cool again.

If you _must_ add water when the engine is still a _little_ warm, add the water while the engine is running in Neutral. Follow the instructions at the beginning of this chapter to park where you can safely get out and open your hood. Then, to avoid the possibility of burning yourself, follow the instructions in Chapter 14 for opening a radiator pressure cap and adding liquid to the system safely.

Sometimes very hot weather causes vapor lock, which makes your car stop without warning and refuse to go again. You can find the simple remedy for this problem in the "Fuel" section, earlier in this chapter.

Overheating When It Isn't Hot Outside

Although hot weather is the most common cause of overheating, many other factors can cause the same problem. If your vehicle overheats in traffic in normal weather, one of the following may be the culprit:

✔ **The water and coolant level in the radiator is low.** If you haven't checked your fluid level in a while (or ever), check it now, either by looking at the level through the side of the coolant recovery system or by following the instructions in "Check the Radiator" in Chapter 3.

✔ **There's a leak in the cooling system.** Chapter 14 has an entire section that explains where to look for leaks in various parts of the cooling system and what to do after you find them.

✔ **If you can't locate any leaks, your thermostat may be malfunctioning.** Obviously, you can't replace the thermostat at the side of the road, but Chapter 14 has instructions for doing so cheaply and easily once you're safely back home. In the meantime, you can eliminate this malfunction as a possibility if you wait until the engine cools down _completely_ and use those instructions to remove the old thermostat and reconnect the hoses. If the car starts up and runs well without the thermostat, the old one was probably screwing up the works.

Get a new thermostat immediately if you find that your old one isn't working. If you drive for long distances without a thermostat, you can damage your engine.

✔ **If none of these seems to be the problem and your vehicle continues to overheat, check out "Overcoming Overheating" in Chapter 14.**

If Your Car Won't Start

Before I end this chapter, consider those wonderful days when your car won't start. If you left your lights, heater, radio, or some other electrical gizmo on after you parked the car, you know what the trouble is: Your battery is dead. Of course, there are other possible reasons that your car won't start. The next section, "Won't-start symptoms," lists them. The last section, "Jumping a start," explains the safest way to jump-start your vehicle.

Won't-start symptoms

Your car may not start for a number of reasons. The following list outlines the most common circumstances and tells you what action you can take to try to remedy each situation:

- ✔ **The car is silent when you turn the key in the ignition.** Check the battery terminal cable connections (see Chapter 3). If they look very corroded, force the point of a screwdriver (with an insulated or wooden handle) between the connector and the terminal post and twist it to lodge it firmly. Then try to start the engine. If it starts, you need to clean or replace your cables. You can find instructions for cleaning them in Chapter 3.

- ✔ **The car makes a clicking noise but won't start.** This sound usually means a dead battery. If not, check the wiring to and from the starter for a loose connection.

- ✔ **The car cranks over but won't start.** Check the fuel supply to your engine (see "Fuel" earlier in this chapter, and Chapter 13). If that's okay, check whether the electrical spark is getting through (see "Fire," earlier in this chapter, and Chapter 12).

- ✔ **The engine starts but dies.** If your car has a carburetor, check your carburetor adjustment and your choke to see whether the choke is first closing and then opening. (Chapter 13 has instructions for both of these checks.) If you have fuel injection, you'll need professional help.

- ✔ **The car won't start on rainy days.** Check inside the distributor cap for dampness (see "Servicing Your Distributor" in Chapter 12). If you find moisture, get some mechanic's solvent from your friendly service station — they use it to clean car parts — or buy an aerosol can of it at an auto supply store. To evaporate any dampness inside the distributor cap, turn the cap upside down and pour or spray some solvent into it. Swish it around and pour it out. Then dry the cap as best you can with a clean, lint-free rag and replace the cap.

Use only *clean* solvent; even a tiny speck of dirt can foul the points. Gasoline won't do because a spark can ignite gasoline fumes and cause an explosion or a fire.

✔ **The car won't start on cold mornings.** For vehicles with carburetors, check the choke. Is it closed? Does it open? See Chapter 13 for details. If you have fuel injection, you'll need to have a professional diagnose the cold-start problems.

✔ **The engine misses while idling.** Check the points (if your car has a non-electronic distributor) and the spark plugs (see Chapter 12). Also check the fuel pump, fuel filter, and carburetor, if you have one (see Chapter 13).

✔ **The engine misses or hesitates during acceleration.** Check the accelerator pump in the carburetor (if equipped), the spark plugs, the distributor, and the timing (see Chapters 12 and 13).

✔ **The engine knocks or pings.** Check your timing (see Chapter 12); also check the octane rating of the fuel you're using. The owner's manual can tell you whether your vehicle needs regular unleaded or premium gasoline. Check the cooling system (see Chapter 14). Do a compression check on the engine cylinders (see the section "Checking the Compression in Your Cylinders" in Chapter 13).

Jumping a start

If your battery has died, you may be able to use jumper cables to jump a start from some Good Samaritan's car — with one important exception.

If either vehicle has an electronic ignition system, the use of jumper cables *may* damage it. If your vehicle is one that may be damaged in this way, you may find a warning to that effect in the owner's manual or on a decal under the hood. Even if you don't find a warning, it pays to be sure, so call the service department at your dealership and ask about your vehicle's make, model, and year.

If you can safely use jumper cables on your vehicle, make sure that the battery on the Good Samaritan's vehicle has at least as much voltage as your own. It doesn't matter whether your car has negative ground and the GS's car has positive ground, or your car has an alternator and the GS's car has a generator, as long as you hook up the cables properly (and the proper way is the same in every case).

To safely jump a start, follow these steps:

1. **Take out your jumper cables.**

   It's a good idea to buy a set of jumper cables (see Chapter 2) and keep them in the trunk compartment. If you don't have jumper cables, you'll have to find a Good Samaritan who not only is willing to assist you but has jumper cables as well.

2. **Place both cars in Park or Neutral, with their ignitions shut off and their emergency brakes on.**

3. **Remove the caps from both batteries (unless they're sealed).**

   Batteries produce explosive hydrogen gas, and a spark could set it off. If the caps are open, you can avoid such an explosion. (Sealed batteries have safety valves.)

4. **Connect the cables.**

   The positive cable has red clips at either end, and the negative cable has black clips. It's important to attach them in the proper order:

   1. First, attach one of the *red* clips to the *positive* terminal of *your* battery (it has "POS" or "+" on it, or it's bigger than the negative terminal).

   2. Attach the other red clip to the positive terminal of the GS's car.

   3. Attach one of the *black* clips to the negative terminal on the GS's battery.

   4. Attach the last black clip to an unpainted metal surface on your car that *isn't* near the carburetor (if your car has one) or battery.

   Figure 21-3 shows how both the positive and negative cables should be connected.

5. **Try to start your vehicle.**

   If it won't start, make sure that the cables are properly connected and have the GS run his or her engine for five minutes. Then try to start your car again. If it still won't start, your battery may be beyond help.

6. **Disconnect the cables, thank the Good Samaritan, and resume your life.**

   Don't shut off your engine; drive around for a while to recharge your battery.

If your alternator light stays on or the gauge on the dashboard continues to point to "Discharge" after your car's been running, make sure that your fan belt is tight enough to run your alternator properly. If your battery keeps going dead, have a professional check both the battery and your alternator.

In any case, never drive around with a light or gauge that reads "Trouble"; have it checked out immediately — that's why those gauges are in there!

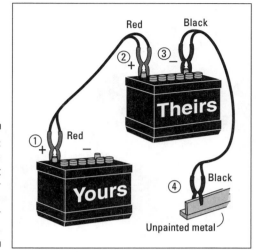

Figure 21-3:
Make sure
to connect
jumper
cables in
the proper
order.

Chapter 22

When All Else Fails: Finding and Dealing with a Good Mechanic

In This Chapter

▶ Choosing the type of repair shop that's right for you

▶ Paying attention to the certification of the mechanic and/or shop

▶ Evaluating automotive service facilities

▶ Maintaining a good relationship with a mechanic

▶ Getting satisfaction on *any* complaint

*Y*ou just moved to a new town, and your trusted former repair facility is too far away to be of any use to you. Or you bought a new car, and your old mechanic doesn't work on that particular type of vehicle. Suddenly, you're lost in an unfamiliar marketplace without the faintest idea of where to go when your vehicle requires service that's beyond your abilities and where to get help in an emergency. The Yellow Pages are full of ads, and the streets are full of service stations, but how can you tell which shops are reliable and which are just waiting to take advantage of you? Relax, dear friend; you've come to the right place for advice.

In this chapter, I tell you how to find a good mechanic, give you tips for establishing a good relationship with one, and provide you with a winning strategy for getting satisfaction on *any* type of consumer complaint.

CAR SMARTS

What's in a name?

Because most vehicles now rely on sophisticated electronic systems rather than mechanical ones, in recent years the term *technician* has replaced *mechanic* at many automotive service facilities. In the interest of variety, I use both terms in this book, but I suggest that you use *technician* if you want to make a good impression on the professionals at your repair shop.

Choosing a Repair Shop

Several kinds of shops repair and service vehicles: dealerships, chain stores, specialists, and independents. How do you decide which is the right shop for you? Each has its drawbacks as well as its advantages. The following sections describe each of these service options so that you can choose the type that's best for you.

Dealerships

When they buy a new vehicle, many people assume that they have to use the dealership's service facilities, at least until the warranty period is over. Be aware that, in most cases, you can have warranty service (but not repairs) done by any licensed independent mechanic, as long as all the service requirements in your owner's manual are fulfilled. (There are some exceptions, so read your warranties before going elsewhere for specialized work.) Of course, you may want to stay with the dealer who sold you the vehicle, because dealerships may offer the following advantages:

- ✔ **They often provide extra services to ensure goodwill.** Not only can they make more profit on years of service to your vehicle, but they also want you to come back to them when it's time to buy another one.

- ✔ **They usually have a variety of factory-trained specialists right on the premises.** The advantage is that you can have brake work, transmission work, and sometimes even bodywork done at the same place.

- ✔ **They stock a wide variety of original parts and equipment (OEM) made specifically for your vehicle.** This not only assures you of satisfaction if parts fail, but original parts may increase the resale value of your vehicle.

- ✔ **If you have a complaint, you're dealing with an established company that's financially able to reimburse you and that's insured to cover any major lawsuits that may result.**

However, dealerships have disadvantages to consider as well:

- ✔ **Dealerships are often more expensive than other types of service facilities.** Independent shops usually have a lower overhead to support.

- ✔ **The sales and service departments of a dealership are often operated as separate entities.** You may find that the service department doesn't really care all that much about your goodwill and whether you buy another vehicle from the dealership. Instead, the attitude may be, "We have more work than we can handle, so if you're not happy here, you can go somewhere else."

✔ **You probably won't receive the personalized service that you may get from an independent mechanic.** You generally deal with a service writer at the dealership who then assigns your car to whichever technician is available when its number comes up. Of course, if you build a good relationship with the service writer, he or she may honor your request for a specific technician who is familiar with your vehicle and its foibles.

Chain and department stores

Large chain stores and department stores that have automotive service departments offer another set of pros and cons:

✔ **They're generally less expensive than dealerships.**

✔ **They usually stock a wide variety of parts, many of which are made to their specifications and carry their brand name.** How these parts compare in price and quality to the original equipment supplied by the car manufacturer varies, depending on which chain you deal with.

The only time you absolutely don't want to use anything but original equipment is when you're restoring a classic car.

✔ **They usually provide good guarantees on parts and labor.** And if you have a complaint, they're generally motivated to keep your goodwill.

✔ **Large chain stores maintain branches nationwide that honor their warranties and guarantees.** If you move or travel frequently, this feature can be very beneficial.

Chain stores also have their disadvantages:

✔ **Large chains also use service writers, and the work may tend to be impersonal, with a new technician working on your car each time.**

✔ **Technicians at some chains get a commission on the parts they sell.** This may motivate them to sell you a new part instead of repairing an old one, or to perform work that your vehicle may not really need.

Here's a feature of large chains that has both positive and negative aspects:

Large chains are good training grounds for inexperienced technicians who are just out of school and are working at their first professional jobs. Your car may turn out to be a guinea pig, as well as a gas hog, if it falls into incompetent hands. On the other hand, it may be lucky enough to be tended to by bright, enthusiastic young people with all the latest techniques at their fingertips.

Independents

An independent service facility can offer the best — or the worst — alternative:

- **Honest, reliable, and experienced independent mechanics can provide personalized service based on high standards of excellence.** They can offer you the opportunity to communicate directly with a professional who knows you, knows your vehicle, and cares a great deal about maintaining a good reputation, because most independent business comes from referrals.

- **Many independent shops are less expensive than dealerships.** Others, especially those that service only luxury cars or high-performance sports cars, may offer the finest workmanship at relatively exorbitant rates. A cherished few provide fine workmanship at low prices — these mechanics are probably saints disguised in greasy coveralls!

- **Expertise, the availability of specialized tools, and the variety of parts in inventory may vary from one independent shop to another, so check carefully to be sure that you're getting a reliable one.** A good independent knows where to find the proper talent, borrow the tools, and buy OEM parts at a good price. An unreliable one patches things together, uses cheap parts, and hopes for the best.

The type of facility you select may vary, depending on the kind of service your vehicle requires. You may find the best buys on tires at a major chain and depend on an experienced independent mechanic for the best deal on reliable, competent service at a good price. See the section called "Finding a Reliable Service Facility" for more information.

Specialists

There are two types of specialists: A specialized chain store or independent mechanic deals with a specific type of repair, such as brake work, transmission work, or muffler replacement. The other type of specialist is an independent shop that works only on specific makes or types of vehicles, such as Ferraris, Volvos, motorcycles, vans, or classic cars.

Here are the pros and cons to consider:

- **A reliable specialist can provide the experience, specialized tools, and extensive inventory that may be unavailable at a shop that handles everything in general and nothing in particular.** If you know that the trouble with your vehicle resides in a particular automotive system, you may want to look for a well-established specialist who focuses on that type of work.

✔ **Some specialized chains that sell and install cheap parts may be more interested in selling new parts than in repairing old ones.** Their "lifetime guarantees" may keep you coming back to pay more for the labor to install those "free" replacement parts than you'd spend on higher-quality parts that last longer.

Check out national chains that specialize in the type of repair you need in consumer publications such as *Consumer Reports* to be sure that the one you choose has a good reputation for durable parts and quality service.

Finding a Reliable Service Facility

Several organizations test, rate, and certify good service facilities or individual technicians. If you're unsure about a particular shop, you can feel pretty secure if you see a sign or a patch on a technician's uniform showing that the shop or the individual has achieved recognition from one of the following sources:

✔ **AAA- and CAA-approved repair facilities:** Both the American Automobile Association (AAA) and the Canadian Automobile Association (CAA) have rating programs for auto repair. These organizations visit and evaluate shops to make sure that they meet high standards for reliable service at a fair price and willingness to resolve complaints. To qualify, shops must provide customers with written estimates of all costs and offer a minimum warranty on parts and labor of 180 days or 6,000 miles. Any history of customer complaints about the shop is taken into account in the evaluation. Because this program operates on a cost-recovery basis, a shop can't "buy" Association approval. They also don't impose price limitations on approved shops. The program covers the full spectrum, from low-cost to high-priced repair facilities.

Both the AAA and the CAA are willing to arbitrate disputes between members and approved shops, in most cases, if negotiations between the shop and the member aren't successful. The exceptions to this are the following:

• They won't get involved simply because you've found that you could have had the job done elsewhere for less.

• They won't decide whether a specific job is covered by a manufacturer's warranty.

To find an Approved Auto Repair Service Program in your area, look for the AAA or CAA logo on display at a shop, contact your local or regional association office, or contact national headquarters at the following addresses and phone numbers for a list of Approved Repair Facilities.

Approved Auto Repair Program
Automotive Engineering and Road Division
American Automobile Association
1000 AAA Drive
Heathrow, FL 32746
407-444-7761
www.aaa.com

Approved Auto Repair Service Program
Canadian Automobile Association
1145 Hunt Club Rd., Suite 200
Ottawa, Ontario
Canada K1V 0Y3
613-247-0117
www.caa.ca

If you are a member of one of these clubs and you have an unresolved complaint about an approved shop, contact the Approved Auto Repair Service Program at your local club or national headquarters.

✔ **ASE-certified technicians:** The National Institute for Automotive Service Excellence (ASE) certifies technicians by testing them on a variety of automobile repair specialties, including brakes and transmissions. To date, more than 440,000 technicians have passed these voluntary tests. Look for the blue and white ASE patch on your technician's uniform (ASE certifies the individual, not the shop) or obtain a list of ASE-certified technicians in your home state by contacting the ASE:

National Institute for Automotive Service Excellence
13505 Dulles Technology Drive, Suite 2
Herndon, VA 20171-3421
703-713-3800
www.asecert.org

✔ **ADS (Authorized Diesel Specialists):** If you own a diesel-powered vehicle that is out of warranty and you are looking for a reliable diesel mechanic, look in your local Yellow Pages under "Automobile Repair & Service" for a shop that displays the ADS logo. ADS-authorized shops must send their technicians to factory schools to keep abreast of new parts, techniques, and systems. They must meet high standards for cleanliness, and they must stock sufficient tools and parts to deal efficiently with most diesel repair and maintenance jobs.

✔ **IGO (Independent Garage Owners Association):** An IGO shield or sign indicates that the owner of the garage is a member of this association. The IGO does not qualify individual technicians, but it has a code of ethics that members pledge to live up to if they want to stay in the organization.

✔ **Service and achievement awards:** Check out the framed certificates hanging in the shop manager's office. Reliable facilities often receive awards for participating in community and civic organizations and for customer service excellence. Look also for certificates awarded to individual technicians who have completed factory-training programs that qualify them to operate specialized electronic equipment, and for grateful letters from satisfied customers.

✔ **Better Business Bureau:** Check with your local Better Business Bureau to see whether a shop has been the subject of numerous consumer complaints.

✔ **Referrals:** I've always felt that the best way to find a good mechanic is the same way you find a doctor, lawyer, or plumber — through referrals. Ask people who drive the same make vehicle as you do where they go for repairs, and then check out the shops that are the most conveniently located. As a fringe benefit, you'll also know which shops to avoid, because many of the people you ask will have horror stories to tell you, too.

Evaluating a Facility

A quick way to do a preliminary check is to call a shop and ask for its basic prices on regular maintenance jobs like tuning the make and model vehicle you drive, flushing the cooling system, and changing the oil and oil filter. You should also ask what the hourly labor rate is and whether the shop uses OEM parts for your particular vehicle. A telephone interview can give you a good idea of whether a shop's prices are competitive and provide you with a feeling for the shop's "vibes." If the people you talk to are surly and uncommunicative over the phone, chances are that you're going to run into trouble if you have to deal with them in an emergency. *Before* you need service, follow up a positive phone interview with an unannounced visit to check on the following things:

✔ **Is the place clean and well-organized or filthy and cluttered?** Appearance is a good indication of general attitude. Auto repair is a trade that calls for patience and precision. If the shop is sloppy and disorganized, the work may be, too.

✔ **Does the shop have modern electronic diagnostic and testing equipment?** These machines save time by pinpointing trouble areas and checking adjustments and tolerances. Saving time means saving money when it comes to paying those labor charges. Of course, this equipment is only as good as the person using it. Ask if shop technicians attend factory schools and seminars run by manufacturers to learn how to use the more sophisticated analyzers and keep up-to-date on new systems.

Modern vehicles require sophisticated, specialized, diagnostic computer equipment, sometimes specific to the make and model of vehicle. Find out whether your vehicle is in that category. If it is, you may have to take it to your local dealer for any work involving computer-controlled functions.

✔ **Does the shop have a good, up-to-date service manual for your vehicle?** I usually buy one for my car's year, make, and model and offer to lend it to the mechanic. After all, service facilities can't stock manuals for every vehicle in the world.

Before you hand over your manual, scan the section that deals with the system in question. If you know which parts are involved and have at least a general idea of the work required, you'll be able to communicate intelligently with the service writer and have a basis for questioning any parts or labor charges that seem excessive.

✔ **Does the shop have the necessary tools to do your job?** Ask whether any part of the job will have to be sent out to a specialist. If this is the case, ask whether they will simply pass those charges on to you, or mark them up to compensate themselves for the time and effort of delivering the vehicle to the specialist and picking it up afterward.

If the entire job has to be done by an outside specialist, consider taking the vehicle there directly instead of having your shop serve as a middle-man. Avoid conflicts with the service facility by saying that you want another estimate.

✔ **What form of payment does the shop accept?** Credit cards? Checks? Or only cash? The advantage of using a credit card is that, in the event of a dispute, you can withhold payment until the credit card company investigates the situation.

✔ **How does the shop guarantee its repairs?** Guarantees usually range from one month to a year. If a shop doesn't think that its work will endure for at least three months, go elsewhere.

✔ **Can the shop provide references?** Most shops will allow you to call a few of its customers to see whether they were satisfied with service. A vehicle that you've paid thousands of dollars for is certainly worth the time it takes to get these assurances.

How does the shop structure the price you pay for repairs? This not only has a great impact on your wallet, but on the quality of the work performed, as well. The following review of the advantages and disadvantages of various pricing systems is based on an article by automotive expert, David (Dre) Solomon, editor/publisher of *Nutz & Boltz,* an automotive newsletter.

✔ **By the clock:** Any type of automotive repair facility may determine the cost of a job by multiplying a fixed hourly labor rate by the time it took to complete the work.

• *Advantages:* This system is simple and easy to understand and encourages technicians to take the time to do their best work.

- *Disadvantages:* It also makes it difficult to accurately estimate what the job will cost because unexpected technical problems can seriously raise the price.

✔ **Pre-established price lists:** Specialists and major chains, such as brake, muffler, and transmission shops, often set fixed prices for specific jobs. Sometimes several basic services are combined into one package.

  - *Advantages:* Prices are easy to understand and are usually competitive. You don't pay more if the job goes slowly.

  - *Disadvantages:* There are none, unless the only service you need can only be done as part of a package.

✔ **Flat rates:** Most shops base their prices on a *Flat Rate Manual*, which lists every job that can be done, as well as the amount of time it should take to accomplish the job on a specific vehicle.

  - *Advantages:* Estimates are accurate because they aren't affected if a job takes longer than normal.

  - *Disadvantages:* You may be charged for the amount of time listed in the manual, no matter how little time the work actually took. Few shops will keep a technician who can't "beat the book" by a substantial amount of time, which means that mechanics may skimp and cut corners to complete repairs as quickly as possible.

✔ **Variable flat rates:** Some dealerships price jobs not only by the *Flat Rate Manual*, but also by the level of skill necessary to do the work properly.

  - *Advantages:* Maintenance jobs are usually priced at a lower rate than more sophisticated repairs. You aren't penalized if the job takes longer than expected.

  - *Disadvantages:* You may have to pay for expensive repairs when the problem could have been corrected in a quicker and cheaper fashion. For instance, some automatic transmission problems are caused by insufficient transmission fluid, but some shops will rebuild or replace the entire transmission instead of simply adding enough fluid to bring the level up to the "Full" line on the dipstick.

✔ **Flat rates and parts commissions:** At many chains or department stores, the mechanic shares in the profits on the sale of parts.

  - *Advantages:* You aren't penalized if the job takes longer than expected.

  - *Disadvantages:* In addition to the disadvantages of flat rates, you may have to pay for a part that could have been cheaply and easily replaced or for parts that you never needed in the first place.

Getting the Best Possible Deal

As I've said before, a big repair job is like major surgery. Not only do you want the best possible surgeon, but you also want to be sure that the surgery is necessary and that it's done under the best possible terms. Therefore, whenever you bring your vehicle in for maintenance or repair, follow these guidelines:

- ✔ **If you're dealing with a new shop or you're faced with major repairs,** *get at least a second opinion and an estimate of costs* **from another repair shop.** If there's a big discrepancy, additional estimates and opinions are in order. If one shop is much lower in price than the others, this is not necessarily the best place to go. Be sure that the work will be of the same quality before you go for the cheapest job.

- ✔ **Ask for a written estimate.** Many states require one anyway and require the shop to call you if they find that the job will cost more than originally estimated. Beware of general statements; try to get as detailed an estimate of what's involved as possible.

- ✔ **Ask that all the parts that are replaced be returned to you, regardless of whether the laws in your state require it.** That way, you can be sure that you're getting what you pay for.

- ✔ **Ask for credit for the core charge on any rebuildable part that's going to be replaced with a new part.** If you're buying a rebuilt part as a replacement, the core charge should be deducted from the price of the part that you buy in exchange for trading in your old part, which will then be rebuilt and sold to someone else.

Check the invoice carefully

Make sure that the invoice for the job includes a written guarantee on parts and labor, and find out whether any of the parts installed comes with its own warranty. (This is especially important if it's a big job that involves expensive parts.) Knowing just where the responsibility lies in the event of a dispute or a malfunctioning part always pays off.

A standard mechanic's invoice has separate areas, each of which serves a different purpose. To decipher an invoice, match the number preceding each of the following items with the corresponding number on the invoice shown in Figure 22-1:

❶ **Description of the work:** This area should list each job that needed to be done. When you pick up your vehicle from the shop, check this area item by item to see that everything was taken care of.

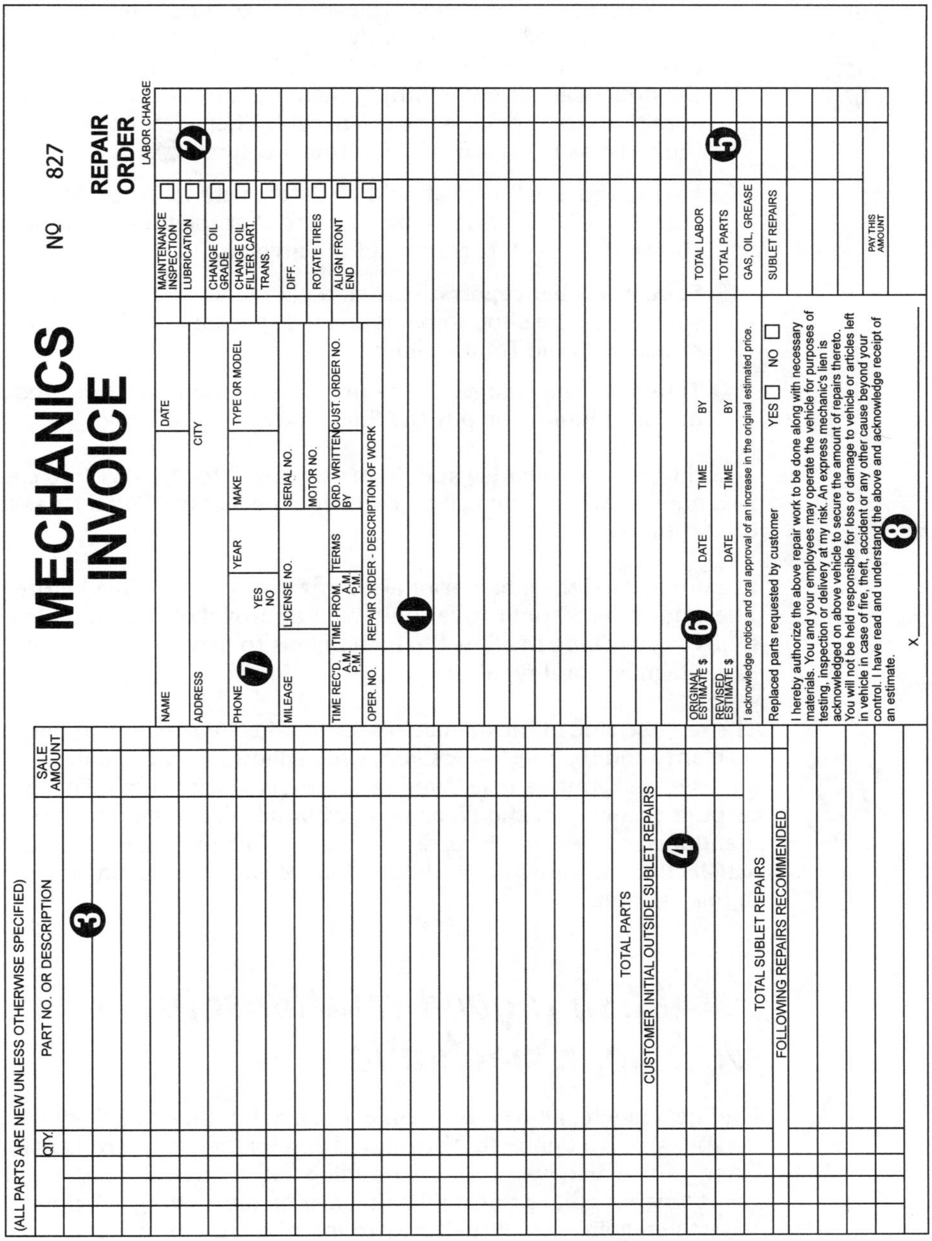

Figure 22-1:
A standard mechanic's invoice.

❷ **Labor charges:** These charges are shown in fractions of an hour. If a job seems to have taken an excessively long time, ask to check the *Flat Rate Manual,* which is a listing of every job that can be done on a vehicle, with the amount of time it should take to accomplish it.

Most shops charge you for the amount of time listed in the manual, *no matter how little time it actually takes them to do it,* and few shops keep a mechanic who can't "beat the book" by a substantial amount of time. If the hours seem right, multiply them by the shop's hourly rate to make sure that they've done the math right. Then check that the labor total is the same as that shown in the Totals column ⑤.

③ **Parts used:** Each part should be listed, with its price. Make sure that the costs have been added correctly and that the total is the same as that shown in the Totals column of the invoice.

④ **Subcontracted repairs:** This area should show all the work that was sent out of the shop to be done by a specialist. The total costs should be repeated in the Totals column.

⑤ **Totals:** All the charges in the previous sections are repeated and totaled in this column. You pay the final figure.

In addition, every invoice should have a space for ⑥ a written estimate and ⑦ a number where you can be reached if necessary. You'll be asked to sign the estimate.

Be sure to read the small print above ⑧ the signature line before you sign. The small print should cover only your approval of the estimate and the fact that you're willing to allow the technicians to drive your vehicle in order to test, diagnose, and repair it.

The reverse side of the invoice often contains information about the shop's warranty and the mechanic's lien, which allows service facilities in some states to sell your vehicle if you refuse to pay for services. For this reason, if a dispute occurs, you should always pay your bill and *then* seek restitution. As I mentioned earlier, credit cards really come in handy in these situations. To get satisfaction, be sure to read the section called "Complaining Effectively," later in this chapter.

Establish a good relationship with your mechanic

Finding a mechanic who is reliable, honest, intelligent, efficient, and relatively inexpensive isn't enough. You should aim for "most favored customer" status. Once you've discovered an outstanding automotive shop, the ball is in your court when it comes to establishing a good and lasting relationship that will have them going out of their way to make you happy. Even though most small businesses are struggling to stay alive these days, a good independent service facility is an exception. Every outstanding one that I've encountered has had more business than time to deal with it.

When I moved to a new city and needed someone I could trust to do major work or emergency surgery on Honeybun, my precious little classic car, I literally had to beg the specialist in classic Mercedes who came most highly recommended to take me on as a customer. He hadn't accepted a new customer in more than five years, and it took a referral from an outstanding car restorer, plus my credentials as an automotive writer and car freak, plus the fact that I had restored Honeybun myself, plus all my charm and my assurances that I would never bother him with piddly maintenance, to get him to agree to be there for me if something came up that I couldn't handle myself. We became good friends, in no small part because I faithfully followed these guidelines:

- ✔ **Call for an appointment.** Don't just show up and expect the shop to drop everything and take care of you.

- ✔ **Get your vehicle into the shop early (by 8:30 or 9:00 a.m. at the latest) if you hope to get it out the same day.** If you're on your way to work, allow sufficient time to give the technician or service writer a full account of what you want done or what you've found to be wrong with the car. Sometimes a test drive helps to demonstrate the problem, so make sure that you have the time to accompany the mechanic if possible.

- ✔ **Bring along a written list of the things you want serviced or repaired.** Include a phone number where you can be reached if questions arise or if the work is going to cost more than was originally estimated.

- ✔ **On your list, be as specific as possible about the symptoms you've experienced.** This is of great use to the technicians who work on the vehicle. It helps to organize the information in the following way:

  - *What* is happening ("The car stalls, pulls to the right, runs roughly, seems to be losing power, or is overheating.")

  - *When* it happens ("The car hesitates when I accelerate, won't start when it rains, smokes when I change gears, or pulls to the left when I brake.")

  - *Where* the trouble seems to be located ("I smell the gas more powerfully when I sit in the rear seat, there's a vibration under the front seat, or there's a squeak under the right front fender.")

To give you an idea of what kinds of things to look for, important symptoms include

- Warning lights and abnormal gauge readings

- Changes in acceleration, gas mileage, handling, steering, and fluid levels

- Drips, leaks, odors, vibrations, and smoke signals

- Unevenly or prematurely worn belts, tires, and hoses

(You can find a whole list of symptoms in Chapter 20.)

If you can provide enough information to help the shop diagnose the trouble easily, you won't have to pay for test drives and electronic diagnostic procedures that may cost more than the simple adjustments or repairs that are necessary.

✔ **Provide the clearest information you can regarding all the symptoms, but *do not diagnose the problem yourself!*** If you tell a shop that your vehicle needs a specific job done on it, then that's the work that will be done, and you will pay for it, *whether the vehicle needed it or not.* If you want to inquire whether the trouble *might* be caused by a malfunction in a specific part, then do so, but keep it in the form of a question. The final diagnosis must be up to the repair shop so that it can be responsible if the diagnosis turns out to be wrong.

✔ **Keep a maintenance record on your vehicle and bring a photocopy for the shop's records if it hasn't done the past maintenance.** I've provided a blank Maintenance Record and a Specification Record that you can use at the back of this book.

✔ **Don't press to get the job done fast unless you're really in a bind.** Making a diagnosis, getting the proper parts, doing the work, and testing the results takes time. Nobody likes to work under pressure. A great way to get the pressure off everybody is to see whether the shop has a spare car, or *loaner,* that you can borrow while work is being done on your vehicle.

✔ **Call to make sure that your vehicle is ready before you come to pick it up.** If it isn't, try to be understanding (unless the shop is chronically slow about getting work done). If it's a matter of parts that were ordered but not delivered on time, there's little that the shop can do about it. If it's just that the shop is overbooked with work, be polite but firm about your need to get the vehicle back as soon as possible.

✔ **When the vehicle is ready, ask what was wrong and what they did to repair the problem.** Keep a repair log, and add the information to it for future reference.

✔ **Be prepared to spend a little time test-driving to be sure that the job's been done to your satisfaction.** You're better off returning immediately with your complaints than showing up several days later, when any number of things may have happened to mess things up.

✔ **Show your appreciation for a job well done.** A phone call to the manager or a letter that the shop can display, praising a technician's work, means a lot to a service facility.

If you know that your favorite technician likes a particular beverage or snack, bring some along in a paper bag and pick your car up at the end of the day. If you're lucky, you may get invited to share it. I've received some of my most valuable tutoring strolling around a garage after working hours, can in hand, while my mechanic expounded on the secrets of his art.

Complaining Effectively

Even if you've followed all my advice about finding good mechanics and staying on the best of terms with them, there's still a chance that someday you'll get into a dispute over the services they've performed. If you've maintained a good relationship with a shop, you'll usually find them willing to be cooperative about redoing work that fails to correct a problem, replacing defective parts they've installed, and the like.

If you approach the shop assuming that the people there are going to treat you fairly and honestly, chances are that they will. If you attack immediately on the assumption that they're out to get you, you'll put them on the defensive and make things much harder for yourself.

Getting satisfaction on any complaint

I learned the following technique from an excellent human-potential trainer, and I pass it on to you. It's based on this "Golden Rule":

> *The best way to get what you want is to maintain a friendly attitude in all disputes — and refuse to be swayed from your purpose!*

Follow these steps to get satisfaction:

1. **Before you contact anyone, decide exactly what you want done.**

   Presenting a specific plan for remedial action is much more powerful than waiting passively for someone else to decide what they're willing to do for you.

2. **Time your campaign carefully.**

   Don't call just before lunchtime or closing time. Someone who's hungry or eager to get home won't want to spend a lot of time trying to help you.

   Try calling 24-hour customer-service numbers in the middle of the night. Chances are they'll be grateful for a bit of diversion.

3. **Approach the proper person in a friendly way, assuming that he or she will do everything possible to settle the issue fairly.**

   To find out which person to approach, see the next section, "Climbing the complaint ladder."

4. **Open with a bit of friendly conversation.**

   The key is to establish a relationship as human beings. If the person you encounter goes into robot mode, it's even more important to get through to his or her essential humanity. If possible, get on a first-name basis.

Most complaint personnel have been trained to deal with suspicion, anger, and aggression. Very few were taught to expect friendliness, trust, and compassion. When they encounter it, their battle tactics are useless.

5. **Clearly state the problem and what you'd like the person to do about it.**

   Tell your story as though you were talking to a sympathetic friend, without blaming anyone. Keep it as short as possible, and don't cloud the issue with unnecessary details.

6. **Be prepared to back up your request with as much documentation as possible.**

   This is why it's so important to keep maintenance records, invoices, guarantees, and warranties.

   If you're asked to document your case, *never part with your originals; just send copies.* It's foolish to place your strategic weapons in the hands of a company that has everything to gain by "losing" them!

7. **Listen patiently to the person's responses without interrupting.**

   If he or she gives you a hard-luck story to explain someone's negligence or inability to give you satisfaction, be sympathetic. Showing that you care about the person's problems will encourage him or her to care about yours.

8. **In a friendly fashion, keep reiterating your problem and what you want them to do to rectify the situation.**

   Say things like, "Gee, that's really a problem. I know how hard it must be to deal with something like that — *and* what can you do to help me?" Be reasonable. If the person can't do exactly what you've suggested, be willing to consider other alternatives, *as long as the problem is resolved.*

9. **Encourage the other person to see the problem through your eyes.**

   Say, "Jim, put yourself in my place. How would you like to schlep yourself to work on the bus for a week, only to find your car still doesn't work when you pick it up and won't be ready for another ten days?"

10. **If the person says that he or she can't help you, ask who has the authority to do so.**

    It's usually a supervisor.

11. **If you're told that it's company policy not to provide a remedy for your problem, stay cheerful — but refuse to accept it.**

    Kid the person out of it. ("Oh, come on, Charlotte, there has to be someone who can take this load off your shoulders. I'm sure your company wants to deal fairly with its customers, so who has the power to 'temper justice with mercy'?")

12. **Repeat the process with every person you're referred to. Keep repeating it until you get satisfaction.**

    A whole hierarchy of people can help you if you're willing to take the time to hang in there on your own behalf.

This combination of friendliness, sympathy, and inflexibility really pays off. I've seen people go out of their way to help me after they realized that I expected them to be the kinds of compassionate and creative people who could remedy the situation and that I cared about the difficulties they may have had in doing so. So try it. What can you lose? You can always bring out the big guns as a last resort!

Climbing the complaint ladder

It's always good policy to take a complaint first to the person you dealt with and then work your way up to people at higher levels of power if necessary. Going over someone's head rarely pays off unless that person has proven to be unsympathetic or unable to help you. However, if the lower echelons fail to give you satisfaction, it pays to jump to the highest authority you can. Even if "The Big Boss" sends your complaint back down the ladder, it will have come from the Executive Suite — and the "underlings" must deal with the chance that the boss will follow up to see how well your complaint has been dealt with. Here's a list of the steps to climb if you're working your way up the automotive complaint ladder:

1. **The *technician* who did the repairs.**

2. **The *manager* of the shop, or the service manager if it's a dealership or large chain.**

3. **The *owner* of the shop or dealership.**

4. **The *factory representative* at the car manufacturer's nearest regional office.**

    Write to the representative and tell what happened and what you want in order to resolve the issue. Be sure to include the following information:

    - The name and address of the establishment.

    - The names and titles of the people you've already dealt with while trying to get satisfaction.

    - The make, year, and model of your vehicle and its Vehicle Identification Number (VIN). You can find it on your registration or up near the windshield where it can be seen from outside the vehicle.

    - Copies (not originals) of any documentation that you think is required, such as invoices, warranties, previous correspondence, and so on.

If it's an option, pursue arbitration in Canada

The Canadian Motor Vehicle Arbitration Plan (CAMVAP) offers binding arbitration as a "fair, fast, friendly, final, and free alternative to court proceedings" to Canadians who have followed an auto manufacturer's dispute resolution process and have given the dealer and the manufacturer a reasonable number of opportunities to resolve their problems concerning warranties or alleged manufacturing defects. This decision cannot be contested by either party. CAMVAP may also help settle the problem without arbitration.

CAMVAP is available to residents of Canadian provinces other than Quebec, who bought their vehicles from an authorized Canadian dealer. Vehicles must be employed primarily for personal and family use and be no more than four model years old. For more information, contact CAMVAP at 800-207-0685. Its brochure provides all the steps involved in its proceedings.

5. *The president* or *CEO* of the corporation that built the vehicle.

   Some people suggest going to the corporate public relations department first, but I disagree. I've found that both the chief executive and the PR department often send the matter back to the regional office for action, so I'd rather have the president's or CEO's initials on the letter when it shows up at regional headquarters again.

6. If you still "can't get no satisfaction" or you have problems with an independent shop that refuses to settle the matter properly, write to your local *Better Business Bureau,* your local *Bureau of Automotive Consumer Affairs* (if there is one), and your state's *Consumer Protection Agency.*

   These organizations may suggest taking the matter to a mediation service, or they may apply pressure of their own. Some states have special bureaus dedicated solely to handling auto repair disputes.

7. If the shop has AAA, CAA, ASE, IGO, or ADS accreditation, write to those organizations with the full specifics of your complaint.

8. If your problem is with a dealership, write to the following address to see whether your state has a mediation service (these services have no clout with independents, however):

   National Automobile Dealers Association (NADA)
   8400 West Park Drive
   McLean, VA 22101

9. You can also take either an independent or a dealership to *small claims court.*

   In many states, new laws have raised the maximum of small claims settlements to levels that cover all but the most expensive auto repair disputes. The fees involved are generally negligible, and you don't need a lawyer. From my experience, small claims procedures are usually swift and fair and aimed at allowing "the little guy" to bring a case of litigation without the need for legal or technical expertise or for great amounts of time and money. If all else fails, don't hesitate to avail yourself of this alternative.

Many establishments would prefer to settle a dispute personally than to lose valuable time in court and have the fact that they've been sued by dissatisfied customers known to the general public and to the Better Business Bureau.

10. **If you're *really* riled, you can complain to the *Federal Trade Commission* at the following address (the FTC also has regional offices that you can contact):**

Federal Trade Commission
Bureau of Consumer Protection
Pennsylvania Ave. at 6th St. NW
Washington, DC 20580

11. **To register complaints about defects and obtain data on recalls, fuel, tires, child seats, seatbelts, and other safety-related issues, call the *Auto Safety Hotline* at 800-424-9393.**

12. **Another excellent guide to obtaining satisfaction is the *Consumer's Resource Handbook.*** It's full of valuable information on a variety of topics. Request the handbook from the following address:

The Consumer's Resource Handbook
Dept. 579L
Pueblo, CO 81009

13. **Contact the *Consumer Federation of America.*** This group of 240 non-profit organizations represents consumer interests through advocacy and education. You can reach them at

CFA
Complaint Resolution
1424 16th Street NW
Washington, DC 20036
202-387-6121

A word of caution: No matter which line of recourse you decide to follow, paying the disputed bill first is always a good policy *if your state honors the mechanic's lien mentioned earlier in this chapter.* If you use a credit card, you may be able to have the credit card company withhold payment until the matter is investigated. If not, it's better than having your vehicle towed away and sold for a fraction of its value. So pay up first, and then go get 'em!

Part V

Helping Your Car Look Its Best

The 5th Wave · By Rich Tennant

She keeps running after I turn her off.

Have you tried jiggling the handle?

al's PLUMBING

In this part . . .

Presumably, you take care of yourself: You bathe regularly, you keep your fingernails neatly groomed, you treat bumps and bruises with bandages and the appropriate salves and ointments. You probably also take care of your home: You sweep, mop, dust, vacuum, and clean out the gutters occasionally. So why wouldn't you also take care of your vehicle? Like anything else, it'll last longer and remain "healthier" if you do. Washing, waxing, removing small dings, cleaning the interior, you name it — this part covers everything you need to keep you vehicle looking great.

Chapter 23

Keeping Your Car Clean and Beautiful

- -

In This Chapter

▶ Washing your car efficiently

▶ Caring for clear-coat finishes

▶ Cleaning and polishing your car to create a brilliant shine

▶ Protecting your vehicle from the elements with wax

▶ Caring for glass, chrome, vinyl, leather, and more

▶ Keeping your engine clean

▶ Cleaning your vehicle's interior

- -

A car is more than a collection of parts and systems. When you drive your vehicle or try to trade it in or sell it, it's judged on its appearance as well as its performance. Contrary to popular belief, the main reason for washing your car often and keeping a good coat of wax on it is not to keep it looking good, but to wash away the salt, mud, and chemical-laden dust and dirt that provide breeding grounds for rust and accelerate paint deterioration.

If you don't care how your car looks and intend to drive the same machine until it spontaneously destructs like the "Wonderful One-Horse Shay" (which, according to the poem, ran perfectly for 100 years and then abruptly ceased to exist when everything failed at once), consider this: After years of driving and restoring cars, I've found that clean vehicles run better! After all, humans, plants, and animals respond to being kept clean and cared for, so why shouldn't your car? And if you think that a vehicle is an insensitive object, you haven't been reading this book very carefully. At any rate, why not try it and see? All it costs you is a little elbow grease and a few soap bubbles.

Cleaning the Exterior

Keeping the exterior of your vehicle clean isn't a matter of being a fanatic who spends every second of free time washing and waxing and dusting; just spending an hour or two each week can keep your new set of wheels young or brighten up Old Faithful.

Washing your vehicle

If you live in an area near the seashore, where a lot of salt is used on the roads in the winter, or where there is industrial air pollution, it's imperative that you wash your vehicle as often as once a week. If you have no access to a hose or a place to wash your car, or if the weather in your area gets so cold that the water freezes on the windshield, drive to one of those coin-operated do-it-yourself car washes and use its facilities. The steamy hoses keep both you and your car warm enough to wash away the mud and salt in the winter and can do an even better job than you could do at home, especially if your water pressure is low.

Most people think that there's nothing special to know about washing a car, but this isn't the case. Doing the job efficiently saves you time and effort and the car comes out looking great. If you work in a haphazard way, the task takes much longer, and you run the risk of scratching the finish, streaking the surface, and leaving the body vulnerable to rust.

If your vehicle was built after the mid-1980s, it probably has a *clear-coat finish* that requires special handling. See the section "Clear-coat finishes," later in this chapter, for details before working on these vehicles.

Follow these general instructions to wash your car safely and efficiently:

- ✔ **Never wipe or dust the body with a dry cloth.** The tiny particles of dust and grit on the surface can scratch the paint, leaving it looking cobwebby wherever the sun hits it.

- ✔ **Never wash a vehicle in the hot sun.** The cool water will cause the hot metal to contract, which can crack the paint and ruin the finish. Park the car in the shade or wait until morning or evening. That way, you can water the garden, too!

- ✔ **Use cold or lukewarm water and a hose rather than a bucket of water to wet and rinse the car.** A bucket holds a finite amount of water. As you rinse out your rag or sponge, the dirt is transferred to the water and back to the rag, where it can scratch or streak the paint. A hose with a spray nozzle can project a stream of water forceful enough to loosen the mud, bugs, bird waste, and other baddies that stick to the surface.

✔ **If you've never washed the vehicle with a hose before, spray lightly around the edges of the windows and the rear deck lid for a short time and then check to see if the weather-stripping leaks.** If it does, consult the instructions in Chapter 24 for patching or replacing weather-stripping, and try to avoid spraying these areas until you remedy the problem.

✔ **Conserve water.** Don't let the hose run while you work. Use it only to wet and rinse the car, and shut it off when you don't need it. Car Wash Association studies have found that people often use as much as 140 gallons for a single car wash, which isn't surprising when you consider that a ⅝-inch hose can deliver 14 gallons of water per *minute*.

✔ **Use just enough water pressure to wet the exterior efficiently.** Blasts at extremely high pressure may loosen and chip paint and parts.

✔ **Use a sponge, soft rag (old terrycloth towels or T-shirts are wonderful), or cotton wash mitt.** To avoid cobwebby scratches, follow the contours of the surface rather than going in circles. Rinse the rag often to get rid of grease and dust particles. Be thorough but gentle. Vigorous scrubbing can scratch and remove the paint.

✔ **Before you wash the car body, hose it down to get rid of the surface dust, and then clean and polish such exterior surfaces as vinyl hardtops, convertible tops, glass windows and sunroofs, chrome bumpers and trim, side mirrors, wheel covers, whitewalls, and tires.** Then, when you wash and rinse the car itself, you'll be sure to get off the last residue of all the substances you used for those jobs. Later sections of this chapter explain how to clean and restore some of those special surfaces.

✔ **Use gentle cleansers unless you intend to rewax your car.** Your car's sensitive skin requires gentle cleansers just as your own body does. Don't use laundry or dish soap or detergent; use a commercial car-washing product instead. Soap and detergent remove the wax and other protective finishes from the surface.

✔ **Use biodegradable washing and cleaning products to minimize environmental pollution.** Unlike the wastewater that is decontaminated and/or recycled by commercial car washes, the dirty, soapy water that you use travels down the sewers and into the waterways and oceans. If your car is really filthy and oily, it may be better to take it to a car wash.

✔ **Always wash a car body from the top down so that soap scum and sludge don't muck up freshly washed areas.**

✔ **Remember to get to all the corners where dirt can collect and rust can form: behind the wheels, inside the fenders, and behind the bumpers.** Don't forget the underbody — this is usually the muddiest and greasiest place of all and the most prone to rust.

✔ **Don't use the hose under the hood.** Cleaning under the hood requires a different technique, as I explain later in the section called "Cleaning Your Engine."

Safety tips for using commercial products

A commercial product can be just the thing you need to keep your car in great shape, but as with any store-bought cleaning supply, it's in your car's — and your — best interest to pay attention to a few commonsense and safety rules:

✔ **Always read and follow the directions on the package.** Some products can damage your skin or your car's surface if left on too long or if applied and removed improperly.

✔ **Never use a spray in an unventilated area.** And never get your face close enough to inhale it or risk getting it in your eyes.

✔ **Don't smoke when using chemicals or petroleum products.** As a matter of fact, don't smoke, period!

✔ **Wash one section of the car at a time: Hose it down, soap it up, and rinse it off.** When you've finished the entire vehicle, hose it all down again to get off every last bit of soap. Use a medium stream of water that flows off in sheets and makes drying the car easier. Make sure that no water collects in the tiny rust-prone spaces around the trim and behind the bumpers.

✔ **Don't scratch at hard-to-remove dirt.** *Soak* it loose by placing a wet rag on it. If your vehicle is befouled with tar or dead bugs, commercial solvents can get rid of them safely. Be sure to remove these intense cleansers thoroughly and wash the surface with soap and water immediately afterward.

✔ **Towel-dry the car immediately with terry towels, diapers, or a synthetic chamois to get rid of water spotting that can mar the car's surface.** Chamois are good for this purpose and can be washed, rinsed, and used for years. But they're more expensive, and I find that old, dry terry towels work pretty well, too. Besides, what else can you do with towels that have not only become too faded for the bathroom but are too torn even for the beach?

Clear-coat finishes

Most modern vehicles are painted in a two-step process that produces a *clear-coat finish,* which can far outlast the acrylic lacquer or enamel used on older vehicles. The first step applies the color and optional metallic sparkle. The second step adds a transparent coating that provides protection and gives the surface a sense of depth and gloss. Although a clear-coat finish protects and enhances the paint, it is extremely sensitive to abrasion and chemicals. If it wears away, the paint beneath it will deteriorate rapidly.

If your vehicle has a clear-coat finish, take these special steps to protect it:

- ✔ **Wash, clean, and wax the vehicle only with products that are designed especially for clear-coat finishes or are labeled "clear-coat safe."** Use the least abrasive products available.

- ✔ **Wash the car often, but don't scrub hard or use power buffers or polishers.** Don't scratch at tar, tree sap, and dead insects; place a wet rag over them and try to soak them off. If necessary, use a product designed to remove them.

- ✔ **Before you use a product designed to remove tar, sap, and bugs, read the label to make sure that it will not damage the finish.** Test it first on a door jamb or other hidden painted surface. Wash off bird droppings and sap immediately with mild soap and water. If left to harden, they're much harder to remove and can permanently damage the finish.

- ✔ **At regular intervals, apply a coat of wax or sealer designed for clear-coat finishes.** A high-quality polymer sealant provides the best protection because it binds with the paint. By making the surface more slippery, it retards water spots and makes it easier to remove bugs and tree sap. A good sealer can last up to six months. Carnuba wax gives a deeper shine but lasts only a couple of months. Follow the instructions in the "Waxing your car" section to get the best results.

Windows

Clean the glass windows and mirrors with the same products you use to clean glass in your home. Many of these products simply spray on and wipe off without rinsing. (If you're a really hardy soul, you can use ammonia with very good results if you follow the directions on the bottle.) Just keep the following in mind:

- ✔ **Be sure to use a lint-free soft rag or sturdy paper towels to avoid scratching the glass.**

- ✔ **Use vertical strokes on the outside and horizontal strokes on the inside of each window so that you can see at a glance which side the streaks are on when you're wiping off the cleaner.** (I always carry a little spray bottle of glass cleaner and a clean soft rag in my car to spruce up the windshield when visibility gets cloudy.)

- ✔ **Lift your windshield wipers away from the glass to clean under them, and don't forget to wipe the wipers, too.** A dirty blade can streak or scratch the glass. Check for dead leaves that may have accumulated in the well under the wipers and remove them by hand or with a vacuum that can handle larger objects.

If you have a convertible with a plastic rear window, that window may become cloudy from oxidation, especially if the hot sun shines on it constantly. Excellent conditioners designed to keep plastic windows clear and supple without scratching them are available. If your car's rear window is already clouded beyond visibility, Meguiar's Plastic Cleaner is a unique heavy-duty product that polishes the cloudy stuff right off the window, leaving it relatively clear again. If you must park your car where the sun can shine directly on its plastic window for long periods of time, cover the outside of the window with an old towel to protect it from the sun.

Chrome and metal trim

Several excellent polishes are designed specifically to clean chrome without scratching the delicate layer of plating. These preparations not only clean the metal without scratching it but also retard rust and leave the surface bright and shining. You can use chrome polish on other metal surfaces, too. Here are some tips for polishing chrome and metal trim:

- ✔ **Try not to get the polish on the surrounding paint.** The polish can discolor the paint.

- ✔ **Be sure to do the *inside* surfaces of the bumpers, too, if you can reach them.** And don't forget the metal hubcaps or wheel covers and the metal frames around the lights and side mirrors.

- ✔ **If you find rust on any metal area, get rid of the stuff immediately!** For instructions, rush directly to the section on rust removal in Chapter 24.

- ✔ **After you clean the metal surfaces, wax them to prevent rust from forming.** Use a special wax designed for chrome bumpers and metal surfaces, because these areas require more protection than painted surfaces do. Other types of wax may prevent the chrome from getting the oxygen it needs to preserve its shine.

Tires

Be sure to clean the tires whenever you wash your car. (You wouldn't take a bath without washing your feet, would you?) Use mild soap or dish detergent to remove dirt and grease. A brush or kitchen scouring pad removes the stubborn stuff, but before you go at it like you're scrubbing your bathroom grout, be sure to wet the tires.

Never use gasoline or kerosene to clean tires. If your car has whitewalls that are extremely dirty or greasy, you may have to resort to a special whitewall cleaner to restore them to their original pristine good looks.

If you want your tires to look extremely shiny and spiffy, here's an inside tip: Car dealers and people with show cars have been known to wax their tires with Lemon Pledge furniture polish! Extremely scuffed tires can be painted with "tire black," a preparation for that purpose sold at auto supply stores. Whether or not you're going for appearances, I suggest that you spray your tires with a silicone lubricant every once in a while to preserve the rubber.

Convertible tops

If you have a convertible with a cloth top (also known as a *ragtop*), keep it clean by vacuuming it often or by using a whisk broom to get the dust out of the areas around the trim. This is not just a matter of cleanliness; the dirt can cause the fabric to rot away if it's allowed to remain there. Do the following to keep your ragtop in good shape:

✔ **Check the top occasionally to make sure that it's not getting caught in the mechanism that raises and lowers it.** This can leave greasy streaks on the fabric, weaken it, and cause it to tear. If your top has a plastic rear window, make sure that it isn't getting scrunched by the mechanism when the top is down and follow the instructions in the earlier section "Windows" to clean it without scratching it.

✔ **Go over the metal mechanism that raises and lowers the top and polish it occasionally to keep it shiny and beautiful.** Put a coat of wax on the metal to retard rusting, and oil the hinges now and then to keep things working smoothly. Use the oil sparingly to avoid staining the top.

✔ **Remember to dust or vacuum the well into which the top folds and to keep it free of objects that can puncture or mar the top.** I remember a friend who had a convertible with a glass rear window. The top was up for most of the winter, and that well seemed like an ideal place to stash her umbrella and other paraphernalia. Then one day the sun shone, and she happily put her top down. Crunch! End of story.

✔ **Check for weak spots or tears, and check the seams for threads that are beginning to break.** Seams that are loosening up can be restitched by hand before they become major problems. Try to use the same holes as the original stitches, stitching right on top of them, and use strong thread in the same color as the original.

✔ **If you see a weak place or a small hole, reinforce it by placing a patch on the *inside* of the top, and glue it in place with a good adhesive or stitch it down securely.** Convertible tops are under considerable tension, and a tiny rip can swiftly tear right across the top.

Vinyl tops

Vinyl tops usually clean up easily with mild soap or dish detergent and water. If the top is very dirty, you may want to try a commercial product made especially for vinyl tops. Use a fairly soft brush to get the dirt out of the tiny crevices in the finish (a recycled toothbrush or nail brush easily gets into the areas around the trim). Brush in circles, because the crevices run in every direction, and rinse often to wash the dirt away. Vinyl hardtops respond nicely to a light coat of wax or the proper silicone preservative.

✔ **If you find that your vinyl hardtop has bubbles in it, prick the areas with a pin and try to press the air out.** If any adhesive comes out of the holes, wipe it off the vinyl immediately. When the air is out, press the vinyl against the roof to reseal it. If the adhesive has dried out, you can use a glue injector to insert a tiny amount of vinyl adhesive under the surface. Dealing with air bubbles is important because they can create holes in the vinyl if something catches them.

✔ **If you find holes or rips in the vinyl, use a vinyl repair kit to correct them.** You can find many of these kits on the market: tiny bottles of liquid vinyl that fill in scratches, major repair kits that include vinyl liquid that can be mixed to match the color of the surrounding area, patches, and sophisticated adhesives. Before you buy anything, read the instructions right there in the store to be sure that you select the simplest kit that suits your purposes.

✔ **If your vinyl top has faded and become discolored, excellent sprays are on the market that can renew the color for you.** Before you use these sprays, be sure to mask the surrounding areas of the car. Always choose the same color or a slightly darker shade to cover up spots.

TIP

The lazy person's guide to "good housekeeping"

If you have no time or inclination for cleaning your car, my advice to you is simple: Hire someone to do it for you. The expense more than pays off in the increased life of your vehicle. At the very least, take the car to a car wash every week or two and be sure that they clean and vacuum the interior as part of the deal.

Car washes vary considerably in efficiency and reliability. Be aware that your vehicle will probably respond to the rather rough and impersonal scrubbing it will receive from the machines at some car washes by acquiring scratches and losing a bit of paint around the edges. Spinning car-wash brushes are especially lethal for cars with clear-coat finishes. To keep the damage to a minimum, find a low-cost "brushless" or "touch-free" car wash that uses curtains of jiggling strips or one that washes cars by hand.

Forget about the optional hot-wax sprays offered by car washes. They're simply not strong enough to provide sufficient protection. Unless the car manufacturer warns that waxing will mar a special finish, most vehicles need a good coat of wax or one of the new polymer products to protect it from rust and fading. This should be done at least twice a year, in the spring and the fall, to protect the car from hot sun, rain, salt, and snow. If you don't want to wax the car yourself, hire someone to do it *by hand.*

If you drive a convertible or a luxury or classic car and you can't keep it clean yourself, hire someone to wash it by hand at least every couple of weeks. Running such a special car through a commercial car wash is tantamount to murder. You would be better off selling the car to someone who will give it the treatment it deserves and buying yourself a durable old clunker or a cheap, flashy "disposable" model every couple of years.

Cleaning and polishing your vehicle

Let me be clear on the distinction between *washing* and *cleaning and polishing* the exterior of a vehicle. Washing, the first of the preceding sections, gets rid of the dirt on the surface. Cleaning and polishing goes a little deeper. As a car gets older, especially if it's exposed to the sun and other elements, the top layers of paint or clear coat begin to fade and *oxidize,* giving the body a hazy or smoky-looking surface. Regular washing and waxing usually retards this process, but an occasional good cleaning and polishing actually removes tiny scratches and dead paint.

When you clean and polish a vehicle that's been painted with acrylic lacquer or enamel, you use special products that actually remove a *very* thin layer of paint. When this layer goes, so do the scratches, the oxidation, and the thin coat of grime that regular washing doesn't get rid of, leaving even a well-kept vehicle shining with unusual brilliance. With clear-coated vehicles, you want to avoid removing the thin clear-coat layer. See the earlier section called "Clear-coat finishes" for tips on handling this type of surface.

To clean and polish a lacquered or enameled car, follow this general sequence: First, wash the car and all its surfaces, as explained in the earlier section "Washing your vehicle." Then use car polish (or a rubbing compound if your car's finish is in really bad shape; see the sidebar "Rubbing compounds" for details) to remove the scratches. Finally, to protect your vehicle from the elements, wax it — instructions are in the next section, "Waxing your vehicle."

A variety of cleaning and polishing products are available, including some that combine wax with a car cleaner to reduce the number of steps you have to go through. These combined products are easy to use and work well if the vehicle isn't too filthy, but they can't substitute for a thorough waxing when it comes to long-term protection. Most commercial car-polishing products contain fine particles of abrasive, which effectively remove an infinitely small top layer of paint and grime. For this reason, don't use these products more than once a month.

If your car is a dark color or has a delicate lacquer or clear-coat finish, look for a polish or wax/cleaner designed for these finishes that contains chemicals rather than abrasives, because scratches really show up on these finishes. Don't use an abrasive cleaner on chrome or plastic unless the label specifically says that you can. If you do, you run the risk of scratching the surfaces and removing the chrome plating.

Rubbing compounds

Whereas most polishes have a mild abrasive action, the abrasives in rubbing compounds are designed to dig a bit deeper into the surface, discard the top layers of paint, and get down to the fresh stuff underneath (assuming that there is any). As a general rule, avoid any polishing preparation that contains such strong abrasives because it can go right through your car's painted finish. However, if your car is in really sad shape, with paint that has faded and dulled to the point that it has little shine, and you're considering painting the car anyway, you may want to try using a rubbing compound to restore the finish before you spring for a paint job. Some cars are painted with acrylic lacquer, or enamel that has a hardener in it, which helps protect the finish and keep the color from fading for a long time.

Newer cars have clear coats that serve the same purpose. These cars should not require rubbing compound to keep their colors bright; on the contrary, rubbing compound can ruin a clear-coat finish.

Rubbing compounds come in fine, medium, and coarse grades. Always try the fine grade first, because the others may be too harsh. The coarse grade removes so much paint that it's usually used for prefinishing jobs, during which the surface is taken down, restored, and repainted. Use rubbing compound sparingly. Follow the directions on the package and don't bear down too hard. Go easy at first to avoid removing patches of paint that have loosened from the surface, bubbled, or chipped around the edges. You can always apply a bit more elbow grease if your initial efforts prove to be too gentle. Always wax the car after using a rubbing compound — unless, of course, you're going to paint it.

Waxing your vehicle

If washing removes the surface dirt, and cleaning and polishing removes the dead layers of paint, waxing a vehicle preserves that clean and shiny finish and seals its "pores" against dirt, water vapor, and rust. If water doesn't bead on the surface of the car when it rains or when you hose it down, it needs waxing badly. *Don't neglect this step.* Even if you use a car-washing product that has wax in it, you must still give most vehicles a thorough waxing at least twice a year, in the spring and fall, to protect them from heavy weather. *Nothing* is more vital than a thorough wax job if you want to keep your vehicle rust-free and young-looking for years to come.

Always be sure to wash the car before you wax it, no matter how clean it looks, to avoid scratching the surface and trapping minute particles of dust.

After applying wax or polymer sealant, use a terrycloth towel to break up the hazy surface by rubbing in one direction. Then rub with a cloth diaper in the other direction and bring out the shine.

Electric buffers

You may have seen professionals use electric buffers to apply cleaners and wax and to shine a car to a high gloss. Although lambswool pads are available that can be attached to the shaft of an electric drill, don't use these, or any other high-speed gadgets, to buff or polish your vehicle.

Professional buffing equipment works gently at slow speeds to avoid scratching or grinding the paint right off the surface. Most of this power equipment requires the light, experienced touch of a professional.

Again, if you drive a dark-colored vehicle or one with a clear-coat or sensitive lacquer finish, make sure that the cleaners and waxes you use have no abrasives in them. If you're unsure as to whether the finish on your car requires special handling, check your owner's manual or call your dealership for instructions.

Unless your vehicle came with specific instructions from the manufacturer, you can choose from a variety of waxes, ranging from combination products (that have both cleaners and wax together) to liquid, soft, and hard waxes. Or you can use a polymer sealant. Here's a closer look at your options:

✔ **Liquid waxes:** Generally speaking, liquid waxes are very easy to use but don't last as long as soft or hard waxes, although some of the abrasive-free liquid wax/cleaners specially formulated for cars with delicate finishes are quite effective. Liquid wax is excellent for a touch-up between major waxings or for general use to replace the wax you lose if you wash your car with a wax-free detergent or soap.

✔ **Soft waxes:** These are my favorites. Soft waxes are light and fluffy and very easy to apply and remove. My favorite is mixed with a light cleaner and leaves the car shining beautifully. (I don't let this keep me from washing it thoroughly first, however.) Apply these products with the applicator pads provided or with a soft terry rag. Simply wipe on the wax, following the contours of the surface; allow it to dry to a haze; and wipe the haze away. The soft waxes that contain no cleaner are excellent for sealing the surface if you've used an abrasive cleaner or a fine-grade rubbing compound.

Because the waxes that contain cleaners usually contain abrasives, do not use them for every car wash or more often than once a month. In between, use the liquid car washes that come with a little wax already in them.

✔ **Hard or paste waxes:** These types of waxes provide the most protection and should be used for your semi-annual major wax job. They last longer than anything except polymer preservatives. These waxes are harder to apply and require rubbing and buffing to bring up a high-gloss shine. Always do a small area at a time to avoid letting the wax harden to a point where it's hard to remove. Apply the wax according to the directions on the can with an applicator or soft rag. Use another clean, soft rag to remove it, and use still another clean, soft rag to rub the body all over until it shines.

✔ **Polymer preservatives:** Products that contain polymer substances protect a vehicle more effectively than wax and for longer periods of time. They literally bond with the surface of the paint and prevent it from fading and oxidizing. At the auto supply store, you can buy poly-sealants that are easy to apply and are supposed to protect your car for six months to a year.

✔ **Polyglycotes:** Professionals and auto manufacturers offer polyglycotes that are supposed to last from two to three years. If you want to use one of these products, be sure to wash the car thoroughly and give it a good cleaning and polishing first. Some of these products say that they can be applied over wax, but I prefer to get all the wax off the car before applying them. When the surface is really clean, shiny, and dry, apply the protective coating, following the directions on the label. Make sure that it gets into all the little crevices around the trim and on the painted metal inner surfaces of the doors and deck lid. Because I'm a fairly cautious person, I still inspect my car regularly for rust to make sure that this miracle stuff is really doing its job.

Cleaning Your Engine

Many car owners never bother to deal with the dirt under the hood on the assumption that what you can't see can't hurt you. Although it's true that only people who exhibit show cars or are compulsively fastidious set much store by having the engine area constantly at its pristine best, there are practical reasons for removing a gross accumulation of grease, oil, gasoline, and dirt from under the hood and for making an effort to keep things under control from then on.

Engines are made of metal and depend on rubber hoses and gaskets and wiring if they are to work properly. Because all the aforementioned baddies can cause rust to form or can seriously deteriorate nonmetal parts and wiring, keeping the under-the-hood area as clean as possible is a good idea. If the area under the hood of your vehicle is beginning to look grubby, get a rag and wipe off as much of the dirt and grease as you can. If the situation has reached the unspeakable stage, I strongly urge you to have a professional steam-clean the area.

Although engine degreasers are available at auto supply stores and coin-operated steam-cleaning facilities at do-it-yourself car wash centers, I don't recommend that you try either of these alternatives for the following reason: Most engine cleaners and degreasers must be washed off thoroughly — usually with a hose — and there's a risk that moisture will penetrate the distributor cap and prevent the engine from starting. The steam produced by the steam cleaners is even more insidious. There have been cases where a car started and went home, only to fail to start the following morning after the moisture from the steam had condensed. That's why I urge you to have your engine cleaned professionally if it's too dirty to wipe clean yourself. When the job is done, you should be able to keep it in good condition by wiping off the area every now and then.

If you're planning to sell your vehicle, think twice about having the engine area cleaned. Although cleaning certainly spiffs up the under-the-hood area, potential buyers may assume that it was done to obliterate signs of unsuccessful surgery on the engine.

If, in spite of my warnings, you're determined to do the job yourself, here are some tips:

✔ Be sure to remove the air cleaner and cover the distributor and the carburetor throat with plastic bags to prevent water from getting into them. Try not to spray the hose directly at these areas.

✔ Follow the directions on the bottle of engine cleaner carefully.

✔ Avoid getting chemical cleaners on the body of the car. They can remove the wax and stain the surface.

✔ Hose off the cleaner thoroughly after it has had time to act.

✔ Unless directed to do otherwise, start the engine after cleaning it and let it idle long enough to dry out the under-the-hood area.

✔ If your engine fails to start, you can try to remove the moisture from inside the distributor cap by following the instructions for starting the car on a rainy day in the section called "If Your Car Won't Start" in Chapter 21, but I'm not promising anything. Never try to remove moisture from inside the distributor cap with gasoline! A spark from the distributor can cause an explosion.

Whenever you have the engine cleaned, make sure that the blow-by on the inner surface of the hood above the engine is cleaned, too, and that the mud and dirt that have accumulated on the inner walls of the car body and near the wheel wells are removed.

If you find that oil accumulates very quickly on your newly cleaned engine, first check the PCV valve to see whether it's plugged up. This little gadget is responsible for rerouting the exhaust fumes from the crankcase back to the engine, where they're burnt again and then released through the exhaust system. If the valve gets plugged, pressure can build up in the crankcase and create oil leaks around the engine. A PCV valve can be checked and replaced very easily. Read all about it in the section called "Checking and Servicing Your PCV Valve" in Chapter 13.

Oil may also seep from under the valve cover gasket if the cover needs to be torqued down properly or the gasket needs to be replaced. If this seems to be your problem, check with a mechanic.

If you think that cleaning your engine is compulsive, think of my uncle, who sprayed the under-the-hood area of his secondhand Cadillac with gold paint so that he could impress the service station attendants!

Cleaning the Interior

The interior of your vehicle is like your living room at home: It's "decorated" with carpeting, paint, fabric, plastic, vinyl, and glass. Some cars have leather and wood as well. Although, unlike the interior of your house, your car stands out in public and reflects your personal habits (and you certainly don't want everyone to think that you're a slob!), keeping the interior clean is more than a matter of pride. Because dirt contains grit and chemicals that can eat away the surfaces of your "furniture," it's vital to practice the same good housekeeping techniques on your car that you would on your home if you want to keep it in decent condition for a long, long time.

Generally speaking, the same procedures and products that you use in the house work quite well in your car. If you're an old hand at housework, read the following information just to make sure that you don't forget anything. If good housekeeping has never been your bag, or if you've spent your life in hotels, the following sections tell you how to clean and care for the interior of your vehicle.

When you're ready to go on your cleaning campaign, try to pick a day when you have time to putter about. Line up all those groovy bottles of special cleaners, festoon the area with clean terrycloth rags or other softies, and tackle the entire interior in one glorious effort. Unless you habitually drive out into the wilderness or chauffeur a horde of wild kids armed with ice cream cones and other goodies, or the weather gets really terrible, you probably won't have to go through this task more often than once a month — less often if you're very fastidious and don't travel around a lot.

Keeping things tidy

The most effective thing you can do is to vacuum the carpets and seats and dust the dashboard, rear window shelf, and other surfaces regularly. If getting your usual equipment to the car is a hassle, you can use little hand vacuums that work on batteries or plug into the cigarette lighter. Keep the little vacuum in the trunk so that you can use it if a spontaneous fit of cleanliness overtakes you. Here are a few other ways to maintain order and cleanliness in your vehicle:

- ✔ **Keep the clutter under control and the seats free of everything but you and the seat belts.** Objects left lying on seats may rip or stain them as people move about or enter and leave the car. Maps and guidebooks belong in the glove box. Store the flashlight, tools, and a copy of this book in the trunk or under the front seat.

- ✔ **Your fire extinguisher takes precedence over any other candidate for under-the-front-seat storage.** You have to be able to reach it quickly in case of an emergency (and the trunk is right over the gas tank). Store the fire extinguisher in a suitable bracket so that it can't roll out from under the seat and interfere with your driving.

- ✔ **Don't keep heavy objects on the rear window ledge or on the dashboard.** They can obscure visibility and can fly around and hurt someone if you have to stop suddenly. Small objects like pencils and coins can fall behind the dashboard and damage the air vents, so find a better place for them as well. Apply a conditioner with UV protection regularly to reduce sun damage and keep the vinyl, plastic, or leather surfaces from cracking and fading.

- ✔ **If you have children who require a supply of toys, store the toys safely.** Keep them on the floor in an open carton that fits snugly between the rear seat and the back of the front seat and make putting them away a regular part of each driving experience.

- ✔ **If your car doesn't have a cup holder, buy one.** Auto parts stores and discount stores sell clip-ons and between-the-seat consoles that keep coffee cups and soft drink cans under control. A spilled cup of hot coffee can do more than ruin your clothes, upholstery, and carpeting; it can scald you and cause an accident.

- ✔ **Don't allow old food and drink containers to clutter up your car.** They attract ants and other insects that can "bug" your vehicle's equipment and wiring.

- ✔ **Follow the instructions in your owner's manual when cleaning seatbelts.** Ordinary household cleaners and solvents can weaken the webbing.

- ✔ **Remember to vacuum and clean the trunk compartment.** It's part of the vehicle's interior, too!

Cleaning upholstery and carpeting

You can use the same products to clean car upholstery and carpeting that you use to clean your chairs, sofas, and rugs. Keep the following in mind:

- ✔ **Avoid using large quantities of water; you don't want to get the padding under the fabric wet or rust the upholstery buttons, if there are any.** Avoid sponges and work with damp rags wherever possible. If you think that you've gotten things too wet, use a portable hair dryer to dry the padding quickly and evaporate water from around the bases of the buttons.

- ✔ **The best products for fabrics and rugs are the ones that spray on, turn to powder, and are removed by vacuuming.** Stain-repellent sprays are excellent if the fabric is clean and new; otherwise, they simply preserve your stains forever. See the section called "Fighting stains and odors" for more information.

- ✔ **To keep upholstery from fading and deteriorating, park the car in a different direction as often as possible so that the sun doesn't keep hitting the same surfaces.** Keep a window or sunroof open a crack to prevent heat from building up. It can dissolve fabric adhesives and crack vinyl seat covers.

Vinyl and plastic

Vinyl seats and interiors and plastic surfaces such as dashboards, steering wheels, and interior moldings usually respond well to water and a mild soap or dish detergent, but you may have to resort to special vinyl-cleaning products if you have really allowed things to get out of hand. You can use a soft brush on vinyl to get at the dirt in the graining, along the welting, and around upholstery buttons, if there are any.

- ✔ **Water can soak down to the padding between the stitching and around the buttons of vinyl-covered seats, too, so use it as sparingly as possible.**

- ✔ **Protect all vinyl and plastic surfaces from sunlight and heat with products such as Armor All.** While you're at it, use it or a spray silicone lubricant on dashboards, weather-stripping, vinyl or rubber floor mats, and tires, too, to prevent them from cracking and drying out and to keep them supple. Avoid oil- and petroleum-based products that can damage vinyl and leave it brittle.

- ✔ **Never use a dry rag to clean the plastic that covers the gauges on your instrument panel.** Small, dry particles of dust and grit can scratch the surface. Use a plastic cleaner sparingly with a *damp* terrycloth rag or sponge. Excess moisture can damage electronic instruments.

Leather

If you're lucky enough to have leather seats in your vehicle, take care of them properly. Leather looks and feels wonderful, and it smells good, too. Because leather "breathes," it doesn't get as wet and sticky as vinyl does on hot days. If properly cared for, leather can last a long time, but like all skin, it dries out and ages prematurely if it's not kept clean and moisturized.

- ✔ **Use a high-quality product like saddle soap to clean and preserve leather seats.** Neatsfoot oil waterproofs, softens, lubricates, restores, and preserves leather that has been cleaned first.

- ✔ **If you must park where the sun can get at your leather seats, lean them forward or drape something over them to protect them.** If conditions are severe, think about installing window film that blocks UV rays. If this is impossible, take comfort from the fact that leather seats don't get as hot as vinyl ones, so you can probably sit down on them without screaming.

Fighting stains and odors

Because stains are caused by a wide variety of substances and can be enlarged or set permanently if you try to remove them improperly, in the interest of brevity and because I believe in leaving specialized areas to the specialists, I suggest that you refer to a stain-removal guide before tackling stains on fabric upholstery or carpeting. Practicing these stain-fighting tactics may also help:

- ✔ **Be sure to get the stain while it's fresh; the older a stain gets, the harder it is to remove.** If something spills and you can mop it up swiftly and dab at it with some water to dissolve it, it's probably worth a try. You may want to stow a small spray container of stain remover in the trunk so that you can attack stubborn stains before sunlight and heat set them.

- ✔ **Avoid drastic measures that can harm the upholstery.** Some people say that chewing gum can be removed more easily if you freeze it with an ice cube first and then chip it off. That may be, but be sure not to scratch at it or you risk ruining the nap of the fabric or scratching or tearing vinyl upholstery. I tend to consult the experts on things like chewing gum, tar, blood, and other hard-to-remove substances.

- ✔ **To avoid spreading a stain, work from the edges in toward the center.** Use a minimum of liquid and dab rather than scrub. When the stain is gone, dry the surface with a hair dryer if you have one handy.

- ✔ **You may be able to cut the stains off high-napped carpets and then camouflage the resulting bald spots with loops cut from a hidden area and glued in with clear adhesive.** Try this trick on an area that doesn't show first, to see whether your handiwork would look better than the original stain.

✔ **Odors are considered stains, too — even though they assault your nose rather than your eyes.** Proctor & Gamble pioneered olfactory stain removal with Febreze, a spray that encapsulates odor stains, lifts them out of the fabric, and destroys them rather than masking them with stronger odors as most air fresheners do.

Repairing tears and holes

Auto seats get considerable wear and tear, and reupholstery is very expensive. If you catch small tears and holes early, you can save yourself a lot of money in the long run. Try the following:

✔ **Sew up tears in fabric seats with strong thread or use patch kits that allow you to put the patch under the fabric and seal the "wound" with a colorless adhesive.**

✔ **Repair small tears and holes in vinyl seats with the special kits that are on the market.** If you have to patch an area where the vinyl no longer exists, be sure that the patch is at least half an inch larger than the hole so that when you slip it under the hole, the adhesive doesn't contact the padding.

✔ **Check out the various vinyl repair kits available and choose the simplest one that can do the job.** If your seats need major surgery, go to a professional who can do the work properly.

Caring for headliners

Headliners — the material (usually cloth or vinyl) that covers the inside of your car roof — are cleaned and repaired just like upholstery, but you have to do the work upside down. Many headliners are held in place by adhesives that can be dissolved by cleaning materials or pulled away by strong vacuuming, causing the headliner to sag. For this reason, treat it gently. Work on small spots, using a damp rag and cool water. Blot dry with a terry cloth towel to avoid drips, and use a hair dryer to hasten the process. If the headliner is badly stained or torn, either spend the bucks to have it professionally repaired or replaced, or live with it until you get a new vehicle.

Cleaning floor mats

Floor mats are useful for protecting floorboards that lack carpeting. (The vinyl floor coverings that substitute for rugs on many new vehicles don't look very sturdy to me.) Mats not only cushion areas that get a lot of wear but also help keep the noise level down. You can also use mats to protect existing carpets, especially in rainy or muddy areas, and to hide carpets that are stained or torn.

Clean vinyl and rubber floor mats with cold water and soap. You can take them right out of the car and hose them down as you wash the car. Be sure to rinse them thoroughly. Use a brush on vinyl mats and a kitchen scouring pad on rubber ones to remove caked-on dirt.

Place old or worn mats on the floor of the trunk or hatchback area to reduce the noise level and protect the interior.

Caring for other surfaces

In addition to the upholstery, seats, floor, and so on, other interior surfaces need attention when you're cleaning. Here's how to deal with these areas:

- ✔ **Glass:** Clean the *interiors* of all your windows, sunroof, and the rearview mirror to remove the film caused by smoke and by the vapors that vinyl and plastic give off. Wash them the same way you wash your windows at home, or refer the section "Washing your vehicle" for instructions.

- ✔ **Chrome and metal trim:** Clean interior metal and chrome in the same way that you deal with the exterior surfaces (refer to the earlier section called "Chrome and metal trim"). And don't forget the door handles and window cranks if your car has metal ones.

- ✔ **Wood:** Ah, for the days of wooden steering wheels and dashboards! There are very few left now. If your car has these elegant appurtenances, be sure to oil and polish the wood often to keep it from cracking and drying out. Use the same stuff you would use on fine furniture — which it is, when you come to think of it!

Remembering Those Final Touches

Just to touch all the bases, oil the hinges of the doors, hood, and rear deck lid now and then, and spray the door and trunk locks with graphite to keep them working smoothly. Be happy that you don't have to put fresh flowers in a little crystal vase in the passenger compartment, as some chauffeurs used to do! (But if you're lucky enough to have one of the reissued Volkswagen Beetles — complete with dashboard bud vase — stop by the florist on your way home from the auto supply store and pick up one of your favorite blossoms.)

Car covers

Once you have your vehicle looking wonderful inside and out, it pays to keep it that way. If you have no garage and you must park the car outdoors, you may want to invest in a car cover to protect it from the sun and keep the dirt and dust off of it. The first thing you should realize is that you do not use a car cover to protect a vehicle from moisture (except to the extent that it keeps a strong rain from driving water in through the windows). Many people go out and buy vinyl or waterproof car covers to keep their cars dry and innocently cause more trouble than they prevent: Moisture gets under the car cover anyway, from underneath, and then is trapped under the cover and prevented from evaporating quickly. Thus a vehicle that's covered with a waterproof cover remains damp longer than one that's been unprotected and has dried in the air and sunlight following a storm.

Now that you know *not* to buy a vinyl or waterproof car cover, here's what to look for:

✔ The best covers on the market are cotton or cotton and polyester, woven so closely that they keep out the sunlight, prevent a good deal of moisture from getting through, dry out quickly, allow the moisture to evaporate easily, and are durable enough to last a couple of years. The fabric is also soft enough to avoid scratching the paint. These covers come in shapes and sizes designed to fit specific vehicles, and you order them by year, make, and model. The best can cost up to a couple hundred dollars, but they save you money in the long run if you have an expensive car to protect.

✔ Some covers come with cables that slide under the car and lock onto the cover to keep it from being stolen. You may want this option, especially if your vehicle sits unattended for long periods of time. Some people simply paint their names or license numbers on the cover in supergraphics. If you do so, just make sure that the paint is waterproof and won't dry hard enough to scratch the surface of the car.

✔ The cheaper car covers designed for small, medium, and large models work fairly well. If you buy one of these, make sure that it has no metal cleats or grommets that can scratch the car, and that it will stay on securely in gusty weather. Look for mail-order ads in car magazines for some of the best buys.

Chapter 24

Getting Rid of Dings, Dents, and Other Hard Knocks

- -

In This Chapter

▶ Knowing when to call in the pros rather than do it yourself

▶ Evaluating body shops and checking a finished job

▶ Finding, eliminating, and protecting your car from rust

▶ Getting rid of small dents, dings, and other imperfections

▶ Understanding when and how to use plastic body filler

▶ Finishing the job with primer and paint

- -

*T*hese days, when "Forever Young" seems to be more of a national anthem than an old love song, many people have begun to devote a regular portion of their time to "bodywork." Bicycle lanes are crowded with people who eschew their cars for the pleasures of combining errands with exercise; streets are packed with joggers as well as walkers; and aerobic dance and yoga classes are filled. We've faced the fact that the only way to stay forever young is to be vigilant about keeping our bodies in shape and to repair minor damage before it has a chance to develop into something really difficult to deal with.

I guess you know what I'm leading up to by now, but I'll say it anyway: Yes, your car's body is subject to the same ravages of time and hard knocks that your own body is — and is exposed to weather a great deal more. If you want Old Faithful (or the new pony) to stay forever young, you must keep a careful eye on it and forestall major damage by taking care of the minor stuff as soon as possible. Earlier chapters in this book deal with proper nutrition and regular maintenance for your vehicle's innards and how to keep it clean inside and out. This chapter deals with the dings and dents that the world deals your car and America's number-one car killer: *rust*.

If you're motivated to upgrade your vehicle by doing minor bodywork yourself, this chapter tells you how to replace or install worn weather-stripping, and Chapter 20 shows you how to get rid of squeaks, vibrations, leaks, and other easy-to-remedy defects. Your car will love you for it!

Seeking Professional Help

The following word of warning applies to all the tasks outlined in this chapter:

> *No matter how optimistic and ambitious you are, do not tackle any body damage larger than a couple of inches in size.*

Repairing a small area is relatively easy. But if your car has suffered fairly extensive body damage, such as major rusting or large holes, dents, creases, or tears in its metal or fiberglass skin, forget about trying to fix it yourself. Instead, rely on a professional body shop for appropriate surgery. (You wouldn't try to set a broken leg yourself, would you?) Even if you remove the dent or rust successfully, you still need to mask, sand, apply the filler, shape the filler to the contours of the car, sand some more, and then prime and paint the surface.

Unless you have considerable skill in working with your hands and you really enjoy challenging and time-consuming jobs, you'll probably find that having a professional tackle the big stuff is well worth the money. That way, you can spend your time doing something that will be profitable enough to pay the restorer's charges, and you can both walk away happy. Your vehicle will look better, too. Amateur attempts usually give themselves away with uneven surfaces or uneven color, and you run the risk of having the filler or paint wear away prematurely from an improperly prepared surface.

Evaluating Body Shops

Body shops run the gamut from small back-alley paint booth operations to high-tech specialists with space-age lasers, computerized sonar, electric eyes, and robots that scan, measure, and repair damage and alignment electronically. Some shops still mix colors by eye and formula, and others use CD-ROMs and scanners that match even faded colors perfectly.

If you care about the environment, find a shop that filters, recycles, and disposes of waste materials in an ecologically sound manner, even if your state or province doesn't require it. If you need to locate a reliable body shop, consult the section in Chapter 23 on finding and evaluating a good service facility. Then use the following tips to pick the best one:

> ✔ **Take a look around the shop to see whether they're removing or at least masking chrome, trim, rubber, locks, door jambs, and handles thoroughly to prevent paint from getting on them.** Look along the sides of finished vehicles. The light reflected off the restored surfaces will reveal whether they are smooth and shiny. Does the color match the rest of the car exactly?

✔ **Get at least three estimates.** Each should include a list of all the parts that need to be replaced or rechromed (such as trim, lights, and bumpers). Straightening and rechroming has become very expensive, and this type of work must be done properly to keep the chrome from flaking off quickly.

✔ **Ask the owner or manager the following questions:**

- **Do you have the latest high-tech equipment?** If your vehicle has been damaged extensively and is covered by insurance, go for the most sophisticated setup you can find. If damage is relatively minor and you're paying for it yourself, you may want to trade extremely high-end technology for a good job done with more traditional equipment at a lower price.

- **Do you do all the work in-house, or do you send some of it out?** Tell them that you want to see invoices for any new parts and outside labor involved. If chrome trim must be sent to a rechromer, you may save money by arranging to take it there and pick it up yourself.

- **What guarantees or warranties apply for parts and labor?** Unless your insurance company guarantees the work it authorizes, make sure that you'll be covered if problems occur.

- **How do you prepare the surface of the vehicle before you paint?** If metal body panels are to be replaced, will the new ones be galvanized to protect them from rust? If old paint is stripped away, will the bare metal be treated if the galvanized zinc layer has been stripped away? What kinds of primers do you use to ensure that new paint will adhere properly?

- **Which sealants, coatings, catalysts, and hardeners do you use to protect the newly restored surfaces?** They should be the same — or at least as good — as those on the rest of your vehicle, or the restored areas will age prematurely when exposed to the elements.

Checking Bodywork

When the work is finished, check it carefully before you leave the shop:

✔ Check light reflected along the repaired surface for ripples, bumps, or depressions.

✔ Make sure that the edges of the hood, rear deck lid, sunroof, and doors are smoothly aligned with the body of the vehicle.

✔ Check whether the inside edges of the doors, hood, and trunk are neatly painted, or whether the old paint shows through.

> ✔ Look for unpainted spaces around the edges of door handles, chrome, and other fittings. These parts should be removed, rather than masked, so that the paint extends under them and protects the area from rust. If inadequate masking has allowed the paint to overspray these and other unpainted surfaces, refuse to pay until the unwanted paint has been completely removed.
>
> ✔ Compare newly painted parts to other areas to be sure that the color matches the older paint exactly.

Because bodywork requires such expertise, buying a new bumper or piece of trim (or locating an unflawed one at a wrecker's) is often less expensive than restoring the damaged part. Many modern vehicles have thin, relatively inexpensive body panels that are designed to be replaced rather than repaired. They crumple so easily that they're as difficult to straighten as tinfoil, and it's cheaper and easier to have a new panel installed and painted.

If extensive areas of a metal car body need to be repaired, have those damaged body panels replaced rather than filled in with plastic body fillers. Unless you're a metalworker and are really familiar with torches, have this work done professionally. It's a good idea to ask each body shop you consult whether they plan to replace large, damaged areas with sheet-metal body panels welded in place of the old ones, or if they plan to straighten the old panels and finish them with a thin skin of plastic body filler wherever necessary.

Getting Rid of Rust

Rust, the "heavy" of this chapter, should probably be called "car cancer." It arrives unheralded, eats corrosively into the car's body in unsuspected nooks and crannies, and — if you're foolish enough to simply paint over it — goes right on with its deadly work unseen. This imagery may seem unduly grim, but I honestly believe that, over the years, more fine vehicles have given way to the ravages of rust than have been demolished in accidents.

The first line of defense against rust is to wash and wax your vehicle regularly. See Chapter 23 for tips on doing these and other cleaning chores.

Checking for rust

If you live in an area where the streets are still salted in winter, where it rains or snows a great deal, or near the seashore — in other words, anywhere your car is exposed to moisture and/or salt — you must be especially vigilant about detecting and getting rid of rust quickly. However, even if you live in a dry climate, you must still make a habit of checking carefully every few months. If you find rust forming, get rid of it before it can do major damage.

The paint on your car is there not only for beauty, but for protection as well. Paint and clear-coat finishes help retard rust. As long as your paint job is unmarred, metal body surfaces are safe. But something as seemingly innocuous as a small scratch that nobody but you notices can spell the beginning of trouble. Check the following trouble spots:

✔ **Small scratches, nicks, and spots where the paint may have flaked off:** If you find any, touch up the paint in those areas before rust can form on the bare metal. You can find instructions in the "Priming and Painting" section later in this chapter.

✔ **Dark spots in the paint, which may indicate that the metal is rusting out from underneath:** If you find these spots, read the following section, called "Dealing with any rust you find," to find out how to take care of the problem.

✔ **Pitted places in the paint and on the chrome and metal trim:** Treat these spots with rust remover, following the directions on the package. With most rust removers, you simply apply the paste or liquid, let it work for several minutes, and then wash it off thoroughly. Look for a rust remover that's safe to use on painted surfaces, and test the stuff on a small hidden area first to make sure that it doesn't affect the color — no matter what the package says.

Another prime breeding ground for rust is anyplace on a vehicle where grime, dirt, or salt can accumulate. These areas are usually around fenders, under trim, and so on. Pay special attention to the following places when you look for rust:

✔ **Each time you wash the car, take a flashlight and check around the fenders, in the wheel wells, and behind the bumpers.** Accumulated salt, mud, and dirt will accelerate rust's growth.

✔ **Shine the light into the little crevices between the car body and all the trim and moldings that are affixed to it.** Dirt and moisture tend to collect in these areas. Look all around the lights, the windows, the side mirrors, the sunroof, and the antenna, too.

✔ **If you live in a damp area, check the metal surfaces *inside* the car.** Don't forget to check around the window frames.

✔ **One of the most insidious places where rust forms is under your car, where you can't see it. Next time you have the car serviced, have them put it up on the hoist and check its underbody thoroughly.** If you're afraid that the service people won't be thorough enough, ask your favorite mechanic to put the vehicle up and let you have a look around. (While you're at it, get the mechanic to show you all the fascinating things under there — the transmission, the oil pan, the brake lines, the emergency brake, the differential, and so on — if you don't already know where to find them. It's quite an education!)

Even if you have a car with a fiberglass (and therefore rustproof) body, the underbody is metal and, therefore, still the most sensitive area where rust is concerned. I have ridden in venerable old cars where the floorboards had rusted through so completely that you could see the road flash by underneath. And if rust attacks the frame, the car can be on its way to the Great Car Lot in the Sky before you know it.

Dealing with any rust you find

Okay, the worst has happened: You've found some rust spots on your car. Don't panic: You still have time to save the patient — unless the rust has gone too far. If the rust is underneath the car, on the underside of the body or bumpers where it doesn't show, or still confined to very small areas that can be touched up easily, you can probably take care of the matter yourself. Here's what to do:

1. **Gently scrape away the rust with a single-edged razor blade or *fine* sandpaper.**

   For slightly larger painted areas, use a brush with stiff (but not metal) bristles. Use coarse sandpaper to grind the rust off large areas that are out of sight and not surrounded by paint.

   Always work *inward* from the edges to avoid extending the area by damaging the paint. Don't make a large job out of a small one by carelessly damaging the surrounding paint! Rust remover can make this job easier if you apply it after you get the crusty stuff off the surface.

2. **After you've removed all the rust, apply some rust arrestor to keep the rust from spreading further.**

   Rust, like fire, is a form of oxidation. Products like Meta-Prep and Extend change the chemical nature of the rust and prevent it from further oxidizing the metal. You just brush or spray on most rust arrestors, wait for them to turn from white to black, and then wash them off thoroughly. (Be sure to follow the directions on the package.)

3. **As soon as the area is dry, prime and paint it to protect the surface and restore it to its former beauty.**

   See the upcoming "Priming and Painting" section for details.

If you see large rust holes in the body of the vehicle, or if the frame has been badly weakened, get a couple of estimates from reliable body shops on what repairing the damage would cost. Then check those estimates against what your vehicle is worth by calling your local bank, insurance company, or loan agency. You can also look in the newspaper to see what vehicles of that year, make, and model are selling for these days. If you have access to the World Wide Web, you can look up the blue book value of your car at the *Kelley Blue Book* site (www.kbb.com). Or try the Edmunds Web site (www.edmunds.com)

for additional consumer-oriented auto pricing information. You can also surf over to `www.carpoint.com` for similar information. If the vehicle seems worth the effort and money and is mechanically sound, bite the bullet and get it fixed. Otherwise, it's time to get yourself another set of wheels.

Undercoating to prevent rust

Special undercoatings, which prevent rust from forming on the undersurface of a vehicle, work quite well if the vehicle is so new that absolutely no rust exists. If you're considering having your vehicle undercoated (or doing it yourself), consider these points:

- ✔ **If rust is already present on the underbody, undercoating simply locks the rust away, where it continues its insidious work unseen.** So before you have your car undercoated, make sure that it's absolutely rust-free. If it isn't, have all the rust removed and a rust arrestor used to destroy any rust that may have been overlooked, and then have the undercoating applied.

- ✔ **If your vehicle is fairly new and hasn't begun to rust, having it undercoated still may be a good idea, especially if you live in a snowy area.** Make sure that they treat the underside of the car with a rust arrestor first, just to be sure, and that the undercoating won't void any warranties.

- ✔ **Many new vehicles come with undercoating as part of the package; this option is fine and worth bargaining for.** If undercoating is an "optional extra," you may find it cheaper to have the work done by an independent professional undercoating shop. Get an estimate of costs before you deal for the car so that you know where the best deals are, and make sure that the outside work won't void any warranties.

- ✔ **Spray undercoatings designed for amateur use are probably better than nothing, but continue to watch closely for rust after applying them.** If you decide to try one of these spray undercoatings, work in a well-ventilated area. Don't spray the undercoating (or anything else, for that matter) on any cables, pipes, or parts under the car that get hot; otherwise, they'll smell awful when the heat hits the undercoating. And before you use the stuff, *remove every bit of rust and coat the surfaces with rust arrestor.*

Removing Small Dents and Dings

Although you need special tools and equipment to yank, hammer, or otherwise coax large dents back into place, taking care of little dents and dings is another matter. This type of damage responds to simple measures and may not require much work at all. You have nothing to lose by trying to do minor bodywork yourself. If you fail, you can always take the car to a body shop anyway! Here are some situations that you may want to tackle:

✔ **If the paint has simply flaked or has been scratched off the surface,** follow the instructions for touching up paint later in this chapter.

Before you prime and paint the vehicle, take care of any rust, dings, or dents that you find. By taking care of all these things at once, you can then put the final coats on all of them at the same time and have a car that looks wonderful.

✔ **If the metal has been pushed in and hasn't been badly creased,** you can try to pop the metal back into place with a rubber plunger (the kind they call a *plumber's helper*). Just moisten the edge of the rubber, place the plunger over the dent, establish suction by pressing down on the handle, and then pull it toward you. It may take a couple of tries before the metal pops back to normal. This technique works especially well on large expanses of metal, such as doors and fenders, if they have only been bent inward.

✔ **If you have small dents,** you can attempt to hammer them out by placing a flat piece of metal (with a rag wrapped around it to protect the paint from scratching) on the outer side of the car and banging the dent from the underside with a flat-ended hammer. Be very careful to bang the underside of the dent only, and not the surrounding area, or you'll end up with a couple of new bumps to deal with. Work from the shallow sides of the dent toward the deeper areas and avoid overworking the metal, which stretches it.

✔ **If you have very small dings or places where the paint has chipped,** you can fill them in with glazing putty, which is very easy to handle. Use a putty knife to apply it, following the directions on the package, and then prime and paint the area. If the damaged area is larger than a very small, shallow ding, you need to resort to a plastic body filler. The next section tells you how to use one.

The new specialty shops that just fix dents and dings are inexpensive. Take your vehicle in and get an estimate before you commit yourself to doing any bodywork yourself. It may cost you so much less in time and effort than struggling through a learning process that having the work done professionally will be cheaper in the long run!

Filling Small Dents and Holes

Dents and holes can be repaired in one of two ways. As I mentioned earlier, you should have large damaged areas repaired by having a professional replace or straighten the body panels. You can fill smaller indentations with plastic body filler.

Many people refer to the process of using plastic body filler as *bondoing.* Although "bondo" has become a synonym for all car body fillers, Bondo is really the commercial name of a variety of auto body-repair products put out by one company.

Many plastic compounds are on the market for filling small holes, dents, and creases in the surface of your car. Buy a good-quality product (the cheap stuff may break loose or flake away) and follow the directions on the package closely.

Most kits contain at least two substances: the filler itself and a hardener, which you mix with the filler before you use it. An all-purpose kit may contain filler, hardener, spot-and-glaze putty, screening for filling holes, applicators, and a can of spray primer. Check carefully at the auto supply store to find the kit with the easiest instructions that can do the job for you as simply as possible. The salespeople should be helpful if you tell them that this is your first attempt at bodywork.

To give you an idea of how to apply plastic body filler, here are a few general instructions that suit most situations (but be sure to read and follow the directions on the product you buy):

1. **Clean the body area thoroughly to remove all traces of dirt, wax, or rust.**

   You can find instructions for cleaning your car in Chapter 23.

2. **Sand the area before you apply the filler, using #180 or #220 aluminum oxide sandpaper (you can find it at an auto supply store).**

   Because body fillers don't stick to paint, you *must* sand the area. When sanding, be sure to *feather-edge* (blend) the paint edges to prevent the old paint from chipping up through the new paint in the future and to ensure a good bond. Work inward from the edges of the dent to avoid enlarging the damaged area.

3. **Mix only as much hardener-filler as you're going to use right away.**

   The hardener-filler combination starts to harden immediately, so mix only what you need. Mix up a relatively small batch at a time, using the proportions recommended on the can, and then mix up more when you need it. This process enables you to work without rushing and gives you time to allow each layer to dry before applying the next layer.

4. **If there's a *hole* in the vehicle's body, place fiberglass screening or fine aluminum chicken wire beneath the hole (on the underside of the body) to keep the filler from falling out.**

   Be sure to clean the area under the edges of the hole thoroughly to get rid of any dirt or paint that may be present. Then mix a very small proportion of filler and hardener and apply it to the edges of the screen and the edges of the area to be patched, to hold the screen in place. If the kit contains no applicator, use a putty knife or plastic kitchen scraper to apply the filler. Let the screen patch dry for several hours before going on with the work.

5. **Apply the plastic filler, working slowly and carefully to avoid spreading the filler outside the dent or hole and marring the surrounding area.**

   After you finish, the filled portion should be slightly higher than the surface of the car around it.

6. **As soon as the plastic filler starts to harden (about to the consistency of hard cheese), use a perforated file to bring the level down almost to the level of the paint.**

7. **Wait at least 20 to 30 minutes until everything is bone dry; then sand the area with medium sandpaper until it conforms perfectly to the surrounding body surface.**

   If you're working on a curved surface, like a fender, this sanding may take some skill.

8. **When everything is smooth and even, prime the area and touch up the paint.**

   You can use primer as a last layer of filler to fill tiny holes or irregularities. Apply several layers of primer, sanding each layer with a sanding block, until the area appears perfectly smooth. (To check, wet the primer and look at the way light reflects off the surface.)

Priming and Painting

The techniques used to paint the body of a car can vary, depending on the size of the area you're working on and the original paint and finish. Many vehicles are painted with processes that require special primers, layers of different colors, metallic flake, and special clear coats after the color is laid on. Repainting such a vehicle can be difficult for professionals and absolutely disastrous for a novice.

Unless you have an experienced and steady hand (and the car's original paint has not faded or changed color since it was new), concealing that you repainted anything larger than a small area is almost impossible. Larger areas require spray-painting, which must be done in a well-ventilated area that's free from dust and dirt. A good spray gun can cost a lot — not to mention the air compressor used to power the gun — and a spray gun can wreak havoc if it runs amok in inexperienced hands. So if the area you need to paint is large, it will probably cost you less in time, money, and effort to have the job done by a professional who can match the paint and do the job right.

Never attempt to do a major paint job on a good car without trying your hand on an old wreck first. If you fail to prepare and prime the surface properly, the new paint will peel, blister, or flake away before long. If you practice on a junker, you can afford to make mistakes — because even a *bad* paint job can increase the resale value of a car that's practically worthless to begin with.

If you want a cheap but decent job that will last a year or so, find out where local car dealers take the used cars they get as trade-ins to have them spiffed up before resale. To save money, you can remove any rust, spot-fill and paint the small areas yourself, and then have the rest of the job done professionally. Of course, if even a cheapo job is beyond your budget, doing your best with a can of spray paint is certainly better than simply letting a vehicle rust away.

On the other hand, touching up a *small* spot with a little bottle of touch-up paint is easy. Before you start the job, mask the surrounding area well and use even, sweeping strokes to apply the paint. (Follow the directions on the can carefully.) Practice on a piece of scrap metal before you tackle the car, and don't expect the results to look terrific.

1. **To find the right paint color you need, look on the firewall of your car — you should see a little plate with the body number and paint code number on it.**

   If you can't find the paint code number, consult your owner's manual or ask your mechanic or car dealer to point it out to you.

2. **Buy a little bottle of touch-up paint that matches the code number at the parts department of a dealership representing the auto-maker that produced your vehicle.**

   If that's not possible, try a professional auto paint supply house. They're also often good sources of semiprofessional advice. If neither source is available, your local auto supply store should have a chart that indicates the proper paint to match your car's make, model, and year.

   These little bottles of paint usually come with a brush or applicator in them. You also need a small bottle of primer, unless the paint specifies that it doesn't require it.

3. **Make sure that the area is rust-free.**

   If the damage is only a deep scratch or a tiny spot, you may need just a dab of rust arrestor to stop the rust from continuing to form under the new paint. If the area is any larger, you must remove *all* the rust carefully, following the directions in the earlier section called "Dealing with any rust you find."

4. **Sand the spot carefully with a tiny bit of #220 sandpaper to rough up the surface so that the primer adheres properly.**

   Work in teeny dabs, feathering the edges and working inward from the surrounding area to avoid enlarging the spot.

5. **Wash the area thoroughly to remove any rust arrestor, dust, dirt, filler residue, and wax; then let the area dry completely before you go any further.**

   Primer is used to seal the surface of the metal against rust (caused by air and moisture) and to provide a surface for the paint to adhere to. Primer also fills in tiny holes and imperfections in the surface. The paint then protects the primer from the sun, dust, and heavy weather. And, as you know, wax protects the paint.

   If you're dealing with a surface scratch or a chip that hasn't gone down to the bare metal, you can probably get away with simply applying the paint. But never apply paint to bare metal. If any metal is exposed, or if the spot is larger than a fraction of an inch, prime the area first.

6. **Use a tiny brush or a matchstick to apply the primer sparingly.**

   You shouldn't need more than a drop to cover the damaged area. Avoid getting primer on the original paint. If you do, wipe it off immediately. Let the primer dry thoroughly before going on with the job.

   If you used glazing putty to fill the dent, you can probably paint right on top of it without priming first.

7. **Mix the paint in the bottle thoroughly to blend the color pigments properly.**

   Unless your car is very new, the color probably won't match exactly (which is another reason for keeping the area as small as possible). The paint on new cars doesn't fade as quickly or badly as old paints did.

8. **Apply the paint, covering the surface of the spot completely, working inward from the edges.**

   If you're painting a scratch or a very small area, you can cut down the brush or use a matchstick or toothpick instead. The paint should be no thicker than the surrounding surface or it will show, run, bubble, or peel off.

9. **Wait several days for everything to dry completely, and then polish the car to blend in the painted area and bring everything to a high gloss.**

10. **Give the car a coat of wax or polymer to protect your hard work.**

    Chapter 23 has instructions for polishing and waxing.

Installing New Weather-Stripping or Patching the Old

Whistles and leaks inside your vehicle are usually the result of worn, torn, or faulty *weather-stripping* (the rubber gaskets that you find around the doors, windows, sunroof, and trunk opening). If the interior or trunk gets wet when you wash the car or when it rains, use a garden hose to locate the areas on the weather-stripping that have been letting the water in. If the car windows whistle when you drive with them closed, check the weather-stripping for the cause of the sound effects. (If you notice leaks *under* the car, see Chapter 20 for ways to find the source and end the problem.)

If the weather-stripping is old, dried, cracked, or worn, you can probably buy a whole new piece designed for your vehicle's year, make, and model at your dealer's service department. To install new weather-stripping, follow these steps:

1. **Check to see whether the new weather-stripping is the same as the old piece you're replacing.**

   The piece should be the same shape and thickness and should have holes, channels, and rubber studs on the inner side that match the ones on the original.

2. **Remove any screws and gently peel off the old weather-stripping, prying any rubber studs out of the holes they're inserted in without damaging the paint or scratching the metal window trim.**

   If the weather-stripping is hard to remove, spray weather-stripping remover around the area and wait until the adhesive softens before continuing.

3. **Use weather-stripping remover to remove any old adhesive that remains on the frame after the seal is gone.**

4. **Insert the new weather-stripping into the frame to make sure that it fits the holes and contours of the frame. Then gently remove it.**

5. **Make sure that the new weather-stripping is clean.**

   You can rinse it off and dry it thoroughly or use fine sandpaper to remove any unauthorized bumps and rough spots.

6. **Apply weather-stripping adhesive (it comes in a tube) *sparingly* to the strip and to the surface of the frame.**

   You don't want the adhesive to squish out the sides because if it gets on anything, it may become permanently affixed to the surface. (Back to the weather-stripping remover!)

7. **Before the adhesive dries, replace the new weather-stripping, making sure that every rubber stud or other fastening device is in its hole securely.**

8. **Replace any screws that you removed, and make sure that the ends of the weather-stripping meet and are glued down securely.**

If your old weather-stripping is in pretty good shape but is admitting air or water in one or two small areas, try applying weather-stripping adhesive under the loose portions, or use a clear silicone sealer (which comes in a tube) to seal around the areas that are leaking.

A quick and easy way to patch things up, if you don't care how they look, is to get a roll of black household weather-stripping about ½ inch wide with an adhesive back and simply stick small pieces of it onto or under the weather-stripping in the trouble areas. This stuff is also useful for keeping camper hatches and sunroofs from leaking or banging if they don't fit quite perfectly, and for keeping rain from coming past the rubber sleeve where the camper shell meets the cab of a truck. You can always use it around the house, too!

Part VI
The Part of Tens

The 5th Wave   By Rich Tennant

@RICHTENNANT

TUNE UP $35¢

'S GARAGE

J&K
SARCOPHAGUS
TRANSPORT

"I keep hearing a 'thump thump' followed by a
low moaning sound."

In this part . . .

Want to know about the ten most important preventive maintenance measures for your vehicle? Want to find out how to save fuel — and be a little kinder to the environment in the process? You can find this helpful information in this part.

Chapter 25

The Ten Most Important Preventive Maintenance Measures

In This Chapter

▶ Things you can do to make your vehicle last longer

▶ Things you can do to make driving your vehicle safer and more enjoyable

*T*he major goals of preventive maintenance are to keep your vehicle from breaking down on the road, to catch minor problems before they become major expenses, to prevent premature wear and tear by keeping parts from wearing each other away and by removing objects that could damage your vehicle's interior and its occupants, and to safeguard warranties and guarantees on your vehicle and its parts. The tips in this chapter tell you what you need to do and help you find information in this book that will keep your vehicle running better, longer.

Change the Oil Frequently and Regularly

Oil reduces the friction in your engine and keeps the vehicle running smoothly. The most important thing you can do to extend the life of your vehicle is to change the oil every 3,000 miles or three months, whichever comes first, or as frequently as every 1,000 miles if you drive mostly short distances in stop-and-go traffic. Turn to Chapter 15 for instructions for changing your oil. It can be easier than cooking dinner!

Do a Monthly Under-the-Hood Check

If you take 15 minutes to do the under-the-hood check in Chapter 3, you can prevent 70 percent of the situations that can cause your vehicle to break down on the road! At the very least, be sure to check the following fluid levels at least once a month: oil, coolant, automatic transmission fluid, brake fluid, power steering fluid, and windshield washer fluid. Refill or replace these fluids as necessary.

Check the Tire Inflation and Alignment

Underinflated tires wear out faster, create excessive heat, increase fuel consumption, and make your vehicle more difficult to handle. Tires that are not properly balanced or are out of alignment wear out rapidly, increase wear and tear on the steering and suspension system, and may take you for a bumpy or unsafe ride. You can avoid many of these problems simply by checking the air pressure in your tires and by looking for signs of wear and misalignment at least once a month and before every long trip. Chapter 19 shows you how easy it is to read tire tread-wear patterns for signs of faulty inflation, alignment, and balancing.

Keep the Interior Clean

The cleaner you keep the interior of your vehicle, the more enjoyable it will be for you to drive, and the longer the upholstery and carpets will remain in good condition. Remove the mats and vacuum them — and the upholstery, headliner, and floor of your vehicle — whenever they start to get dirty or every time you wash your vehicle, whichever comes first. Wipe up spills as they occur, *before* they have a chance to set and become permanent.

If it's too late to prevent stains, consult a stain-removal guide for the appropriate method to avoid making the stain bigger or even permanent. Use an odor remover to keep the interior smelling fresh, rather than simply masking odors with perfumed products. Chapter 23 offers advice for cleaning your vehicle's interior and dealing with nasty stains and odors.

Keep trash and personal effects in receptacles, and keep kids' toys stashed in a box that fits snugly on the floor behind the front seat. If you have to stop short, these things can become lethal projectiles.

Wash the Vehicle Frequently and Keep It Out of the Sun

Wash your vehicle once a week to protect against paint deterioration and rust and keep it looking its best. Do so in a shady spot to avoid ruining the finish.

If water doesn't bead on the surface of the vehicle when it rains or when you hose it down, it needs waxing. Wax your car at least twice a year, in the spring and fall, to protect it from weather extremes and preserve its clean and shiny finish, sealing its "pores" against dirt, water vapor, and rust. Chapter 23 tells you everything you need to know to keep your vehicle clean and protect it from the elements.

Get Rid of Rust

Rust can start out as a small spot in an unsuspected nook or cranny and then spread like cancer through the rest of your vehicle. Turn to Chapter 24 for tips on checking for rust, removing rust, preventing the formation of more rust, and restoring your car's finish.

The best way to prevent rust is to wash and wax your car regularly. (See Chapter 23 for instructions on cleaning your vehicle's exterior as well as the interior.)

Change the Filters

Changing your air, fuel, and oil filters regularly can help extend the life of your vehicle, increase its fuel efficiency, and improve its performance.

The air filter keeps dirt out of your fuel injection system or carburetor. Your vehicle runs on a mixture of fuel and air, so if air can't flow freely through a dirty filter, you pay the price in fuel consumption and performance. The air filter should be changed every 20,000 miles — more frequently if you drive in a dusty area such as the desert. If your car has a carburetor, you can easily change the filter yourself. If your car has a fuel-injection system, changing the air filter *may* be a job for a professional mechanic. (See Chapter 13 for more information about checking and replacing the air filter.)

The fuel filter helps prevent rust and sediment from entering the engine. You should change the fuel filter every time you tune your vehicle — more often if you tend to ride around with an almost-empty fuel tank (which you shouldn't do if you want your engine to last a long time). Turn to Chapter 13 for more information about checking and replacing the fuel filter.

The oil filter cleans the oil and removes metal and dirt particles that would otherwise circulate through your engine and cause friction between moving parts that can damage it or cause it to wear out prematurely. Change the oil filter every time you change your oil. (Chapter 15 tells you how to change the oil filter during an oil change.)

Change the Coolant at Least Once a Year

Coolant helps your vehicle keep its cool, and changing it is a job that you can handle yourself. Change the coolant at least once a year or every 30,000 miles, whichever comes first — more often if your car has been losing coolant for some time or overheats easily. See Chapter 14 for instructions for checking and changing your coolant.

Lubricate the Moving and Rubber Parts

A lube job involves applying various kinds of grease and oil to some of your vehicle's moving parts to keep them moving freely, and to some of the rubber parts to keep them supple. Older cars with ball joints and grease fittings should be lubricated every 3,000 miles, and Chapter 16 tells you how to do this kind of lube job. Vehicles built after the mid-1980s have sealed joints that don't need to be periodically refilled with grease, but *all* vehicles still have transmissions and other parts that need to be checked and serviced on a regular basis. Many garages offer to check these areas as a freebie when they change your oil. Take advantage of the offer.

To prevent friction that can wear parts away prematurely, investigate and eliminate all squeaks and rattles as soon as they occur. Chapter 20 helps you troubleshoot strange sounds and other symptoms.

Get Scheduled Maintenance to Keep Warranties Valid

Performing scheduled maintenance prolongs the life of your vehicle, ensures that your warranties remain valid, and may improve the vehicle's resale value when you're ready to part with it. Check your owner's manual or ask the dealership for your vehicle's maintenance schedule and warranty information.

You don't have to have scheduled maintenance done at a dealership. Licensed independent mechanics can do the work without voiding the warranty as long as they use parts from the auto manufacturer or use parts that meet the manufacturer's specifications.

Chapter 26

Ten "Eco-Logical" Ways to Save Fuel

*I*f you've become involved to the point where you regularly change your own oil and generally keep your car at peak efficiency, you're probably already happily aware that you are getting better mileage than you did in the past. But there are several other ways to save fuel. Fuel crises may come and go, and we may all be rolling in money someday, but unless every driver learns to drive efficiently, we're going to go on wasting fuel and dumping the unburned residue into the environment.

This chapter gives you some ways to do your bit when you and your car are on the road. I call it "eco-logical" because it makes sense to view your vehicle and your driving techniques from an environmental perspective as well as from an automotive point of view. As we've learned the hard way, the two are intimately related!

Take a Look Under the Hood

Take a look at these parts of your vehicle and make sure that they're in good condition and are functioning properly:

> ✔ **If your air filter is dirty, you can lose 1 mile per gallon at 50 mph.** If you can cut your fuel consumption by only 10 percent, you can save an average of 77 gallons a year! Chapter 13 tells you how to check and replace your air filter.

- ✔ **If your PCV valve is not functioning properly, you're running your engine less efficiently, and you may be burning and polluting your oil, too.** Chapter 6 tells you what the PCV valve does, and Chapter 13 shows you how to check and replace it.

- ✔ **If your spark plugs are misfiring, the problem can cost you up to 25 percent in gas mileage.** Find out about spark plugs in Chapter 5. Chapter 12 tells you how to check, adjust, and replace them.

- ✔ **If your ignition system is overdue for a tune-up, do it — or have it done — *now!*** A simple tune-up can reduce carbon monoxide and hydrocarbon exhaust emissions by 30 to 50 percent. It also saves you fuel and improves your vehicle's performance. See Chapters 5 and 12 for more on the ignition system.

- ✔ **If the accessory belts that connect your fan, water pump, alternator, and a variety of other devices are too loose or too tight, a serious loss of efficiency can be the result.** A belt should have about half an inch of "give" and should not be frayed or badly worn. Chapter 3 shows you how to check these belts, and Chapter 13 provides instructions for adjusting and replacing them.

- ✔ **If a brake is poorly adjusted, it may "drag" while the vehicle is in motion.** Moving the wheel against the dragging brake takes more power, and the result is that your brake linings — and the gas in your tank — won't last as long. To check for dragging brakes, jack up each wheel (see Chapter 1) and spin it. If a brake shoe or brake pad is dragging, you can feel it as you try to turn the wheel on the hub. Chapter 10 tells you everything you need to know about brakes.

- ✔ **If you hear a rumbling sound, your wheel bearings may be worn and may need to be replaced.** Chapter 18 has instructions for checking and repacking wheel bearings.

Start Up without Warming Up

When you start your car in the morning, do you warm it up before you drive off? If you do, no good! Most manuals caution you not to indulge in lengthy warm-ups. They waste fuel, pollute the air, and increase wear on your vehicle.

If your vehicle isn't starting up immediately, try the following:

- ✔ **If your vehicle has fuel injection,** an automotive technician will have to set things right. Check out "What to Do When All Else Fails" in Chapter 13.

- ✔ **If your car has a carburetor,** see Chapter 6 to locate and check your choke and Chapter 13 for instructions on making choke and carburetor adjustments.

> ✔ **If you have trouble starting up on cold mornings,** Chapter 8 can help you locate your thermostat, and Chapter 14 shows you how to replace it if necessary.

Drive Eco-Logically

View your driving techniques in terms of fuel consumption. For example, if you're driving at 55 mph and you accelerate to 65 mph and then have to brake after a block or two, you have wasted the gasoline it took to accelerate the vehicle because you had to return to the original speed so soon.

Before putting on extra speed, check to be sure that you won't have to waste the effort by slowing for a blinker, crossroad, or curve ahead. Remember, every time you step on the brake pedal, you cancel the speed that you used fuel to achieve!

Here are some other driving techniques that can help you save fuel:

✔ **Arrange your car seat as comfortably as possible.** Research has shown that a comfortable driving position helps you tread more lightly on the gas pedal, and a light foot on the gas pedal saves gas. By driving at 50 mph instead of 70 mph, a "featherfoot" can cut fuel consumption by 20 percent! Increased wind resistance at the higher speed also causes your car's chassis to age twice as fast.

✔ **Start and accelerate slowly and smoothly.** Moving a vehicle from a stationary position takes power. You can either apply that power efficiently by starting and accelerating slowly, or you can blow the whole thing by slamming on the gas pedal for a quick getaway. A fast start may cost you 8 miles per gallon for the first 4 miles. A slow start can carry you 50 percent farther on the same amount of gas. Try not to speed — at least for the first mile!

✔ **Obey the speed limits, especially in city traffic.** Traffic lights are set for the local speed limit. So if you maintain a nice, steady, legal speed, you'll find that the lights magically turn green as you approach them. The result: less work for you and 15 percent less fuel consumed.

✔ **Try to stay in your lane.** Each time you change lanes to pass another car on the highway, you waste fuel because you have to accelerate to pass and then usually have to step on the brake to avoid hitting the vehicle in front of you when you get back into the lane. The result is up to 30 percent more fuel wasted.

✔ **Set a steady pace.** Anticipate slowdowns and halts in traffic so that you don't have to stop short. If you're not speeding, you may be able to account for a lot of slowdowns just by taking your foot off the gas pedal. By decelerating rather than braking, you won't wear out your brakes as quickly, and you'll save fuel.

- ✔ **Build up speed slowly *before* you get to a hill.** The extra momentum will carry you at least part of the way up. Don't accelerate to maintain your speed while you're climbing unless you're holding up traffic. Keep the gas pedal steady, and never crest the top of a hill at a high speed; you'll only have to brake on the way down, wasting the gas that got you up there so quickly in the first place.

- ✔ **Try coasting down hills,** using the weight of your vehicle and its momentum to carry you down, with your foot off the accelerator.

- ✔ **Use Overdrive.** Doing so can save you another 10 percent in fuel.

- ✔ **If you have a manual transmission, shift into higher gears as soon as possible.** Practice doing so at the lowest speed the vehicle can handle without laboring or lugging the engine.

Structure Trips to Save Gas

Keep a list and combine lots of little trips into one longer one. A 1-mile trip on a cold engine can cut fuel economy by as much as 70 percent. If you can, skip the trip altogether and use the phone, fax, or Internet. Ride your bike or the bus. Try to shop locally. If the prices are a little higher, you might compensate by what you save in time, effort, and fuel. Carpools are great fuel-savers, too, and they often result in new friendships as well.

It takes more fuel to make a left turn than a right turn because you usually have to wait, idling at 0 miles per gallon, until traffic clears and then overcome inertia to get the car moving again. For the same reason, a trip around the block can use less fuel than a U-turn that involves a lot of stopping and starting.

Fill 'Er Up Eco-Logically

Fuel economy involves more than altering driving techniques. What you do at the pump affects your fuel consumption and can save you money as well. Keep the following points in mind the next time you fill up at the gas station:

- ✔ **In hot weather, fill up in the early morning or evening, when the air is cooler.** Like everything else, gasoline expands with heat. An increase of only 30 degrees can cause 10 gallons of gas to expand by as much as four-fifths of a quart — that's as much as a bottle of whiskey!

✔ **Never overfill the tank.** When the filler hose clicks off automatically, resist the temptation to squirt in that extra little bit. An overfilled tank will run over and spill gasoline on the ground if you travel up a hill or park in the heat of the sun. Not only does this spillage waste fuel and dissolve asphalt on driveways and roadways, but the fumes also contribute substantially to air pollution.

Keep Your Side Windows Shut

Open side windows increase wind resistance. Try to use the interior vents, a sunroof, or vent windows if you're lucky enough to have them. Air conditioning may seem to be a good answer in terms of wind resistance, but it costs you mileage: First, the car has to carry around the weight of the air conditioner and its coolant. Second, it has to put out extra power to make the air conditioner work. You pay your money and you make your choice — air conditioners can consume an extra 2½ miles per gallon!

Keep Your Tires Properly Inflated

Underinflated tires consume about 1 mile per gallon of extra gasoline. They wear out faster, too. Air costs nothing, so make sure that your tires are getting all they need. Chapter 19 shows you how to "read" your tires' treads to see whether they're properly inflated and how to find the proper pressure range on the sidewalls of your tires. To get an accurate reading, always put air in your tires in the morning before you drive the car (except to get to the nearest air pump, of course). After a car has been driven for a while, the tires heat up and the air in them expands.

Get the snow tires off the car as soon as possible, too. They consume a lot more fuel. Next time, buy all-weather tires.

Clean the Junk Out of the Trunk Compartment

You use extra fuel to haul that weight in the trunk around. Every 500 pounds you carry costs you from 2 to 5 miles per gallon, so it pays to keep your vehicle as light as possible by cleaning out the trunk.

Keep Your Car Waxed

Did you know that a highly waxed car cuts wind resistance dramatically? And it looks good, too. Chapter 23 shows you how to wash and wax your vehicle and how to keep the interior clean.

Use a Trailer Instead of a Roof Rack

Those light-looking roof racks are deceptive. They create quite a bit of drag, especially when fully loaded, and the ensuing wind resistance substantially interferes with the air flow around the car. As a matter of fact, a small trailer loaded with the same gear is probably not as big a liability because trailers travel in the "wake" of the car and meet with less air resistance. Of course, they weigh more, too, but once underway, they follow along easily if you don't speed. Besides, you always disconnect the trailer when you don't need it, but you tend to carry the empty roof rack around even when you have no load to put on it.

Appendix A

A Practical Glossary of Automotive Terms

[Words appearing in this font *are defined elsewhere in the Glossary.]*

ABS brakes: See anti-lock braking system.

accelerator: The gas pedal.

accelerator pump: The part of the carburetor that provides an extra squirt of fuel to enrich the fuel/air mixture, thus enabling the car to respond swiftly to increased acceleration when you suddenly depress the gas pedal.

accessory (or drive) belt: A V-shaped or serpentine belt that's driven by a crankshaft pulley and transmits this drive to various accessories, such as the alternator, air conditioning compressor, fan, power steering pump, and water pump.

additives: Substances that may be added to gasoline, diesel fuel, coolant, or lubricating oil. Popular additives clean gasoline and diesel fuel injectors, add water pump lubricant and corrosion preventers to coolant, and add viscosity extenders to lubricating oil.

air cleaner: A container located on or in the air intake duct to the fuel injection system or carburetor that contains an air filter, which removes dust and dirt from the air before it enters the engine. Also acts as a flame arrester in case of backfire.

air filter: The element in the air cleaner that removes impurities from the air. Some air filters are disposable; others can be cleaned and reused.

air intake duct: The passage through which air travels to the air cleaner and the fuel injection system or carburetor. See also venturi.

air springs: Rubber boots filled with air that are computer controlled to cushion the bumps and vibrations of driving. See also suspension system.

airbag: An inflatable bladder that pops out of the dash, steering wheel, or side panels during a collision to protect the vehicle's occupants.

air-cooled engine: An engine that uses air instead of water in its cooling system.

alignment: The position of the car wheels relative to the car body. Proper wheel alignment improves handling and performance and reduces tire wear. The front wheels — and on some cars, the rear wheels — have adjustments to allow the alignment to be changed. See also camber, caster, toe-in, toe-out, steering-axis inclination, turning radius.

Allen wrench: An L-shaped rod designed to remove certain screws and fastenings with hexagonal holes in their heads. These wrenches come in sets of assorted sizes and are sometimes called hex wrenches.

all-wheel drive: A vehicle on which the drive train delivers power to all the wheels, rather than just to the front or rear wheels. Full-time all-wheel drive operates constantly and improves handling even on dry pavement. Selectable all-wheel drive is engaged manually at the driver's discretion. See also four-wheel drive, traction control.

alternative fuel: A substance other than gasoline or diesel fuel, such as electricity, natural gas, hydrogen, and fuel cells.

alternative power plants: Hybrids, fuel cells, and other innovations designed to replace the internal combustion engine.

alternator: Generates electric current that's stored in the battery and used to start the car and run the electrical equipment. Alternators generate alternating current (AC), which is converted to DC before being fed to the battery. Alternators have replaced generators that produced direct current (DC) but otherwise performed the same functions on older cars.

antifreeze: See coolant.

anti-lock braking system (ABS): Anti-lock braking systems have become increasingly popular because they enhance traction in slippery conditions and allow you to keep steering control of a vehicle, even in a skid. There are two-wheel and four-wheel anti-lock systems.

automatic choke: A choke that automatically adjusts the amount of air entering the carburetor by sensing changes in engine temperature. See also thermostatic coil choke, thermostatic spring choke.

automatic transmission: A transmission that selects gears automatically by means of a hydraulic converter and a system of bands and clutches.

axle: A solid metal shaft to which the wheels of a vehicle are attached.

backflushing: See flushing the cooling system.

balancing: See wheel balancing.

ball joint: A movable joint found on the steering linkage and suspension system of a car that permits rotating movement in any direction between the parts that are joined. See also boot, grease fitting, zerk fitting.

bands: Automatic transmissions rely on hydraulic pressure to change gears by means of a system of friction bands and clutches. These bands can be adjusted externally without taking the transmission apart. Adjusting the bands is part of normal transmission service.

battery: A box filled with a solution of water and acid called electrolyte. The box contains metal plates that store current generated by the alternator and deliver it to the parts of the car that operate electrically. See also ground, negative terminal, positive terminal, electrical system.

bearings: Antifriction devices that are usually found between two moving parts. For example, the babbit bearings found between the connecting rod and the crankshaft are lubricated and cushioned with oil, and the front wheel bearings must be repacked with grease at regular intervals. Bearings can be ball- or roller-type.

biocide: A product that kills any fungus or microbes that may have contaminated diesel fuel.

bleeding a system: To remove air bubbles from a brake system, a fuel injection system, or a cooling system so that they don't impede the flow of liquid through that system.

block heaters: Devices that keep the engine warm when a car isn't used in very cold weather. These are especially important for starting diesel engines at extremely low temperatures.

blow-by: Combustion products that blow past the piston rings during the piston's power stroke. These products form acid and sludge in the crankcase and cause smoking from the oil filler hole.

blue books: Listings of the current prices for new and used cars, based on age, condition, and optional equipment; published in the Kelly Blue Book, the NADA Used Car Guide (published by the National Automobile Dealers Association), and the Red Book (published by National Market Reports).

Blue books are available at bookstores, auto supply stores, banks, loan offices, libraries, insurance companies, and on the Internet at www.kbb.com and other Web sites.

boots: The rubber or plastic covers located at either end of a spark-plug cable to insulate the connections between the cable ends and the spark plug and distributor terminals. Always grasp the cable by the boot when removing it. Also, the protective cover of ball joints and constant velocity joints that holds the grease. See also grease fitting.

bore: The width or diameter of the cylinder hole. See also stroke.

brake backing plate: A metal plate, located inside the brake drum, on which the wheel cylinder, brake shoes, and other brake parts are mounted.

brake booster: If your car has power brakes, a brake booster is located between the brake pedal and the master cylinder to increase the force applied to the pistons in the master cylinder. There are two common types: the vacuum booster, which uses engine vacuum and atmospheric pressure; and the hydro-boost unit, which uses hydraulic pressure from your car's power steering system. Some vehicles with anti-lock brakes have a hydraulic pump to generate pressure for booster operation.

brake discs: Also known as rotors, these are used universally on front braking systems and on some rear braking systems. Brake fluid under pressure pushes pistons in brake calipers, which clamp a set of brake pads around one corner of the rotating disc and slow it down, thus slowing down the car. See also brake drums, brake fluid, brake pads, brake system.

brake drums: Metal drums mounted at the rear wheels on some cars. The brake shoes press against the inner surfaces of the drums to slow or stop the car. See also brake system.

brake fluid: The liquid used in the hydraulic brake system to stop or slow the car. See also brake discs, brake lines.

brake lines: A system of hoses and metal tubes through which the brake fluid flows from the master cylinder to the brakes at each wheel. See also brake system.

brake lining: A high-friction material that's attached to the brake shoe. When the shoe is pressed against the brake drum, the lining grabs the inside of the drum, which stops the wheel and thus the car.

brake pads: Friction material on a metal backing plate that, during braking, is clamped around a brake disc by brake caliper pistons to slow down the wheel to which it is attached. See also brake system, brake fluid.

brake shoes: Curved pieces of metal on which are bonded high-friction brake linings that are forced against the brake drums to slow or stop the car.

brake system: A system that uses hydraulic pressure to enable your car to slow and stop safely. Consists of the master cylinder, brake lines, and disc or drum brakes at each wheel. See also brake discs, brake drums, brake fluid, brake lines, brake lining, brake shoes, parking brake, power brakes, wheel cylinder.

breaker plate: The movable plate inside the distributor to which the points and the condenser are affixed.

breaker points: See points.

bushing: A protective liner that provides a cushion between moving metal parts.

butterfly valve: A small metal disc that controls the flow of air into the carburetor. See also choke, throttle.

calipers: Devices on disc brakes that hold the brake pads and press them against the disc to stop or slow the car.

cam: A metal disc with irregularly shaped lobes used in the camshaft to activate the opening and closing of the valves and, in the distributor, to force the points to open.

cam lobes: The bumps on a camshaft that contact and activate cylinder head intake and exhaust valves, either directly or via such devices as camshaft lifters or push rods.

camber: A wheel alignment adjustment of the inward or outward tilt on the top of the wheel when viewed from the front of the car. Improves handling and cuts tire wear.

camshaft: A shaft with cam lobes that causes the valves to open and close. See also cam, overhead camshaft, push rods, rocker arms.

camshaft sensor: A trigger device found on some distributorless ignition systems that synchronizes when the proper ignition coil should be fired.

carburetor: A device that vaporizes fuel and mixes it with air in proper quantities to suit the varying needs of the engine.

carburetor barrel: The tubelike part of the carburetor through which air flows and is mixed with vaporized fuel. The choke butterfly valve is located at the top of the carburetor barrel, and the throttle valve is located at the bottom. Midway through, the barrel narrows, and this part is called the venturi. Carburetors can have one, two, or four barrels. See also dual carbs, four-barrel carburetor.

caster: A wheel alignment adjustment that positions the wheels correctly, like the casters on a chair or shopping cart, so that the tires follow naturally in a forward straight line. On a turn, the wheels will tend to straighten out when the steering wheel is released.

catalytic converter: A pollution-control device found on many newer cars that acts like an afterburner to reburn unburned gas in the tailpipe.

centrifugal advance: A device that advances or retards the ignition spark to correspond with changes in engine speed and load. See also spark advance, spark retard.

cetane rating: A method of rating diesel oil by measuring the time lapse between fuel injection and ignition to determine how easily the oil ignites and how fast it burns. See also octane rating.

charging system: A system that, using an accessory belt driven by the engine, enables the alternator (or generator) to generate electrical current, which is stored in the battery and delivered to the electrically operated parts of the car.

chassis: The parts of a truck or SUV that are left when the body and fenders are removed.

cherry condition: A popular term for a car that has been kept in, or restored to, perfect condition.

choke: The device that limits the amount of air allowed to enter the carburetor, thus enriching the fuel/air mixture and enabling the car to start and run more easily when cold. Automatic chokes have a thermostatic coil or thermostatic spring that actives a butterfly valve at the top of the carburetor barrel. Older cars have manually operated chokes.

circuit: The path of electrical current through an electrical system.

classic car: A car that is generally considered to be one of the finest models ever built. Unlike antique cars, classic cars don't have to be extremely old. Ford Mustangs and Volkswagen Beetles built in the late 1960s are considered to be classics by many people.

cloud point: The lowest temperature at which diesel oil tends to thicken and cloud up.

clutch: In a manual transmission, a device that disconnects the engine from the transmission to allow the car to change gears, and then allows the engine and transmission to resume contact and turn together at a new speed. In an automatic transmission, a clutch performs a similar function, disconnecting the drive while gears change. See also clutch disk, clutch pedal, engine flywheel, free pedal play, pressure plate, throw-out bearing.

clutch disk: In a manual transmission, a spinning plate located at the end of the driveshaft facing the engine flywheel and covered with an asbestos surface. When the clutch is engaged, the clutch disk is forced against the flywheel, causing the engine and the transmission to turn at the same speed.

clutch pedal: A pedal located on the floor of the car to the left of the brake pedal on cars with manual transmission. When the clutch pedal is depressed, it disengages the clutch so the engine and the crankshaft can turn independently of the transmission and the driver can change gears.

CGN: See compressed natural gas.

coil: See ignition coil.

coil springs: Large metal coils like bed springs that cushion and absorb the shocks and bumps as the car is driven. Coil springs are usually found near the front wheels, but many cars have them in the rear as well. Often the shock absorbers run up the center of the coil springs. See also suspension system.

combustion: The intense burning of the fuel/air mixture in the combustion chamber.

combustion chamber: The part of the cylinder where the fuel/air mixture is compressed by the piston and ignited by a spark from the spark plug.

compressed natural gas (CNG): One of the most popular alternative fuels designed to replace gasoline as a source of automotive power.

compression gauge: A device used to check the amount of pressure created in a cylinder when the piston is at its highest point (TDC) and is squeezing the fuel/air mixture into the smallest possible space. A poor compression-gauge reading can indicate the need for a valve grind, new piston rings, and so on.

compression ratio: A measure of the amount of pressure applied to the fuel/air mixture in the combustion chamber. It's determined by comparing the volume of the combustion chamber, with the piston at its highest point (TDC), to the volume of the cylinder when the piston is at its lowest point.

computer: See engine management computer.

condenser: A small metal cylinder, usually located inside a non-electronic distributor, that prevents electricity from arcing across the gap when the points are open by acting as a "sponge" for the excess current.

connecting rod: The metal rod that connects the piston to the crankshaft and converts the up-and-down motion of the piston into the circular motion of the spinning crankshaft. The term "throwing a rod" refers to a broken connecting rod breaking through the side of the engine block.

constant velocity joints (CV): Found mostly at either end of the driveshafts in front-wheel-drive cars, and on the driveshafts of some rear-wheel-drive cars with independent rear suspension systems, these joints are specially designed to transmit engine torque while allowing full steering and suspension movement. They allow movement combinations that U-joints are incapable of handling. See also universal joints.

contact gap: See point gap.

contact points: See points.

control arms: The upper or lower A-shaped suspension components that are mounted on the frame and support the ball joints and steering knuckles. See also suspension system.

coolant: An ethylene glycol solution that raises the boiling point and lowers the freezing point of the water in the cooling system, prevents rust and corrosion, and lubricates the water pump. Also called *antifreeze.*

coolant recovery system: A bottle or tank that acts as a reservoir for liquid expelled from the cooling system through the overflow pipe and then returns the liquid to the system when it cools down. A special radiator pressure cap is also part of the kit. Also called a *closed cooling system* when it's part of the original equipment.

cooling system: A system that stores, circulates, and cools a mixture of water and coolant that flows through water jackets in the engine block and through the radiator, to keep the engine from overheating as you drive. See also fan, pressure cap, thermostat, water pump.

core charge: *Core* is an acronym for *cash on return.* A sum of money is refunded for a rebuildable part that's exchanged for a rebuilt part of the same type. A common core charge is for brake shoes that need relining.

core plugs: Metal plugs in the sides of the engine block that can pop out because of excessive pressure and prevent the engine block from cracking. These plugs sometimes develop leaks and should then be replaced. Also called *freeze plugs.*

cotter pin: A locking device shaped like a pin but split up the center. It's usually inserted in a hole drilled through a nut

and bolt and is intended to lock the nut in place so that it can't unscrew. After insertion, the legs of the cotter pin are bent around the nut to keep it in place.

crankcase: The lower portion of the engine where the crankshaft is located. The oil pan is located at the bottom of the crankcase.

cranking: The act of engaging the starter by turning the key in the ignition switch, which makes the engine turn over. In the old days, a hand crank was used to do this, hence the term *cranking.*

crankshaft: The main rotating shaft in the engine. The connecting rods transmit power from the pistons to the crankshaft, which, in turn, transmits power to the transmission, then to the driveshaft, and eventually to the drive wheels.

crankshaft pulley: A grooved wheel attached to the front end of the crankshaft which is connected by accessory belts to the fan, alternator, power steering pump, water pump, air conditioning compressor, and other devices so that the rotating crankshaft can drive these other parts as well. The crankshaft pulley usually has timing marks located on it, and these are necessary for checking and adjusting timing with a timing light. Also called a *harmonic balance wheel.*

crankshaft sensor: A trigger device that tells the ignition module when to fire the spark plugs on cars with distributorless ignition systems.

creeper: A platform on wheels that allows you to move around easily while lying on your back when you work under your car.

cross-shaft lug wrench: See lug wrench.

cruise control: An optional feature that keeps your car cruising at a preset speed unless overridden by the brake pedal.

CV joint: See constant velocity joint.

cylinder: A hollow tube-shaped pipe in the engine block. The piston rides up and down in the cylinder to compress the fuel/air mixture that drives the engine.

cylinder block: See engine block.

cylinder head: The part of the engine above the engine block that contains the combustion chambers and the valves. The spark plugs screw into the top or side of the cylinder head. On most cars, a valve cover, camshaft cover, or a rocker-arm cover is located on top of the cylinder head.

cylinder sequence: The order in which the cylinders are located on a particular car. It's necessary to locate the #1 cylinder to check and adjust timing with a timing light. The #1 cylinder may be at the front of the engine on a U.S.-made straight 4- or 6-cylinder engine or at the rear of the engine on a foreign-made car. See also firing order.

diesel engine: An engine without a carburetor that burns diesel fuel instead of gasoline. The diesel oil is injected directly into the combustion chamber, where it's ignited by the heat caused by intense compression, rather than by a spark from a spark plug, as in a carburetor.

diesel fuel: Fuel for cars with diesel engines. Similar to home heating oil, kerosene, and jet fuel. Also known as *diesel oil*. See also cetane rating.

dieseling: An engine that continues to run after the ignition key has been switched off is said to be dieseling. This condition is often due to using fuel with too high an octane rating.

differential: A box of gear wheels, situated in rear-wheel drive cars between the rear wheels, that turns the power of the rotating driveshaft at right angles to drive the rear axle and rear wheels. In front-wheel drive cars, the differential is located in the transaxle, usually directly below the transmission. The differential also allows each of the drive wheels to turn at a different speed when cornering.

dipstick: A metal stick that's inserted into a reservoir to check the level of the fluid in the reservoir by means of markings on the stick. The most common dipsticks check the levels of oil, transmission fluid, and power-steering fluid.

disc brakes: Brakes that have calipers with high-friction brake pads, which grab a brake disc (sometimes called a *rotor*) attached to the wheel and force it to stop turning, thus stopping the car. Older cars have disc brakes on the front wheels and drum brakes on the rear wheels. Many other cars have disc brakes on the front and rear wheels.

displacement: The volume of the inside of the cylinders — that is, the amount of fuel and air they can hold before compression takes place.

distributor: The part of the ignition system that distributes the proper amount of electrical voltage to each spark plug, in the correct sequence, at the precise moment, for efficient combustion. See also condenser, distributorless ignition, points, rotor, spark advance, spark retard.

distributor cap: A cap that covers the distributor. It has an outlet for each spark plug wire, plus an outlet where the wire from the coil enters the cap to conduct electrical current to the rotor. The cap keeps dirt and moisture from getting into the distributor.

distributor hold-down clamp: A metal bracket at the base of the distributor that has a nut or bolt that can be loosened to allow the distributor to be moved on its shaft to readjust ignition timing or to open the points for gapping.

distributor shaft: The metal shaft inside the distributor that's driven by the engine and drives the distributor rotor.

distributorless ignition: An ignition system in which each spark plug has its own coil. Spark commands are issued from the engine management computer.

downshifting: Shifting the car manually to a lower gear to accelerate or provide more power to climb a steep hill.

drive train: The path of power from the engine to the drive wheels. Consists of the clutch, transmission, driveshaft, differential, transaxle, or rear axle.

drive wheels: The set of wheels that are connected to the driveshaft and actually drive the car forward and backward while the other set of wheels simply turns in response to the car's motion.

Vehicles are now identified as having front-wheel drive, rear-wheel drive, four-wheel drive, or all-wheel drive.

driveshaft: In rear-wheel-drive cars, the spinning metal shaft that transmits power from the transmission to the differential, the rear axle, and the rear wheels. In front-wheel-drive cars, a shorter driveshaft transmits power from the transaxle to the front wheels.

drum brakes: Brakes that use hydraulic pressure to force curved brake shoes against the inner walls of a hollow metal drum attached to each wheel. See also brake system, disc brakes.

dual carbs: Two carburetors on the same engine.

dwell: On vehicles with non-electronic ignition systems, the distance the distributor shaft rotates while the points are closed. Also called cam angle. The dwell is given in degrees.

dwell meter: A device for determining whether your points are correctly gapped to allow the distributor to deliver a spark of proper intensity and duration to the spark plugs in a non-electronic ignition system. See also tachometer.

electric vehicle (EV): An alternatively powered vehicle designed as an environmentally safer improvement over the internal combustion engine.

electrical system: A system that generates, stores, and distributes the electrical current required to start and run your car and such electrically operated equipment as the radio, headlights, power seats, windows, air conditioner, and engine management system. See also charging system, ignition system, starting system.

electrodes: Metal rods attached to the center and side of the spark plugs to conduct current and create a gap across which the spark must jump.

electrolyte: The mixture of sulfuric acid and water that's found in the battery.

electronic ignition system: An ignition system with a distributor or distributor-less engine management computer that transmits electrical current to the spark plugs by electronic means, eliminating the need for replacing points or condensers and for checking dwell.

electronic sensing devices: Electronic devices found on cars with fuel injection that sense various conditions such as intake manifold fuel/air pressure and temperature, throttle position, and engine speed. This data is fed to the engine management computer, which in turn determines the amounts of fuel to be injected into the combustion chambers and the timing of the spark so that the engine can run at peak efficiency under all conditions.

emergency brake: An auxiliary brake attached to a rear wheel or to the transmission that keeps a vehicle from moving accidentally. Also called a *parking brake.*

emissions control system: See exhaust system.

engine block: The metal block in which the cylinders and the crankshaft are located. Also called the cylinder block.

engine flywheel: A spinning plate located at the end of the crankshaft on cars with manual transmissions that engages the clutch disk, causing the

engine and the transmission to turn at the same rate of speed. Also helps to dampen engine vibration. See also clutch.

engine management computer: Also known as a computer command control system, electronic engine control system, or engine control computer. This computer is fed information from numerous electronic sensing devices and, using this information, precisely controls the operation of the engine by metering the correct fuel/air mixture and timing the spark for the prevailing conditions. See also distributorless ignition system.

EPA estimates: Estimates of the average amount of fuel consumed in city and highway driving by a particular vehicle, based on tests administered by the Environmental Protection Agency. These estimates should be used for comparison only because they vary with the driver, the load, and road conditions.

EV: See electric vehicle.

exhaust gases: The burned residue of the fuel/air mixture that must be refined and expelled from the car via the exhaust system.

exhaust manifold: A set of pipes that carry exhaust gases from the engine to the exhaust system and out of the car through the tailpipe. See also intake manifold.

exhaust port: The opening that enables the exhaust valve to conduct the fuel/air mixture out of the combustion chamber.

exhaust system: Sometimes called the emissions system, this system conducts the exhaust gases from the exhaust manifold to the rear of the car and into the air. Along the way, pollution-control devices are sometimes used to burn off harmful substances, and a muffler (and resonators in some cases) controls the noise of the escaping gases. See also catalytic converter.

exhaust valve: The valve that opens to allow the exhaust gases to pass from the combustion chamber to the exhaust manifold.

fan: Electrically driven and mounted in front of the radiator — or, in older cars, driven by an accessory belt and situated between the radiator and the engine — the fan draws air through the radiator to cool the liquid in the cooling system when the car is standing still, operating at low speeds, or when the air conditioner is running. In some cars, an electrically driven fan is controlled by a thermal sensor in the cooling system.

fan belt: A single flexible rubber belt that connects the fan and the alternator on some older vehicles. The operation of the engine turns the fan, and this turns the belt, which drives the alternator, enabling it to generate electric current. See also accessory belt.

feeler gauge: A device for measuring the distance, or gap, between two surfaces. Use a wire feeler gauge to gap spark plugs and a flat feeler gauge to gap points and adjust valves.

firewall: The insulated partition that runs from the windshield down between the interior of the car and the engine area. Protects the driver and passengers from engine fires, noise, and fumes during accidents.

firing order: The sequence in which the cylinders fire on a particular car to distribute the shock of combustion evenly and reduce engine vibrations. This should not be confused with cylinder sequence, which refers to the location of the #1 cylinder on a specific vehicle, and where the other cylinders are located in relation to #1.

five-speed transmission: A manual transmission with a fifth gear that functions as an overdrive to allow the wheels to turn faster than the engine. On freeways, where cars can achieve higher speeds and then coast without needing much power, this is a real gas saver.

flash point: The temperature at which diesel fuel ignites.

flat rate manual: A listing of almost every job that can be done on a car with the average time required for a mechanic to complete it; it's used by service facilities to estimate labor charges. Many shops require their mechanics to "beat the book" yet charge their customers for the full time suggested by the flat rate manual.

float bowl: A small chamber in the carburetor that holds a small ready supply of fuel to be vaporized and mixed with air by the carburetor. The level of the fuel in the float bowl is controlled by a small float and a shutoff valve in the chamber. As fuel is sucked out of the float chamber to run the engine, the float goes down, thus opening a shutoff valve to allow more fuel from the fuel tank into the float chamber. When the float chamber is full again, the float goes up and pushes against the shutoff valve to prevent more fuel from going into the float chamber and flooding it.

flushing the cooling system: Circulating water through the cooling system to remove old liquid and clean the system of rust and dirt. *Backflushing* means circulating the water from the engine to the radiator (reversing the normal direction of flow) in order to clean the system more efficiently.

four-barrel carburetor: A carburetor with four barrels that works like two 2-barrel carburetors. Usually found on older, large V-8 engines.

four-stroke power cycle: Refers to the four movements of the piston — down up, down and up — that draw the fuel/air mixture into the combustion chamber (intake stroke), compress the mixture (compression stroke), transmit the power created by the combustion to the crankshaft (power stroke), and expel the exhaust gases from the cylinder (exhaust stroke).

four-wheel drive: Allows a driver to adjust a vehicle to operate in difficult terrain. How this is accomplished differs from one model to another. Four-wheel drive should be used only when needed because it doesn't work efficiently under normal road conditions. See also all-wheel drive, traction control.

free pedal play: The distance the clutch pedal can be depressed before it begins to disengage the clutch. About ¾ to 1 inch of free pedal play is normally required to assure that the clutch will be fully engaged when not in use. Without free pedal play, the throw-out bearing, and/or the clutch, would wear out.

freeze plugs: See core plugs.

friction: The rubbing of two moving parts against each other. Friction creates heat and wears down moving parts. The lubrication system uses oil to reduce friction and to increase the life of your car. Friction is used between brake pads and brake discs and between brake shoes and brake drums to slow down and stop your car.

front-end alignment: See alignment.

front-wheel drive: A vehicle that's "pulled" by its front wheels, rather than being "pushed" by its rear wheels, has front-wheel drive. This eliminates the long driveshaft and the center floor hump found on cars with rear-wheel drive. See also transverse engine, transaxle, constant velocity joints.

fuel/air mixture: A vaporized, mistlike combination of fuel and air that's compressed in the cylinders and ignited to produce the power that drives the engine and the car.

fuel cell: A power plant that creates electrical current from hydrogen and oxygen that is passed over a catalyst, usually a microscopically thin sheet of platinum. The electrical current is then fed directly to the vehicle's electric motor for propulsion. See also alternative power plants.

fuel filter: A small device that removes impurities from the fuel before it gets to the fuel injection system or carburetor. In fuel-injected cars, usually found in or close to the fuel tank. In carbureted cars, usually found near the carburetor in the fuel line that leads from the fuel pump (in-line fuel filter), or inside the carburetor or the fuel pump (integral fuel filter).

fuel injection: A fuel system without a carburetor that employs an electronic fuel management system to deliver a specific amount of fuel to each combustion chamber in response to changes in engine speed and driving conditions. See also fuel injectors.

fuel injection pump: Found on diesel engines, it sends fuel to its mini-pumps, and from there to the fuel injector nozzles.

fuel injectors: Devices that work like hypodermic needles to inject the proper amount of fuel into the combustion chambers in response to signals from an electronic sensing device on cars with fuel injection systems.

fuel lines: The hoses or pipes through which the fuel passes from the fuel tank to the carburetor.

fuel pressure regulator: A spring-loaded diaphragm that maintains proper fuel pressure and meters unused fuel back to the fuel tank.

fuel pump: A pump that draws the fuel from the fuel tank and sends it through the fuel lines to the carburetor or the fuel injectors.

fuel rail assembly: A hollow pipe in a fuel injection system that supplies fuel to the set of fuel injectors connected to it.

fuel supply pump: See fuel transfer pump.

fuel system: A system that stores, cleans, and delivers the fuel to the engine in proper quantities to meet the varying needs that arise as you drive. Consists of the fuel tank, fuel lines, fuel pump, fuel filter, and fuel injection or carburetor.

fuel tank: The storage compartment, under the trunk in most cars, that holds the fuel for the car. Also called the *gas tank.*

fuel transfer pump: One of a series of mini-pumps on diesel engines, each of which is responsible for delivering fuel from the fuel injection pump to one of the fuel injector nozzles at a pressure of more then 1,000 pounds per square inch.

fuses: Fuses control the flow of current to the electrical components on your vehicle the same way they do at home. They are located in a fuse box that's usually found under or near the dashboard. Your owner's manual can help you locate it.

gap: The space between the spark plug electrodes, or between the points when they are as far apart as they can get. Adjusting this space is called "gapping." See also point gap, spark plug gap.

gapper: See feeler gauge.

gas gauge: A dashboard device that indicates the amount of fuel in the fuel tank.

gas tank: See fuel tank.

gasket: A rubber, cork, paper, or metal plate that's inserted between two parts to prevent leakage of gases or fluids.

gear ratio: The speed of the engine compared with the output speed of the transmission, and/or the differential, in a given gear.

gear selector: A gearshift located on the side of the steering column, in a console, or on the floor between the front seats on vehicles with automatic transmissions.

gearshift: The stick (usually located between the front seats) that the driver uses to select and change transmission gears. See also gear selector, stick shift.

generator: See alternator.

glow plug: An electrical element located in the combustion chamber of a diesel engine that helps to heat up the air in the chamber so that the diesel fuel is ignited more quickly.

grease: See lube grease.

grease fitting: A device that seals in and allows the addition of more grease or some other type of lubricant to cushion two moving parts, allow them to move freely, and prevent them from wearing each other away. See also ball joint, steering knuckles, tie-rod ends, zerk fitting.

grease gun: A device that can be loaded with grease and used to lubricate your car. Grease guns come with extenders for hard-to-reach places and with adapters for lubricating various types of ball joints and zerk fittings.

grease seal: A circular, metal-backed, rubber device, that keeps grease from leaking out and protects wheel bearings and similar parts from dust and water.

ground: An object that makes an electrical connection with the earth, to safely complete an electrical circuit. For example, one terminal of the battery is wired to the metal frame of the vehicle to utilize the frame as a path for returning electric current to the battery and thus completing the electrical circuit. All U.S. vehicles are "negative ground" — because the negative terminal is wired to the frame of the car. In some countries, this is called "negative earth."

guarantee: A promise by the manufacturer to fix or replace a specific part if it doesn't last for a specific time period or distance. See also warranty.

harmonic balance wheel: See crankshaft pulley.

head gasket: The seal between the cylinder head and the engine block. This gasket keeps the coolant out of the cylinders and free from contamination by exhaust gases. A "blown" head gasket causes a serious loss of compression.

headliners: Fabric or vinyl upholstery on the interior of the roof of a vehicle.

heater core: A device that heats the passenger compartment. Hot coolant and water circulate through it from the engine and heat air that is then blown by an interior fan into the vehicle.

hex wrench: See Allen wrench.

horsepower: The energy required to lift 550 pounds one foot in one second — or 33,000 foot-pounds per minute.

hose clamps: Adjustable metal rings placed around a hose where it connects to another part to prevent leaks and to keep the hose in place.

hubcap: The cap that fits over the outside of a wheel on some vehicles to keep dust and water away from the wheel bearings and brakes. Considered a decorative accessory on many cars, it's also a safety device that causes quite a racket if a lug nut falls off and tumbles around inside it.

hybrid: An alternative power plant that combines a small internal combustion engine and an electric motor to get maximum power with minimum emissions and maximum fuel economy. See also alternative power plants.

hydraulic: A system that uses fluids under pressure to transmit force or power. Hydraulic devices on a vehicle may include automatic transmission, power steering, and brake systems.

hydrometer: A device to determine the specific gravity of a liquid. It's used to test battery electrolyte and the percentage of coolant in the cooling system.

idiot lights: Popular term for the dashboard indicators that light up only when your car is already in trouble from lack of oil, overheating, and so on (as opposed to gauges, which indicate levels of oil and engine temperatures, thus enabling the driver to prevent breakdowns and damage).

ICE: See internal combustion engine.

idle: The engine speed when the car isn't moving.

idle air bleed screw: A screw found instead of the idle speed screw on some carburetors. It allows air to enter the carburetor when the throttle is closed so that the car can idle.

idle mixture screw: A screw located on the outside of the carburetor that controls the proportion of the fuel/air mixture. It's now illegal to adjust these if limiter caps are present.

idle speed screw: A screw located at the bottom of the carburetor on the outside that keeps the throttle from closing completely when the car is idling, thus controlling the idle speed. See also idle air bleed screw, idle mixture screw, idle stop solenoid.

idle stop solenoid: A small cylinder located on the outside of the carburetor on some vehicles. It prevents the car from continuing to idle after the ignition switch is shut off (this is called dieseling).

ignition coil: The part of the ignition system that receives a small amount of electrical voltage from the battery, amplifies it into a big jolt of voltage, and sends it to the spark plugs via the distributor.

ignition module: A transistorized component in an electronic ignition that triggers the ignition coil to fire high voltage. It replaced the breaker points on older cars.

ignition switch: The slot in which you turn the car key to activate a vehicle's electrical circuits and start the car. When the key is removed, the electrical circuits are disconnected from the battery.

ignition system: A system that provides the electric current used to ignite the fuel/air mixture in the combustion chambers of the cylinders. Its parts include the coil, which amplifies the voltage it gets from the battery and sends it to the distributor, which directs the current to each spark plug at the proper time. In cars with distributorless ignitions, the engine management computer directs low-voltage current to the spark plug coils and then to the spark plugs.

ignition timing: The timing of the spark plug spark in the combustion chamber during the piston's compression stroke. This timing is preset by the auto manufacturer, and in cars with electronic ignition systems rarely needs to be adjusted. In cars with engine management computers and distributorless ignitions, no adjustment can be made.

inlet valve: See intake valve.

in-line engine: An engine in which the cylinders occur in a single row with the crankshaft running along the bottom. Also called a *straight engine*. See V-type engine.

intake manifold: A set of pipes through which the engine draws a fuel/air mixture from fuel injectors or a carburetor into each cylinder. See also exhaust manifold.

intake port: The opening that enables the intake valve to conduct the fuel/air mixture into the combustion chamber. See also four-stroke power cycle.

intake valve: A valve that opens to allow the fuel/air mixture to enter the combustion chamber. Also called the *inlet valve*.

integral equipment: Any device or system that's designed for and installed in a car by the manufacturer, rather than being added to a finished vehicle at a later date.

internal combustion engine (ICE): An engine that works on power released by vaporized fuel and air burning inside the engine itself, rather than on an outside source of combustion as, for example, a steam engine does.

jack: A device for lifting the car, or part of the car, off the ground to facilitate repairs. The most popular jacks are the tripod, scissors, and hydraulic jacks.

jack stand: A safety device that keeps the car from falling to the ground if the jack is removed or faulty. Most jobs require two jack stands for safety.

journal: The area on the crankshaft that fits into the lower portion of the connecting rod. A layer of oil and metal bearings cushions the movement of the connecting rod around the journal to prevent premature wear.

jumper cables: Cables used to jump a start by conducting current from one car battery to another. This allows a car whose battery has run down to start and begin to generate its own power. See also positive terminal.

knocking: A sound that occurs in the cylinders when the fuel/air mixture is ignited too soon and the subsequent explosion hits the piston as it travels up the cylinder on the compression stroke. Usually, it's due to faulty timing, low-octane gas, or fragments of burning carbon in the cylinders. Also called *pinging* or *pre-ignition*. It sounds like marbles rattling in a can and can be heard best when accelerating up hills. This sound can also be caused by impending mechanical failure within the engine due to extreme wear of a piston or bearing. See also four-stroke power cycle.

leaf springs: A series of steel plates, placed one atop the other, which bend flexibly to absorb the bumps and shocks of driving. Most often used in the rear suspensions of trucks and some sport-utility vehicles. See also suspension system.

leasing: Payment of a sum each month in return for the use of a vehicle instead of buying it outright. The two basic types of leases are open-end leases, under which you pay an additional amount at the end of the term and acquire ownership of the vehicle; and closed-end leases, under which ownership reverts to the leasing agency at the end of the term.

lube grease: Super-thick lubricating oil that has a paste-like consistency. Used to lubricate the steering linkage, the suspension system, and other moving parts outside the engine.

lube job: The greasing and lubrication of the suspension system, the drive train, and other parts of the car that need it.

lubrication system: A system that stores, cleans, cools, and recirculates oil through the engine to lubricate and cool its moving parts. The system components are the oil pan, oil pump, oil filter, and dashboard oil gauge. You can check the level of oil in the system with the oil dipstick.

lug nuts: The nuts that hold the wheel onto the car. You must remove them with a lug wrench to change tires.

lug wrench: A wrench used during tire changes to remove the lug nuts that hold the wheel onto the car. The cross-shaft type provides the best leverage. Carry one in your trunk compartment.

manifold: See exhaust manifold, intake manifold.

manual transmission: A transmission system in which gears are selected by the driver by means of a hand-operated gearshift and a foot-operated clutch. Also called a _standard transmission_.

master cylinder: A device that stores brake fluid and hydraulically forces it through the brake lines to the brakes when you step on the brake pedal. Clutches have master cylinders, too.

mechanics lien: Recourse available to repair facilities in some states by which they can confiscate and sell your vehicle to compensate themselves if you don't pay your bill.

misfiring: The failure of the fuel/air mixture in one or more cylinders to undergo combustion while the car is running. Misfiring can be due to poor compression caused by worn or improperly adjusted valves, worn piston rings, or a faulty head gasket. Or it can be caused by poor ignition due to worn or dirty spark plug electrodes, worn or improperly gapped spark plugs, poor fuel delivery, faulty ignition wiring, or faulty distributor components. It can be detected by placing a stiff piece of paper at the end of the tailpipe and listening for an irregular puffing sound.

motor mounts: The rubber-covered brackets that hold the engine and transmission to the frame of the car and cushion vibrations.

mph: An abbreviation for miles per hour.

muffler: A device for controlling the noise of the exhaust gases before they are released into the air through the tailpipe.

negative ground: See ground.

negative terminal: The battery terminal that conducts electric current back to the battery. The negative terminal usually has either "neg" or "-" on it.

NOS (new old stock): Duplicates of parts for out-of-production cars that are issued by the original manufacturer for the restoration of older vehicles. See also OEM.

octane rating: A method of rating gasoline by measuring its ability to resist knocking, or pinging, in internal combustion engines. Engines with higher compression ratios require higher-octane gasoline. See also cetane rating.

odometer: A dashboard device for measuring and indicating the number of miles a car has traveled. A trip odometer that can be set to zero in order to register the mileage on a particular trip can be found on some vehicles as well.

OEM (original equipment manufacturer): Parts supplied by the original manufacturer of a particular vehicle. See also NOS.

oil: A substance that lubricates and cools the moving parts of the engine and reduces the formation of rust and corrosion. Oil comes in varying weights suitable for efficient operation in cold and hot weather and for engines in varying states of wear. See also viscosity.

oil drain plug: The plug that secures the drain hole in the oil pan. In many (but not all) cars, an oil plug gasket lies between the plug and the hole and should be replaced if leakage occurs. In some cars, there is no gasket because the metal-to-metal connection between the drain plug and the oil pan is tapered and leak-free.

oil filler hole: A hole at the top of the engine through which new oil can be added after the filler hole cover is removed.

oil filter: A canlike device that screws onto the outside of the crankcase and cleans the oil as it circulates through the lubrication system. Oil filters should be replaced at least every other oil change.

oil pressure gauge: A dashboard device that indicates the oil pressure as the oil is pumped through the engine. If this gauge shows a sharp drop, reads "Low," or lights up, stop the car immediately and find the reason for your loss of oil pressure before driving any farther. Without oil pressure, you can burn out your engine in less than a mile. This low indication doesn't necessarily mean that you're low in, or out of, oil in your oil pan. It could mean that the oil pump is defective or has failed.

oil pan: The chamber at the bottom of the crankcase that stores oil. The oil drain plug at the bottom of the oil pan can be removed to allow old oil to flow out of the car during an oil change.

oil pump: A small pump located in the crankcase that circulates the oil from the oil pan to the moving parts of the engine.

optional equipment: Any equipment or feature of a new car that isn't included in the basic price and is provided only if the purchaser requests it. Beware of new car deals that force you to buy a vehicle equipped with options you don't need.

original condition: An older vehicle that has all of its original paint and equipment and has not been restored or modified is said to be in original condition.

overdrive: An optional special gear that allows the rear wheels to turn faster than the engine. This lowers fuel consumption during sustained high-speed driving on freeways.

overhaul: See rebuild.

overhead cam (OHC): A camshaft located above the cylinder head rather than below the cylinders in the engine block. Overhead camshafts eliminate the need for push rods to activate the valves. DOHC engines have double (two) overhead camshafts: One operates the intake valves, and the other operates the exhaust valves.

owner's manual: A handbook provided by the car manufacturer to give the owner basic instructions for operating the various devices on a vehicle. Many owner's manuals contain specifications for items associated with maintenance, but very few offer instructions for doing-it-yourself. See also service manual.

ozone checking: Cracks or hard spots usually found on the sidewalls of tires. Caused by the action of the ozone in the air on the rubber, this condition is normal but could be dangerous on tires that are more than 40,000 miles old or have been exposed to ozone for a long time.

parking brake: An auxiliary brake attached to a rear wheel or to the transmission that keeps the car from moving accidentally. Also called an emergency brake.

passing gear: An automatic transmission gear that shifts a car into a lower gear for a short burst of extra power to pass other cars on the highway. This gear is engaged by sharply depressing the gas pedal. When the pedal is released, the car returns to a normal driving gear.

PCM (Powertrain Control Module): A computer that controls the operation of the fuel, ignition, and emission-control systems on newer cars.

PCV valve: Part of the positive crankcase ventilation system, which reroutes crankcase blow-by to the intake manifold and back to the engine, where it's reburned in the cylinders as part of the fuel/air mixture. This cuts emission pollution and increases fuel economy because unburned fuel in the blow-by is consumed the second time around. It also keeps the blow-by and water vapor from fouling the oil in the crankcase, thus reducing the formation of engine sludge.

Phillips screwdriver: A screwdriver with a pointed tip that's shaped to fit the crossed slots in the heads of Phillips screws.

pinging: See knocking.

piston: A cylindrical part, closed at the top, that moves up and down inside the cylinder to compress the fuel/air mixture and drive the engine by means of a connecting rod, which is attached to the piston at one end and to the crankshaft at the other. See also journal, piston rings.

piston rings: Metal rings located in grooves on the outside of the piston that keep the fuel/air mixture from leaking past the piston into the crankcase during compression and that keep oil from going up into the combustion chamber. Faulty rings can cause poor compression, severe blow-by, and excessive smoking from the tailpipe.

planetary gearset: A set of gears consisting of several *planet* gears rotating around a central *sun* gear.

planetary-gear system: A gearset used in automatic transmissions that features a central gear, called a *sun* gear, surrounded by two or more smaller *planetary* gears that mesh with a ring gear. How picturesque!

point gap: On vehicles with non-electronic ignitions, the space between the points when they're fully open. Adjusting this gap is a primary part of the basic tune-up because the spark that jumps this gap is affected, both in intensity and in duration, by the width of the gap. See also feeler gauge.

points: Two or more metal terminals, located inside the distributor on vehicles with non-electronic ignitions. These terminals are brought into contact and then separated by the movement of the cam wheel on the rotating distributor shaft. The points regulate the intensity and duration of the current that's conducted to each spark plug by interrupting the flow of current from the coil as they open and close. Also called *contact points, breaker points,* or *ignition points.* See also gap.

polymer coating: A coating that prevents paint from oxidizing, protecting a car from premature fading and rusting. Do-it-yourself polysealants last for from 6 months to a year; professionally applied polyglycotes can last from 2 to 3 years.

positive terminal: The battery terminal that leads to the electrical system on cars with negative ground. The positive terminal usually has "pos" or "+" on it. Jumper cables and other devices that connect to the battery usually have red clips for the positive terminal and black clips for the negative terminal and ground.

power booster: A device that uses engine vacuum to assist you in braking the car. Helps the brake pedal activate the hydraulic pistons in the master cylinder.

power brakes: A brake system that uses a power booster to make braking easier.

power steering: A device that uses hydraulic power to help the driver steer the car more easily. Cars with power steering usually have a reservoir in the power steering pump, which requires the occasional addition of power-steering fluid (sometimes automatic transmission fluid).

Powertrain Control Module: See PCM.

pre-combustion chamber: A small chamber located outside the combustion chamber of some cars in which a small amount of rich fuel/air mixture can be ignited to start the combustion process to increase fuel efficiency and cut emissions. Found principally on diesel engines and certain gasoline engines. Also called *prechambers.*

pre-ignition: See knocking.

pressure cap: A radiator cap that allows the cooling system to operate under pressure at higher temperatures for greater efficiency. Safety pressure caps can be used to help release the pressure before the cap is removed to prevent injuries due to escaping steam or hot coolant.

pressure plate: A disc that's forced by springs against the clutch disk, which forces the disc and the engine flywheel against each other, causing the engine and the transmission to turn at the same rate of speed. See also clutch.

primary terminal: The clip found inside the distributor on vehicles with non-electronic ignitions that allows electric current to pass from the points to the condenser and provides the insulation to keep the current from contacting other metal parts. See also ignition system.

psi: An abbreviation for pounds per square inch, a measurement of pressure. The term is used to measure the amount of air pressure in tires and the amount of compression of the fuel/air mixture in the combustion chamber. In the metric system, pressure is measured by kilometers per square centimeter.

push rods: The rods that run between the camshaft or camshaft lifters and the rocker arms. The lifters and the push rods are pushed up by the cam lobes, causing the rocker arms to make the valves open and close. Engines with overhead cams don't need push rods because the camshaft cam lobes contact the valves directly.

radial tires: See tires.

radiator: A device that cools the liquid in the cooling system by allowing it to circulate through a series of water channels, which are exposed to air ducts.

radiator cap: See pressure cap.

radiator fill hole: An opening at the top of the radiator through which a 50-50 mix of water and coolant can be added. The pressure cap seals the fill hole. See also coolant recovery system.

radiator pressure cap: See pressure cap.

ratchet: A device that allows you to turn a screw or bolt in one direction and then move the handle of the wrench or screwdriver back, without force, in the opposite direction to prepare for the next stroke, without removing the tool from the screw or bolt. See socket wrench.

rear axle ratio: The number of times the rear wheels turn compared to a particular transmission speed. The higher the rear axle ratio, the slower the engine can run and still allow the car to achieve a given speed.

rear-wheel drive: A vehicle that is *pushed* by its rear wheels, rather than *pulled* by its front wheels, has rear-wheel drive. This means that its engine and transmission are separate (rather than combined in a transaxle), and it has a long driveshaft located under a center hump in the floor and a differential between the two rear wheels. See also front-wheel drive.

rebuild: To disassemble a particular device, clean it thoroughly, replace worn parts, and reassemble it. Engines, clutches, carburetors, and brakes are sometimes rebuilt as part of the maintenance or restoration of older vehicles. You can rebuild a part yourself with a kit containing instructions and part replacements, or you can buy a rebuilt part and turn in your old part for a core charge. Rebuilding is sometimes called *overhauling.*

reproduction: A cars or car part that has been duplicated by other manufacturers because the original is no longer widely available.

resonator: A small auxiliary muffler found on some vehicles that further reduces the noise of the escaping exhaust gases.

restoration: Restoring a car to its original condition (including original parts, paint, rechroming, and so on) rather than merely rebuilding or repairing one. See also OEM, reproduction, rebuild, cherry condition.

retreads: Used tires that have been refurbished by grinding the tread off and winding a strand of uncured rubber around the tire. Then the tire is placed in a mold, where the rubber is cured under heat and pressure and the tread itself is shaped. Finally, the tire is painted. The quality of retreads can vary; to be safe, only buy retreads from well-known manufacturers.

rings: See piston rings.

rocker arm cover: A metal lid located on top of the cylinder head on cars that have valves activated by an overhead cam or rocker arms. See also valve cover.

rocker arms: Curved levers, each of which has one end attached to a push rod and the other end attached to a valve stem in order to make the valves open and close in response to the pressure of the cam lobes on the spinning camshaft. Cars with overhead cams don't always require rocker arms, because the valve stems may contact the cam lobes directly.

rotor: A device that sits atop the distributor shaft and rotates with it to conduct electric current to each spark plug terminal in turn. The discs on disc brakes are sometimes referred to as rotors. See also ignition system.

rpm: An abbreviation for revolutions per minute. A tachometer measures engine revolutions in terms of rpm.

rubber: All the rubber seals, mats, and pads that cushion and protect car windows, trim, handles, bumper sections, carpets, and so on. A restoration should include replacement of all damaged or missing rubber with OEM rubber parts or exact reproductions of it.

rubbing block: A little block located on the movable point that contacts the distributor cam wheel and causes the points to open. (A spring causes the points to close.)

rubbing compound: A polish that contains abrasives harsh enough to remove layers of "dead" paint. Useful in radical restoration procedures, rubbing compounds should not be used on new cars or those with delicate finishes.

safety pressure cap: See pressure cap.

sealed beam unit: A headlight that usually contains twin high/low filaments, a reflector, and a lens and is sealed to keep out dirt and moisture. When the headlight fails, you replace the entire unit. Sealed beam units are usually found on older vehicles. Newer ones have halogen headlights.

sealer: A substance you can add to the liquid in the cooling system to seal leaks. Also called *stop-leak*. Other kinds of sealing compounds are used to coat surfaces before installing hoses or gaskets. These are effective in preventing leakage but usually make the hose or gasket hard to remove.

service manual: A handbook published by a car manufacturer or a specialized publishing company that contains instructions and specifications for the maintenance and repair of specific vehicles. Most service manuals deal with only one make, model, or year, and nearly all are intended for professionals or the very experienced amateur. They're useful for locating various parts on your car and for parts specifications. See also owner's manual.

service writer: At many dealerships, the person responsible for receiving cars brought to the service department, in order to estimate the nature and cost of repairs and when the work will be completed.

shock absorbers: Devices located near each wheel to cut down the vertical bouncing of the passenger compartment on the springs after the wheels go over a bump or the car stops short. Shock absorbers also improve handling on rough road surfaces. See also suspension system.

sludge: A combination of oxidized oil, gasoline, coolant, and blow-by that can foul an engine. Some engine oils have detergents to break down sludge.

socket wrench: A wrench that completely covers the head of a bolt rather than fitting around its circumference. A socket set usually consists of a variety of sockets plus at least one handle (usually a ratchet handle), a couple of extenders, and sometimes a spark plug socket as well.

solenoid: A device connected to electrical current that induces mechanical movement in another device. See also idle stop solenoid, starter solenoid.

spark advance: To adjust the ignition timing so that the spark plugs will fire sooner than they have been firing. See also spark retard.

spark plug: A device that delivers the electrical spark to the combustion chamber. This ignites the fuel/air mixture and produces the power that drives the engine. See ignition system, spark plug gap.

spark plug gap: The space between the center and side spark plug electrodes, across which the spark must jump to ignite the fuel/air mixture in the combustion chamber. Adjusting this gap is a major part of the basic tune-up, because the width of the gap affects the intensity of the spark. See also feeler gauge.

spark plug socket: A metal cylinder with a rubber lining that fits over the exposed end of the spark plug to make it easy to remove the plug without damaging its porcelain surface. Can be purchased separately or as part of a socket wrench set.

spark retard: To adjust ignition timing so that the spark plugs will fire later than they have been firing. See also knocking, spark advance.

specifications: The size, description, or part numbers for various items needed to maintain or repair a car. See also owner's manual, service manual.

speedometer: A dashboard device that measures and indicates how fast the car is going. The speedometer cable should be lubricated when the needle starts to move erratically, or if the cable begins to make noise.

spindle: The small shaft located at each front wheel on which the front wheels revolve in rear-wheel-drive cars.

splash shield: A removable device found on disc brakes that helps to keep water and dirt from fouling the brakes.

springs: Devices to cushion and absorb shocks and bumps and to keep the car level on turns. A car can have air springs, leaf springs, coil springs, torsion bars, or a combination of these. See also suspension system.

stabilizers: A variety of devices used to keep the passenger compartment of a car from swaying and lurching on sharp curves and turns. Also known as anti-roll bars. See also suspension system.

standard transmission: See manual transmission.

starter: A small electrical motor that causes the engine crankshaft to begin to turn, which starts the engine running and so starts the car. Also called the cranking motor. See also starting system.

starter solenoid: A device that uses electrical current to start and engage the starter. See also solenoid.

starting system: The portion of the electrical system that starts the car. Consists of (1) the ignition switch, which closes the circuit and allows current to flow from (2) the battery to (3) the starter, via (4) the starter solenoid, and in some cases a relay. Also called the cranking circuit.

static shield: A device found on some distributors on cars with non-electronic ignitions that reduces radio interference caused by the working of the ignition system.

steering knuckles: A type of ball joint located at the ends of the tie rods on the steering linkage. See also grease fittings.

steering linkage: The system that connects the steering wheel to the front wheels and allows the wheels to change direction in response to commands from the driver. Contains grease fittings to cushion against wear and friction. See also alignment.

steering-axis inclination: An alignment adjustment that allows the steering wheel to return to the straight-ahead position when the car comes out of a turn.

stickshift: See gearshift.

stop-leak: See sealer.

stroke: The vertical distance that the piston moves as it travels from the top to the bottom or from the bottom to the top of the cylinder. See also bore and four-stroke power cycle.

strut: An efficient type of shock absorber. See also suspension system.

supercharging: A method of increasing engine power by forcing larger amounts of air into the cylinders using an accessory belt-driven air compressor. Unlike turbocharging, which uses an air compressor driven by an exhaust driven turbine, supercharging decreases fuel economy.

suspension system: A system that cushions the passenger compartment of the car from the bumps and shocks caused by the wheels moving over irregular road surfaces. Includes springs, shock absorbers, steering linkage, upper and lower control arms, torsion bars, and stabilizers. See also grease fittings, bushings, zerk fittings.

synchromesh: A manual transmission device that allows two gears to mesh more smoothly by causing them to spin at the same rate of speed before coming together.

tach/dwell meter: See tachometer.

tachometer: A device for measuring engine rpm. Many cars with manual transmissions have a dashboard tachometer to aid in changing gears. A portable tachometer is used to adjust idle speed as part of a basic tune-up. Often, a tachometer is combined with a dwell meter in a single unit called a *tach/dwell meter.*

tailpipe: The last link in the exhaust system. Conducts exhaust gases from the muffler to the rear of the car and into the atmosphere.

TDC: An abbreviation for top dead center.

thermostat: A device that keeps the hot coolant confined to the engine cooling passages to help the engine warm up more quickly. After the engine has warmed up, the thermostat allows the coolant to flow to the radiator, where it's cooled and recirculated through the engine to prevent overheating. See also cooling system.

thermostatic coil choke: A sensing device mounted on the carburetor that automatically controls the choke

butterfly valve by sensing the heat of the exhaust manifold. See also choke.

thermostatic spring choke: A sensing device that automatically controls the choke butterfly valve by sensing the heat of the intake manifold. See also choke.

throttle: A device that controls the power produced by the engine at any given moment. The throttle regulates the fuel/air mixture that goes into the cylinders. It consists of a throttle arm, located on the outside of the carburetor or throttle-body fuel injection system, and connected to the gas pedal, which activates a throttle butterfly valve at the base of the intake barrel, where it joins the intake manifold.

throw-out bearing: A part of the clutch, activated by the clutch pedal, that allows the clutch to disengage. If you allow the car to idle in gear with the clutch pedal depressed, instead of shifting to Neutral, you can wear out the throw-out bearing. Also called the *clutch release bearing.* See also free pedal play.

tie-rod ends: Ball joints located at the ends of the tie rods, which are part of the steering linkage.

timing: The capability of the valves, ignition system, and other engine-driven parts of the car to work together for maximum efficiency. Timing is checked as part of the basic tune-up because, if the timing is off, the car can't perform well, just as all the pieces in an orchestra must not only be in tune but must play together to achieve a good performance. Timing is regulated by checking it with a timing light and then adjusting the distributor or the timing chain. See also distributor hold-down clamp, ignition timing, spark advance, spark-retard, timing belt, timing marks, valve timing.

timing belt: A crankshaft-driven "toothed" belt that drives an overhead camshaft or camshafts and, in some cars, a water pump. The camshaft(s), in turn, via their cam lobes, open and close the cylinder head intake and exhaust valves. This belt should be changed at the mileage interval recommended in your owner's manual or service manual, usually between 60,000 and 90,000 miles. See also valve timing.

timing chain: A crankshaft-driven chain that drives an overhead camshaft or camshafts, which, in turn, open and close the intake and exhaust valves. In many modern vehicles, this part has been replaced by a timing belt. See also valve timing.

timing light: A device used to check ignition timing. The light is hooked to the first cylinder spark plug and blinks on and off as the plug fires. When aimed at the timing marks, this stroboscopic effect causes the marks to appear to stand still opposite a pointer.

timing marks: A series of marks or notches usually located on the crankshaft pulley (also called the *harmonic balance* wheel). When a timing light is aimed at these marks, they appear to stand still, enabling you to see if the proper mark is lined up with a stationary pointer located nearby. The proper timing marks are part of a vehicle's specifications.

tire valve: A small valve mounted on the wheel rim of a tubeless tire that allows air to be added to the tire with a properly equipped air hose and allows air to be withdrawn from an over-inflated tire by pressing on the little stem at the end of the valve. Some tire valves have little caps to protect against leaks and keep dirt from fouling the valve.

tires: Critical parts of your car that allow braking, accelerating, and cornering on wet or dry roads and contribute significantly to the vehicle's ride quality. All cars today use radial construction tires. Sidewalls are usually reinforced with polyester or nylon. Treads are reinforced with a combination of polyester, steel, and sometimes nylon. See also alignment, ozone checking, tire valve.

toe-in: An adjustment of front-wheel alignment so that the tires are slightly pigeon-toed when the car is standing still. Toe-in is required for proper steering and tire wear.

toe-out: A wheel alignment adjustment to control the way the car tracks on turns. Tires should never be toe-out.

top dead center (TDC): The point at which the piston has reached the top of its stroke and has compressed the fuel/air mixture to the greatest extent. BTDC and ATCD mean before and after top dead center. These terms are used to refer to timing marks. See also combustion chamber.

torque: Turning or twisting force. See also torque wrench.

torque converter: A fluid coupling in an automatic transmission that transfers power from the engine to the transmission's input shaft.

torque wrench: A special wrench that measures the exact amount of torque being applied to tighten a nut or bolt.

torsion bars: On Chrysler products, these are often connected to the control arms to compensate for uneven loads and to allow the front wheels to move up and down freely on uneven road surfaces. See also suspension system.

traction control: A feature that senses when one wheel is spinning faster than the others. It may automatically apply the brakes, cut off power to that wheel, and/or reduce acceleration to improve traction and maintain stability.

trailer-towing packages: Optional equipment that usually includes a heavy-duty suspension, a larger radiator, a transmission cooler, and a rear bumper with a trailer hitch and wiring for the tow vehicle's lights.

transaxle: A single unit combining the transmission, the differential, and the clutch (on a manual transmission). The transaxle connects directly to the driveshafts on front-wheel drive or rear-engine vehicles.

transfer case: A unit mounted between the transmission and driveshafts of four-wheel drive vehicles that controls the flow of power to the front and rear drive axles when you shift back and forth between two-wheel and four-wheel drive.

transistor: A tiny electronic component, with at least three connections but no moving parts, that functions as a switch, amplifier, or detector by controlling the flow of current.

transmission: A box of gear wheels that allow your car to move forward and backward with varying amounts of power to meet a variety of driving situations. Manual transmissions are operated by means of a clutch and gearshift. Automatic transmissions are driven by hydraulic pressure.

transmission fluid: A super-thin oil that fills the automatic transmission system so that it can run on hydraulic pressure. Also found in many power-steering pumps.

transmission input shaft: The turning shaft that carries the power from the engine *into* the transmission.

transmission output shaft: The turning shaft that carries the power *out* of the transmission to the driveshaft.

transverse engine: An engine that's mounted between the drive wheels, often found on front-wheel drive cars. See also transaxle.

tread-wear indicators: Bars of hard rubber that appear across the treads of tires that have been worn below $\frac{1}{16}$ inch of surface.

triggering mechanism: A device that controls the timing of the ignition module or ignition coils on vehicles with electronic ignition systems.

trim: Nonfunctional metal or plastic moldings, frames, and other decorative additions to car bodies and interiors.

tune-up: The process of replacing fuel filters, air filters, and spark plugs to ensure that air, fuel, and spark are available in good condition to obtain maximum engine efficiency.

turbocharging: Using an exhaust-driven turbine to drive an air compressor that compresses air into the cylinders and increases the power of the engine. See also supercharging.

turn over: An engine is said to turn over when the starter has caused the crankshaft to begin to turn, which starts the pistons moving so that combustion can begin to take place in the cylinders, providing power to move the car.

turning radius: The relation of one front wheel to the other on turns. If your tires are "squealing" on turns, have your front-end alignment checked to be sure that bent steering arms haven't affected the turning radius of the car.

U-joints: An abbreviation for universal joints.

undercoating: A protective material applied to the undersides of new cars to prevent the formation of rust.

universal joints: Couplings located at either end of the driveshaft on a rear-wheel drive vehicle that allow the shaft to move freely, without affecting the more rigid transmission shaft, and to absorb the movement of the axle and wheels. Also called U-joints. On cars with transverse engines, these are called constant velocity joints.

vacuum advance: A device located to the side of the distributor that advances the ignition spark in response to the vacuum produced by the operation of the engine.

vacuum modulator: A small, easily replaceable, and inexpensive part found on some vehicles that can give the impression of transmission failure if it malfunctions. If the car tends to stay in low gear, shifts with difficulty or produces whitish smoke, has an automatic transmission, and is constantly low in transmission fluid, try replacing the vacuum modulator before undertaking major repairs. Most vacuum modulators simply screw into place.

valve cover: A metal lid located on top of the cylinder head on cars with overhead cams. The valve cover is removed when the valves need adjusting.

valves: Metal devices that open and close to allow fuel and air to enter the combustion chamber and exhaust gases to leave it. Operated from the camshaft by means of valve lifters, push rods, rocker arms, and overhead camshaft lobes, the valves can be adjusted with feeler gauges so that they open and close at the proper times. (These adjustments can't be made to valves that are operated by valve lifters). See also exhaust valve, intake valve, timing belt, timing chain.

vapor lock: Bubbles formed in the fuel line when the fuel boils because of extreme heat. These bubbles prevent the fuel from reaching the carburetor and cause the car to stop running. A wet rag will cool the line and get rid of the problem, and a piece of tinfoil wrapped around the line will prevent its recurrence in extremely hot weather. Fuel injection systems rarely experience vapor lock because the entire fuel system is kept at a fairly high pressure, thus preventing the fuel from vaporizing.

vaporize: To convert a liquid into a mist by breaking it into small particles and mixing it with air. The carburetor vaporizes gasoline to produce a combustible fuel/air mixture.

venturi: The part of the carburetor barrel that's narrowed to increase the ability of the air to mix with vaporized fuel by creating a vacuum that draws more fuel out of the float bowl.

viscosity: The thickness or pourability of a liquid. Oil comes in a variety of thicknesses, or *weights.* It also comes in single viscosity (single-weight oil) and in a blend of viscosities (multi-weight oil), which enable it to flow easily in cold weather and reduce thinning in hot weather. The higher the weight, the greater the viscosity of the oil. You can find the weight of the oil noted on the outside of the bottle.

voltage regulator: An electrical device that controls or regulates the electric voltage generated by the alternator.

V-type engine: An engine in which the cylinders occur in two rows set at an angle to each other, with the crankshaft running through the point of the V. The most popular engine of this type is the 8-cylinder V-8 engine. V-6 and V-4 engines are also available; Jaguar, Mercedes, and BMW even make V-12 engines! See also in-line engine.

warranty: A promise by a car manufacturer or a car dealer to fix or replace parts on a new car if they malfunction before a specific time or distance has elapsed.

water jackets: Channels in the engine through which water and coolant circulate to cool the engine. See also cooling system.

water pump: A device that circulates the liquid through the cooling system by pumping it from the engine water jackets to the radiator.

water separator: A device found on diesel cars that removes any water that may have contaminated the diesel fuel.

wheel alignment: See alignment.

wheel balancing: A procedure that ensures that the weight of a wheel is distributed evenly so that your car moves smoothly on the road at any speed, with no vibration in the steering wheel or rear seat. *Static* balancing distributes the weight of the wheel evenly around the axle or spindle and is done with the wheels off the car. *Dynamic* balancing distributes the weight evenly as the wheel and tire hang down vertically and also balances the brake drum. (This can be done with the wheels on the car.)

wheel bearings: The inner and outer bearings found at each wheel cushion the contact between the wheel and the spindle it sits on. They're packed with grease to prevent wear from the friction produced by the turning wheels. See also bearings.

wheel cylinder: A small cylinder located at each wheel brake that uses brake fluid to exert hydraulic pressure, which forces the brake shoes against the brake drums and stops the car.

zerk fitting: A small valve that allows grease to be added to a ball joint with a grease gun and prevents the grease from leaking out when pressure is placed on the area. See also grease fitting.

Appendix B

Specifications and Maintenance Records

· ·

On the following pages, you'll find a Specifications Record and a Maintenance Record. If you make photocopies of them before you fill them in, you'll have them for several vehicles and be able to take them to the store with you when you go to buy parts and have a history to take to a service facility when you go in for maintenance and repairs.

Specifications Record

Make, model, year	
Number of cylinders	
Automatic or manual transmission	
Type of transmission fluid or grease	
Type of power steering fluid	
Engine displacement	
Type of fuel injection or carburetor	
Air conditioned?	
Smog devices?	
Horsepower	
Electronic ignition/distributorless ignition (some 1985 and newer vehicles)	
Dwell (pre-1975 vehicles)	
Contact point gap (pre-1975 vehicles)	
Spark plug gap and size	
Cylinder firing order	
Ignition timing (not applicable for distributorless ignition vehicles)	
Oil weight (summer/winter)	
Oil capacity	
Oil filter number	
Coolant capacity (½ total cooling system capacity)	
Air filter number	
Fuel filter number	
Tire size (spare, too)	
Min. & max. tire pressure (front/rear/spare)	
Disc or drum brakes (front/rear)	

Maintenance Record

Vehicle:_____   From:_____   To:_____

I. Under-the-Hood Checklist

	J	F	M	A	M	J	J	A	S	O	N	D
* Checked coolant level	❏	❏	❏	❏	❏	❏	❏	❏	❏	❏	❏	❏
Flushed system and changed coolant (once a year)	❏	❏	❏	❏	❏	❏	❏	❏	❏	❏	❏	❏
* Checked fan belt	❏	❏	❏	❏	❏	❏	❏	❏	❏	❏	❏	❏
Changed fan belt (if frayed)	❏	❏	❏	❏	❏	❏	❏	❏	❏	❏	❏	❏
* Checked battery	❏	❏	❏	❏	❏	❏	❏	❏	❏	❏	❏	❏
Replaced battery (as needed)	❏	❏	❏	❏	❏	❏	❏	❏	❏	❏	❏	❏
* Checked oil level	❏	❏	❏	❏	❏	❏	❏	❏	❏	❏	❏	❏
Changed oil (every 3 months or 3,000 miles)	❏	❏	❏	❏	❏	❏	❏	❏	❏	❏	❏	❏
Replaced oil filter (every oil change)	❏	❏	❏	❏	❏	❏	❏	❏	❏	❏	❏	❏
* Checked automatic transmission fluid level	❏	❏	❏	❏	❏	❏	❏	❏	❏	❏	❏	❏
Added automatic transmission fluid	❏	❏	❏	❏	❏	❏	❏	❏	❏	❏	❏	❏
* Checked brake fluid level	❏	❏	❏	❏	❏	❏	❏	❏	❏	❏	❏	❏
Added brake fluid	❏	❏	❏	❏	❏	❏	❏	❏	❏	❏	❏	❏
* Checked power steering fluid level	❏	❏	❏	❏	❏	❏	❏	❏	❏	❏	❏	❏
Added power steering fluid	❏	❏	❏	❏	❏	❏	❏	❏	❏	❏	❏	❏
* Checked windshield washer fluid level	❏	❏	❏	❏	❏	❏	❏	❏	❏	❏	❏	❏
* Checked windshield wiper blades	❏	❏	❏	❏	❏	❏	❏	❏	❏	❏	❏	❏
Replaced windshield washer blades	❏	❏	❏	❏	❏	❏	❏	❏	❏	❏	❏	❏
* Checked tire pressure (don't forget the spare!)	❏	❏	❏	❏	❏	❏	❏	❏	❏	❏	❏	❏
Replaced tires (record details in Section IV)	❏	❏	❏	❏	❏	❏	❏	❏	❏	❏	❏	❏

(continued)

I. Under-the-Hood Checklist *(continued)*

	J	F	M	A	M	J	J	A	S	O	N	D
* Checked wiring	❏	❏	❏	❏	❏	❏	❏	❏	❏	❏	❏	❏
Replaced wires (record details in Section IV)	❏	❏	❏	❏	❏	❏	❏	❏	❏	❏	❏	❏
* Checked hoses	❏	❏	❏	❏	❏	❏	❏	❏	❏	❏	❏	❏
Replaced hoses (record details in Section IV)	❏	❏	❏	❏	❏	❏	❏	❏	❏	❏	❏	❏

II. Tune-Up Checklist

Electronic ignitions: Every 18,000 miles or 2 years

Non-electronic ignitions: Every 12,000 miles or 1 year — more often if necessary

	J	F	M	A	M	J	J	A	S	O	N	D
* Checked air filter	❏	❏	❏	❏	❏	❏	❏	❏	❏	❏	❏	❏
Replaced air filter (once a year or every 20,000 miles)	❏	❏	❏	❏	❏	❏	❏	❏	❏	❏	❏	❏
Checked fuel filter	❏	❏	❏	❏	❏	❏	❏	❏	❏	❏	❏	❏
Replaced fuel filter (every tune-up or as manufacturer recommends)	❏	❏	❏	❏	❏	❏	❏	❏	❏	❏	❏	❏
Checked PCV valve	❏	❏	❏	❏	❏	❏	❏	❏	❏	❏	❏	❏
Cleaned or replaced PCV valve (every 12,000 miles)	❏	❏	❏	❏	❏	❏	❏	❏	❏	❏	❏	❏
Checked spark plugs (cleaned and regapped them)	❏	❏	❏	❏	❏	❏	❏	❏	❏	❏	❏	❏
Changed spark plugs (every tune-up, or more often if burnt or worn)	❏	❏	❏	❏	❏	❏	❏	❏	❏	❏		
Checked points, dwell, & point gap (pre-1975 vehicles)	❏	❏	❏	❏	❏	❏	❏	❏	❏	❏	❏	❏
Changed points, condenser, & rotor (every tune-up, or more often if burnt or worn)	❏	❏	❏	❏	❏	❏	❏	❏	❏	❏	❏	❏

* Do once a month or every 1,000 miles.

	J	F	M	A	M	J	J	A	S	O	N	D
Checked timing (not applicable for distributorless ignitions)	❏	❏	❏	❏	❏	❏	❏	❏	❏	❏	❏	❏
Adjusted carburetor (pre-1980 vehicles)	❏	❏	❏	❏	❏	❏	❏	❏	❏	❏	❏	❏
Cleaned or rebuilt carburetor (when needed)	❏	❏	❏	❏	❏	❏	❏	❏	❏	❏	❏	❏
Cleaned fuel injection throttle housing (every 18,000 miles)	❏	❏	❏	❏	❏	❏	❏	❏	❏	❏	❏	❏
Cleaned fuel injectors (when needed)	❏	❏	❏	❏	❏	❏	❏	❏	❏	❏	❏	❏

III. Lubrication and Brake Checklist

	J	F	M	A	M	J	J	A	S	O	N	D
Checked grease fittings (every 3,000 miles)	❏	❏	❏	❏	❏	❏	❏	❏	❏	❏	❏	❏
Lubricated steering & suspension (every 3,000 miles or as needed)	❏	❏	❏	❏	❏	❏	❏	❏	❏	❏	❏	❏
Had complete professional lube job (once a year or as needed)	❏	❏	❏	❏	❏	❏	❏	❏	❏	❏	❏	❏
Checked brakes (every 10,000 miles)	❏	❏	❏	❏	❏	❏	❏	❏	❏	❏	❏	❏
Had brakes rebuilt (record details in Section IV)	❏	❏	❏	❏	❏	❏	❏	❏	❏	❏	❏	❏
Checked wheel bearings (every 10,000 miles)	❏	❏	❏	❏	❏	❏	❏	❏	❏	❏	❏	❏
Repacked wheel bearings (every 20,000 miles or as needed)	❏	❏	❏	❏	❏	❏	❏	❏	❏	❏	❏	❏
Checked shock absorbers	❏	❏	❏	❏	❏	❏	❏	❏	❏	❏	❏	❏
Replaced shock absorbers (as needed)	❏	❏	❏	❏	❏	❏	❏	❏	❏	❏	❏	❏
Had front-end alignment (as needed)	❏	❏	❏	❏	❏	❏	❏	❏	❏	❏	❏	❏
Had automatic transmission serviced (every 20,000 to 25,000 miles)	❏	❏	❏	❏	❏	❏	❏	❏	❏	❏	❏	❏

IV. Parts Replacement Record

Part	Date and Details
Wiring (coil wire, ignition wires, spark plug boots, etc.)	
Hoses (top or bottom radiator hose, vacuum hoses, fuel lines, etc.)	
Brakes (pads/shoes relined, rotors/drums machined, etc.)	

Part	Date and Details
Tires (Which one? Where did new tire go? Mileage on odometer at tire change?)	
Other parts	

Index

IDG BOOKS WORLDWIDE BOOK REGISTRATION

We want to hear from you!

Visit **http://my2cents.dummies.com** to register this book and tell us how you liked it!

- ✔ Get entered in our monthly prize giveaway.

- ✔ Give us feedback about this book — tell us what you like best, what you like least, or maybe what you'd like to ask the author and us to change!

- ✔ Let us know any other *...For Dummies*® topics that interest you.

Your feedback helps us determine what books to publish, tells us what coverage to add as we revise our books, and lets us know whether we're meeting your needs as a *...For Dummies* reader. You're our most valuable resource, and what you have to say is important to us!

Not on the Web yet? It's easy to get started with *Dummies 101*®: *The Internet For Windows*® *98* or *The Internet For Dummies*®, 6th Edition, at local retailers everywhere.

Or let us know what you think by sending us a letter at the following address:

...For Dummies Book Registration
Dummies Press
7260 Shadeland Station, Suite 100
Indianapolis, IN 46256-3917
Fax 317-596-5498

BESTSELLING
BOOK SERIES

Auto Repair For Dummies®

BESTSELLING
BOOK SERIES

Cheat Sheet

How to Take Anything Apart — and Get It Back Together Again

1. **Get a clean, lint-free rag and lay it down on a flat surface, near enough to reach without having to get up or walk to it.**

   As you remove each part, you're going to lay it on this rag. Consequently, the rag shouldn't be in an area where oil or dust or anything else can fall on it and foul the parts. If you're going to use something that blasts air for cleaning purposes, leave enough of the rag uncluttered to lap it over the parts resting on it.

2. **Before you remove each part, ask yourself the following questions, and if you're worried about forgetting, make notes:**

   ✔ What is this thing?

   ✔ What does it do?

   ✔ How does it do it?

   ✔ Why is it made the way it is?

   ✔ How tightly is it screwed on (or fastened down)?

3. **As you remove each part, lay it down on the rag in clockwise order, with each part pointing in the direction it lay when it was in place.**

   When you're ready to reassemble things, the placement and direction of each part tell you when to put it back and how it went.

4. **If you're making notes, assign each part a number indicating the order in which you removed it — part #1, part #2, and so on.**

   You can even put numbers on the parts with masking tape if you're afraid that the rag may be moved accidentally.

5. **When you're ready to reassemble everything, begin with the last part you removed, and then go counterclockwise through the parts.**

...For Dummies®: Bestselling Book Series for Beginners

Auto Repair For Dummies®

Cheat Sheet

Safety Rules

- Don't smoke while you're working on your vehicle.

- Never work on your vehicle unless the parking brake is on, the gearshift is in Park or Neutral, and the engine is shut off (unless it has to be running for you to do the work).

- Be sure that the parts of the engine you're working on are nice and cold so that you don't get burned.

- Never jack up a car unless the wheels are properly blocked.

- Use insulated tools for electrical work.

- Before using a wrench or ratchet on a part that's "stuck," make sure that, if it suddenly comes loose, your hand won't hit anything. To avoid the possibility of bruised knuckles, *pull* on wrenches whenever possible rather than *pushing* them.

- Take off your rings, long necklaces, and other jewelry and tie back long hair.

- If you're using toxic chemicals, such as antifreeze, cleaners, and the like, keep them away from your mouth and eyes, wash your hands thoroughly after using them, and either store them safely away from pets and children or dispose of them in a way that's good for the environment.

- Know that gasoline is extremely dangerous to have around. Not only is it toxic and flammable, but the vapor in an *empty* can is explosive enough to take out a city block.

- Work in a well-ventilated area. If possible, work outdoors in your driveway, your backyard, or a parking lot. If you must work in your garage, be sure to keep the garage door open, with the vehicle as close to the door as possible.

- Keep fire extinguishers handy. Place one in your garage and one in the passenger compartment of your vehicle.

Monthly Under-the-Hood Check

If the idea of commiting yourself to a regular under-the-hood checkup seems less than alluring, consider this: *Spending 15 minutes a month on this under-the-hood check can prevent 70 percent of the problems that lead to highway breakdowns!* Convinced? Then check these things once a month or every 1,000 miles (Chapter 3 tells you how):

- Check the air filter
- Check the accessory belts
- Check the battery
- Check the coolant
- Check the hoses
- Check the oil dipstick
- Check the automatic transmission fluid dipstick
- Check the brake fluid
- Check the power-steering fluid
- Check the windshield wipers and windshield washer fluid
- Check the wiring
- Check the tires